In Praise of Worship

In Praise of Worship

An Exploration of Text and Practice

Edited by
DAVID J. COHEN *and* MICHAEL PARSONS

☙PICKWICK *Publications* • Eugene, Oregon

IN PRAISE OF WORSHIP
An Exploration of Text and Practice

Copyright © 2010 Wipf and Stock Publishers. All rights reserved. Except for brief quotations in critical publications or reviews, no part of this book may be reproduced in any manner without prior written permission from the publisher. Write: Permissions, Wipf and Stock Publishers, 199 W. 8th Ave., Suite 3, Eugene, OR 97401.

Pickwick Publications
An Imprint of Wipf and Stock Publishers
199 W. 8th Ave., Suite 3
Eugene, OR 97401

www. wipfandstock.com

ISBN 13: 978-1-60899-145-7

Cataloging-in-Publication data:

In praise of worship : an exploration of text and practice / Edited by David J. Cohen and Michael Parsons.

xvi + 298 p. ; 23 cm. Includes bibliographical references.

ISBN 13: 978-1-60899-145-7

1. Liturgics. 2. Public worship. I. Cohen, David J. II. Parsons, Michael. III. Title.

BV15 .I25 2010

Manufactured in the U.S.A.

Dedicated to
Paul and Merrill Kitchen,
serving people faithfully in the footsteps of Jesus

and

David and Wendy Bryan,
alter Christus, in the overflow of grace

Contents

Foreword by David Coffey, OBE (Baptist World Alliance) / ix
Preface / xi
List of Contributors / xiii
List of Abbreviations / xv

PART ONE: Worship and Text

1. Worship as Community Creation: Deuteronomy's Vision of Worship—*David G. Firth* / 3
2. Journey to the Center of the Heart: Psalm 19 as Transformance—*David J. Cohen* / 17
3. Nourishing Our Missional Identity: Worship and the Mission of God's People—*Michael W. Goheen* / 32
4. Worship and the Presence of God: Seeing with Ezekiel —*John W. Olley* / 54
5. Worship in the New Testament—*Alastair Campbell* / 70
6. The *Proskuneō* Myth: When a Kiss Is Not a Kiss —*Chris Jack* / 84
7. On the Mountain: Worship as Community Experience in Matthew—*Stephen Haar* / 98
8. Time and Location: Aspects of Realized Eschatology, Paul, and Our Worship—*Michael Parsons* / 120

PART TWO: Worship and Practice

9. The Trinity and Lament—*Robin Parry* / 143
10. Art for God or to God through Art?—*Angela McCarthy* / 162

11	Worship as Information, Formation, and Transformation —*Nancy Ault* / 176	
12	Pastoral Rituals and Life-cycle Themes in Family and Individual Worship—*Alan Niven* / 193	
13	Rhythm and Worship: In Search of Pachelbel —*Travis Fitch* / 211	
14	In Praise of Worship: The Trinitarian Nature of Christian Devotion—*Michael O'Neil* / 232	
15	Worship and the Quest for Justice—*Brian S. Harris* / 250	
16	The Preacher as Worshipper—*Michael J. Quicke* / 262	

Bibliography / 279

Foreword

It has been my privilege during the past twenty-five years to experience the worship of the world church and my life has been enriched immeasurably by the breadth and diversity of the people of God at worship. I have stood on the banks of the River Zaire in a rural region of the Democratic Republic of the Congo and witnessed the baptisms of over one hundred believers. Some families had walked for three hours in order to be present for this special occasion in the life of the Baptist community.

I recall a visit to a Russian Orthodox Church in Moscow when more of my senses were activated in worship than is usual. There was the awesome sight of the magnificent iconostasis screen, the pungent smell of the incense, and the glorious sound of the choir singing the liturgy of St John Chrysostom.

My visits to African American churches in the USA are too numerous to itemize, but I can testify as a preacher that nothing surpasses the enervating thrill of a congregation that joins you vocally when you are quoting from a scripture passage, supports you when you appear to be flagging during the second point of your sermon, and then on the final lap cheers you home all the way to the finish.

It was in the awesome setting of St Paul's Cathedral, London, that I attended the Memorial Service for the British victims of the Asian Tsunami of 2004. As we stood in silent memory of those who had died, hundreds of flower petals representing the deceased were released from the roof of the cathedral as the choir sang poignantly, "God be in my head and in my understanding." The prayerfully-shaped liturgy of lament was a tender pastoral support to the families who were grieving for their loved ones.

I have worshipped with a church community based in a disused factory warehouse in one of the poorest districts of Lima, Peru. In material terms the worshippers possessed nothing, yet their vibrant singing, praying, and dancing was a revelation of their abundant joy in the Lord. In this Peruvian place of worship I saw a "wealth of generosity" that reminded me of the apostle's pastoral insight into the life of a materially poor congregation (2 Cor 8:1–2).

Global worship has an overflowing richness of diversity. Because of this diversity the pragmatics of how we worship have never truly united Christians. Battles over the "how" of worship are centuries old. When Augustine attempted to change the pattern of the Good Friday service by introducing readings from all four Gospels, people were shocked by the departure from the tradition of reading solely from Matthew. When J. S. Bach first performed his *St Matthew Passion*, St Thomas Church, Leipzig, reduced his salary and the church council warned Bach that if he continued to lead worship in this way, within two years the organ would be ruined and most of the congregation deaf.

Today, when a congregation sings, "Open our eyes Lord we want to see Jesus," or "Come Down, O Love Divine" it is offering a prayer for that spiritual anointing which will renew a church community through worship. Worship in spirit and truth always involves fresh revelations of the mystery of why it is our joy and duty to offer thanks and praise to the almighty and eternal God; worship sustains us in the costly challenges of discipleship and grants us the perseverance to endure to the end; worship confronts the corrosive effects of sin and magnifies the redeeming work of grace; worship alerts our minds to the false and foolish claims of idolatrous cultures; in worship our ears become attuned to the word of God and we learn to go with the grain of God's will and learn the works and ways of the Lord. Through worship God constantly reshapes us to re-imagine mission in the world from his perspective; the open hands of the worshippers receive the gifts of the Spirit necessary to accomplish the mission of God in a broken world. Worship emboldens us to have a living hope in Christ and take the long view.

In this broad and grace-filled context, the great value of the essays in this book is the excellent and diverse attempt by the writers to provide fresh ways of thinking about why and how we worship as individuals and as communities. It is the "why" and the "how" of worship that needs rethinking and renewing. This excellent volume begins that process.

David Coffey, OBE
President of the Baptist World Alliance
Pentecost, 2009

Preface

Martin Luther once spoke of worship as "one of the precious holy possessions" of the body of Christ, placing it squarely in the context of "reform, sanctification and the will of God." We believe that, essentially, he was right. However, today, in contrast, there is a great deal of contemporary discussion that places significant emphasis on music and singing as, somehow, defining what worship is. From a variety of perspectives this book challenges that limited, and *limiting*, perception of worship and asks its readers to see worship as the Bible appears to, as all-embracing, having to do with the whole of life, without in any way reducing the significance of what we might see as concentrated moments of individual and corporate devotion.

The contributors to this volume follow the biblical understanding with scholarly competence and enthusiasm. We are grateful to them for their willingness to contribute to the project from their own particular perspective. What has been interesting is the consistency of biblical, theological, and pastoral conclusions on the nature and practice of worship. We are grateful as well to the editors of Wipf and Stock, and their imprint, Pickwick Publications, for their interest in the work and for publishing it. Thanks, too, go to David Coffey for his generous Foreword.

We are also thankful for the support of Vose Seminary in allowing us the time and space to bring this book to fruition and our wives and families, both for their interest in our work and their ongoing personal support. Our hope is that many will find encouragement and inspiration in these pages.

David J. Cohen and Michael Parsons
August, 2009

Contributors

DAVID G. FIRTH, Old Testament Tutor, Cliff College, Calver, UK.

DAVID J. COHEN, Head of Biblical Studies, Lecturer in Hebrew Bible, Vose Seminary, Perth, Australia.

MICHAEL W. GOHEEN, Geneva Professor of Worldview and Religious Studies, Trinity Western University, Langley, Canada.

JOHN W. OLLEY, formerly Principal and Lecturer in Old Testament, Vose Seminary, Perth, Australia.

ALASTAIR CAMPBELL, formerly Lecturer in New Testament at Spurgeon's College, London, and at the United Theological College of the West Indies, Kingston, Jamaica.

CHRIS JACK, Lecturer in Applied Theology, London School of Theology, UK.

STEPHEN HAAR, Academic Dean, Australian Lutheran College, Adelaide, Australia.

MICHAEL PARSONS, Director of Postgraduate Research, Lecturer in Christian Thought, Vose Seminary, Perth, Australia.

ROBIN PARRY, Editorial Director of Paternoster, UK.

ANGELA MCCARTHY, Lecturer in Theology, University of Notre Dame, Fremantle, Australia.

NANCY AULT, Lecturer in Practical Theology, Murdoch University, Perth, Australia.

ALAN NIVEN, Vice-Principal and Lecturer in Pastoral and Family Studies, Churches of Christ Theological College, Melbourne, Australia.

TRAVIS FITCH, Pastor for Worship and Fine Arts, Churchlands Christian Fellowship, Perth, Western Australia.

MICHAEL O'NEIL, Senior Pastor, Lesmurdie Baptist Church, Perth, Western Australia.

BRIAN S. HARRIS, Principal, Lecturer in Practical Theology, Vose Seminary, Perth, Australia.

MICHAEL J. QUICKE, C. W. Koller Professor of Preaching, Northern Seminary, Chicago, USA.

Abbreviations

AAR	*Australian Art Review*
AB	Anchor Bible
ABD	*The Anchor Bible Dictionary*
ABJT	*Asian Baptist Journal of Theology*
ACR	*Australasian Catholic Record*
Adv Haer	*Adversus haereses*
ANRW	*Aufstieg und Niedergang der römischen Welt*
BCPE	*Bulletin du Centre Protestant d'Etudes*
BDAG	*A Greek-English Lexicon of the New Testament and Other Early Christian Literature*
Cant R	Canticles Rabbah
ChM	*Churchman*
ChrCent	*Christian Century*
CT	*Christianity Today*
CurTM	*Currents in Theology and Mission*
DLNTD	*Dictionary of the Later New Testament and Its Development*
DPL	*Dictionary of Paul and His Letters*
EBC	*Expositor's Bible Commentary*
EDNT	*Exegetical Dictionary of the New Testament*
EpRev	*Epworth Review*
Ex R	Exodus Rabbah
GTJ	*Grace Theological Journal*
ICC	International Critical Commentary
Int	*Interpretation*
IJST	*International Journal of Systematic Theology*
IRM	*International Review of Mission*
JBL	*Journal of Biblical Literature*
JBQ	*Jewish Bible Quarterly*
JETS	*Journal of the Evangelical Theological Society*

J Past Th	*Journal of Pastoral Theology*
JPC	*Journal of Popular Culture*
JPT	*Journal of Pentecostal Theology*
JSNT	*Journal for the Study of the New Testament*
JSOT	*Journal for the Study of the Old Testament*
JSRI	*Journal for the Study of Religions and Ideologies*
Lev R	Leviticus Rabbah
LW	*Luther's Works*
Midr Ps	Midrash Psalms
ModTheol	*Modern Theology*
NBD	New Bible Dictionary
NIB	*New Interpreter's Bible*
NICOT	New International Commentary on the Old Testament
NIDNTT	New International Dictionary of New Testament Theology
NIDOTTE	New International Dictionary of Old Testament Theology and Exegesis
Num R	Numbers Rabbah
Pan	*Panarion hareses*
Pesik R	Pesikta Rabbati
Pss Sol	Psalms of Solomon
ResQ	*Restoration Quarterly*
SBB	Stuttgarter Biblische Beiträge
Sci Chr Belief	*Science and Christian Belief*
SJT	*Scottish Journal of Theology*
SPJMS	South Pacific Journal of Mission Studies
SR	Studies in Religion
TB	Tyndale Bulletin
TDNT	Theological Dictionary of the New Testament
THKNT	Theologischer Handkommentar zum Neuen Testament
Tob	Tobit
TToday	Theology Today
VT	*Vetus Testamentum*
WBC	Word Biblical Commentary

PART ONE

Worship and Text

1

Worship as Community Creation

Deuteronomy's Vision of Worship

DAVID G. FIRTH

INTRODUCTION

ALTHOUGH NUMEROUS STUDIES ON worship in Ancient Israel have been published, there is a tendency for them to fall into a familiar structure that examines holy places, holy people, and holy seasons. Robin Routledge has recently provided a fine example of this approach, though he has also considered additional elements such as the place of prayer and music and the relationship of the sacrificial system to forgiveness.[1] These elements are central to the vision for worship across the Old Testament as a whole, and especially the Pentateuch (though the Psalms are also important), and so it is entirely appropriate that they are placed in the foreground of such studies.[2] Nevertheless, there is an inherent danger in any work that surveys the whole of the Old Testament (or ancient Israel as a social context)—that in emphasizing that which is common to the whole of the Old Testament we effectively marginalize that which is in some sense distinctive.

In addressing this issue, there is a vital first question that must be asked. Put simply, what is worship? How we define worship will shape

---

1. Routledge, *Old Testament*, 175–208.

2. For similar examples, see Brueggemann, *Worship*; Childs, *Old Testament*; 145–74, Dyrness, *Themes*, 143–60; Eichrodt, *Theology*, 98–177; Robinson, *Religious Ideas*, 130–58; Smith, *Old Testament*, 311–36.

our investigation of the Old Testament, and Deuteronomy in particular, as we reflect on its theology of worship. Many options are available, and to some extent it may depend on whether our definition starts with contemporary practice or with the biblical material. After all, it is clear that contemporary Christian worship takes many forms that are quite distinct from those described in the Old Testament. If we started with contemporary practice in many churches, we might conclude that worship is equated with singing praise songs. I have often enough sat in worship services where the leader announces after a time of prayer or reading of the Bible that we are now about to "have a time of worship," which is inevitably the cue for the band to pick up their instruments and the data projector to show the words of the next song. Somehow, prayer, hearing the Scriptures, and preaching appear to have become something less than worship. In truth, this is probably more to do with a sloppy use of language, but it models an approach to worship that is limited to musical praise and encourages a limited understanding of worship that has no place for confession or struggle which rightfully have a place in it. But starting with our own practice is inappropriate here for more profound reasons than the fact that our own language of worship is often poorly formed. More importantly, it leaves us without the ability to discover the breadth of how the Old Testament understands worship, even if we stay for the moment within the now traditional boundaries. Yet, if we start with the biblical material itself we are also left without an exact definition since there is no point where the Old Testament actually defines worship. What we can suggest, though, is that a synthesis of the biblical material is possible, and that emerging from this it is possible to argue that worship is "the relational phenomena between the created and the Creator, which finds expression in both specific events and lifestyle commitments."[3] The importance of this definition is that it enables us to see both the function of the holy places, people, and times and also that the Old Testament views worship as a lifestyle, not something that only occurs in the gathering of God's people. The danger is that we make everything worship so that the concept itself ceases to be meaningful, but so long as we can demonstrate that the lifestyle discussed derives its shape from the specific events and moments that shaped Israel's worship then that problem can be covered.

---

3. Pierce, *Enthroned*, 3.

TERMS FOR WORSHIP

Before turning to examine Deuteronomy's perspective on worship, we need briefly to examine the main terms that are used for worship in the Old Testament. Broadly speaking, worship is conceived as an act of homage, and the terms the Old Testament employs recognizes this fact.[4] It is an act of homage before the holy God, one whose worth is the center of all that we do, though worship is not restricted to these terms. Indeed, none of these words occur in the section of Deuteronomy we will consider with this specifically theological sense, but studying them briefly is still important for establishing the context for worship.

There are three main verbs that we need to note, each of which is sometimes translated as "worship."[5] The first is *ḥwh*, which means "to bow down."[6] It is not a word that is restricted to religious use—in the book of Esther (which never mentions God) Haman is infuriated by Mordecai's refusal to bow down (*ḥwh*) before him. In fact, the term is derived from the act of doing obeisance before a king in the court, but is applied by extension to the act of worship in that Yahweh is the great king. In the context of worship, it is most commonly used to describe worship that is carried out within the cult, the formal procedures for worship associated with the priestly system, but need not be restricted to it—as, for example, in the case of Exodus 34:8, where Moses simply responds to the presence of Yahweh. Nevertheless, if it is understood that the cult is the place where Yahweh's presence is regularly invoked, then we should understand that the homage offered there comes from an awareness of his presence. A second verb, *sgd*,[7] is also used to mean "bow down," but it is only ever used for bowing down to another human (Dan 2:46) or an idol (Isa 44:15). However, *ḥwh* can also be used for this function, so we should recognize that it is the dominant word, though

---

4. Smith, *Old Testament*, 312.

5. Hill, *Enter His Courts*, 1–9, points to a slightly wider range of terms, but for our purposes it is sufficient to stay with these three. VanGemeren, ed., *NIDOT*, 214, suggests a wider range again, while also linking the terms for worship to concepts such as bending, kneeling, ministry, service, toil and work. As is evident in the discussion above, none of these terms is restricted to a purely theological sense.

6. Old grammarians (still reflected in BDB) analyzed this verb as coming from the root *šḥh*, but this is now known to be incorrect.

7. This root thus occurs in both Hebrew and Aramaic, though it is more common in Aramaic texts.

there is clearly a sense in which Israel felt it appropriate to apply it to Yahweh, whereas *sgd* apparently could not be used in this way.

The third verb of some significance is *ʿbd*, which means "to serve." The derived noun *ʿăbôdâ* is also used with the meaning "service." The terms come from the realm of slavery, since the verb frequently has the sense of compulsory service, as in the case of a slave, though Hebrew does not actually distinguish between slavery and free service. When this is applied by extension to Yahweh, we have a situation similar to that of *ḥwh*, in that it is understood that Yahweh is the great king and that people are therefore his servants simply because of his personal authority. Psalm 100, which uses *ʿbd* is an important text because of the ways it stresses that this worship is given with great joy. Yahweh is not being coerced by the worship of his people, unlike the dominant ancient Near East perspective; rather, it was the joyful submission of his people to the one who was over all. This is particularly evident in the Psalms.

What emerges from this is that the Old Testament as a whole tends to use language for worship which is drawn from other realms, and that even the language for worship is itself metaphoric, structuring the worship of Yahweh with what would be expected on coming into the presence of an ancient king. But this also points to the element of lifestyle as an expression of this worship, because it was expected that a king could realistically expect a certain lifestyle from his people. The language of worship shows that it involved offering homage to Yahweh as the great king and also that this involved a continuation of his service.

THE PERSPECTIVE OF DEUTERONOMY: CREATION OF COMMUNITY BEFORE GOD

In discussing "Worship in the Old Testament" it is always possible to be so broad that we don't discover anything new, or have our thinking challenged in any way. We know from the language employed that worship is the adoration of God, the giving of glory to him, and on a skim through the Old Testament we might find that reflected, just as we knew we would. So, rather than taking a broad overview, we need to focus on one specific text in the Old Testament to discover what it has to say about worship. Our task is more to discover the *theology* of worship than its form, so that we might ponder the question of how that can be reflected in our own worship. Obviously, we will not reproduce the *form* of worship that we find in the Old Testament, because it is no longer relevant to us. Sacrifices and offerings are no longer required. But the theology that lies behind Israel's worship is of vital importance.

In taking a text in the Old Testament, one might immediately think of Psalms as the place to discover what the Old Testament has to say on worship. And to some extent, it is a very clear example of that. But to start there is to miss the point. Israel's life and worship were to be grounded in the *tôrâ*, and much of what is in the Psalms is a reflection of that. It is therefore preferable to examine some of the texts in the Pentateuch that provide the foundation for Israel's theology of worship.

When we examine the Pentateuch, it is quite apparent that a large proportion of Exodus 25—Numbers 10 is concerned with the topic of worship in its various forms. That is more than we can reasonably cover here. However, the book of Deuteronomy provides a much more manageable set of laws for our purposes, with most of the relevant material covered in 12:1—16:17. Moreover, a number of studies have pointed to the way Deuteronomy is structured as a covenant text in which the king directs his subjects.[8] Since the Old Testament's language of worship is based on the metaphor of life in the presence of the king, this makes Deuteronomy a particularly suitable location for this sampling. Even taking this smaller block of material, it is apparent that we will be skimming through to some extent, but it should be possible for the main themes to emerge clearly for us.

At the risk of oversimplifying what we find here, we can suggest that Deuteronomy's theology of worship can be summed up by saying that worship's primary goal is the creation of community in response to Yahweh, though we discover this by looking at it in light of the definition of worship given above. Yahweh has created a people, and their worship must live out what it means to be his people. Although other themes can be brought out from these chapters, three main ones emerge to guide our reflection—worship is faithful obedience to God, worship is a response to God's goodness in daily life, and worship is concern for the marginalized within the community. These three themes run through these chapters, and to some extent define their theology of worship.[9] All

---

8. See Williamson, *Sealed with an Oath*, 111–15.

9. It has also been suggested that the exposition of laws in Deuteronomy 12–26 is shaped by the Ten Commandments. Hence, Olson, *Deuteronomy*, 62–78, ties this section to the first three commandments (according to the Lutheran–Roman Catholic system of enumeration). Christensen, *Deuteronomy*, 221, accepts this analysis, though because he follows the more traditional Protestant numbering of the commandments

three are present in each section of these chapters, though one tends to be dominant in each.[10] Thompson also stresses the fact that the choice of worship as the first element in the legal code of Deuteronomy was doubtless intentional, because it emphasizes the need for Israel to be properly related to Yahweh before all else.[11]

Worship Is Faithful Obedience to God (Deut 12:1—14:21)

Worship as faithful obedience to Yahweh is particularly prominent here. Three different elements are stressed in response to this—Israel must worship where Yahweh chooses, she must worship Yahweh alone, and her culture must reflect her obedience to Yahweh.[12]

WORSHIP WHERE YAHWEH CHOOSES (DEUTERONOMY 12)

In chapter twelve we have a long discussion of what is known as "the altar law." In a fairly extended way, it stresses that Israel is to worship at the place Yahweh will choose. Presumably, there is only one place intended at any given point in time, though the possibility that the place will change over time is admitted. Although this place was ultimately Jerusalem (1 Kgs 9:3), it need not have been the original intent in Deuteronomy, for which the language of the one place is more closely related to Israel's occupation of the land.[13] As Millar observes, "The aim is *not* to identify this place, but to urge Israel to conform her worship to the divine command."[14] Consistently through this chapter, Israel is told that when they worship, they should worship at the one place. This does

---

treats them as covering the first four commandments. See also, Walton, "Deuteronomy," 213–25. Although this could strengthen the case made here, it does not depend upon this view.

10. Helpful and accessible commentaries on these chapters are Christensen, *Deuteronomy*; Craigie, *The Book*; McConville, *Deuteronomy*; Thompson, *Deuteronomy*, and Wright, *Deuteronomy*. Of these, Wright is particularly helpful in making clear the missiological dimensions of Israel's worship as it is expounded in Deuteronomy, stressing the links between chapters 12–29 and 1–11.

11. Thompson, *Deuteronomy*, 161.

12. Deuteronomy 15:19–23 can also be considered under this heading, but has been omitted for reasons of space.

13. It is often assumed that Deuteronomy 12 has been written in full awareness of the choice of Jerusalem, but this is not a necessary assumption. Cf. Hagedorn, "Placing (a) God," 193; Millar and McConville, *Time*, 117–23; McConville, *Deuteronomy*, 214–17. It should be noted that Deuteronomy speaks only of a place for an altar, not a temple.

14. Millar, *Now Choose Life*, 110 (original emphasis).

not exclude worship in the home. The point of reference is the sacrificial system and the feasts that would be attended every year. But the "formal" aspects of worship were to occur in the one place. Israel was to show her obedience in this way.

The reason for this is that Canaanite worship apparently tended to set up any number of shrines, usually at a "high place" or under a "green tree." This is especially clear in 12:1–7 where Israel is directed to destroy Canaanite sanctuaries and only worship at the place Yahweh shall choose. Israel's worship was not meant to be capable of being misunderstood. Many of the forms of worship she employed were in fact similar to those used by the Canaanites and most ancient peoples. That is why the chapter ends with a stern warning in 12:29–31.[15] Israel's worship may well use forms that are similar to those used by others, but the whole point of her worship must also be apparent.[16] She can use the worship tools of her time, which are not unique to her, but her obedience to Yahweh must be apparent in how she uses them. Thus, when we have the point stressed that Israel is not to "do as they do" (12:4, 31) it is not a prohibition on the offering of sacrifices, which Israel's neighbors would have understood all too well. It is that Israel is to offer a radical re-interpretation of her activities, and yet still utilize the culturally acknowledged forms. There is thus a missiological purpose in these commands, in that Yahweh asks Israel to offer worship to him that is understood from within a given cultural milieu, and yet at the same time to offer a radical reinterpretation of it. Israel's worship is thus to be comprehensible to her neighbors, yet Israel is also to articulate a different theology that defines what is distinctive of her worship of Yahweh.

Yet obedience is not arbitrary, and the heart of this law in verses 8–28 indicates that obedience is a joyful acceptance of Yahweh's provision which is also concerned to provide Israel with mechanisms to enable faithfulness. Thus, obedience arises from experiencing the blessing of being settled in the land by Yahweh so that attendance at the sanctuary is a matter of joy that also remembers those who had no inheritance of their own (12:8–14). Obedience thus prepares for other themes which

---

15. Note that 12:32 in English is 13:1 in Hebrew. English verse numbers are used throughout.

16. Thus, the various sacrifices that are offered by Israel are typical of the sacrifices that would have been offered by her neighbors, but it must be understood that they are a response to the gracious command of Yahweh and not an attempt to placate the gods.

emerge. But Yahweh's provision was not just of a sanctuary, but also a means of ensuring that Israel did not fall prey to the temptation to offer sacrifices wherever animals were slaughtered. This is achieved by allowing for the slaughter of animals in a non-sacrificial manner (12:15–25), though obedience was still required here as blood could not be consumed. What emerges from this is that obedient worship is a response to God for all his provision, both the gift of the land and the gift of a means of worshipping faithfully, all of which is marked by joy.

Worship Yahweh Alone (Deuteronomy 13)

Chapter twelve closes by expressing concern about the danger of being led astray by other gods, and this theme becomes dominant in chapter 13. Constantly, the concern is with the danger that other gods pose. It becomes apparent as we proceed into chapter 13 that the opening commands of the Decalogue are constantly in the background.

Three possible scenarios are raised—a false prophet, a member of the family, or a town that follows other gods. What is distinctive is that these dangers come from within, either from an apparent religious commitment or the call of family or clan. The danger that these gods posed is that they distracted people from Yahweh so that their total devotion was not to him. One cannot be a member of the community of Yahweh's people and not honor Yahweh above all else. What Deuteronomy is saying here is that those who worship Yahweh must understand the radical nature of that commitment—no other can claim such devotion. Israel's worship simply cannot be mixed. At the same time, it insists that authentic worshippers must recognize the temptations that exist and lead them away from devotion to Yahweh, because such temptations always exist. Certainly, Israel was aware of influential teachers and preachers, of family members or communities that would somehow appear to offer something significant and worthwhile. But as these different groups sought to dilute the absolute demands of Yahweh, so they would dilute what was distinctive of Israel. Significantly, therefore, worship could not be just a "heart response" to Yahweh—there had to be an application of the mind and thought processes as well. Idolatry was always a threat to be countered.[17]

---

17. Wright, *Deuteronomy*, 178, observes, "One of the most critical missiological tasks facing the church today is to recover, rethink and reapply a full biblical understanding of idolatry, with a sober, painful evaluation of the extent of its penetration, not only to the roots of western culture, but into the very bloodstream of the church."

The means by which this idolatry was to be countered was the destruction of those who sought to lead the nation into apostasy. Through the three examples there is a progression from those most likely to influence the people to apostasy (a prophet counseling false worship, 13:1–5) to members of one's own family (13:6–2) through to the existence of a town which practices and encourages the worship of other deities (13:12–18). Israel's response to this was to be twofold. Positively, Israel was to adhere absolutely to Yahweh but conversely, whatever the social status of the persons concerned, they were to be utterly destroyed. In effect, they are to be treated like Canaanites because they are encouraging Canaanite practice.[18] Israel is Yahweh's people, bound to him as their king in covenant, and no rival can therefore be tolerated. Such a rigorous penalty for apostasy seems harsh today, but it is based on the essence of Israel as free people with Yahweh. Apostasy denied what Israel was, taking from them what they had. Unity with Yahweh produces freedom, but apostasy enslaves the people again which is why it is rejected with such vigor.[19]

Israel's Culture Must Reflect Her Devotion to Yahweh (Deut 14:1–21)

For most contemporary readers, this list of material does not seem overly interesting in and of itself. What it does, though, is demonstrate that Israel must testify to her faith in Yahweh through obedience to him at the basic level of culture. Thus, this passage is thematically very close to the preceding one, even if the topic of apostasy and unclean foods might seem a little remote to our ways of thinking. The point is that absolute obedience to Yahweh is to be demonstrated in all circumstances.

The opening two verses reject Canaanite practices of mourning for the dead, whilst verse twenty-one could reject some form of magic ritual for fertility, though it must be admitted that the interpretation of this law is uncertain.[20] In between is a list of clean and unclean foods which is similar to that of Leviticus 11. This is not on the whole inspiring reading, and some of the animal identifications, and especially those of the birds,

---

18. Arguably, the death of Achan in Joshua 7 and destruction of Gibeah in Judges 19–20 are an application of this law.

19. See McConville, *Deuteronomy*, 241.

20. It also occurs in Exod 23:19 and 34:26, both times concluding a block of material.

are not entirely clear. But, they all suggest Israel's need at the level of her cultural practices – how she mourns, eats, and waits for rain—to demonstrate her obedience to Yahweh. Israel as a people is to be holy, to demonstrate that she is Yahweh's treasured possession.[21] We are not sure of the reasons behind all of what is included here, but this basic truth remains, and whereas in Leviticus the list is more concerned with maintaining purity, its placement here seeks to promote a life that is distinct from Canaanite practice and which demonstrates Israel's holiness. In fact, this passage links all three main themes—her actions are to demonstrate that she is a community living in obedient response to Yahweh, so that even when she sits down to eat a meal, Israel is in worship, and what she eats is a pointer to the one whom she serves in obedience.[22]

In all three of these passages we see that the shape of worship is determined by one's obedience to Yahweh. Moreover, the shape of this obedience moves from the central sanctuary to the home, so that worship is seen to involve a lifestyle that derives from an absolute commitment to Yahweh rather than simply the practice of cultic acts.[23]

Worship Is a Response to God's Goodness in Daily Life (Deut 14:22–29; 16:1–17)

Although the main portion that reflects this theme occurs in 16:1–17, we also see it in 14:22–29. Israel's worship is in response to Yahweh, it is in obedience to him, but it flows out of their daily experience of him. It should be noted that the whole of 14:22—16:17 is structured around times of periodic observance, which is why matters which might seem to be more appropriately considered as acts of social justice are treated as worship in Deuteronomy.

THE TITHE (DEUT 14:22–29)

In 14:22–29 we see this in the setting aside of tithes, which is essentially the positive counterpart to the prohibitions in 14:1–21. The tithe is an

---

21. Millar, *Now Choose Life*, 117, notes that calling Israel Yahweh's treasured possession (*sᵉgullâ*) is invariably linked to Israel's election and thus the covenant.

22. This law, of course, does not bind Christians, but the principal is one applied by Paul in his discussion of foods in Corinth. All foods are clean but we may not eat in such a manner that we cause a fellow Christian to stumble.

23. Christensen, *Deuteronomy 1:1—21:9*, 287, argues that the whole of 12:1—16:17 is a chiasm with 14:1–21 as its center.

amount, perhaps not fixed,[24] which was to come out of the annual produce of the Israelite family. Since the tithe was to be eaten, and if the central sanctuary was too far away it was sold to raise the cash for a feast, this is not the passage that church treasurers normally consider. However, two key elements come out of this passage in terms of this theme.

First, worship given to Yahweh comes out of the daily experience of his goodness. It is not expressed in abstract, spiritual terms. It is expressed in physical terms. God has, each year, given a crop. That crop is continual evidence of his goodness and provision. One does not need some startling spiritual experience to affirm God's goodness. Rather, worship is rooted in the normal experiences of life as seen in the year's crop, something especially important since Israel was largely a subsistence farming economy. Second, worship was to be marked by joy. It celebrates what God had done in normal life and uses this in worship, thus enabling Israel to "learn to revere Yahweh your God always" (14:23).

The Festivals (Deut 16:1–17)

We see the same pattern in the description of the festivals in 16:1–17, where we have Passover, Weeks, and Tabernacles described. Passover, of course, celebrates Israel's deliverance from Egypt, though it is notable that in an agricultural society Israel would have celebrated then anyway with the start of planting. However, 16:1, 3 make it clear that the basis for celebrating Passover is the deliverance from Egypt, though that it was to be celebrated at the central sanctuary also shows that entry into the land is an important element. The exodus was not complete without the land, and it is the land that enables Passover to be celebrated.[25] Discussion of Passover is followed by Weeks (16:9–12) which carefully fuses the deliverance from Egypt with enjoyment of the harvest in the land, whilst Tabernacles is here described exclusively in terms of agricultural produce and human craft. Other emphases occur for Tabernacles elsewhere, but in Deuteronomy it is the agricultural cycle that is predominant. Again, the emphasis is on joy that is a response to the goodness of God in daily

---

24. Cf. Mayes, *Deuteronomy*, 245.

25. Elsewhere, the nature of Passover as family worship is stressed, but as McConville, *Deuteronomy*, 272, argues, it is always understood also as a community activity, which is why it is appropriately celebrated in the sanctuary.

life (16:15), which is why it is essential to appear with an offering at the sanctuary three times a year.

Both of these passages insist, therefore, that Israel's worship must be a joyful response to Yahweh for his activity in daily life. The story of salvation becomes meaningful through integration with daily experience. Hence, the starting point of all worship is the reality that God is active in all of life, and worship is fundamentally a response to that. Moreover, the use of agricultural produce in worship meant that people were encouraged to reflect on their own experiences whilst also observing the experience of the whole community, so in addition to the Sabbath cycle of weeks and years, each year was also structured to the rhythm of worship that celebrated Yahweh's presence and provision. Finally, by placing these events in the sanctuary, Deuteronomy insists that worship finds expression in the life of the community as a whole. Where the food laws have stressed the possibility of worship as something that happens in the home, the feasts stress the importance of the gathered community.

Worship is the Concern for the Marginalized in the Community (Deut 15:1–18)

We noted that worship in Deuteronomy is the creation of community in response to Yahweh. So far, we have the response to Yahweh, so we now consider the creation of community.

Here we must return to 14:22–29 before considering chapter 15. We noted there that worship is rooted in daily experience, but the joyful worship it describes is not only for those who have been personally blessed. Although most people had small farms, not all did—notably, Levites, widows, orphans, and resident foreigners, each of whom did not control access to land.[26] What would happen to them in the midst of all this feasting? Deuteronomy 14:22 is quite specific—in the midst of their feasting, Israel is not to forget the Levites, for they have no land. In addition, Deuteronomy also divides the six working years of the seven-year Sabbath cycle into two groups of three years. At the end of each three years, those with land were to make a special offering on behalf of those without land. This was not to be a token sum, for these people were to be "satisfied" by what they ate. Indeed, a consistent theme that runs through

---

26. Although the groups here are often considered to be equivalent to the poor—and no doubt many were—the issue here is access to land since the tithe derived from usufruct. Cf. McConville, *Deuteronomy*, 252.

these chapters is the need to remember the marginal and provide for them in worship. Such provision is integral to what it means to worship. In addition, this enables Deuteronomy's vision of worship to move out from the family to the community as a whole.

This theme is developed in 15:1–18, where the concern is probably first with Israelites who owned land (15:1–11) and then with those who did not (15:12–18).[27] In verses 1–11 we have the year of release described in which debts were either cancelled or suspended for the year of the land's release.[28] The point that is consistently made is that Israel is to give generously to their poor, a term which covers all those in need. Their own deliverance provided their model, but the practical reality was rooted in the character of Yahweh as the one who insisted that the basic needs of all should be met. Deuteronomy knows that this is not easily achieved (compare 15:4 and 11), but it does not change the fact that a worshipping community expresses this by sustaining those in need.

This is also evident in 15:12–18 with the release of Hebrew debt-slaves at the end of every seventh year. On release, the master must provide for them generously—verse 14 literally requiring them to be "necklaced" with abundance. We notice, though, that the decision as to whether or not someone stayed in slavery was dependent upon the slave, not the master. They were given rights because they were a member of the community, and Yahweh's blessing was related to this.

These details about the seventh year were not simply a piece of economic social engineering.[29] They are a part of a seven-year cycle in which the seventh year was set aside for Yahweh, trusting him to sustain the people rather than maintaining normal economic activity. It was a Sabbath. At such a time the greatest temptation is to rely on one's available economic resources—calling in loans or requiring slaves to carry out the necessary labor. But as a community in worship, this is unacceptable, and these laws provide a different focus. If the whole nation was to be in worship, then provision must be made for all to have enough. Community must be built if the nation is to be a people of worship.

---

27. Wright, *God's People*, 147–48, 253.
28. On this disputed issue, see Wright, *God's People*, 167–73.
29. Though, see Hamilton, *Social Justice*.

CONCLUSION

This is all too brief a look at these chapters, and much more could be said. However, they raise challenging concerns for us about how we conduct contemporary Christian worship, especially the extent to which our worship seeks to create an inclusive community as opposed to the individualism present in much of western society. We are perhaps generally aware of the need for our worship to be given in obedience, and clearly given to God in Christ through the Spirit. But many contemporary worship services happen without any obvious reference to the daily life of those who participate in it. Even when we move away from the sloppy language that equates worship with singing praise songs, the idea that worship constitutes a set of lifestyle commitments is not often evidenced. How do our singing, our prayer, and our testimony point us to God's continued activity in our lives, activity for which we should worship him? How do we ensure that concern for the marginalized as a means of the creation of community (and not simply as an act of charity for someone with whom no close relationship) becomes a dominant feature of what we do? We live in an individualized age, and community is not always a strong point. But if the church is an inclusive community of those brought together in the body of Christ, then Deuteronomy challenges us at the core of what it means to worship God.

2

Journey to the Center of the Heart

Psalm 19 as Transformance

David J. Cohen

INTRODUCTION

A DEFINITION OF WORSHIP, and how we practice it, can prove to be elusive. Yet, the Bible clearly affirms the significance of worship as an activity for both the community of faith and individuals. Despite this affirmation, questions linger such as "What is worship?" and "Why would we worship at all?" In addition, one might wonder what effect worship might have on human beings who do engage in worshipping God. We might also ask where best to look in the biblical text to reflect on the meaning, practice, and context of worship. I suggest here that Psalm 19 is one such place. Although the psalm does not offer a definitive or comprehensive answer to the questions posed above it does provide language, images, and interconnections which prove valuable for reflecting on some of the issues.[1] Through an exploration of Psalm 19 we are invited to grapple with the elusive idea of worship and discover some interesting biblical perspectives on what it is, how it might be practiced, and what effect it might have.

---

1. In fact McConnell points out that "the OT never defines worship [but] it does provide clues about its understanding of the topic." Cf. McConnell, "Worship," 929.

PSALM 19

Of course, one might ask why Psalm 19 is the chosen focal point, and legitimately so! There are various sections of the biblical text from both the Old and the New Testaments that we could examine for discussion and reflection. However, Psalm 19 presents a unique and broad view of the notion of worship. This is because of its content, structure, *and* its inclusion in the Psalter—historically a devotional prayer/hymnbook for people of Judeo-Christian faith. In identifying Psalm 19 as a superlative example of expressing worship C. S. Lewis described Psalm 19 as "the greatest poem in the Psalter and one of the greatest lyrics in the world."[2] The fact that this psalm is poetic and, at the same time, a song reinforces the power of such writing to evoke powerful images, emotions, and even a different manner of living for worshipping individuals and communities who use it. John Eaton concluded that Psalm 19 "in fact has an inexhaustible richness of theme, making it one of the greatest treasures of religious devotion."[3] Again, this underlines the arguably superlative nature of this psalm, certainly among psalms, as an expression of devotion and worship to God. But what is it about Psalm 19, particularly, that elicits responses such as these?

Although Psalm 19 clearly expresses worship towards God with a variety of language and images it does not use any of the common Hebrew words that tend to be translated as "worship" in most English versions of the Old Testament.[4] These Hebrew words for worship, when used elsewhere in the Old Testament, encompass anything from the action of bowing down (ḥwh) to fearing (yārēʿ) or serving (ʿbd) God. The spectrum of worship in Hebrew vocabulary is perhaps best summarized as an attitude most often expressed in some kind of action. Despite the absence of these words from Psalm 19 ideas reflected in the common Hebrew vocabulary used to describe worship can be inferred from the text. Certainly, one only has to begin praying or singing the psalm to be

---

2. Lewis, *Reflections*, 63.

3. Eaton, *The Psalms*, 108–9.

4. McConnell provides an extensive discussion of the various Hebrew words for worship and how they are used in his article. He notes interestingly at the outset of his discussion that the English word "worship" derives from the old English "worthship" implying something is "worthy of praise." He goes on to conclude that "the OT authors would agree that Yahweh is worthy of worship but they never use such terminology." McConnell, "Worship," 929–30.

captivated with the psalmist's, and creation's, sense of worshipful expression to God.

Notwithstanding the content of the text I suggest that it is the way in which the psalm is structured that contributes significantly to its capacity to engage an individual or faith community in worship. It provides a gathering point for embarkation on a journey that begins in the heavens and ends in the human heart. Also, worth noting is that Psalm 19, as part of the Psalter, need not be a one-off journey, from origin to destination, but a journey that can be travelled repeatedly. This journey can be one of *active participation and reflection* as we use it to express prayerful worship and, in turn, it offers us an opportunity for transformance. Transformance is a process that signifies a participation marked by subsequent personal transformation.[5] As a text through which transformance can take place Psalm 19 involves engagement with God in the theaters of the cosmos, everyday life, and one's heart. Within these three theaters this beautifully crafted psalm enables the worshipper to join with, and yet individuate from, the cosmos in an act of worshipful devotion while being enlivened to the possibility of personal transformation through the act of worshipping God.

Before we explore what Psalm 19 says about worship and how it might facilitate transformation, we need to examine briefly the unity *and* diversity expressed through the structure of the psalm. On first reading Psalm 19 one might wonder how such a broad expanse of imagery and ideas can co-exist in the same piece of writing. As a result the integrity of the psalm has been a topic of much discussion among biblical scholars. Should we view Psalm 19 as an integrated whole or is it simply a result of later editorial work combining largely unrelated ideas? There has been a variety of responses to this question, two of which are helpful in the present discussion. Vos concludes his observations stating that he "regard[s] the psalm as a wisdom poem in which creation, the Torah and mankind bear witness to God's mighty deeds." While I think Vos' observations are helpful in highlighting the psalm's diversity I am more hesitant than Vos to settle definitively on a particular genre identification. In some ways this

---

5. Driver, *Liberating Rites*, 28. Driver coins this term specifically to describe what can happen when a person engages in ritual activity. As biblical psalms have been/are often used as a part of ritual worship for individuals and communities of faith, rather than simply analyzed and explained, the term "transformance" is appropriate here.

psalm defies any attempt to definitively categorize it.[6] Fishbane is more reluctant to be definitive noting that, "the concerns and references of this psalm raise this question about it: Is it a hymn, a didactic praise of Torah, or a petition? An attentive reading of its totality suggests that it is, in fact, all three."[7] Both Vos' and Fishbane's observations highlight the dilemma but, in different ways, acknowledge how the structure unifies a diverse collection of ideas.[8] It is apparent from the structure that the psalm falls naturally into three sections reflecting the diversity, highlighted by Vos and Fishbane, and these three sections correspond to the three theaters I am proposing.[9] This discussion will treat the psalm as a whole while considering the value and significance of the three proposed "theaters." I will suggest that it is within these theaters that prayerful worship, reflection, and the possibility of transformance is offered. On this basis then the structure of Psalm 19 can be formulated in the following way:

- The theater of the cosmos (vv. 1–6)
- The theater of everyday life (vv. 7–11)
- The theater of the human heart (vv. 12–14)

In light of these observations we will now explore what we discover in these three theaters and how they interconnect with each other in the overall structure of the psalm. To do this we will examine each theater in turn and ponder the potential implications they raise in understanding what it means to worship God, why we worship God, and how such an activity might transform us.

---

6. Vos, *Theopoetry*, 114, provides an excellent summary of the discussions around this issue. Of course, linked to the integrity of the psalm is the identification of its genre which, in some ways, has been just as problematic as the psalm's integrity.

7. Fishbane, *Biblical Text*, 85.

8. Craigie, *Psalm*, 179. Interestingly, he also notes that "the psalm in its present form is a unity, either composed as a single piece, or else the author took a fragment of an old hymn (vv. 2–7) and extended it by means of a theological commentary and comparison." No doubt discussions will continue, and so they should, but the participant in the psalm is still left with a text which *is* now a whole entity, regardless of its provenance.

9. It is also worth noting that Gerstenberger (*Psalms*, 101) provides an extensive list of scholars who choose to divide Psalm 19 into two sections; vv. 1–6 and 7–15. However, for the purposes of this discussion it is helpful to further divide vv. 7–15 into vv. 7–11 and vv. 12–15.

The Theater of the Cosmos (vv. 1–6)

The first theater of Psalm 19 is the theater of the cosmos where we enter to eavesdrop on the heavens as they not only reveal but also express something of the "glory of God." In fact the verb used to describe what the heavens do suggests a "retelling" or a "rehearsing" taking place in this theater. However, this is not a dress rehearsal. It is revealed as a performance for all to see. However, unlike any ordinary theater, where one normally enters before the performance begins, Psalm 19 introduces us to a "perpetual" theater operating in worshipful devotion towards God. The fascination of this theater is that it neither needs nor demands the presence of humankind for its functioning and efficacy. God is worshipped irrespective of human involvement. Yet the psalmist invites those who would be worshippers to enter this theater and to witness and ultimately take part in the unfolding drama.

The theater of the cosmos should not be viewed as light entertainment for a casual observer. As Kraus notes, the use of *kābôd* to describe the "glory of God" (v. 1) adds an emphatic "notion of weightiness, of weighty prestige (*gravitas*)" to what is being recounted by the heavens.[10] However, despite this grand scene within the theater of the cosmos a strange phenomenon becomes almost immediately apparent. There is speech and knowledge but there are no words or sounds (vv. 2–3). This paradox of speech and silence could lead us to consternation or even a stalemate in our understanding of what is happening here. Or conversely, perhaps it could spur us on to "listen" more closely to the text. "Creation speaks but its language is peculiar. It is not verbal, *but it is steady, and it is heard.*"[11] Alter is helpful at this point preferring to translate the verb *nābaʿ* as "breathe."[12] In other words, the heavens verbalize nothing and yet "say" much about God in worship as they "breathe."[13] What's more, with phrases such as "day after day" coupled with "night after night" (v. 2), the unspeakable and unremitting nature of this worship is, at least momentarily, captured within human language and time.

---

10. Kraus, *Psalms*, 270.

11. Murphy and Carm, "Wisdom," 6 (emphasis added). Murphy and Carm also note the observations of Karl Barth and Gerhard von Rad on Job 38–41 where "Creation had a voice which spoke differently to Job than the chorus of the three friends."

12. Alter, *The Books*, 60. In fact he goes on to say that "the literal, or at least etymological, sense of the Hebrew verb . . . is to 'well forth.'"

13. Kraus, *Psalms*, 275.

In a journey of twists and turns we are then presented with a further paradox. The heavens, which declare God's glory, and yet have no speech or sound, have a "voice [which] goes out into all the earth" (v. 4). Worship of God in the theater of the cosmos is not confined by spatial limits. Notwithstanding the unrestricted nature of the proclamation Craigie suggests that "the reflection of God's praise in the universe is perceptible only to those already sensitive to God's revelation and purpose."[14] While his line of argument suggests the possibility that at least some human beings may be able to perceive God's glory he goes on to surmise that for others "*reflection* may open up an awareness of the knowledge of God, the Creator, who by his hands created a glory beyond the comprehension of the human mind."[15] Certainly we could continue to speculate on the nature and level of human perception in this environment. However, what Craigie does alert us to is the idea that an awareness of, and participation in, the theater of the cosmos is not completely beyond human grasp. Nonetheless, the opening verses of Psalm 19 do clearly affirm that, irrespective of human participation, God is continuously worshipped and only God is worthy of praise.[16]

The Theater of Everyday Life (vv. 7–11)

From the cosmos the psalmist transitions, rather abruptly, into the theater of everyday life. Although in some ways one could argue that the transition has already begun with the announcement that "their [the heaven's] voice goes out into all the earth, their words to the ends of the world" in v. 4. Worshipping God, by declaring God's glory, while rather ambiguous to this point, now becomes more grounded in the concept of Torah. Here I am using Torah in the sense of "teaching" or, one could say "moral and ethical guidance for life."[17] Levine states that, "unlike the

---

14. Craigie, *Psalm*, 181. In contrast to this Kraus (*Psalms*, 275) calls this "transmission" but argues that "it is a message that cannot be perceived by humans."

15. Ibid., 180, (emphasis added).

16. Fishbane, *Biblical Text*, 85. He highlights the ideas of Sarna who suggests that there could be a "polemical" edge to the psalmist's presentation of the sun here. Clearly, in Psalm 19, the sun is subordinated to God in contrast to "ancient Egyptian, Hittite and Mesopotamian hymns to the sun." Craigie (*Psalm*, 181) adds to this noting that Gen 1:3–19 is an antecedent for the text of Psalm 19.

17. *JPS Hebrew-English Tanakh*. It is interesting to note that the *JPS* TANAKH translation uses the term "teaching" in contrast to many English versions. One exception to this is the *NLT*, which uses the term "instruction."

heavens, the Torah speaks loudly, clearly, and articulately of God's will for humankind, and especially for Israel."[18] In the context of Psalm 19 Torah could be seen to verbalize the "non-verbal" declaration of God's glory by the heavens, thereby articulating worship of God. But does living out Torah demonstrate worship of God or, in the words of v. 1, declare the glory of God?

If the psalmist is correct in statements made about Torah in vv. 7–11 then Torah is not only a reflection of God's will for humankind, as Levine points out, but also, when lived out, it becomes an expression of worship, declaring God's glory in the theater of everyday life. So in this sense the living out of Torah declares God's glory together with the heavens. This shows a worshipful response to the Divine by both the cosmos and humankind, giving a "voice" which can be "heard" even by those who may be unable to perceive the presence of God in our world.

Torah in the theater of everyday life is presented as a series of couplets from vv. 7–11:

- The law of the LORD is perfect, refreshing the soul (v. 7c).
- The statutes of the LORD are trustworthy, making wise the simple (v. 7b).
- The precepts of the LORD are right, giving joy to the heart (v. 8a).
- The commands of the LORD are radiant, giving light to the eyes (v. 8b).
- The fear of the LORD is pure, enduring forever (v. 9a).
- The ordinances of the LORD are sure, and all of them are righteous (v. 9b).

It is interesting to note at the outset that in the previous section of Psalm 19 (vv. 1–6) God is referred to by the Hebrew 'ēl. However, in this second section, from v. 7 onwards, God is referred to by the Divine name YHWH possibly signaling an emerging sense of intimacy with God for the psalmist.[19] In addition, each couplet, except the last two, highlights the aspects of potential personal transformation for those living Torah in the theater of everyday life. It is worthwhile at this point to consider

18. Levine, *Sing Unto God*, 20.
19. Fishbane, *Biblical Text*, 86.

some of the vocabulary used in each couplet to more fully understand how the living out of Torah in the theater of everyday life has transformative potential.

Torah is first described as *tāmîm* (v.7a) which is a term pointing to completeness and a purity or without blemish. The effect of this is literally "a bringing back of the soul" (v. 7b). In simple terms, then, Torah is life-giving, soul refreshing, and liberating as opposed to the view of some that Torah, with its more common translation as "law," is restricting and life sapping. It seems the intent here is to communicate that Torah lived out in the theater of everyday life can be equated with both glorifying God (worship) and personal life-giving change.

In the second couplet (v. 7b) *ēdût* is substituted for Torah with these "statutes" being described as something which can be implicitly trusted. Once again a concrete result is voiced: "making the simple wise." The outcome of adherence to God's trustworthy "statutes" can be viewed as part of a foundation for gaining wisdom.[20] The third term used to reflect the idea of Torah is *piqqûdîm* and is translated by many English versions as "precepts" (v.8a).[21] These "precepts," being described as *yāshār* ("right"), are synonymous with the previous terms, "perfect" and "trustworthy." Again, the effect of these "right" precepts is made clear. They gladden the heart.

The next couplet reveals yet another term conveying the idea of Torah. However, in contrast to the plural, "precepts," the term *miṣwâ* is used in the singular form (v. 8b). It is perhaps more reasonable to suggest that rather than the focus here being on individual "commands" we should consider a more all-encompassing idea for such *miṣwâ* as God's "command" for living.[22] Here the "command of the Lord" is acknowledged to have an intrinsic purity or cleanness but its effect on human enlightenment is also stressed. Clines identifies allusions to the creation account here suggesting that, "The terminology used to describe the law of Yahweh in Ps. xix 8ff. is reminiscent of the description of the tree of

---

20. This contrasting of the "wise" and "simple" has echoes of other psalms, such as Pss 1 and 119 together with wisdom literature found in Proverbs, Job and Ecclesiastes.

21. Cf. NRSV, TNIV, NIV, NJB et al. Interestingly, within the Psalter this term is found almost exclusively in Psalm 119 except for this and two other occurrences (cf. Pss 103:18 and 111:7). The focus of Psalm 119 is clearly on Torah and living in a wise manner as a result of faithfully adhering to Torah.

22. I view the idea of *miṣwâ* here in a similar sense to how I described Torah earlier as "ethical and moral guidance for life."

knowledge of God and evil. It is here suggested that the author of Ps xixB intended by his allusions to Gen. ii–iii to assert the superiority of the law to the tree of knowledge as a means of obtaining wisdom."[23] This is an interesting observation which, if valid, suggests that the living Torah is a proactive way of gaining wisdom in contrast to the self-serving grasp for knowledge narrated in Genesis 3 with disastrous effects on the Divine-human relationship. It also reinforces the idea that lived Torah "grounds" the worship of God in the theater of everyday life as a consistent expression of faithful devotion to God. Another way of viewing this is to note that "just as the sun dominates the daytime sky, so too does Torah dominate human life."[24] Inherent in these verses is the way in which Psalm 19 involves humankind in the practice of worship by connecting the theater of the cosmos with the theater of everyday life using the concept of Torah. One cannot leave this psalm imagining that there is an unbridgeable gap between the two. In observing this Eaton says that "the marvel of this psalm lies somewhere in its connect of the vast natural phenomena with the individual's moral way."[25]

Clearly the first four couplets presented here provide a pattern of cause and effect focused around the idea of worshipping God through living Torah in the theater of the everyday. But what do we make of the final two couplets? (v. 9) These appear to be more propositional statements which are made with seemingly no need to provide further clarity or definition. Mays points out that the phrase "fear of the Lord" (v. 9a) occurs very rarely in the Hebrew Bible. However, on the two other occasions the phrase is used it clearly points to a wise way of living life.[26] Here in Psalm 19 "fear of the Lord" appears to be stated simply as a valuable attitude to uphold, regardless of any potential outcomes. The second statement uses the term *mishpāṭ* as a synonym for Torah, again, shifting back to the plural form and these ordinances are described as "entirely righteous" (v.9b). For Craigie this "draws together the sum total of the law, which is righteous as a consequence of its origin in God, and

---

23. Clines, "Tree of knowledge," 8. He goes on to point out that the image of "giving light to the eyes" is sometimes used metaphorically "to cause someone to become aware of something by means of supernatural insight" (11).

24. Craigie, *Psalm*, 183.

25. Eaton, *The Psalms*, 111.

26. The other two occurrences are Ps 111:10 and Prov 1:5.

righteous with respect to its destination, mankind."[27] The couplets themselves, together with Craigie's observation, suggest that even if Torah, human beings, or presumably the heavens, were not to declare the glory of God the nature and glorious character of God remains a reality which cannot be challenged. It stands irrespective of what is, or is not, said and done. Nonetheless, from a human perspective these two propositions cannot be divorced from the outcomes voiced within the previous couplets suggesting the active participation of the individual and the resultant transformative power of Torah. Human beings are called to respond to God in worship by aspiring to live Torah in the theater of everyday life. Thus, declaring God's glory *with* the heavens and being transformed in the process.

In a manner only poetry can achieve the essence of Torah is then encapsulated in two metaphors which capture both the imagination and the senses (v. 10). As if to further "ground" the concept of Torah, in the theater of the human heart, we are enticed by something which is "more precious than gold" and "sweeter than honey." These metaphors capture something of the aesthetic nature of Torah as well as its practical nature. In other words one's worship of God by living Torah in the theater of everyday life is not obligation, nor merely a desire to do the right thing. It is a way of living that produces a life of goodness and beauty. This then aesthetically pleasing and emotionally satisfying to both the worshipper and those with whom the worshipper relates.[28] This is a further reflection of the nature and character of God. So these metaphors, combined with the preceding couplets, are focused on the individual being transformed *in* the theater of everyday life. This transformation comes about because of God's revelation in the heavens and in lived out Torah prompting Klouda to conclude that, "the rehearsal of Yahweh's marvelous works and the teaching of Torah synthesize God's revelation."[29] A recognition and participation in this revelation is foundational to both the concept and practice of worshipping God. What's more, it encompasses not just everyday life but, in fact, the cosmos in total.

---

27. Craigie, *Psalm*, 182.

28. Paul reflects a similar concept in NT terms stating, "For we are to God the pleasing aroma of Christ among those who are being saved and those who are perishing." (2 Cor 2:15)

29. Klouda, "Dialectical Interplay," 186.

Verse 11 presents us with a summary statement for the couplets and metaphors identified in vv. 7–10 and a vital link with the final section of Psalm 19, the theater of the human heart. In doing so a powerful verb is employed to make the link and underline the idea that this worshipful encounter with God is not simply one of observation or even intellectual assent but, rather, transformation. The word zāhar is translated in many English versions with the primary idea of "warning." However, Harris et al. suggest that the root meaning is probably "teaching" in the sense of "admonishing" or "warning" (v. 11a).[30] Perhaps the *New Jerusalem Bible* captures the idea most fully by translating v. 11 as follows: "Thus your servant is *formed* by them; observing them brings great reward."[31] The idea of "formation" encapsulates both the admonishing role of Torah (warning) and the positive aspect of Torah (shaping or forming). So, the one who worships God in the theaters of the cosmos and everyday life enters a formative experience which brings first, a recognition of the need for change and, second, a recognition of the possibility of change.

So in attempting to summarize the diversity of Torah nuances found here in verses 7–11 Mays states that, "This eclectic gathering of terms is a procedure used also in Psalm 119 . . . [S]uffice it to say that [it] suggests that the psalmist found the instruction of the Lord in a variety of sources."[32] This observation also suggests that the presence of Torah, in the theater of everyday life, cannot be encapsulated in just one term alone or explained in one way. Craigie concurs suggesting that "from a poetic perspective, these terms may be seen as synonymous, though from a theological perspective, they may be seen as all-embracing."[33] Torah is difficult to summarize in a simple way and yet, for the psalmist, it offers the key to worshipping God in the theater of everyday life and living life as God intended. However, the focus on Torah in verses 7–11 highlights a dilemma as the psalmist moves into the theater of the human heart.

---

30. Harris et al., *Theological Wordbook*, 236–37.

31. Emphasis added. It is interesting that the pronoun "them" used here is ambiguous as to its referent although clearly it alludes to the various expressions of Torah in vv. 7–10.

32. Mays, "The Place," 5.

33. Craigie, *Psalm*, 181.

The Theater of the Human Heart (vv. 12–14)

As Psalm 19 moves into this final theater (beginning in v. 12) it becomes an intimate reflection of the human heart in general and the psalmist's heart in particular. A powerful rhetorical question offers a doorway to self-awareness as an entrance into the theater of the human heart. It is one thing to be aware of a place we might call the interior of the human heart but quite another to be mindful of state of the human heart. Fishbane perceptively points out that "the chasm between God's words of revelation and man's corresponding acts are bridged by the words and act of prayer. The psalmist is revealed as a creature in need of redemption."[34] There is a sense here of vulnerability, but not hopelessness, as a human being engages with God. The exposed "need of redemption," as Fishbane puts it, also reveals a gracious God who can address this "issue" of the human heart.[35]

Interestingly, English translations of verse 12a tend to reverse the Hebrew word order and offer a freer, rather than more literal, parallel line in v. 12b. The Hebrew provides perhaps a starker description of what one sees, and what one hopes for, in the theater of the human heart:

v.12a   errors—who discerns?
v. 12b   from hiding—acquit me.

Dramatically the rhetorical question which forms a doorway into the theater of the human heart leads to a "petition-prayer [which] is the gift of hope received in its recitation."[36] The prayer is one which points to a transformance being in process (the question) while it petitions for transformation to take place (the request). Fishbane concludes that, "the true subject of part 3 (vv. 12–14) is . . . redemption."[37] So then, the initial observation of "errors" and "faults" (v. 12) within the theater of the human heart opens the way into a redemptive transformation bringing hope out of potential despair.

Craigie insightfully links the final direction of Psalm 19 back to the concept of Torah, voiced in vv. 7–11 saying, "[I]t is the Torah of God

---

34. Fishbane, *Biblical Text*, 89.

35. Of course this kind of process is not without precedent. Another example is the experience described in Isa 6 that demonstrates vulnerability, mindfulness (on the part of Isaiah), and redemption.

36. Ibid., 90.

37. Ibid., 89.

alone that reveals to mankind that he has a place in the universal scheme of things. It is not a place which gives ground for human boasting or declaration of human might over the cosmos: when the psalmist's praise of God's revelation in the Torah dawns upon him personally, it issues immediately in a prayer for forgiveness and acceptance."[38] The action of Psalm 19, which began with a recognition of the heavens declaring the glory of God, draws to a climax in the theater of the human heart. Here, bringing glory to God now becomes a petition-prayer for personal transformation. In some ways the final words of the Psalm present a kind of *inclusio* that harks back to the opening of the psalm. The personalized expression, "O Lord, my Rock and my Redeemer," shows that the God in the theater of the cosmos, and the God in the theater of everyday life is also the God of the theater of the human heart.

REFLECTIONS

As we began this discussion I posed three questions that formed the basis of this exploration.

- What is worship?
- Why might we worship at all?
- What effect might worship have on human beings?

In an attempt to address these questions I have suggested that Psalm 19 provides some responses as we journey into three theaters—the theater of the cosmos, the theater of everyday life, and the theater of the human heart.

The theater of the cosmos reminds us that whatever worship is, it is focused exclusively on God and declares God's glory. This is a stark reminder for a decidedly egocentric humanity that we are not the beginning, nor the end, of worship. In fact the theater of the cosmos suggests that declaring God's glory does not necessarily need human support or participation. Declaration of God's glory, as an act of worship, is something that continues unabated through the existence of the heavens. So, in this sense worship is something which is supra-human.

However, before we dismiss *our role* in worshipping God, the psalmist reminds us of the centrality of living Torah, God's guidance for the life of faith in the theater of the everyday. In Psalm 19 Torah provides the

---

38. Craigie, *Psalm*, 183.

everyday expression for worship of God. For the psalmist worshipping God looks like living out Torah in all its wonderful colors and shades. In presenting this as an expression of worship we are reminded that worship is not exclusively something supra-human, nor is it a one-off event but a whole of life journey. The heavens declare God's glory in the theater of the cosmos "day after day" and "night after night" and reflecting on this the psalmist reminds us of our responsibility to constantly live Torah in the theater of everyday life. Thus, the Torah focused life becomes a human reflection of "The heavens declare." This is what worship might look like for the psalmist but why would human beings worship God in this way? Torah, in its broadest sense can be understood as "hitting the mark." That is, in living Torah, as an act of worship we are most fully becoming who God intended us to be in the first place; human beings expressing the image of the creator.[39]

The final theater of Psalm 19 brings us to the most personal and intimate point of worship; the human heart providing an insight into what might result when human being engage in worshipping God. Here, worship blossoms from despair in brokenness to joy in a hope-filled picture of redemption. The one whose glory is declared by the heavens is also the one who reaches out to broken humanity as an ancient world redeemer would care for family members in need. So why would we worship at all? The conclusion to Psalm 19 would, in part, suggest that *we respond* in worship because we are acutely aware of our need and that the Redeemer has already heard our cry of desolation, initiating a consoling hope.

Finally, we have noted that the three theaters do not invite us to enter as detached observers to watch a performance as an audience. They invite us in as active participants. Through this active participation the content and the structure of the psalm itself suggests a process of transformation. This begins in witnessing the glory of God, as declared by the heavens, and ends with a transformation at the center of one's heart. The process we observe here in Psalm 19 is one of transformation for the psalmist but suggests something greater for those of us who pray the psalms. Perhaps in the very action of praying or singing psalms like

---

39. Harris et al., *Theological Wordbook*, 403. They highlight that "The basic idea of the root yārâis 'to throw' or 'to cast' with the strong sense of control by the subject . . . [T]he three most frequent uses of this root deal with shooting arrows, sending rain and teaching." Hence, the emphasis here is an activity which has a specific "goal" or "mark."

Psalm 19 we can unlock for ourselves a process of transformance. The action itself encourages transformation to begin in the center of the human heart.

While each of these theaters presents a different and yet complementary picture of what worship might look like they also provide the impetus for worshipping God more fully. They remind us that we worship in a context far greater than any one individual or community of faith. We worship God from deep within the human heart, expressing this worship in everyday life, and together with the whole of creation.

This journey, albeit potentially transforming, cannot be confined to the individual. The picture we have in Psalm 19, and within the broader context of the Psalter, suggests that while we worship as people of faith we do not worship alone. We worship with one another, declaring God's glory and we also worship with the cosmos as it declares the same. This act of collaboration with one another and with the cosmos in worship leads inexorably towards a deeper sense of reflection on and mindfulness of God's ongoing redeeming work in our world. Reflecting on our humanity leads to an insistent yearning for redemption from the brokenness of our world including that of humankind. Yet this is the miracle. That an encounter, such as the one we witness in Psalm 19, which could potentially leave us bereft of all hope, turns out to be the very essence of hope. The God we worship is the God who desires to transform us and our world so that it might be on earth as it is in heaven. The heavens declare God's glory so that we and our world might be redeemed and made whole again.

3

Nourishing Our Missional Identity
Worship and the Mission of God's People

Michael W. Goheen

INTRODUCTION

Today the church in Western culture faces a potentially disastrous crisis.¹ There are two sides to this plight. The first is ecclesial—we have lost an understanding of the role and identity scripted for God's people in the biblical story. The second is cultural—there is confusion concerning the church's place in the surrounding cultural context. Wilbert Shenk correctly locates the root of this crisis as the loss of missional consciousness. On the one hand, the biblical identity of the church is fundamentally missional; yet that missional self-understanding has been forgotten. On the other hand, the proper relation of the church to its cultural milieu is in terms of a missionary encounter; yet we have been co-opted into the dominant culture and taken captive by its idols. What is urgently needed is a recovery of both our "inner mission consciousness" (missional self-understanding) and our "outer mission consciousness" (missionary encounter with culture).²

---

1. By "Western culture" I refer to a cultural block that shares many foundational beliefs that are product of European history. In terms of scope, I would subscribe to Samuel Huntington's definition: "The West, then, includes Europe, North America, plus other European settler countries such as Australia and New Zealand" (*Clash of Civilizations*, 46). Perhaps South Africa should be included as well.

2. Shenk, *Write the Vision*, 86–99.

Paul H. Jones argues that a big step toward the recovery of a missional consciousness will be our worship. "We are *how* we worship." He continues,

> For the Church, corporate worship is the most visible and profound occasion for individuals to encounter both the gospel and the understanding of what it means to be a Christian in the world. When the community of faith assembles, the normative texts are read and interpreted, the formative rites are celebrated, and the faithful are equipped for service in the world. Inasmuch as the Church is anchored in the gracious acts of God, corporate worship sustains and transmits Christian identity formation.[3]

Indeed, our worship is essential for our missional identity formation, and in this essay I want to probe the way the psalms accomplished this for Israel.

WORSHIP AND MISSION

Before proceeding to the Old Testament story it is important to say a few introductory words about worship and mission. Thomas Schattauer has articulated three ways that worship and mission are related to each other.[4] The first is the more traditional approach he calls "inside and out." Here worship and mission are understood as two different activities. Worship is what takes place on the inside and mission on the outside. Worship is the means by which the church is nurtured for its mission in the world. The second is a contemporary approach that has reacted against this bifurcation of worship and mission which he labels "outside in." Advocates of this view want to bring mission directly into worship either as an opportunity for evangelism (evangelicals) or as a rallying point for social and political action (liberals). Worship is collapsed into missional activities.

Schattauer offers a third way beyond these alternatives—"inside out." He believes this approach to be both "thoroughly contemporary" and "radically traditional" because it takes up the correct insights of the first two approaches and places them in the context of the *missio Dei*. Mission is first of all a matter of what God is doing for the renewal of the world rather than specific activities undertaken by the church. Thus

---

3. Jones, "We are *How* We Worship," 347.
4. Schattauer, *Inside Out*, 2–3.

the church is a people gathered in by God's mission, and as such their worship is itself a witness to God's saving work. The church's worship is directed outward toward the world, not by transforming worship into evangelism or social action, but by celebrating the mighty deeds of God especially as revealed in Jesus Christ in the midst of the world as a witness to what God has done and is doing for the sake of the creation.

Crucial to Schattauer's model is a reorientation of our understanding of mission. Mission is often conceived primarily or exclusively as tasks carried out by the church in the world for the sake of God's kingdom. Indeed, this is part of the church's mission but such tasks are derivative. A proper understanding of mission begins by recognizing the priority of God's redemptive initiative—God's mission.

Christopher Wright has given us some helpful reflection on the *missio Dei*. He believes that God's mission is the key to unlocking the Bible's grand narrative. Classical definitions of the *missio Dei* that have dominated missiological discussion for the past half century have been primarily systematic and shaped by the metaphor of sending: the Father sends the Son, the Son sends the church in the power of the Spirit.[5] Although Wright appreciates this development, he believes it neglects the importance of the Old Testament, and so he wants to reframe it in two ways: first, to expand it beyond the metaphor of sending, and second, to make it more narrative.[6] For Wright, "the whole Bible renders to us the story of God's mission through God's people in their engagement with God's world for the sake of the whole of God's creation."[7] God's mission is his long term purpose to renew and restore the whole creation and the life of humanity. The mission of the church must be understood within this framework. "Fundamentally, our mission (if it is biblically informed and validated) means our committed participation as God's people, at God's invitation and command, in God's own mission within the history of the world for the redemption of God's creation."[8]

Thus, the mission of the church is first of all a call *to be* something not *to go* somewhere or *to do* something. Of course, going and doing are

---

5. For a brief history and understanding of the term *missio Dei* see Bosch, *Transforming Mission*, 389–93. For an early and important theological articulation see Vicedom, *The Mission*.

6. Wright, *Mission of God*, 23, 62ff.

7. Ibid., 51 (original emphasis).

8. Ibid., 22–23 (original emphasis).

important as elements of our participation but these initiatives must be understood in a subordinate way as part of a wider mission.

One more definition that Wright offers is helpful: "God's mission involves God's people living in God's way in the sight of the nations."[9] This definition gives us a sense of how God will employ his people in his mission. He will make them a display people who embody God's original creational intention and eschatological goal for human life. He will come and dwell among them and give them his Torah to direct them to live in the way of the Lord. As such his people will be an attractive sign before all nations of what God intended in the beginning and the goal toward which God is moving—the restoration of the creation and human life from the corruption of sin.

Essential to embodying God's creational design and eschatological purpose for human life will be a "missionary encounter" with other stories, other ways of viewing, understanding, and living in the world. Israel is set in the midst of the nations, and their call to make known Yahweh and his redemptive purpose *necessarily* means an encounter with and challenge to the pagan ways of life of the surrounding peoples.[10]

ISRAEL'S MISSIONAL ROLE AND IDENTITY IN THE OLD TESTAMENT STORY

Theodore Mascarenhas offers fruitful reflection on the role of the psalms in the missional calling of Israel.[11] To begin he correctly observes that the "Psalter is placed within the larger work of the Old Testament and as such the idea of the missionary function must be traced first within the Old Testament."[12] And so, in the first section he reflects generally on the

---

9. Ibid., 470.

10. "Missionary encounter" is the language of Newbigin, *Foolishness*, 1. By missionary encounter Newbigin refers to a clash of ultimate and comprehensive stories—the biblical story and the cultural story. When this happens the foundational religious beliefs and reigning idolatrous assumptions shared by the cultural community are challenged. The people of God offer a credible alternative way of life to its contemporaries. There is a call for a radical conversion, an invitation to turn from its idolatrous beliefs and to come live in the true story of Yahweh's mighty deeds especially revealed in Jesus Christ.

11. Mascarenhas, *Missionary Function*.

12. Ibid., xiii. William Richey Hogg also encourages us to understand the missionary calling of Israel as the "necessary context" for understanding the psalms. He sketches Israel's history as the covenant people of the One Creator God set in the midst of the

"missionary function" of Israel in the Old Testament story. Missionary function is the role Israel sees for itself in God's mission to restore humanity and the creation to himself.[13]

Israel is chosen by God to play a central role in the unfolding of God's redemptive purposes. Since God's renewing work is directed toward all nations "Israel relates itself not only to its God, but is his chosen one before the nations. It views and understands its origin, existence, and history in relation to the peoples and the nations."[14] Israel's missionary function is consistently elaborated in three words common in ecclesiological reflection—sacrament, sign, and instrument of salvation.[15] Israel is a sacrament, that is, a visible embodiment of God's salvation in the midst of history; Israel is a sign, that is, a picture of the renewal that is coming as the goal of universal history; Israel is an instrument that God uses in his ongoing work of redemption.

Mascarenhas believes that "the missionary function of Israel is perhaps best expressed in three metaphors: blessing to the nations, kingdom of priests, and light to the nations."[16] The following section of his book analyses Abraham as a blessing to the nations (Gen 12:2–3), Israel as a kingdom of priests (Exod 19:3–6), and Israel as a light to the nations (Isa 42:1–6; 49:1–6).

It is clear that Mascarenhas has put his finger on key texts in the Old Testament that help us understand the missional role of Israel

---

nations as a light to make God known and to bring blessing to all people as the story in which one must make sense of psalms ("Psalm 22," 241–42).

13. Ibid., 10. When expositing the views of Mascarenhas I employ his terminology of "missionary." Generally speaking I prefer the word "missional" in this context. For a helpful analysis of the use of the terms "mission," "missions," "missionary," "missional," "missiology," and "missiological" see Wright, *Mission of God*, 22–25. About "missionary" Wright says, "Because of the dominant association of the word *missionary* with the activity of sending and with crosscultural communication of the gospel—that is, with a broadly centrifugal dynamic of mission—I prefer not to use the term in connection with the Old Testament." A better adjectival form of "mission," he believes, is "missional" (23).

14. Ibid., 18.

15. The Vatican II Document *Lumen Gentium* calls the church "a kind of sacrament—a sign and instrument, that is, of communion with God and unity among all people" (LG, 1; cf. LG 8,9). Subsequent Roman Catholic theology has continued with this threefold ecclesiological description. This terminology has become common in ecumenical Protestant ecclesiological reflection as well (Gassman, "The Church as Sacrament," 1–17).

16. Mascarenhas, *Missionary Function*, 18.

within the story of God's mission. In this he follows many who recognize the central importance of these texts for the Old Testament story.[17] Nevertheless, it is not so clear that the notion of metaphor adequately grasps the fundamental significance of these texts, especially Genesis 12:2–3 and Exodus 19:3–6. Indeed, when these texts are seen in terms of their pivotal place in the unfolding narrative of God's mission in the Old Testament, it becomes clear that they play a much more important role—they function together as a hermeneutical lens to read the entire story of the Old Testament. We will briefly trace this story through the hermeneutical lens formed by these two texts.

Genesis 12:2–3: Blessed to Be a Blessing

This "stupendous utterance" made to Abraham in Genesis 12:2–3 is set in the context of the first eleven chapters of Genesis.[18] These chapters are universal in scope—God is the creator of the heavens and the earth, and is Lord of all the nations. Sin pollutes all cultures of humankind and likewise God's judgment on sin is universal. In reference to Genesis 3–11 Gerhard Von Rad speaks of the author's "great hamartiology," his focus on sin, its effects, its consequences, and God's judgment.[19] Now, in Genesis 12 the biblical story narrows from its universal scope (all nations) to a particular focus (one man, one nation). The bad news of sin, alienation, curse, and judgment on all nations is met with a promise of good news: God has chosen one man to bring blessing back to his creation and to all peoples.

Paul Williamson speaks correctly of a "twofold agenda" in Genesis 12:1–3.[20] Abraham is first of all to be formed into a great nation and to be a recipient of God's covenantal blessing. The purpose is so that all nations on earth might be blessed. This final clause "all peoples on earth will be blessed through you" is "the principal statement of these three verses." It is a "result clause" that indicates that the final goal of God's election and blessing of Abraham is the salvation of the nations.[21] Thus

---

17. For example, Blauw, *Missionary Nature of the Church*, 15–28; Martin-Achard, *A Light to the Nations*, 32–41; Bailey Wells, *God's Holy People*; Dumbrell, *Covenant and Creation*; Kaiser, "Israel's Missionary Call," 25–34.

18. Wolff, "The Kerygma of the Yahwist," 140.

19. Von Rad, *Old Testament*, 1:154.

20. Williamson, "Covenant," 145.

21. Dumbrell, *Covenant*, 64–65.

"God's calling and election of Abraham was not merely so that he should be saved . . . It was rather, and more explicitly, that he and his people should be instruments through whom God would gather that multinational multitude that no man or woman can number . . . [I]t is first of all election into mission."[22]

We are not told precisely how Abraham will be a blessing to all nations.[23] That will be given further clarification in Exodus 19:3–6.

Exodus 19:3–6: Priestly Kingdom and Holy Nation

The means by which God will bring blessing to the nations is given more detail in Exodus 19. These programmatic verses are set in the context of Exodus which narrates the birth of God's people. The book of Exodus is not a "literary or theological goulash" but rather has a "theological unity" that is reflected in its literary structure.[24] Indeed, the literary structure has profound theological implications for the missional identity and role of God's people in the biblical story.

The first 18 chapters narrate the redemption of Israel from slavery in Egypt. As Redeemer, God acts to free his firstborn son from slavery to Pharaoh to restore him to his rightful place in God's family (Exod 4:22–23). Since Pharaoh was considered to be an incarnation of the Egyptian god Re, and since pagan religion shaped all of the political, social, and economic life of Egypt, this redemption was a profoundly *religious* liberation.[25] Israel was freed from idols to serve Yahweh in every area of their lives. Upon the heels of this redemption God establishes a covenant with his people (Exod 19–24). But why had God—the Lord of all nations—liberated this one small nation and bound himself to them in covenant? What role does God have for them to play? The answer is offered in Exodus 19:3–6 in the covenant task God gives Israel as his people. Here we find the "unique identity of the people of God."[26]

---

22. Wright, *Mission of God*, 263–64.

23. Perhaps Gen 18:18–19 offers a clue: Abraham and his family are commanded to "keep the way of the Lord" and to do "what is right and just." Both phrases point to a life that lives in God's way before the nations.

24. Durham, *Exodus*, xxi.

25. Curtis, *Man as the Image*, 86–96; Middleton, *Liberating Image*, 108–11. See also, Frankfort, *Kingship*.

26. Bailey Wells, *God's Holy People*, 34.

Three terms are used to describe Israel in their identity and role in God's mission: treasured possession, priestly kingdom, and holy nation. Israel was chosen as a treasured possession to play a priestly role as a holy nation. Israel would play a priestly role living as a model before and mediator to the nations. Israel would be a holy nation, living a distinctive life before the nations. We may summarize the significance of these labels in terms of Israel's call to mediate God's salvation to the nations as they lived before the nations a communal life that embodied God's design for human life. As Durham points out, Israel was to "be a display people, a showcase to the world of how being in covenant with Yahweh changes a people."[27] The universal horizon of God's action in so calling Israel is clearly in view in the words "because the whole earth is mine" (v.5).[28]

God's people living in God's way before the nations: this is one way we have described mission. Thus immediately upon the heels of this call the Torah is given to guide Israel in living out their calling as a holy nation (Exod 20–23). This instruction covers the full spectrum of human life. It points back to God's creational intention for human life, now set contextually in this ancient near eastern setting. "The people of God in both testaments are called to be a light to the nations. But there can be no light to the nations that is not shining already in transformed lives of a holy people."[29]

The final chapters of Exodus deal with the tabernacle and the story of Israel's rebellion with the golden calf (Exod 25–40). Together we see that the final brick in the building of God's people in Exodus is God's presence. As holy yet merciful and forgiving (Exod 34:6–7), God comes to dwell in their midst. God will now carry out his mission to bring blessing to the nations as he lives among Israel as their divine king.[30]

---

27. Durham, *Exodus*, 263.

28. Dumbrell rightly notes that the phrase "because [*ki*] the whole earth is mine" should be understood "not as the assertion of the right to choose but as the *reasons or goal* for choice" ("Prospect of the Unconditionality of the Sinaitic Covenant," 146). Fretheim translates this "because the whole earth is mine" and notes rightly that this links this text with the missional purpose of God first articulated to Abraham in Gen 12:3 ("Because the Whole Earth is Mine," 237).

29. Wright, *Mission of God*, 358.

30. On the importance of the presence of God in Israel for their mission, Martin-Achard says, "The evangelisation of the world is not primarily a matter of words or deeds: it is a matter of presence—*the presence of the People of God in the midst of man-*

Thus the book of Exodus renders to us the identity and role of God's people: they are a redeemed people (Exod 1–18), a covenant people (Exod 19–24), and a people in whom God dwells (Exod 25–40). God's work of forming a people finds its focus and goal in the calling to be a priestly kingdom and holy nation before the watching eyes of the surrounding nations (Exod 19:3–6). Durham contends that "this special role becomes a kind of lens through which Israel is viewed throughout the rest of the Bible."[31] Or, as Dumbrell puts it even more strongly, "The history of Israel from this point on is in reality merely a commentary upon the degree of fidelity with which Israel adhered to this Sinai-given vocation."[32]

On Display in the Land: Israel and the Nations

Duane Christensen rightly observes that "'Israel as a light to the nations' is no peripheral theme within the canonical process. The nations are the matrix of Israel's life, the *raison d'être* of her very existence."[33] And so Israel is placed on the land in the midst of nations to shine as an appealing display people visible to the nations. From this point on "Israel knew that it lived under constant surveillance of the then contemporary world."[34] Displayed on the land "Israel was visible to the nations." Indeed, the "life of God's people is always directed outward to the watching nations."[35]

We note, however, an interesting phenomenon in the remainder of Old Testament history in the way Israel's story is told. Even though God's mission to the nations is "the meaning of Israel's history" yet "during the whole history of Israel this comes to realization little if at all."[36] For the purpose of this chapter two brief observations are important.

The focus of the Old Testament narratives is on the work of God in the midst of Israel to form them as a holy nation. There are two sides to this story. The first side is God's work in their midst according to the

---

kind and the presence of God in the midst of His people. And surely it is not in vain that the Old Testament reminds the Church of this truth" (*A Light*, 79—original emphasis).

31. Durham, *Exodus*, xxiii.
32. Dumbrell, *Creation*, 80.
33. Christensen, "Nations," 1037. Cf. Wright, *Mission of God*, 455.
34. Bavinck, *Introduction*, 14.
35. Wright, *Mission*, 371.
36. Blauw, *Missionary Nature*, 27. Cf. Bauckham, *Bible*, 30.

covenant in grace and judgment. The second side is Israel's struggle with the idolatry of the nations that surround them as they carry out their mission to be a holy people. The pagan idolatry of the nations poses a constant threat and temptation to Israel.

Israel's encounter with idolatry is an important thread in the story and this too must be understood in terms of God's mission. Israel's calling is to live in God's way in the sight of the nations. However, those nations are not neutral and passive observers, so to speak. In their cultural lives they do not serve Yahweh but other gods. Thus Israel's calling was one of a missionary encounter with the idolatrous cultures of the surrounding nations, a confrontation of the pagan gods with the claims of the living God. Israel's life was an alternative shaped by God's Torah and as such was a light in the midst of darkness. Sadly, Israel's history demonstrated that instead of being a solution to idolatry they often became submerged in it becoming part of the problem.

Yet even though the narrative of the historical books zooms in on God's work and Israel's struggle with idolatry, we must not forget the bigger picture in which this drama is set—God's work in Israel for the sake of the nations. Put another way: God has a universal goal (all nations, whole creation) but uses particular means (Israel). Much of the focus of the historical books is on the particular means. Nevertheless, the universal goal remains the backdrop of God's mission and Israel's history.

A second observation is important. It is primarily in the psalms and the prophetic books that the universal horizon of Israel's election is unmistakably affirmed. In both present summons and future promise, Israel's mission as a light to the nations emerges in the prophets. Likewise the poets within Israel compose hymns and prayers that set Israel's calling in a universal context. In fact, as Miller points out, "the praise of God is the most prominent and extended formulation of the *universal* and *conversionary* dimension of the theology of the Old Testament."[37] Israel's missional role is constantly nourished by this dimension of their liturgy. W. Creighton Marlowe calls the psalms the "music of missions"[38] while Mark Boda speaks of the Psalter as a "missional collection."[39] Together

---

37. Miller, "Enthroned," 9.

38. Marlowe, "Music," 445–56.

39. Boda, "Declare His Glory." See also, Kaiser, *Mission*, 29–38; Wright, *Mission*, 474–84; Legrand, *Unity and Plurality*, 15–18; Hedlund, *Mission*, 83–92.

the prophets and the psalms interpret Israel's history in terms of their mission to the nations.

PSALMS IN ISRAEL: NOURISHING A MISSIONAL IDENTITY

Until the beginning of the twentieth century the psalms were primarily treated in terms of their theological content. Hermann Gunkel and Sigmund Mowinckel brought about a "sea change" in the scholarly study of the psalms when they developed a new approach to the psalms that investigated their purpose and use in Israel's worship.[40] The psalms are not first of all theology but poetry that is used as the response of God's people in worship and prayer. "The poetry of the Psalms is distinctive because it is prayed poetry . . . the language . . . the worshipping community uses to speak to God and about God, in response to his overtures in history . . . The Psalms are the songs which accompany the People of God on their journey through history."[41]

Thus, as God's people sing or pray, individually or corporately, the psalms foster a faithful covenantal response to God's mighty deeds whether that is in praise, lament, thanksgiving, historical memory, love for God's law, repudiation of idols, or more.[42]

One of the things that the psalms did was to nourish Israel's missional identity: their God was the God of all nations; he was concerned for their salvation; and Israel's election and covenant were directed to that end. Since mission is central to the Old Testament story there is much that can be said about how the psalms did this. In the next few paragraphs I will confine myself to two major themes. First, the psalms nourished a universalistic vision of God as the one true God who is creator and lord of all nations. This stands as a stark alternative to the pagan polytheism and henotheism that reduced the gods to tribal deities. They nourish Israel in the true story fostering a vision of the real world. Second, in numerous ways the psalms direct Israel's attention to the nations as the ultimate horizon of their existence. George Peters counts

---

40. Hogg, "Psalm 22," 239.

41. Anderson, *Out of the Depths*, 23.

42. Much Old Testament scholarship believes that the psalms were Israel's hymnbook for corporate worship in the temple. However, this view is not unanimous. Others believe that this is more of a prayer book for individual devotion. In either case the psalms nourished the covenant life of the people of God as they sang and/or prayed, individually or corporately.

over 175 universal references to the nations of the world and suggests that "the Psalter is one of the greatest missionary books in the world, though seldom seen from that point of view."[43] The psalms not only lead Israel deeper and deeper into the true story of the world, they also continually remind Israel that it is the final goal of their election to make known this true God, this true story, the real world to the nations.

The True God, the True Story, the Real World

The psalms proclaim that there is one God. Israel's God, Yahweh is the one and only, the true and living God who is King over all the earth. While he had made himself known to Israel, and is their God, He is also the God over all nations.[44] At the core of the Psalms is a universal monotheism.[45] God is the Creator of all things (Ps 95:4, 5). Thus, he controls and rules the non-human creation (Ps 18:7–15); he governs the history of the world (Pss 33:10–11; 67:4); his laws of justice apply to all nations (Ps 37). God rules and judges the nations (Ps 83): Thus, all come under his judgment (Ps 7:7–10); the nations must find salvation and refuge in him (Ps 2:8–12); they cannot resist his power and purposes (Ps 33:10–19). Truly, Yahweh is a God of universal power and dominion. He is the King of the whole earth, Creator, Sustainer, Ruler, Lord, and Judge. As Mascarenhas concludes, "The theology of the Psalms, like that of the entire Old Testament, reveals an absolute, exclusive and indisputable monotheism, unique among the religions of antiquity."[46]

It is important for us, as a people who have been grounded in this monotheism all our lives, to be shaken out of our complacent familiarity and get hold of the radical uniqueness of Israel's faith among the nations. Truly, the claims of Israel about their God were "astonishing claims. They were also unprecedented and unparalleled claims."[47] The surrounding nations were henotheistic and polytheistic, and their gods were tribal

---

43. Peters, *Biblical Theology*, 116.

44. Mascarenhas says, "Universalism is one of the characteristic traits of the Psalms. The principal texts invite all the earth to sing to the Lord, the families of the peoples to praise him and affirm that Yahweh reigns over the whole world and governs with justice. This follows from the universalistic theology of the Psalter" (*Missionary Function*, 64).

45. On monotheism in the Old Testament see the fine article by Bauckham, "Biblical Theology," 187–232.

46. Mascarenhas, *Missionary Function*, 67.

47. Wright, *Mission*, 85; cf. Sherwin, "I Am Against You," 149–60.

deities that ruled only particular nations. From the historical records we know that Israel was constantly tempted and seduced by this overwhelming religious power. The psalms nourished an alternative vision of God and the world in contrast to the pagan religions of the surrounding nations. In nourishing a monotheistic vision of God, the psalms engage in a polemic against the idols and pagan religions that surrounded Israel (Pss 115:1–8; 135:15–17). If Israel was to be a light to the nations they must be firmly grounded in a monotheistic and universalistic vision of Yahweh in contrast to the idols of the nations.[48]

If this be God then two appropriate responses are in order. From all the nations, praise. If "the lordship of this God is universal in scope" then it "should bring forth the conversion of every being to the worship of Israel's God." Miller continues, "This call to the nations and peoples to praise the Lord is no incidental or exceptional matter. It is pervasive in the Psalms."[49] The response from Israel is the obligation to make known this God to the nations. As H. H. Rowley has put it, "Monotheism necessarily implies universalism. If God is One and there is no other, then He must be the God of all men, and if men are to have any true religion He it is that they must worship."[50] It is *this God* that makes himself known to Israel and, as Rowley continues concerning Israel, "they to whom knowledge has been mediated are called to share their treasures with all men."[51] Wright expresses similar sentiments: "Israel believed that they had come to know him as the one and only true and living God. In his transcendent uniqueness there was no other god like YHWH. Furthermore, they had a sense of stewardship of this knowledge since it was God's purpose that ultimately all nations would come to know the name, the glory, the salvation and the mighty acts of YHWH and worship him alone as God."[52]

Israel's Missional Obligation to Make the Truth Known

The psalms nourish this obligation to share their treasures with all people by continually orienting Israel to the nations as the ultimate horizon of their election and covenant. The danger for God's people then, as today,

---

48. See Wright, *Mission*, 71–188.

49. Miller, "Enthroned on the Praises," 13.

50. Rowley, *Biblical Doctrine*, 62. See further Bauckham, "Biblical Theology," 187–232; Wright, *Mission*, 75–92.

51. Rowley, *Biblical Doctrine*, 62.

52. Wright, *Mission*, 92.

is that election and covenant can be misunderstood in an insular and introverted sense of privilege that is forgetful of missional responsibility. The psalms contend against such exclusivity. We can briefly summarize this dimension of the psalms in six statements.

- The psalms nourish a vision of universal worship in which a multitude made up of all nations bow before the Lord (Pss 33:8; 46:10; 67:3–4; 102:15; 150:6).
- The psalmists summon and invite all the nations to worship Yahweh (Pss 47:1; 66:8; 67:3, 5; 68:32; 96:7, 10; 100:1; 117:1).
- The psalmists exhort the people of God to proclaim and declare the mighty deeds of God before the nations (Pss 9:11; 18:49; 96:2–3; 105:1).
- The psalmist responds to these exhortations with his own intention to fulfill this obligation (Pss 18:49; 57:9; 108:3).
- The psalmist prays for God's blessing on Israel so that the nations might recognize that God is the true and living God (Ps. 67).
- The psalms picture a future fulfillment when all the nations of the earth will join Israel in the praise of Yahweh (Pss 2; 22:27–31; 66:4; 86:9).[53]

While passages that orient the life of Israel toward the nations are scattered throughout the psalms, there are some psalms whose entire thrust is to remind Israel of their missional calling. Both Mascarenhas and Marlowe see Psalms 67, 96, and 117 in this way.[54] Surely if Israel sang Psalm 67 on a regular basis they could not but recognize that they were a "so-that people"—blessed *so that* they might bring blessing to the nations.

> May God be gracious to us and bless us
> and make his face shine on us—
> *so that* your ways may be known on earth,
> your salvation among all nations.
> (Psalm 67:1ff. TNIV).

---

53. Scott Hahn speaks of a "liturgical hermeneutic" by which he means an interpretation of the story of Scripture that sees its goal as the worship of God by peoples from all nations ("Canon, Cult, and Covenant," 207–35; See also, Piper, *Let the Nations Be Glad!*

54. Marlowe, "Music of Missions," 450–52; Mascarenhas, *Missionary Function*, 67, 96, 117.

WORSHIP AND MISSION IN THE CHURCH TODAY

Perhaps Israel did not sing Psalm 67 enough. In any case, in spite of the nourishment of their liturgy, Israel failed in their calling to be a light to the nations. As their history slides increasingly downhill into rebellion, the prophets emerge on the scene with the promise that God is not finished. A day is coming when Israel will be restored—gathered, purified, and given the Spirit (Ezek 36:24-27)—and God's purposes for the nations and creation will be fulfilled. It is in the work of Jesus that this is fulfilled.[55] During his ministry he limits his focus to re-gathering Israel (Matt 15:24). Israel is purified by the death and resurrection of Jesus Christ, and endowed with the Spirit.[56] The little flock—restored, eschatological Israel[57]—is commissioned to continue the mission of Jesus now not only to Israel but to all nations (Matt 28:18-20; John 20:21).[58]

As Gentiles are incorporated into the Abrahamic covenant (Gal 3:7-9) and engrafted onto Israel's covenant story (Rom 11:17-21) they are likewise incorporated into the missional calling of God's people.[59] There is a difference now. Since Pentecost, they are newly formed as a multi-ethnic and non-geographically based people sent among the nations. Thus the central "missional mandate" of the Old Testament (Exod 19:3-6) is freshly applied to the New Covenant people of God (1 Pet 2:9-12).

Luke gives us a picture of this church in mission in Jerusalem after Pentecost (Acts 2:42-7). Again, worship and the gathering of God's people are central in nourishing this community for their missional calling. They are a people committed to four things—apostles' teaching, fellowship, breaking of bread, and prayer (Acts 2:42). As they are nourished by the true story they embody it in their lives and as such are an attractive community, a light shining in the midst of Jerusalem (Acts 2:43-47).

---

55. Lohfink, *Jesus*, 70-73.

56. Some have seen a contradiction between Jesus' exclusive focus on Israel (Matt 15:24) and the inclusive universality of the prophets and his own message. But this must be interpreted in terms of Jesus re-gathering Israel as the preliminary eschatological event that precedes the mission to the Gentiles. For a defense of this interpretation, see Jeremias, *Jesus' Promise*; LaGrand, *Earliest Christian Mission*. Likewise, Lohfink states, "Now the decisive point is that *the restoration of Israel occurs in order that the Gentiles also seek the Lord* (cf. Acts 15:17)" (*Jesus*, 140—original emphasis).

57. Lohfink, *Jesus*, 9-12; Wright, *Jesus*, 300.

58. Lohfink, *Jesus*, 75-81, 132-47.

59. Cf. Bartholomew and Goheen, *Drama of Scripture*, 198.

Their lives of compassion, justice, joy, worship, and power emit a radiant light and "the Lord added to their number daily those who were being saved" (Acts 2:47).

Here the missional calling of the church is nourished by worship, and the same need remains today as much as with ancient Israel and the early church. What can we learn from the psalms? First, worship today needs to tell the true story of the world inviting God's people to come live in the real world it narrates. A few years ago Bob Webber and Phil Kenyon issued a clarion call to the Western church. It is a summons to growing faithfulness in the midst of huge threats to the gospel and Christian identity at the beginning of the twenty-first century. They say, "Today, as in the ancient era, the Church is confronted by a host of master narratives that contradict and compete with the gospel. The pressing question is: who gets to narrate the world?"[60] Webber believes the three leading contenders are the Muslim story, the liberal capitalist story, and (somewhat surprisingly) the Marxist story.[61] Over against such contenders the authors say, "In a world of competing stories, we call Evangelicals to recover the truth of God's word as *the* story of the world, and to make *it* the centerpiece of Evangelical life."[62] Getting this straight is the first order of business. Later in the document they offer reflections on the importance of worship for this task. They begin, "We call for public worship that sings, preaches and enacts God's story."[63] Jones makes the same point, "The Church is a 'story-formed community' that is rooted in the crucifixion and resurrection of Jesus the Christ . . . In order for the community of faith to endure through time and to withstand the threats of inculturation, the story of what God has accomplished for the Hebrew people and the Christian community must be continually re-told in corporate worship."[64] Truly the Bible must narrate the world for the Christian community.

Neither the intellectualism of Enlightenment-inspired worship nor the self-centered narcissism of some contemporary worship will draw us into the story of Scripture. Rather, worship fashioned on the pattern

---

60. Webber and Kenyon, *Call to an Ancient Evangelical Future*, "Introduction," 3rd paragraph.

61. Webber, "Together in the Jesus Story."

62. Ibid., Section 1, "On the Primacy of Biblical Narrative."

63. Ibid., Section 4, "On Church's Worship and Enacting God's Narrative."

64. Jones, "We Are *How* We Worship," 353.

of the Psalms—focusing on the narrative of God's mighty deeds—can move us more deeply into God's story. Worship enables us to celebrate what God has done in the past but not as a stale history lesson. Since we are part of that story our worship also nourishes our participation in his ongoing work which continues to the present and will continue until God's purposes are fulfilled. John Burkhart claims that "Fundamentally, worship is the celebrative response to what God has done, is doing, and will do."[65] The way the worship is structured, the hymns that are chosen, the way various elements are introduced and related to each other all can focus our attention on the story of God's mighty deeds—past, present, and future—in which we find our place.

This story told in the Bible is the true story in which God's people are called to live. It must, therefore, be held over against all competing stories, and worship will play a crucial role. A particularly poignant example of this is found in the book of Revelation.[66] John's vision, which constitutes the book of Revelation, comes on the Lord's day, the day of worship (Rev 1:10). The church in Asia Minor is threatened by the invincible power of Rome and is in danger of being domesticated. The threat of the imperial cult put pressure on the church to accommodate itself to the idolatry of the empire. Surely the great might of Rome demonstrated that the world it narrated was the real world. Yet the book of Revelation audaciously challenges what appears to be the "sheer facticity" of Rome's established order.[67] To the small and weak community, threatened by overwhelming odds, John makes bold to say that the true story of the world is revealed in a man crucified by the Roman Empire but who now reigns over all and is guiding universal history to its final goal. John offers this vision as an "alternative world."[68] He thus "constructs a counter-narrative disputing the imperial one, opening up a different way of seeing the world."[69] This counter-narrative is the story of the kingdom of God centered in the cosmic Christ and involved in a cosmic battle but assured of a cos-

---

65. Burkhart, *Worship*, 17.

66. Cf. Rodney Clapp's chapter, "The Church as Worshiping Community: Welcome to the (Real) World" in *A Peculiar People*, 95–96.

67. Meeks, *Moral World*, 145.

68. Nissen, *New Testament*, 147.

69. Bauckham, *Bible*, 104. The outstanding last chapter of this book is an important call for the church to embody the biblical story over against the powerful, encroaching story of global capitalism. He uses the book of Revelation as an example of a church that resisted an imperial story.

mic victory. It is this story that is celebrated in the liturgy, songs, and prayers of God's people in Revelation. The worship of the early church in the Roman Empire was both a *witness* to the true story of the world revealed in Jesus Christ and the place where the church was *nourished* in this story so that they might heroically refuse to "compromise with a system they see as aligned with the forces of sin and death."[70]

Here we catch a glimpse of what worship ought to be. The cultural narrative that threatens us today may not be as explicitly hostile but is surely as dangerous.[71] Today's church is being co-opted by this story through entertainment and advertizing, through television and internet, through sports and shopping malls. Unless the church learns to create another reality—the real world—in its worship, the witness of the church will be hopelessly compromised by the powerful idols of our culture.[72] Liturgy today must witness to the real world, the true story, the living God as revealed in Jesus Christ, and thereby form a people ready for a missionary encounter in their various callings.

Worship must enact the true story of the world and nourish believers in their callings. But the second thing we learn from the psalms is that we must be continually directed to the unbelieving world as the ultimate horizon of our calling. We have received the gospel, not simply for our own good, but to communicate it in life, word, and deed.[73] As Israel of old, the church is in need of a worship that directs our lives to the nations.

The same elements of liturgy can direct attention either inward on ourselves or outward, orienting us to the nations and our calling. Usually scholarly attention is directed to the word and sacrament.[74] Indeed, the word and sacraments need to be rescued from an introverted orienta-

---

70. Senior and Stuhlmueller, *Biblical Foundations*, 305.

71. Craig Bartholomew and I have told that story in *Living at the Crossroads*, in three chapters, "The Western Story: The Roots of Modernity," "The Western Story: The Growth of Modernity," "What Time Is It? Four Signs of Our Time in the Western Story."

72. Note the sub-title of Clapp's chapter, "Welcome to the (Real) World" (*A Peculiar People*, 94).

73. The church and Christians are "to *be* the witness, *do* the witness, and *say* the witness" (Guder, *Be My Witnesses*, 91).

74. For example, Clapp, *Peculiar People*, 99–113; Jones, "We Are *How* We Worship," 353–57; Lovas, "Mission-Shaped Liturgy," 354–58; Schattauer, *Inside Out*, 23–86; Goheen, "Narrating the World." Beyond chapters on proclamation, baptism, and communion Schattauer's book also discusses liturgical assembly, liturgical year, liturgical space, music, ritual practice, and occasional service.

tion that only dwells on benefits for believers, and instead utilized to point the church to their calling in the world. Baptism and the Lord's Supper remind us of our mission in an ongoing story. Each of these rites focuses on the mightiest of God's deeds—the cross of Jesus. Yet it matters *how* we focus on Christ's crucifixion. Too often our celebration of these sacraments nurtures a passive reception of the means of grace designed solely to give individual salvation. Yet there is no better place to remind the congregation that this is our call to communal participation in God's mission. The cross is that place where God accomplished his purpose to defeat sin and evil for the sake of the creation he loved. In baptism we are incorporated into the community that shares in this victory and is called to make it known to the world. Baptism is a rite of initiation into a community that continues the mission of Jesus until the end. The Eucharist continually nourishes us for that mission by orienting our lives to the central event where the victory of the kingdom was accomplished and pointing us forward to the culmination of God's purpose. Put simply, both sacraments should be eschatological and missional, and our liturgical celebration of them should foster this view.[75]

Preaching is a central element of worship. The business of preaching is to bring us face to face with Jesus Christ and all his saving power to equip us for our mission in the world. Jesus stands as the fulfillment of a long story. The Old Testament was written to form and equip a people to play their role in God's redemptive purposes for the world. The New Testament tells the story of Israel with Jesus as the fulfillment, applying that story to form a faithful missional people in new cultural contexts. Thus, to preach Christ, in his life, death, and resurrection, is to form a missional people to embody God's purposes in the world. Jesus reveals and accomplishes the end of universal history. Our preaching of Christ is God's power to give us kingdom life and equip us for our mission in the world.[76] Seen from this perspective, the rampant practice of distilling principles from the text to satisfy an immediate gratification for relevance seems a far cry from what is needed. Sermon bits or morsels separated from their redemptive-historical context may be tasty, but, like

---

75. Some of the content of this paragraph is indebted to an unpublished address Newbigin gave to a gathering of Anglican and Reformed church leaders, in an attempt to resuscitate an eschatological and missional understanding of baptism and Lord's Supper over against what he calls a "Christendom" appropriation of the sacraments in the Western church ("How Shall We Understand Sacraments and Ministry?")

76. Wright, *Last Word*, 35–59.

candy, will not nourish us. It may help us feel better or comfort us or guide us or inform us but leave the idolatrous cultural story untouched.

Besides word and sacrament, many other liturgical elements offer an opportunity to nourish a missional consciousness. The way the congregation is gathered, welcomed, and called to worship will cast a certain light on the whole service. The service of confession of sin can be introduced and presented as a time to be cleansed from our capitulation to cultural idolatry, a time to be renewed and empowered for our calling in the world.[77] Confessions of faith can reinforce a missional cast to our faith.[78] Our prayers should move beyond the needs of the congregation and direct us outward to a world in need. The charge to the congregation and benediction at the end can be done in a way that encourages the congregation to think in terms of God's presence accompanying them in their mission.[79] These along with numerous other signals will have a long-term effect in nourishing a congregation in their missional identity—chosen for the sake of the nations.

Our music is exceedingly important.[80] Much music today simply does not nourish an outward orientation; the blessings of the gospel are celebrated only in terms of their benefit to believers. Indeed much music is in grave danger of being co-opted by the selfish me-oriented consumer story of our culture. The gifts of the gospel are more spiritual consumer items to be enjoyed by the Christian community than gifts given for the

---

77. The song, "See How the World Groans," puts confession of sin in a missional setting.

78. An outstanding example of this is the contemporary testimony of the Christian Reformed Church in North America entitled *Our World Belongs to God*. Three things stand out about this delightful document: (1) It is in *narrative* rather than systematic form. (2) It is *missional* to the core. The longest section (paragraphs 41–54) is entitled, "The Mission of the Church." (3) It is written in beautiful *poetic and doxological language* making it especially suitable for worship. It can be accessed at http://www.crcna.org/pages/our_world_main.cfm.

79. Schmidt, "Sent and Gathered," 121–29.

80. In defense of this perhaps it is worth quoting again Luther's well known words from his preface to Georg Rhau's *Symphoniae Incundae*, "Next to the Word of God, music deserves the highest praise. For whether you wish to comfort the sad, to terrify the happy, to encourage the despairing, to humble the proud, to calm the passionate or to appease those full of hate, what more effective means could you find than music? The Holy Ghost himself honors her as an instrument for his proper work when in His Holy Scriptures he asserts, that through her, his gifts were instilled in the prophets . . . The gift of language combined with the gift of song was given to man that he should proclaim the Word of God through Music" (*LW* 53.323).

sake of the nations. Blessed *to be a blessing* and chosen *for the sake of the world*: often in our music it is the "blessed" and the "chosen" that are emphasized, shorn of their ultimate purpose.

Along with older songs there are a host of contemporary songs with rich lyrics and tunes that direct the worship of God's people to their ultimate goal. For example, the hymnbook appropriately entitled *Mission Praise* offers many fresh songs that nourish the missional calling of the church. I conclude this chapter with a list of a few of those songs which express in worship the theme of this essay: "Beauty for brokenness" (806—with the words, "Until the nations learn of your ways, Seek your salvation and bring you their praise."); "An Army of Ordinary People" (32—with the words, "a city, a light to the nations . . . are we"); "For I'm Building a People of Power" (151—with the words, "I'm making a people of praise, that will move through this land by My Spirit"); "From the Sun's Rising" (164—with the words, "To every tongue, tribe and nation He sends us"); "Go Forth in His Name" (955—with the words, "Now is the time for the Church to arise and proclaim Him, 'Jesus, Saviour, Redeemer and Lord.'"); "Great is the Darkness" (835—"In every nation salvation will come to those who believe on your name. Help us bring light to the world . . ."); "Here I Am" (229—with the words, "God's seeking out a very special people to manifest His truth and His might"); "We'll Walk the Land" (743—with the words, "We'll walk for truth, speak out for love . . . to fill the nation with your song"); "Lights to the World" (8—with the words, "kindle in us a mighty flame till every heart . . . shall rise to praise your holy name"); "One Shall Tell Another" (541—with the words, "From house to house in families shall more be gathered in"); "See How the World Groans" (923—with the words, "Someone must care for them, someone must tell, tell of Christ, tell of His power to set men free!"); "That the World May Believe" (847—"How do we start to touch the broken hearts, the barren lives, the lonely and bereaved? Lord, in your name we shall go forth."); "Light to the World" (643—with the words, "touch our lives with such a fire that souls may search and find You there"); "Where It Matters, There You'll Find Us" (866—with the words, "In the streets of every city, bringing hope and healing"); "Let All the Earth Hear His Voice" (403—with the words, "Silent no more we cry out—let the world hear the shout: in the earth the Lord reigns").

Our worship will nourish us to be a certain kind of people—of that we can be sure! May it be a people whose lives are given for the sake of the world. May our prayer be that of the third verse of the song "Lord, Whose Love in Humble Service":

> As we worship, grant us vision till your love's revealing light
> in its height and depth and greatness dawns upon our quickened sight,
> making known the needs and burdens your compassion bids us bear,
> stirring us to tireless striving, your abundant life to share.[81]

May our response be that of the fourth verse, "Called from worship into service, forward in your name we go."

---

81. *Psalter Hymnal*, #603. Text by A. F. Bayley.

4

Worship and the Presence of God

Seeing with Ezekiel

John W. Olley

INTRODUCTION

The opening vision of the book of Ezekiel could not seem more remote from the common experience of contemporary weekly worship. Its language is often tortuous (in Hebrew, as well as in translations), throughout descriptions are introduced by "looked (something) like," "the appearance," with sounds "like," culminating in the double distancing, "the appearance of the likeness of"—and even what things are "like" is often difficult to picture! We can sympathize with Ezekiel in seeking to describe the indescribable, but then what?

Closer reading, not only of the opening vision but of others in the book, opens up a number of features that impinge on what we do in services of worship and can both challenge practices and expand our horizon of expectations. The very strangeness irrupts into comfortable routine or cultural acquiescence and helps us see the God who is with us, and the results of that presence. Ezekiel not only sees God's glory but is enabled to see life and society more clearly.

THE GOD WHO IS PRESENT WHERE EZEKIEL IS

Ezekiel was a priest, far from Jerusalem and the temple, with the group of exiles who had been taken to Babylon, along with king Jehoiachin, at the time of the first attack by Nebuchadnezzar (1:1–3; 2 Kgs 24:1–2, 10–17). The opening vision is only a few years from the final destruction. He was well aware of the centuries-old temple in Jerusalem that was seen as the place of God's glory (1 Kgs 8:10–11; Ps 46): the way to come "before Yahweh," to be "in his presence" was to participate in worship at the Jerusalem temple. This was the place to encounter Yahweh. Yet now, far from the temple, Ezekiel "sees" God's glory: "God reveals the sovereign freedom of his appearing, when and where he wills . . . In the full splendour of his regal glory God met his people in the midst of a heathen land."[1]

The striking, unexpected nature of the location of the appearance may be dulled for later readers, with long experience of worshipping God "where we are" shaped by words such as those of Jesus to the woman by the well (John 4:21–24). But this was an "unclean land" (Amos 7:17); that the people were there was a consequence of their moral impurity, violent injustice, and idolatrous worship, it was a place of despair. Just as modern (or post-modern) worshippers have their places where "we sense the presence of God," so in contrast amongst the exiles is not where one would expect to meet God! Wright's contemporary reflection is apt: "There are times when our doctrinal conviction of God's omnipresence needs to become an experienced reality again. Whether through geographical distance, like Ezekiel's, or through more spiritual or emotional alienation, the experience of exile from the presence of God can be dark and terrible . . . We can certainly pray for the reassurance of the touch of his hand reminding us that God is there, even there."[2]

The opening description of the revelation itself takes the reader back before Jerusalem and the temple, for here is a theophany in the storm, with vivid brilliance of light, a reminder of the God who appeared after the exodus (Exod 19:16–19; 24:10; Hab 3:3–7). Jerusalem may be threatened by the power of Babylon and would soon be destroyed, but the immensity of the windstorm is an awesome reminder of the God of the exodus, who is coming—although, as we will comment below, the initial message will be not deliverance but judgment.

Many readers of the vision will join with John Calvin, "I confess it is very obscure and I do not profess to understand it."[3] Nevertheless it

---

1. Zimmerli, *Ezekiel 1*, 140.
2. Wright, *The Message*, 45.
3. In his *Commentary*, cited by Wright, 45–46.

has been the source and stimulus for much mystical thought and action. From at least the middle of the second century BCE the vision has been referred to as the "Chariot" (Hebrew *Merkabah*), the term first known in Sir 49:8 and the LXX of Ezek 43:3. Yet importantly, while later use of the vision was to enable the worshipper somehow to mystically go up to or into the presence of God, and unlike later apocalyptic writers where the key person is taken to the heavenlies, here the "glory of Yahweh" comes down to Ezekiel where he is "among the exiles."[4]

As a result of archaeological discoveries and comparative studies over more than a century, current readers have access through commentaries to material elucidating the imagery.[5] In using words in ways that show the limitations of language, the only imagery can be that which is culturally available and communicable. Yet in so doing Ezekiel does not domesticate and tame God, but speaks of a God who challenges popular perceptions. Pertinent for our purpose of exploring relevance for contemporary worship is the summary and reflection of Odell:

> Though Ezekiel's vision may well have been a suprarational experience of divine transcendence, the raw materials for the vision are the cultural icons and political rhetoric of the Assyrian empire, which had exerted control over Israel and Judah for centuries . . . Ezekiel's appropriation is radically subversive . . . [he] asserts that the only effective power in the lives of the people of Israel is Yahweh.
>
> In today's world of constitutional democracies, one searches in vain for a metaphor that approaches Ezekiel's in its conveyance of divine universal order. In our contemporary ways of speaking about God, no other metaphor [than that of sovereign] has the potential to still the many voices that clamor for our allegiance, or to rebuke the powers that sabotage our dignity.[6]

Dominant powers, whether political, military, economic, or cultural (generally intertwined), provide all-embracing and permeating images and language of success and power. There is always the temptation to fall

---

4. For later use of the vision see, e.g., Halperin, *The Faces*; Lieb, *The Visionary Mode*; and Himmelfarb, *Ascent*.

5. Allen, *Ezekiel 1–19*, 1–45, espec. 27–37; and Odell, *Ezekiel*, 14–51, esp. 23–31, include sketches and diagrams of relevant ancient Near Eastern iconography and representational art, and see, also, Greenberg, *Ezekiel 1–20*, 51–59; and Block, *Ezekiel 1–24*, 89–109.

6. Odell, *Ezekiel*, 34–37.

in line with such, whether it be like Ahaz and the adopting of Assyrian altars (2 Kgs 16:10–14), or the later Christian adopting of the symbols of imperial power in the Constantinean era, or the material and economic status symbols of much of the modern West.

The imagery of the vision provides a stimulus to examine the adequacy of divine images in contemporary worship and to explore ways in which current "cultural icons and political rhetoric" may be used in a way that is "radically subversive" in the contexts of our congregations, pointing to the One who alone is sovereign and present. It is God who is sovereign, not his people or any other human grouping. The contrast between the vision of God's glory and the attitudes and views of the exiles could not have been greater, but it was the vision of God and what followed that was to be a key factor in changing those attitudes! Drastic situations required a vision of God's glory, and a later vision of "God's glory displayed in the face of Christ" (2 Cor 4:6) is still having world-changing results. Ezekiel's vision is an example of culturally relevant language that critiques that same culture, giving glory alone to God.

WORSHIP ENABLES EZEKIEL TO SEE

Ezekiel's response was that "I fell on my face" (1:28), an act of submission and worship common in many cultures. Immediately he is told to "stand up" and is raised by the Spirit to hear God speak to him (2:1; also 3:24; 43:5). "Standing" is the position of a courtier or other subject awaiting instructions, and in each instance Ezekiel receives a word from God. This was also his response during subsequent visions (3:23; 9:8; 11:13; 43:3; 44:4).

The juxtaposition of awareness of God's presence, submissive worship, being accepted and commissioned with a message is heightened in Ezekiel by the literary presentation and provides a pattern that is readily transposed to worship contexts in general. It may be noted that in the LXX, translated four centuries later, all six instances of "I fell face down" are in the present indicative, a usage "at those places where the author feels that he wishes to draw attention to an event . . . within a discourse unit selected for special significance."[7] As such it brings immediacy, and might also suggest that readers adopt a similar stance!

---

7. Porter, *Verbal Aspect*, 196; see also, Hauspie, "*Piptō*."

The God who speaks is also the One who "sees." The vision narrative opens with "I looked, and I saw" (1:6), but

> this is a vision that likewise *sees* (cf. Ps 11:4), Not only the wheels but the living creatures themselves are replete with eyes (1:18, 10, 12) . . . But, of course, that which is seen ("the appearance of the likeness of the glory of the Lord") sees much more clearly than does the seer (the prophet and, in turn, the reader) who beholds. Indeed that which is seen sees all . . . [The description] concludes with an awareness that it is not Ezekiel who beholds the vision so much as it is the vision that beholds him.[8]

Lieb focuses this movement in arguing that the opening "visions of God" (1:1; a heading for the whole book) becomes not simply that it is God who is seen but rather God becomes the subject, they are "visions *by* God."[9] This is borne out by what follows as throughout the book Ezekiel is enabled to "see" what God makes known to him, especially what is going on in the city of Jerusalem and the temple and what will go on with the new temple and city whose location will be in the middle of the land. Ezekiel is commissioned to communicate what God shows him, initially by speech, but now through a literary work, the book of Ezekiel, which in turn enables readers to see what God sees and what God will do. In this way various aspects of society, in Jerusalem and amongst the exiles, are "exposed" and come under the judgment of God.

There is compromised worship in the temple, with frequent reference to "idols" (*gillûlîm*), 39 times in the book), even secret worship of the sun (8:16; cf. 2 Kgs 21:5; 23:11). Alongside are violence and widespread injustice, with political infighting and prophets who proclaim "peace" (10:9; 11:6; 13:10). Lack of integrity in worship is mirrored in corruption, self-seeking, and injustice.

After the exile worship of images seems to have ceased amongst Jews but later Hellenistic culture was to provide other influences, some of the struggles being represented in the books of Maccabees. It is thus noteworthy, and of continuing significance, that the LXX translators commonly gave as equivalent to this word, and others, the broader *enthumēma* ("thought, invention, imagination"), *epitēdeuma* ("practice, pursuit"), and *dianoēma/dianoia* ("thinking"). Thus attention is widened to (wrong, rebellious) thinking and consequent actions, rather than

---

8. Lieb, *Visionary Mode*, 39.
9. Ibid., 40.

focusing on the futility of objects worshipped. God not only sees the objects, but exposes inner thoughts and motivations.

The visions also exposed false hopes of those who felt secure (7:19–27, 11:2–4, 14–15). A trust in the permanence of the temple and city, irrespective of the behaviour of the worshippers, and in power and wealth, has to be shattered before renewed relationship is possible. The structure of the opening block (chs. 1–11) has movement with detailed descriptions of the vision of God's glory framing messages of judgment. The vision is seen in exile (ch. 1), leading to Ezekiel's call to announce the Lord's word to a "rebellious" people (chs. 2–3), expressed in several messages of judgment, some with symbolic action (chs. 4–7), before he is taken in a vision to see the horrific behaviour of the leaders in the temple (chs. 8–9) and then to see God's glory leaving the temple (chs. 10–11). God's glory cannot be bound to even his own "temple/palace"—liturgy and building are not enough! Not until 39:21 will there be another mention of God's "glory," foreshadowing its return in ch. 43. What is "seen" and experienced first is judgment and destruction of false hope.

THE VISION OF GOD'S PURPOSE EXPANDS

The God who spoke to Ezekiel after "I fell on my face" continues to speak: the God who showed his glory to Ezekiel is going to act "so that they/you may know I am Yahweh." Yahweh is God of all nations; the God whose name has been "profaned" is going to act to "hallow my name." There is a future for Israel and it is linked with the honour of God's name. Worship leads into a continuing openness to hearing God's word, seeing more of God's purposes and making him known.

"That You/They May Know I Am Yahweh"

The oft repeated phrase that people, rebellious Israelites, and the nations, will "know that I am Yahweh," or "know that I have spoken/acted" (around 80 times) points to the centrality of God and his relationship to all peoples as a feature of the book. Every single instance is preceded by some word or action of Yahweh and several continue with a phrase, "Yahweh who . . . ," "Yahweh when I . . ." Theologically and practically significant is that consistently such knowledge is through revelatory actions, in judgment or in restoration, seen by others, and is always in the future, apart from Yahweh "having been known" to Israel in Egypt (20:5,

9, 12). "The remarks preceding the statement of recognition say nothing about any sort of human effort or intellectual exercise... Not one of the 78 (or 80) passages under question... offers us a description of Yahweh's essence or being. It is always a matter of Yahweh's intervention."[10]

Further, revelation of the name "calls the people (and the surrounding peoples) into a movement of recognition that is not a state of enraptured vision, but rather is lifetime activity, and movement towards a goal."[11]

Thus, in the early chapters Yahweh's judgment, seen in destruction of the city, desolation of the land, and scattering of the people, has a clear purpose: so that the people (or whole land) "will know that I am Yahweh" (6:7, 13, 14; 7:4, 9, 27, etc.), but sadly the time when they will "know" is only after judgment has ceased and the people who remain alive realize (5:13; 6:10; 14:23; 15:7; 17:21). The message Ezekiel has to proclaim is that people can only say "we know that he is Yahweh" when they give sole covenantal allegiance worshipping Yahweh alone and following his laws relating to both worship and life in society. To know the meaning of the name Yahweh is to follow his ways: one cannot serve Yahweh and anything else.

While, as expected, Israel ("house of Israel," Jerusalem, "the mountains of Israel," "people of the land," "prophets," "survivors") "will know" (51 times), there are around 32 instances where it is nations or "all flesh" who will know (17:24; 21:4, 10; 16x in chs. 25–32, "Oracles against the Nations"; 5x Edom in ch 35; and 8x "the nations" in chs 36–39). While in chapters 25–32 and 35 the "nations" knowing comes through Yahweh's judgment on them, in chapters 36–39 the major focus is on their knowing through the total restoration of Israel—spiritual and moral, physical and political—and destruction of unrepentant opponents. Part of the process is Israel herself coming to see the link between "Yahweh" and being "the house of Israel" (34:30).

The phrase "know that I am Yahweh" (and not, for example, "know me") points to the goal, not simply that the nations acknowledge that there is a supreme or sole God, but that this God is to be identified with Yahweh, the God of Israel. Yahweh is working in and through Israel that the nations may know. One may link this with Psalms that speak of Yahweh and his glory being known amongst all nations (e.g., Pss 96–99).

10. Zimmerli, "Knowledge of God," 33, 36.
11. Zimmerli, "I Am Yahweh," 10.

What the nations think of Yahweh and their response to him is linked with what they see happening in the life of Yahweh's people. The nations "knowing" and Israel "knowing" are inseparable.

God and Surrounding Powers

Worship that flows into hearing and proclaiming God's word is not separated from political and economic structures and relationships. Again, Israel's relationship provides windows for reflecting on contemporary situations. Israel, rather than living according to the covenant relationship, is looking to other nations for assistance or as models to follow. Thus, there is a need to "see" these powers from God's perspective.

While similar blocks in Isaiah 13–23 and Jeremiah 46–51 are judgment on nations who are either enemies or part of the Babylonian empire, in Ezekiel the Oracles against the Nations (chs. 25–32) show different foci. Thus chapter 25 is a response to nearby nations' attitudes or actions upon the destruction of Jerusalem: their scorn and acquisitive desires are seen as a mockery of what is Yahweh's. Following is a series of oracles and laments concerning Tyre, a city on the Phoenician coast which played a leading role in sea-trade with Egypt and other Mediterranean areas, as well as providing a link with inland Assyria (detailed in ch. 27). Her wealth and secure position were well known, linked with slavery—but she will become nothing. It would appear (26:2) that "the Tyrians welcomed Judah's demise as an opportunity to expand their own commercial interests,"[12] but the oracles move on to arrogant claims of superiority and security (ch. 28). Even that great power will come to an end.

Significantly in the book of Revelation's lament over Babylon, a cipher for Rome (Rev 18, especially vss. 3, 9–19), the language is not taken from prophetic oracles against Babylon in Jeremiah or Isaiah, but from Ezekiel's description of the wealth of Tyre. A probable reason is that Babylon's military might and rule over other nations (with prosperity because of power) is to the fore in Old Testament, whereas Tyre is a commercial power. The portrayal of wealth is a significant feature throughout Revelation, with a contrast between the wealth of Babylon (Tyre/Rome) and that of the new Jerusalem.[13]

---

12. Block, *Ezekiel 25–48*, 32.

13. Kraybill, *Imperial Cult*; Royalty, *The Streets*, 59–65, 177–210; and Kowalski, *Die Rezeption*, 369–78.

The shift to Pharaoh and Egypt (chs. 29–32) is to a power that Jewish leaders looked to for help against Babylonian might. Here was a ruler who claimed sole and absolute sovereignty over territory, who believed his might, based on the constancy of the Nile, provided lasting security.

However all powers end up in one place where there is equality—the realm of the dead. Yahweh is alone sovereign and he "sees" injustice and self-sufficient arrogance. This is a message his people needed to hear as they lived in a turbulent period, with the realities of political, military, and economic strength being evident—and as borne out in Revelation, of continuing relevance. But how are the nations and the people to "know," to "see" what Yahweh "sees"?

The Name of Yahweh, Profaned or Made Holy? Belittled or Honored?[14]

God desires that his "name" be known among the nations, but he has chosen to tie his reputation amongst the nations to the life and circumstances of his people. The revelation to Moses at the burning bush linked the name with "I will be with you" in the journey of deliverance from Pharaoh into to the land (Exod 3:12–17). Through the plagues the text describes how Pharaoh, the Egyptians, and the Israelites come to "know that I am Yahweh" (Exod 7:5, 17; 8:21; 9:16; 10:21 14:18). That the meaning of "Yahweh" is inextricably linked with circumstances of the people is evidenced in Moses' audacious words at the Golden calf incident—a key concern is what the name will mean to the Egyptians (Exod 32:11–13). Other nations come to know the meaning of "Yahweh," that he alone is God who delivers, who is just and compassionate, and who enters into covenantal relationship with people, through seeing his people, their worship and lifestyle, with concomitant blessings (Deut 4:5–8).

But what happens if God's people do not worship him alone and do not live a commensurate lifestyle of obedience, of justice, and righteousness? Ezekiel 20 is a powerful almost revisionist history of Israel, of continuing persistent rebellion! It "sees" the past in different light. The people may want to be like everybody else (20:32), "as if they could abort the Lord's plan for his people, But . . . Israel's future lies in God's hands, and 'no action on the exiles' part can ever interfere with God's determination to see that plan fulfilled, the rebellious purged, cultic pu-

---

14. For more detailed discussion including New Testament material, see Olley, "Hallowed be your name."

rity enforced, and human willfulness quelled in a morass of shame and contrition."[15]

The past history repeatedly provided opportunity for Yahweh to judge, even give up on the people, but this would have led to his name "being profaned," being treated as common and ordinary, by "the nations" (20:9, 14, 22). Now, however, the situation has become so ingrained and desperate that his "mighty hand and outstretched arm," a phrase traditionally associated with the exodus, is to be experienced by them with "outpoured wrath" (20:33, 34). There will be a purging outside the land so that the people will "know that I am Yahweh" and no longer "profane my holy name" (20:38–39).

This motif is developed further in chapter thirty-six, after the complete destruction of temple and city. What Yahweh had earlier avoided has now come to pass: "wherever they went among the nations they profaned my holy name" (36:20). The reason is significant. The nations say, "These are Yahweh's people, and they have left his land." Implied is the nations' interpretation that Yahweh has been either powerless to protect his own or else has been cruel. He is regarded as a local god of no relevance to the nations. Reference to "profaning/ making common my name" is a motif in this small block, in 36:20, 21, 22, 23. In each instance it is "you" who have "profaned my name": the implication is that, not only is it simply their having left the land, but that the worship and lifestyle of the people in exile has had a similar effect.[16]

"I Will Hallow My Name"

This leads to Yahweh's action, restoring the people to the land "not for your sake, but for the sake of my holy name" (36:21, 22). Here (36:23) is the only instance in the Old Testament of God "making holy my name." It is in the Lord's Prayer and it is followed by a great passage (36:24–30) which has been appropriately entitled "A Catalogue of Yahweh's Name-Sanctifying Actions."[17] The renewal is not the people's action or response but his, with the repeated first person verbal subject:

---

15. Darr, "Ezekiel," 1274–75, including a quote from her earlier "Ezekiel's Justification," 102.

16. Cf. Jews in Egypt (Jeremiah 44), the ridicule of idols oracles (Isa 40:19–20; 41:5–7; 42:17; 44:6–22), along with expressions of despair (Ezek 37:11) and criticism of Yahweh's justice (Ezek 18:2).

17. Block, *Ezekiel*, 352.

> *I* will sprinkle clean water upon you, and you shall be clean from all your uncleannesses, and from all your idols *I* will cleanse you. A new heart *I* will give you, and a new spirit *I* will put within you; and *I* will remove from your body [rasab] the heart of stone and [*I* will] give you a heart of flesh [rasab]. *I* will put my spirit within you, and [*I* will] make you follow my statutes and be careful to observe my ordinances. (36:25-27, NRSV, emphasis added)

There is to be a fresh start with a removal of accumulated impurities and defilement of past idolatry and bloodshed.[18] Flowing from this will be prosperity in the land (v. 29), and, interestingly, it is then that the people are aware of their past despicable behaviour. The change is evident to "the nations around you" (v. 36). "Though many of his prophecies deal with the gloomy picture of punishment and destruction, Ezekiel has a positive view of his people's destiny . . . Because the people's destiny does not rest on human deeds but on God's name, their restoration from exile is guaranteed."[19]

There remains, however, one area where the nations have misunderstood the character and action of Yahweh. The attack by Gog and his hordes (chs. 38-39) threatens not only Israel but the reputation of Yahweh. The cluster of "know" phrases in chapter 39 is significant as are the statements following Gog's defeat (39:7, 22-23): the nations are to know that the exile was not due to Yahweh's weakness (a view enabling Gog to attack, just as Babylon had), but due to his deliberate actions. Yahweh is "zealous for my holy name" (39:25): no other god, or lesser power, is to be given the honor due only to Yahweh.

This overarching picture provides a perspective in returning to 36:22 with the statement that Yahweh is not acting for the sake of Israel but "for the sake of my holy name." Zimmerli highlights the starkness: "Here too Ezekiel is devoid of all soft-hearted features and warmer tones. There is no mention of mercy, love, covenant faithfulness, the justice that brings salvation. This whole vocabulary is missing from the book of Ezekiel . . . In place of these . . . the dominant concept is that of the majesty of Yahweh and the revelation of his honor and glory."[20]

---

18. Greenberg, *Ezekiel*, 730, provides links with ritual law of Lev 16, along with Num 19:13, 20.

19. Luc, "A Theology," 143.

20. Zimmerli, *Ezekiel 2*, 247-48.

This action is because God's purposes do not end with Israel, but rather go out to the nations. The honor of Yahweh's name is linked with the people being brought back, cleansed and renewed, made holy, and given peace from enemies. Later will come the vision of a city from which a river flows watering trees that continually provide fruit for food and healing (47:1–12; expanded in Rev 22:2 "of the nations"). From the beginning of the recounting of history in chapter 20 the concern has been attitudes to the name "among the nations." It is to be the restoration of the people and the defeat of Gog from Magog and his armies that there will be proof to all, Israel and nations, that "I am Yahweh."

Admittedly, the question is left open in Ezekiel as to the future of the nations in relationship with Yahweh. Will they participate in the blessings given to Israel? The response of Wright appropriately highlights the dire situation in which Ezekiel prophesied:

> Before we jump to the conclusion that Ezekiel was unconcerned about the salvific destiny of the nations and compare him unfavorably with Isaiah 40–55 we should recall again the desperate situation Ezekiel ministered into . . . The prophecies of Israel can speak of the universal salvation of God going to the nations because they can also speak of the restoration of Israel as though it had already taken place . . . Ezekiel can only offer hope to the nations through the restoration of Israel, a restoration that itself seems almost impossible.[21]

As with the vision that opens the book, the strength of focus on Yahweh and his name comes across to modern readers with the clarity of a black and white sketch that has no greys. There is a "blessing of point zero" as one is forced to focus on the solid core of faith and hope.[22] The reader cannot avoid being confronted—and that is its value for the modern worshipper. Ezekiel helps us to see God's glory and in turn to see ways in which the actions of God's people cause that glory to be tainted. There are actions which bring shame, rather than honour. Like a surgeon's scalpel, the words and images go to the core of worship and the focus of the lifestyle of God's people.

With a common practice being to include the Lord's Prayer in Christian worship, and with the very first petition being "hallowed be

---

21. Wright, *The Message*, quoting in part from an unpublished dissertation by D. A. Williams.

22. The phrase is used by Zimmerli, "Plans for Rebuilding," 113.

your name," Ezekiel provides a key interpretative background to a petition that is often poorly understood. It is no accident that in Matthew the prayer is in the middle of the Sermon on the Mount, a passage which portrays a missiological lifestyle amongst the nations ("a light to the world").[23] The petition can be read as a plea in a world in which the name of the God and Father of our Lord Jesus Christ is so widely unknown or dishonored, and in which God's own people bring dishonor by their behavior, both individually and corporately. It is a plea that God so act amongst his own people, forgiving, cleansing, empowering by the Spirit, removing injustice and false worship, that his name may be known and honored throughout the world.

It is also a prayer of hope to congregations and individuals, no matter what their situation, their failures or successes, weaknesses or strengths. The theocentric message of Ezekiel helps us see the cleansing, restoring work of the Spirit of God. There is hope because God will act "for his name's sake." The prayer of Christ in John 17 provides another interesting commentary on the same themes: there too are brought together "glory," "name," "know," "sanctify"—"so that the world may know." There is to be a mutual sharing in the "love" that characterizes the relationship between Father and Son, so that the world may know the divine character. That this is given to us in a prayer of Christ is an assurance that it will come to pass. The future is certain, there is hope no matter what the circumstances—and of course, the prayer of John 17 is set in the context of Gethsemane. The events surrounding and on the cross seen at one level could not be further from bringing glory to God—and yet the glory of God is revealed, for here "God was in Christ reconciling the world to himself" (2 Cor 5:19). God's glory is to be known, his name honored by those who are one with him, and thence to all nations.

Worship that is theocentric, that is open to hear the word of God, that knows the name of God, is worship that provides clear vision of hope in the midst of turmoil, even despair. It is worship that puts the powers in perspective and exposes false hopes. In writing of the attraction of a liturgical church, Galli commented, "It is precisely the point of liturgy to take people out of their worlds and usher them into a strange, new world—to show them that, despite appearances, the last thing in the world they need is more of the world out of which they've come. The world the liturgy reveals . . . is more real than the one we inhabit day by

---

23. Olley, "'You Are the Light.'"

day . . . We find our gaze directed away from ourselves and toward God and his kingdom."[24]

His concern is with "the prayers, responses and shape of worship," to which could be added the content of the word that is preached, for Israel too had its liturgy but failed to hear and obey the word that should have been proclaimed. There can be worship that does not lead to God, but which has as its end the worship itself or is evaluated on the basis of "what I get out of it." Recently an avowed atheist, a Melbourne journalist, asked for her funeral to be in a church: "I love old hymns, religious poetry, church spires . . . I am a cultural Christian . . . the church belongs to us all."[25] Again, the book of Ezekiel helps us to "see" all, even worship that is less than giving honor to God and making his name known.

IN WORSHIP WE SEE THE FUTURE

Already words given to Ezekiel have enabled him to see aspects of the future as he looks beyond the present exile and destruction, a time of "dry bones" where "hope is gone" (37:3, 11). God's action of "hallowing my name" continues with promise of new life. Given past history, and "God's glory" having left the temple, there comes the amazing promise that "my dwelling place . . . , my sanctuary is among them forever" (37:27–28). Four centuries after the initial return from exile, the LXX used the term *kataskēnōsis*, a word used in classical Greek of "encampment" and used of the "nests" of birds in Matthew 8:20 (// Luke 9:58). Reminiscent of the tabernacle it lacks the royal patronage imagery of a temple, emphasizing the presence rather than the structure. "According to O.T. ideas of the blessed future, man is not translated to dwell with God, but God comes down to dwell with man, and His Presence transforms earth into heaven."[26]

New Testament descriptions of Christ as the "God-with-us," the Word who "made his dwelling (*skēnoō*) with us," who promised "I will be with you"—significantly in a context of "all peoples"—and the sending of the Spirit "to be with you" come to mind.[27] Here is the outworking of the covenant relationship that is now restored. God has not given up, he

---

24. Galli, "A Deeper Relevance."
25. Davis, "Atheist Bone."
26. Cooke, *Ezekiel*, 404.
27. Matt 1:23; John 1:14; Matt 28:20; John 14:16–17.

forgives, cleanses, and renews, "I will be their God and they will be my people" (Ezek 37:27). For the holy God to "take up residence" is an amazing assurance of acceptance and renewal.

That presence is given greater pictorial representation in the vision of chapters 40–48, the new temple and land where God's glory returns (43:1–12; 44:4). As for chapter 1, details and ongoing relevance are debated, but imagery is taken up in the vision in Revelation 21–22 of the new Jerusalem. Here is the presence of God come down to earth in glory, in a city with open gates from which flows a life-giving river. The "violence and oppression" of the past by rulers and leaders, with unjust exercise of power in commerce and business transactions, is to be no more (45:7–12).

The size and architecture also convey powerful images of welcome and openness. The temple complex is more than three times the size of a typical palace compound. Further,

> the close correlation of the removal of votive monuments (43:7, 9) with the command to Ezekiel to describe the measurements of the gates and passageways . . . signify the establishment of authentic worship and, as a consequence, authentic existence . . . God puts an end to . . . petitions by proxy . . . [God's] house must be enlarged to accommodate everyone . . . If the entrances and exits allow the people to approach God in worship, they also allow them to move toward and away from the divine presence as authentic selves, worshipping in freedom.[28]

The vision of the future, guaranteed by the word and presence of God, reaffirmed in worship as the word is read and the presence experienced, transforms the present. Is it coincidental that two New Testament books that provide visions of the heavenly that comes down to earth with encouragement that looks to the future, namely, Hebrews and Revelation, are given to Christians facing pressures and persecution? Revelation in particular is known for its prayers and praises.

In worship as we "see" God (now known as Father, Son, and Spirit) and the divine purposes for creation, we are enabled by the Spirit to give thanks to God for his work amongst us, and open ourselves to that ongoing work of "hallowing his name" that "the nations may know." We are able to go about our daily lives in a way that increasingly honors our God

---

28. Odell, *Ezekiel*, 532–34.

because we "see" differently the world in which we live. Worship is to help us more clearly to "see" God and to "see" ourselves and the world.

> My gracious master and my God,
> assist me to proclaim,
> to spread through all the earth abroad,
> the honor of your name.[29]

---

29. Charles Wesley, "O for a thousand tongues."

5

Worship in the New Testament

Alastair Campbell

INTRODUCTION

The modern reader approaching the subject of worship and seeing a chapter headed "Worship in the New Testament" is likely to expect that we shall be concerned with such practical matters as the style and content of Christian meetings and the emergence of Christian liturgy. "How," we wonder, "did the New Testament Christians worship?" Perhaps we ask the question with the further assumption that if we could only know the answer it would provide some sort of standard by which our own acts of worship could be evaluated and reformed, something that we should try and "get back to." If so, we are likely to be disappointed. The question is not illegitimate, but it proves harder to answer than we might expect. The early missionaries who wrote our New Testament were much more concerned to tell their converts *who* should be worshipped than *how* that worship should be expressed.

WORSHIP AS SUBMISSION

The commonest word for worship in the New Testament is *proskunein* which literally means "to prostrate oneself" before a superior. David Peterson writes,

> From earliest times, this term expressed the widespread oriental custom of bowing down or casting oneself on the ground, kissing the feet, the hem of a garment or the ground, as a total bodily

gesture of respect before a great one. As applied to the honoring of the gods, it meant bending over or falling down before an image or making some literal gesture of homage to a god. At an early stage *proskunein* also came to be used for the inward attitude of homage or respect which the outward gesture represented.[1]

This leads him to conclude that, "Submission is the fundamental disposition indicated by this word." While essentially an attitude of heart and mind this submission may be expressed by outward and physical actions.

We can see this most clearly from the Book of Revelation. Here we find both the worship of God and the Lamb by the heavenly host (4:10; 5:13) and the worship of the Beast (representing the Roman state and its emperor) by the "inhabitants of the earth" (13:8). As Richard Bauckham says, "Worship, which is so prominent in the theocentric vision of Revelation, has nothing to do with pietistic retreat from the public world."[2] On the contrary, it is a political statement and a public act. Worshippers of the beast receive a mark on their hand or forehead that everyone can see. The gritty reality behind this vision is well illustrated by the letter of Pliny to the Roman emperor, Trajan.[3] Pliny was governor of the neighboring province of Bythinia about twenty years after John wrote to the seven churches of Asia, and he says that he required those accused of being Christians to "repeat after me a formula of invocation to the gods" and to make "offerings of wine and incense to your statue (which I had ordered to be brought into court for this purpose along with images of the gods)." By contrast, in the vision of heaven that John describes in chapters four and five the heavenly host express their submission to God by falling down before him and declaring his praise in a loud voice. Presumably this, too, reflects realities "on the ground" and in the churches, and this is confirmed again by Pliny who reports that the Christians chanted "verses alternately among themselves in honor of Christ as to a god." In both cases the intention of what is done is to express submission and allegiance.

That worship is primarily a matter of submission wherever it occurs in the New Testament is confirmed by several famous passages. For example, when the devil promises Jesus that he will give him all the king-

1. Peterson, "Worship," 52.
2. Bauckham, *Theology*, 161.
3. Radice, *Letters*, 294.

doms of the world and their splendor, "if you will bow down and worship me" (Matt 4:9), the thought is clearly of allegiance, albeit allegiance expressed by oriental gesture. Jesus is being called to live by Satan's lies, not engage in any particular ritual or liturgical activity.

In John's Gospel the Samaritan woman tries to get Jesus to pronounce on whether acceptable worship should take place in the temple in Jerusalem or on Mount Gerizim, as the Samaritans claimed. In his reply Jesus shows no interest in whether worship should be in one place or another (the liturgical question), but says, "But the hour is coming, and is now here, when the true worshipers will worship the Father in spirit and truth, for the Father seeks such as these to worship him. God is spirit, and those who worship him must worship in spirit and truth" (John 4:23–24).

"Worship in spirit and in truth" does not refer to a particular style of worship but to the worship of God—truly revealed by Jesus as "Father"—in the power of the Spirit—whom Jesus will make available. As he does throughout the Fourth Gospel, Jesus is calling on both Jew and Samaritan to leave their traditional ways of thinking and to submit to the true God in the way he has come to make possible (John 6:40; 8:31; 14:5–13).

A third example comes from one of the few places in his letters that Paul is actually talking about what should go on "in church." In an attempt to get the Corinthians to value intelligible prophecy over ecstatic but unintelligible utterances he imagines the effect that these might have on outsiders who come into the Christian meeting. If they see everyone speaking in tongues, they will conclude from the resulting bedlam that the Christians have gone mad, whereas, if they will only speak intelligibly, there is the possibility that the newcomer will actually be converted. In Paul's words, "But if an unbeliever or someone who does not understand comes in while everybody is prophesying, he will be convinced by all that he is a sinner and will be judged by all, and the secrets of his heart will be laid bare. So he will fall down and worship God, exclaiming, "God is really among you!" (1 Cor 14:24–25).

Once again, falling down and worshipping God is a matter of submitting to God as God. The language describes the person's conversion and does not refer to liturgical activity.

HOW DID THE EARLY CHRISTIANS WORSHIP?

Proskunein is not the only word translated as "worship" in the New Testament. There is also *latreia* and its cognate verb *latreuō*. When these words refer to cultic activity it is with reference to the worship by Israelites under the old covenant (e.g., Luke 2:37; Acts 26:7, and Hebrews *passim*), or of pagan worship of idols (Acts 7:42; Rom 1:25). When they are used of Christians they refer to the whole of life lived in obedience and submission to God. For example, Paul speaks of "God, whom I serve with my whole heart in preaching the gospel of his Son" (Rom 1:9; cf. Acts 24:14; 27:23; 2 Tim 1:3). Particularly significant is the use of *latreia* in Romans 12:1–2. "I appeal to you therefore, brothers and sisters, by the mercies of God, to present your bodies as a living sacrifice, holy and acceptable to God, which is your spiritual worship. Do not be conformed to this world, but be transformed by the renewing of your minds, so that you may discern what is the will of God—what is good and acceptable and perfect."

Clearly, "spiritual worship" refers here not to liturgical activity of any kind, or to anything that happens "in church," but to the whole of life offered as a living sacrifice to God. Paul, in fact, is using cultic worship as a *metaphor for the Christian life*. Christians are priests; the sacrifice they offer is themselves and the transformed lives they lead in the world; and all this is not to gain God's favor but in grateful response to all his mercies that the previous eleven chapters have eloquently proclaimed.[4] Similar metaphorical use of cultic vocabulary is employed by Paul to describe his own missionary service (Rom 15:16) and its attendant sufferings (Phil 2:17–18), by Hebrews to refer to Christian charity (13:16), and by Peter to refer to the witness of the whole people of God, who form "a royal priesthood" (1 Pet 2:9). The conclusion is plain. When we encounter the word "worship" (or its various Greek equivalents) in the New Testament the reference is not usually to liturgical or congregational activity but to something much broader, namely the recognition of God as God (and Jesus as God) and to the consequent surrender of

---

4. Paul was not the first person to speak in this way of spiritual worship (*logikē latreia*). It was a commonplace among Greek philosophers that God did not require animal sacrifices but rather the righteous behavior of the worshippers. The Corpus Hermeticum actually uses the phrase *logikē thusia*. See Ferguson, "Spiritual Sacrifice," 1152–89, and references there.

heart, soul, mind, and strength to him, and the adoption of the life-style that he commands.

However, the recognition that this is what the vocabulary of "worship" generally refers to in the New Testament by no means invalidates the search for what went on in Christian meetings, to which today we give the name "worship" also. The fact that Paul did not use one of the available words for worship to refer to what Christians did when they assembled together does not prove that they did not in fact worship in this other sense of the word, or that Paul would have thought our interest in this to be misplaced. The question, "How did the early Christians worship God?" is legitimate, but it is not for that reason easy to answer.

There are several reasons for this. First, there is the nature of the New Testament documents themselves—four portraits of Jesus showing the crucified one to be the Messiah and Lord, an account of the spread of the gospel from Jerusalem to the ends of the earth that shows little interest in church order, letters written to address issues of belief and behavior that arose in particular communities, and an apocalypse that, as we have seen, is more interested in who is to be worshipped than in specifying how this is to be done. To put it simply, the New Testament documents contain no liturgical instructions or descriptions of the kind that we find in the *Didache* (c. 100 CE?). Second, while Justin (c. 155 CE) and Hippolytus (c. 220 CE) give us detailed accounts of early Christian worship in the second and third centuries, we cannot assume that this is relevant for the first century.

Third, even where we catch a glimpse of Christian worship in a New Testament document, we cannot assume that what was done somewhere was done everywhere. The New Testament churches were widely scattered and developed in different ways and at different speeds without any central control, so that the glimpses we get of congregational worship, especially in Acts, resemble isolated snapshots which the modern scholar attempts to arrange so as to tell a plausible story. Fourth, we should beware of confusing literary metaphor with liturgical practice. For example, when we read, "As many of you as were baptized into Christ have clothed yourselves with Christ" (Gal 3:27), it is tempting to conclude as many preachers have done that Paul is alluding to the practice of providing the newly baptized with a new garment. But which came first? Did the practice give rise to the metaphor? Or did Paul's metaphor suggest the later practice? Scholars are rightly cautious.[5]

---

5. Dunn, *Epistle*, 204.

Finally, it might be thought that Christian congregational worship could be reconstructed from the worship that took place in the Jewish synagogue—except that our knowledge of the first century synagogue is as scanty as our knowledge of the first century church![6] Indeed, some of the earliest references to synagogue services are provided by the New Testament itself (Luke 4:16–21; Acts 13:14–15). However, we can at least note that the earliest Christians, being Jews, were familiar with a form of congregational worship that did not involve temple or sacrifice, and which probably did involve the three elements of praise, prayer, and instruction, even if the detailed evidence we have for this comes from later sources.[7]

All of this will make us cautious as we seek to answer the question, "How did the first Christians worship God?" The New Testament itself provides our only evidence, but that evidence permits us to draw the following conclusions with reasonable confidence.

New Testament Christians Sang Hymns to God

There are explicit references to their doing so. Paul and Silas sang hymns to God while in prison (Acts 16:25). Paul writing to the church at Corinth says, "When you come together each one has a hymn" (1 Cor 14:26). Writing to the Colossians he urges them, "With gratitude in your hearts sing psalms, hymns, and spiritual songs to God" (Col 3:16; cf. Eph 5:19). While some scholars have tried to distinguish these—"psalms" being taken from the Old Testament or based on Old Testament forms, "hymns" being Christian compositions in praise of the risen Lord, and "spiritual songs" being spontaneous outbursts of praise—others are more cautious and think the writer is just piling up synonyms.[8] Furthermore there are almost certainly actual examples and fragments of early Christian hymns embedded in the New Testament writings themselves.

First, there are the hymns inserted by Luke into his story of the births of John the Baptist and Jesus and placed on the lips of Mary, Zechariah, Simeon, and the heavenly host (Luke 1:46–55; 1:68–79; 2:14; 2:29–32). They contain many echoes of similar songs in the Old Testament and would have equally appealed to Aramaic-speaking congregations in

---

6. Bradshaw, *Search*, chaps. 1 and 2.
7. Martin, "Worship," 985.
8. Martin, "Hymns," 420; Lincoln, *Ephesians*, 346; Best, *Ephesians*, 511.

Palestine and to Greek-speaking Christians brought up on the LXX. As Dunn says, "Luke has almost certainly drawn them from the living worship of the earliest congregations."[9]

Second, there are the hymns of praise in the book of Revelation, notably 4:11; 5:9–14; 7:12; 11:17–18; 15:3–4; 19:7–8. Again, with Dunn we may readily agree that the worship of heaven is "very probably modeled on or represents the worship and language with which the seer himself was familiar," but we do not need to follow him in concluding that this worship consisted of short, spontaneous outbursts rather than longer hymns and psalms.[10] John is an artist and he draws on the praise language with which he is familiar to depict the praise of heaven, but just as the speeches in Acts do not prove that Paul typically spoke for just five minutes at a time, so the use of short acclamations of praise in John's portrayal of heaven may tell us of the language John's churches used to praise God but hardly that their praise was either short or spontaneous.

Third, it is claimed that we can detect hymns or fragments of hymns in Paul's letters, the most widely recognized being Philippians 2:6–11; Colossians 1:15–20; 1 Timothy 3:16; and Ephesians 5:14.[11] The interest of those who have developed this theory has been not so much to depict early Christian worship as to show the character of pre-Pauline Christianity. Did Paul write this passage or is he quoting a well-known "hymn"? If the latter, has he changed it in any way, adding phrases or omitting them so as to bring it into line with his own thought? We are not here concerned to answer such questions but rather to ask whether these passages are rightly regarded as hymns at all. This seems doubtful. The theory depends on being able to discern the presence of a poetic structure marked by balance and rhythm, but in fact in most cases there is no agreement as to what that structure is. Some theories only work if certain phrases are omitted as interpolations by the author of the letter in which they appear. This looks like an attempt to doctor the evidence to fit the theory! We may readily grant that these are "purple" passages employing exalted diction and poetic style, but are they hymns? Paul was quite capable of such writing as the passage on love in 1 Corinthians 13 shows, but although this has sometimes been called a "Hymn to

---

9. Dunn, *Unity*, 133. See further Farris, "The Canticles," 91–112.

10. Dunn, *Unity*, 134.

11. Similar claims are sometimes made for John 1:1–16; Heb 1:3; and 1 Pet 1:8–22. See Dunn, *Unity*, 137ff.

love," nobody so far as I know thinks that it was ever sung as a hymn by Christian congregations.[12] It is surely wiser to think of these passages as something more like creeds carefully constructed for memorization and recitation. Commenting on Colossians 1:15–20, O'Brien says, "In describing the passage in this way [i.e., as a hymn] it should be noted that the term 'hymn' is not employed in the modern sense of what we understand by congregational hymns with metrical verses. Nor are we to think of Greek poetic form. The category is used broadly, similar to that of 'creed,' and includes dogmatic, confessional, liturgical, polemical or doxological material."[13]

He is surely right. A moment's reflection on the dynamics of congregational singing should be enough to tell us that no congregation ever sang Philippians 2:6–11 or Colossians 1:15–20. They are far too complex and employ too many different words to make a good song. The case is different with Ephesians 5:14, "Therefore it says, 'Sleeper, awake! Rise from the dead, and Christ will shine on you.'" This admits to being a quotation and seems to come from a song, very likely a song sung at baptismal services encouraging the baptisands to live out the meaning of their baptism. As such it helps to explain what is meant when a few verses later the writer calls on the readers to "speak *to one another* in psalms, hymns and spiritual songs" (Eph 5:19).

The New Testament Christians Offered Praise and Prayer to God

We would expect this, of course, given that they were heirs of the prayer traditions of Judaism, and recipients of Jesus' distinctive teaching on the importance and character of prayer. Evidence that they did so when they met together is provided by Acts and the Pauline letters. The first reported action of the embryo Jerusalem church after the ascension of Jesus is to meet together to pray (Acts 1:14). Prayer is one of the four activities that Luke names as characteristic of the church after Pentecost (Acts 2:42), both in the temple and in homes where the church met. Just as Jesus himself had done (Luke 6:12), the early Christians prayed to God when selecting leaders. This was true of the Jerusalem church selecting a new apostle (Acts 1:24–25), and of the Antioch church commissioning their first missionaries (Acts 13:1–3). According to Luke, it was while

---

12. Barrett, *Commentary*, 299.
13. O'Brien, *Colossians*, 32.

"they were worshipping the Lord and fasting" that they discerned God's choice of Barnabas and Saul and after further fasting and prayer that they sent them off. The word translated "worshipping" is a participle of the Greek verb *leitourgeō*. While this word is used in a variety of contexts in the New Testament to denote service of various kinds, in the present context, addressed "to God" and paired with "fasting" it surely refers to prayer and is meant to characterize the meeting as a whole as one where the church acknowledged God's sovereignty and sought God's will.[14] Acts provides us with one extended summary of the church at prayer following the arrest and release of Peter and John (4:23–30). God is addressed as "Sovereign Lord," creator of the world and lord of history, making clear that their prayer is an expression of the submission we have seen to be at the heart of true worship. It is to be noted that Luke goes out of his way to emphasize that prayer was a corporate activity of the whole church as it met together (Acts 1:14; 2:46; 4:24), and by implication an important reason for its doing so.[15]

That the early Christians offered praise and prayer to God is also evident from Paul's letters, most of which begin with Paul telling the readers how he gives thanks and prays for them. From this we can deduce that Paul addressed God in prayers of adoration, thanksgiving, and petition. For example,

> Blessed be the God and Father of our Lord Jesus Christ, the Father of mercies and the God of all consolation, who consoles us in all our affliction, so that we may be able to console those who are in any affliction with the consolation with which we ourselves are consoled by God. (2 Cor 1:3–4)

> We always give thanks to God for all of you and mention you in our prayers, constantly remembering before our God and Father your work of faith and labor of love and steadfastness of hope in our Lord Jesus Christ. (1 Thess 1:2–3)

> And this is my prayer, that your love may overflow more and more with knowledge and full insight to help you to determine what is best, so that in the day of Christ you may be pure and blameless, having produced the harvest of righteousness that comes through Jesus Christ for the glory and praise of God. (Phil 1:9–11)

---

14. For a different view see Marshall, "How far did the early Christians worship God?" 218, and Peterson, "Worship," 67.

15. See further, Green, "Persevering," 183–202.

Longenecker notes that the same three types of prayer are to be found in the "Eighteen Benedictions," which even at this early date were a staple of synagogue prayer, and proposes that Paul would have carried this over into the churches he founded.[16] Although these are strictly prayer reports rather than actual prayers it is difficult not to feel that we hear in them the style as well as the content of the Apostle's prayers. This is still truer of the long prayer of blessing that opens the letter to the Ephesians, "Blessed be the God and Father of our Lord Jesus Christ, who has blessed us in Christ with every spiritual blessing in the heavenly places" (Eph 1:3). If, as many think, this letter was not actually written by Paul, it may nevertheless be first-hand evidence for the way Paul was remembered to have prayed. If not, it is evidence for the way prayer developed in the Pauline churches. The same is true of the instruction found in the Pastoral Letters. "First of all, then, I urge that supplications, prayers, intercessions, and thanksgivings be made for everyone, for kings and all who are in high positions, so that we may lead a quiet and peaceable life in all godliness and dignity" (1 Tim 2:1–2).

As Jeremiah urged the exiles to settle down and pray for Babylon (Jer 29:7), so Paul is represented as urging the church to pray for the society in which they live and for its rulers. Corporate prayer is to form an important part of the Christian meeting (1 Tim 2:8).

The New Testament Christians Met to Share in a Meal

In his programmatic summary of the life of the earliest Jerusalem church Luke tells us that, "They devoted themselves to the apostles' teaching and fellowship, to the breaking of bread and the prayers" (Acts 2:42). A few verses later he tells us that, "they broke bread at home and ate their food with glad and generous hearts" (2:46). It is unclear whether he means us to understand breaking bread as a reference to the Eucharist or to shared meals, which after the Jewish custom would have begun with a prayer of thanksgiving to God. The issue is not resolved in the only other places breaking bread is referred to in Acts. The account of the meeting at which Eutychus had to be resuscitated after falling out of the window begins, "On the first day of the week, when we met to break bread" (Acts 20:7), which rather suggests a celebration of the Lord's Supper (this then eventually takes place, Acts 20:11). On the other hand, when he

---

16. Longenecker, "Prayer," 203–27.

tells us that Paul broke bread with the sailors and passengers on board ship (Acts 27:35), Luke appears to be describing an ordinary meal. Yet the way he describes Paul's actions ("he took bread; and giving thanks to God in the presence of all, he broke it and began to eat") strongly recalls the actions of Jesus at Emmaus (Luke 24:30).[17] On balance we should probably understand Luke to refer both to shared meals and to the Lord's Supper, because he knows that at this early period no distinction was made between the two, the words and actions of Jesus being recalled in the context of a real meal at which the poor and needy were welcomed and fed.

This is confirmed by the only explicit references to the Lord's Supper in the New Testament (1 Cor 10:16–17; 11:17–34). The rebuke Paul gives the church at Corinth only makes sense if the church was in the habit of meeting to share a common meal at which rich and poor alike were welcome. The greed and selfishness of the wealthier members has ruined the occasion, so that "one remains hungry and another gets drunk," and those who have nothing are humiliated (1 Cor 11:21–22). So it is a real meal, but not just a meal, since the words of the Lord Jesus are recalled, together with his death and resurrection "until he comes." Those who participate are declared to be the beneficiaries of his sacrificial death and members together of his body (1 Cor 10:16).

Apart from the evidence of Acts and 1 Corinthians there are no other certain references to the Lord's Supper in the New Testament, even where we might expect them, and in the light of later developments that is surprising. Ephesians, for example, can call for unity on the basis of "one Lord, one faith, one baptism" (4:5), but says nothing about one bread or one cup. The Pastoral Letters instruct Timothy to devote himself to "the public reading of scripture, to preaching and to teaching" (1 Tim 4:13), but are completely silent about the Eucharist.

Nevertheless, we have enough evidence to say that a shared meal was an important element of early Christian worship, but in saying this we should note its significance. As it was in the ministry of Jesus, a shared meal was an expression of fellowship and of belonging, and as such its message was a message from God to people, not an offering from people to God. Significantly, it was apparently called by the name *agapē*, or "love feast." In time, and no doubt at different times and in different places, the horizontal dimension of fellowship with one another gave way to the

---

17. Wainwright, "Lord's Supper," 688–89.

vertical dimension of communion with God, Eucharist and *agapē* were separated, and bread and wine, no longer part of a meal became a sacrament and in time a sacrifice. Whether we see this as a proper development in Christian thinking or a sad conformity to the religious thinking of the world around, we should at least agree that it is a development that goes beyond anything we find in the New Testament.[18]

The New Testament Christians Met to Be Instructed

Luke's portrait of the ideal church of the early days begins, "They devoted themselves to the apostles' teaching" (Acts 2:42). At Antioch we are told there were prophets and teachers (13:1). At Troas the church assembled to break bread, but also to allow Paul to teach them at great length (20:7–12). In his farewell address to the Ephesian elders Paul says, "I did not shrink from doing anything helpful, proclaiming the message to you and teaching you publicly and from house to house" (20:20). "House to house" presumably refers to meetings of the church in the homes of some of its leading members. The Acts of the Apostles may fairly be described as the story of the spread of God's word from Jerusalem to the ends of the earth and fittingly it ends with Paul "in his own rented house" teaching about Jesus (Acts 28:30–31).

This picture is confirmed by Paul's own letters. When Paul was present he was no doubt the teacher, but in his absence different members of the church spoke as they were able. From the start there were leaders whose task was to "admonish" the congregation (1 Thess 5:12), but anyone might bring a word from God and was not to be despised (5:19), so that Paul can say to the Corinthians, "When you come together, each one has a hymn, a lesson, a revelation, a tongue, or an interpretation" (1 Cor 14:26). However, even in Corinth we see Paul trying to introduce an element of control into the church's worship: "And God has appointed in the church first apostles, second prophets, third teachers" (1 Cor 12:28). Writing to the Romans Paul makes it plain that not all are equally gifted when it comes to speaking to the church (Rom 12:6). By the time Ephesians is written it is recognized that God has given some to be apostles, prophets, evangelists, pastors, and teachers specifically to equip the rest of the church and build it up (Eph 4:11–12), and, when we reach the Pastoral Letters teaching and preaching is in the hands of Timothy

---

18. Barrett, *Church*, 89–101; Dunn, "Whatever Happened?" 35–48.

and those elders whom he appoints (1 Tim 4:13-14; 5:17). Whether it was brought by many or few, as prophecy or as teaching, instruction and exhortation remained central to the purpose of the Christian meeting throughout the New Testament period and beyond.

CONCLUSION

The New Testament Christians then met to sing praise to God, to pray to him, to share a meal and be instructed in how they should think of him and live their lives for him. In all these ways they expressed that submission to God that is at the heart of worship. Their songs declared his majesty. Their prayers acknowledged his sovereignty and their dependence on him. Their supper was *the Lord's* supper that ruled out any involvement with idols (1 Cor 10:21). They met to hear God's word, whether from Scripture or from another Christian believed to be inspired by God, with the intention of bringing to God "the obedience of faith" (Rom 1:5). What they did not do was to offer any kind of tangible sacrifice, whether an animal or a pinch of incense. They met in homes, not in a temple, and their leaders were teachers and not priests. Their meeting together was predicated on the one, sufficient sacrifice of Christ; their shared meal declared to them God's inclusive grace; and their prayers were a response to God's favor, not an attempt to secure it.

So what does all this have to say to us today? Especially, what does it have to say about the content and conduct of Christian worship in the secondary, liturgical, sense of what we do when we meet together in Jesus' name? We should not try to use the New Testament as if it were a handbook of church order. The patterns of assembly we glimpse in the New Testament were a response to a unique situation. They met in homes because they had nowhere else to go, not as a preferred location for Christian witness. If their meetings were informal, this was a function of who they were, very ordinary people caught up in something utterly new, with few resources or traditional wisdom to guide them, not a result of conscious decision. In any case the New Testament itself presents us with a developing picture, from the informal meetings in Corinth to the relatively ordered church life of the Pastorals. Who is to say that one is more authoritative than the other?

But if the New Testament does not provide us with a pattern, it does provide us with certain principles by which everything we do "in church" can be evaluated and, if necessary, reformed. The first is *truth*.

No one can read the New Testament documents without being brought face to face with their deep concern for the truth, the truth of God as revealed in Christ Jesus. The content of Christian hymns and prayers must always be judged according to the truth they express or fail to express. As Paul said, "No one can say, 'Jesus is Lord,' except by the Holy Spirit" (1 Cor 12:3), and Jesus crucified and risen remains the test of all we do and say, however apparently inspired or persuasive.

The second principle is *love*. The disgraceful conduct of some Corinthians at the Lord's Table is critiqued not in terms of the offence that drunkenness may present to God, but by its loveless disregard of the poorer members. What Paul says about love (1 Cor 13) does not just apply to worship, of course, but it is invoked by Paul in 1 Corinthians precisely to critique the Corinthians' priorities in this regard. As the argument unfolds in the next chapter it emerges that what is loving is what helps or builds up others. Speaking in tongues may be impressive but it fails this test because it is unintelligible, and therefore unhelpful to others who may be present.

This leads directly to the third principle, namely, that of *edification*. Surprising as it may seem, congregational worship in the New Testament is evaluated not by how it might please God, not by any principle of reverence or correctness, but by how far it benefits other people. Corinthian praise and prayer may score highly in terms of enthusiasm or sincerity, but this is of no help if others cannot say, "Amen." Paul says, "You may be giving thanks well enough, but the other person is not built up" (1 Cor 14:17). This emphasis is continued in other places in the New Testament. The "psalms, hymns, and spiritual songs" that we sing are not only sung to God but are a way of speaking *to one another*—for their encouragement and edification presumably (Eph 5:19). Hebrews encourages us to "approach the throne of grace with confidence" (4:16) and "to enter the Most Holy Place by the blood of Jesus" (10:19), but the reason we should meet together is to "spur one another on toward love and good deeds" and to "encourage one another—and all the more as you see the Day approaching" (10:24–25).

All of which is to say that the final test of congregational worship lies not in anything that happens in church but in the transformed lives offered to God in daily life. Congregational worship that is worth anything not only expresses this obedience but also enables it through the renewal it brings to the mind (Rom 12:1–2).

6

The *Proskuneō* Myth

When a Kiss Is Not a Kiss

CHRIS JACK

INTRODUCTION

In recent times, urban myths (or legends) have become a common topic of discussion: those mythical stories or "facts" that, without any real foundation or substance, have established themselves as being true.[1] Did you know that it is possible to stand eggs on end during the vernal (spring) equinox due to the angle of the earth's inclination toward the sun on that one day of the year? Plausible? Perhaps. But not true! Myths also exist in the realm of Christian discourse: theories, statements, sound-bytes that are paraded as fact, despite being neither accurate nor correct. One such is the association of the word *proskuneō*, the most frequent word for worship in the New Testament, with "kiss." Alarmingly, this myth is perpetuated not only at the level of popular discussion but, at times, in more serious, academic writings, as will be evident from the examples that follow.

---

1. An internet search for "urban myth" or "urban legend" yields a diverse array of websites, some of which sport an abundance of tales, "truths," and other assorted folklore—some fun, some fascinating, and some positively disturbing.

THE MYTH: A SAMPLING

Graham Kendrick, in his generally excellent popular-level book on worship, notes the importance of *proskuneō* as the most frequently used word for worship in the New Testament. He then seeks to define the word: "The basic meaning is 'to come towards to kiss (the hand).'"[2] Whilst he at least attempts to identify the nature of the kissing involved, he is incorrect to say that this is part of the basic meaning. Indeed, the whole concept of "basic meaning" as something to be derived from a word's etymology is flawed, as will be shown below. In a more recent book, dealing with the emerging church and its approach to worship, Dan Kimball asserts that *proskuneō* is literally "to kiss toward." He then observes, following Charles Ryrie, that "kissing the earth was an act to honor the deities of the earth, as was prostrating oneself in reverence."[3] The additional observation moves closer to the actual sense of *proskuneō*, yet the fact remains that the concept of "kissing" has been introduced. Kimball later notes, correctly, that *proskuneō* has "the connotation of submissive lowliness and deep respect," only to follow that up with a return to the language of kissing in his assertion that worship gatherings in the emerging church should be ones in which people "kiss toward [God] in reverence and lay prostrate."[4] What exactly does "kissing towards" mean?[5] Based as it is on a strict etymology of *proskuneō*, it neither does justice to the meaning of the word (as will be shown), nor does it offer anything that is especially meaningful, or helpful, in its own right. How many Christian worshippers express their worship by any kind of kissing action or gesture, or anything that remotely equates to it?

Kendrick and Kimball are but two out of the many examples that could be drawn from the more popular end of the spectrum.[6] In a book of more serious scholarship which sets out to provide a biblical theology of worship, Noel Due, whilst rightly observing that *proskuneō* means "I worship, do obeisance to, prostrate myself" adds, without further explanation, "it is commonly agreed that its most basic meaning is 'to kiss.'"[7]

---

2. Kendrick, *Worship*, 23.
3. Kimball, *Emerging Church*, 114.
4. Ibid.
5. I have come across no one who attempts to explain this phrase.
6. Wiersbe, *Real Worship*, 20; Giglio, *Air I Breathe*, 68; Pilavachi, *For the Audience of One*, 35–36.
7. Due, *Created For Worship*, 42. He cites in support "*Proskuneō*," in *NIDNTT*, 2,

There is a double problem here. First, the reference to "basic meaning" mistakenly implies that some sense of "kissing" is fundamental to the word and its use. Second, the concept of "kissing" is introduced without any significance being attached to it. How does it aid one's understanding of worship, if at all? Or is it merely a gratuitous observation? In similar vein, Allen Ross, in his substantial contribution to the biblical theology of worship, informs the reader that the meaning of *proskuneō* is "to bow down." He then adds, in brackets, "(*kuneō*, "to kiss")."[8] Like Due, he does not pursue the matter, but merely provides this seemingly gratuitous piece of information. What it does, intentionally or otherwise, is to bolster the prevailing myth that *proskuneō* has something to do with "kissing."[9]

It may be felt that such allusions to "kissing," even if misguided, should not be viewed too seriously, not least when little, or nothing, is made of them. Since they have some foundation in the word's etymology, is this not a harmless myth, if indeed it is a myth at all? That it is a myth we shall later demonstrate. That it is far from harmless in its capacity to mislead, once the "kiss" concept is identified and extended, may be seen from our next example, Peter Craig-Wild's *Tools for Transformation*. In a book that helpfully seeks to address the challenge of worshipping in relevant and appropriate ways in contemporary contexts, one section stands out as something of an aberration. The chapter on the biblical understanding of worship contains this heading, "The kissing game—

---

7 5. However, this merely reflects the opening statement of the article and ignores the significant explanatory comments that follow. These will be further discussed in due course. Due subsequently introduces a second Greek word used in the New Testament for worship, *latreuō*. He then comments, "At the risk of oversimplifying the relationship between the two words, *proskuneō* and *latreuō*: the first encompasses outward acts of worship, while the second (though not excluding the outward actions) relates to the disposition of one's heart and life." (43). This is not only an oversimplification, but is inaccurate, as we shall later demonstrate.

8. Ross, *Recalling the Hope*, 51.

9. Compare Ross's conclusion to his discussion of *proskuneō*, in which he rightly focuses on the aspect of "bowing down," with Due's comment above, restricting the sense to outward actions. Ross concludes, "To bow down before someone, a king or God, is to show adoration, devotion, submission, and service; and by the physical act of bowing the object of the veneration appears higher and so is exalted. And so when the Bible describes people bowing down before the LORD, it usually means more of what that particular posture represents. This was one posture that would be clearly understood" (52).

proskunein."[10] Craig-Wild begins, "Perhaps the most powerful word for worship in the New Testament is *proskunein*. I remember as a young lad hearing a sermon about this. I heard the word kiss used somewhere, and for years giggled every time I heard it. I thought it was one of those naughty words teenagers look for in dictionaries—and perhaps in a way it is."

After giving a few examples of its use (Matt 4:10; Luke 4:8; John 4:20–24; Rev 5:14), Craig-Wild offers two suggestions as to how best to translate the word: "to fall down in obeisance" or "to approach as if to kiss." What follows is astonishing, to say the least. Craig-Wild asserts that "There is something almost erotic about this verb as it underscores the quasi-physicality of true worship. There is either a falling down in awe and wonder, or a passionate embracing of God."

As if that were not sufficient, in the following section, entitled "More than just a kiss!," Craig-Wild continues. "This passion and intimacy is reminiscent of the word in Hebrew often translated *to know*. That word is *yada*. In this context worship is the ultimate place of coming to know. *Yada* can also mean to perceive, to discern and, crucially, to have sexual intercourse. Worship becomes the place of total interpenetration with God—the place of true knowing—of complete intimacy and intermingling."[11]

Here, way too much has been built on the alleged association of the word *proskuneō* with "kiss." The ramifications are far-reaching indeed!

THE MYTH EXPOSED

What, then, of this association? Does it have any foundation in fact? Yes, it does. The word *proskuneō* is a composite of two Greek words, *pros* and *kuneō*, the former of which is a preposition meaning "to" or "towards," and the latter of which means "to kiss." Employing a "literal," etymological approach, the meaning of *proskuneō* that is commonly derived is "to kiss towards." Here, then, is the source of the myth. That it is a myth, with a veneer of truth, but lacking real substance—that a "kiss" is in reality not

---

10. Craig-Wild, *Tools*, 24. For the benefit of readers who may not be familiar with Greek, *proskunein* and *proskuneō* are different forms of the same verb. There is no universally accepted way of referring to Greek verbs; it is a matter of personal preference.

11. Craig-Wild, *Tools*, 25.

a kiss—will be disclosed by an investigation of the origins, usage, and meaning of *proskuneō*.[12]

The Etymological Fallacy

First, a brief consideration of an important detail of linguistic theory that impacts directly on the task in hand. In his seminal book *The Semantics of Biblical Language*, first published in 1961, James Barr launched a scathing attack on what he perceived to be the inadequate, and even erroneous, usage of linguistic evidence within the field of biblical studies. It caused quite a stir. Whilst he has not won over all his critics, in the ensuing years many of his main theses have gained wide acceptance.[13] Chapter six of the book deals with etymology, the study of the origins of words. Barr highlights the fact that this field of linguistic study is concerned with history rather than meaning (semantics), making the important point that understanding a word's origins, its past, is not a guarantee to understanding its contemporary meaning; the latter is dependent not on how the word originated, but on how it is currently used.[14] This view is strongly endorsed by Moisés Silva in his highly regarded contribution to the application of lexical semantics to biblical studies, *Biblical Words and their Meaning*. His chapter on the discussion of the legitimate and illegitimate uses of etymology concludes,

> To summarize, the idea that etymology provides what is essential to a word persisted through the nineteenth century; unfortunately, today we still hear comments concerning the "basic," "proper," even "real" meaning of a word when the reference is only to its etymology. Modern studies compel us to reject this attitude and distrust a word's history; at the same time, we must use the past history of a word in coordination with its present use by means of the notion of transparency. Even in the closest ties between

---

12. This is not the place to enquire into the nature of meaning. Suffice it to say that our present interest is in what the word denotes. An accessible and reasonably brief discussion of "meaning" can be found in Lyons, *Language*, 136–78.

13. See the summary evaluation offered by Moisés Silva, *Biblical Words*, 18, "Barr's book, *The Semantics of Biblical Language*, was a trumpet blast against the monstrous regiment of shoddy linguistics. Controversial throughout, undiplomatic at times, it has been recognised as a major contribution to biblical studies." See also, Cotterell and Turner, *Linguistics*, 28, 109ff.

14. Barr, *Semantics*, 107.

Jack—*The Proskuneō Myth* 89

historical and descriptive studies, however, the priority of synchrony, the *dominant* function of usage, must be maintained.[15]

Two matters raised here are significant for our study of *proskuneō*. First, the inadequacy of referring to "basic" meaning on the grounds of etymology alone. Too often, once the origins of a word have been established, inferences, or worse, outright claims are made, that this "basic" meaning is what the word *really* means (as opposed, one assumes, to other derived meanings which are to be accorded less significance).[16] Such injudicious use of etymology has been aptly termed "the etymological fallacy."[17] James Barr used the phrase "the root fallacy" to denote essentially the same error.[18]

The relevance of this linguistic point for the study of the word *proskuneō* is immediately evident: taking the two constituent elements of the word, *pros* and *kuneō*, identifying their meaning, putting the meanings together, then maintaining that this is the (basic) meaning of the word, is inadequate, even inept. To approach the word in this way is to be guilty of the etymological (or root) fallacy. Setting aside for a moment the refinements of linguistic theory, an analogous example taken from English (and this could easily be replicated with equal effect from many other languages) readily demonstrates that language does not work in this manner. Take the word "butterfly."[19] It is ostensibly made up of two words, "butter" and "fly." Is that observation sufficient to determine the meaning of the composite word? Does it offer some basic meaning that somehow undergirds other meanings? Far from it! Any argument, moreover, that New Testament Greek functions in a different way, and is in some respect special, or unique in regard to the matter of etymol-

---

15. Silva, *Biblical Words*, 51, (emphasis added). For a further helpful discussion of etymology, and its limitations, see Louw, *Semantics*, 23–31. Note the opening sentence of the next chapter, "Etymology does not provide an original meaning that acts as the basis for every other meaning of a word" (33). For a brief, but helpful treatment of this issue, see Caird, *Language and Imagery*, 44–46.

16. For specific examples of this, together with a stimulating discussion of the issues, see Carson, *Exegetical Fallacies*, 26ff.

17. See Lyons, *Language*, 55.

18. Barr, *Semantics*, 100, 158–60. In this, he has been followed by a number of biblical scholars. For example, Carson, *Exegetical Fallacies*, 26ff., who describes the root fallacy as "one of the most enduring of errors" (26).

19. This example is used by Louw, *Semantics*, 27. He offers, following Harold Conklin, these additional examples: pineapple, grandson, fountain-pen, earring, and strawberry.

ogy, is soon dispatched by reading the relevant sections of works already cited, or by turning to a standard textbook of New Testament Greek.[20] Special pleading of this kind will not do; it does not hold up in the face of the overwhelming evidence against it.

The second key point from Silva's conclusion cited above is that usage is the dominant factor in fixing meaning. Whilst George Caird is perhaps guilty, atypically, of a measure of overstatement when he maintains that "It is nowadays generally agreed that only current usage determines meaning," he is not too far off the mark, for, whereas it may not be the *sole* factor, there is widespread agreement amongst specialists in the field that usage is the *primary* means by which meaning is determined.[21] That is to say, if you wish to know what a word means, look closely at how it is used.[22] So, how is *proskuneō*, the most commonly used term in the New Testament for "worship," used, and what exactly does it mean? We begin by assessing whether the form of the word has any significance, or not. This requires consideration of how *proskuneō* was originally used. The journey back into the word's history is not, however, in order to discover some basic meaning that can then be imposed on its New Testament usage, but to seek an explanation of why it has the form it does. Hopefully, the value of this will become clear as we proceed.

The Earliest Usage of Proskuneō

Experts are unsure of the precise origins of *proskuneō*, as well as its earliest use, though there is general agreement as to its meaning and the concepts it encompasses. So, for example, Heinrich Greeven, in the relevant article in *TDNT*, discusses the extent to which some form of kiss may or may not originally have been involved, whilst at the same time wrestling

---

20. Such as Funk, *Greek Grammar*. The introduction, in discussing New Testament Greek in its historical and cultural context, unequivocally asserts, "The higher unity to which the language of the NT belongs is the Greek lingua franca of its time" (1).

21. Caird, *Language and Imagery*, 44.

22. For the further substantiation of this principle, and for a fuller discussion of matters relating to (lexical) semantics, the following may be consulted. Standard texts on linguistics are given first, in order of increasing complexity; these are followed by works of biblical scholarship that deal with the relevant linguistic issues: Yule, *Study of Language*, 114–26; Cruse, *Lexical Semantics*; Lyons, *Semantics*; Cotterell and Turner, *Linguistics*, 129–87 (there is a helpful summary of the main points, 178–81); Carson, *Exegetical Fallacies*, 25–66 (deals with fallacies, as the title suggests, but covers much relevant ground); Caird, *Language*, 37–84; Silva, *Biblical Words*; Louw, *Semantics*.

with "the element of casting oneself to the ground" which is known to have been associated with the term, but for which there is no foundation within the form of the word itself. To be more precise, part of the word, *kuneō*, at least suggests the concept of "kissing," whereas there is no element within the word itself to suggest prostration on the ground. Greeven concludes, "the adoration of chthonic deities offers a simple explanation of the development of the usual meaning of the term. The man who wants to honor an earth deity by kissing must stoop to do so."[23] In this way, he endeavors to provide an explanation for both elements—kissing and prostration.

Hans Schönweiss and Colin Brown, after acknowledging that the prevailing scholarly opinion is that the basic [*sic*] meaning of *proskuneō* is to kiss, come to a similar conclusion.[24] They draw attention to Egyptian reliefs on which worshipers are depicted "with outstretched hand throwing a kiss to (*pros-*) the deity." They also note that in Greek contexts, where, they maintain, the word becomes a technical term, the focus is on prostration before the deity or deities. In similar fashion to Greeven, they observe that "Probably it came to have this meaning because in order to kiss the earth (i.e., the earth deity) or the image of a god, one had to cast oneself on the ground."[25] The entry on *proskuneō* in *BDAG*, the standard Greek-English lexicon of the New Testament, further reinforces this point: *proskuneō* was "used to designate the custom of prostrating oneself before persons and kissing their feet or the hem of their garment, the ground, etc."[26]

There you have it. Kissing is seen to be a facet of the action(s) denoted by *proskuneō*, after all. Where, then, is the "myth"? Is it really so inaccurate to maintain that the word means "to kiss (towards)"? Well, here we arrive at the nub of the matter. The word evidently *meant* "to kiss (towards)," at times literally, in its earliest usage. That is apparently the reason for the word being coined, and for it having its actual form. However, that is not the end of the story. We must now skip forwards several centuries, since the earliest known occurrences of *proskuneō*, those which provide the data for the discussions above, were "penned" up to four or five hundred years, or more, before the writing of the New

23. Greeven, "*proskuneō*," in *TDNT* 6, 759.
24. Schönweiss and Brown, "*proskuneō*," in *NIDNTT* 2, 875.
25. Ibid., 876.
26. *BDAG*, 882.

Testament. And, as we have already established, it is *usage*, not origins or form as such, that determines meaning. Current usage, that is. Cotterell and Turner summarize the point well. "The history of a word . . . may explain *how* a word came to be used with some particular sense at a specified time, but in order to find out *what* a lexeme means at that particular time we have only to look at contemporary *usage*."²⁷

What we therefore need to ascertain is the way in which *proskuneō* is used, and the meaning it carries, around the time of the writing of the New Testament, as well as within that corpus itself.

Proskuneō in the Septuagint and the New Testament

What is evident, as the relevant literature is perused, is that the alleged "basic" meaning of *proskuneō*—"to kiss (towards)"—is not found; not only has the physical gesture of kissing disappeared, but so has any inference of the concept. No passage, either of the New Testament, or of any contemporaneous literature, in which *proskuneō* occurs, refers, either explicitly or implicitly, to "kissing." Conversely, what is striking is the frequency with which *proskuneō* is accompanied by a physical gesture such as falling down, bowing to the ground, prostrating oneself. So, for example, on twelve out of the sixty occasions *proskuneō* is found in the New Testament, the verb *piptō*, "to fall (down)," also appears in close connection with it, making explicit this gesture.²⁸ This has the effect of heightening the sense of paying respect, even indicating submission. That these are inherent in the term is one of the notable features of definitions of *proskuneō* in standard works of reference.

BDAG offers the following definition of *proskuneō*, "to express in attitude or gesture one's complete dependence on or submission to a high authority figure, (fall down and) worship, do obeisance to, prostrate oneself before, do reverence to, welcome respectfully."²⁹ Not dissimilar is the summary definition found in *NIDNTT*, "worship, do obeisance

---

27. Cotterell & Turner, *Linguistics*, 132, (original emphasis).

28. Matt 2:11; 4:9; 18:26; Acts 10:25; 1 Cor 14:25; Rev 4:10; 5:14; 7:11; 11:16; 19:4; 10; 22:8. The following expressions are all used in conjunction with *proskuneō*: "falling on their knees" (Mark 15:19), "clasped his feet" (Matt 28:9), and "[fall down] at your feet" (Rev 3:9). See the comment by Nützel in *EDNT* 3, 174, and note his conclusion there: "This suggests that homage expressed by *proskuneō* also occurs generally with prostration."

29. *BDAG*, 882.

to, prostrate oneself, do reverence to."[30] What is striking here is (a) the absence of any mention of or reference to "kiss;" (b) the focus on the physical gesture of prostration, or at least falling down; (c) the attitude of reverence or submission (obeisance). What has happened is that the cultural context has changed. Long before the first century CE kissing (the ground, or whatever), which may well have been more a Persian custom than a Greek one, was not a part of the actions or gestures associated with *proskuneō*.[31] By the time one reaches the first century, there is no longer any real association at all in people's minds with "kiss" (as is seen from the lack of it in their actions, or any explicit reference thereto in the contexts in which *proskuneō* is found), any more than an English-speaking person thinks of "butter" on hearing the word "butterfly."

The contention that by New Testament times kissing was no longer a feature of *proskuneō*, either in thought or in deed, finds further corroboration in the Septuagint (LXX). Produced during the second or third century BCE, this Greek translation of the Hebrew Scriptures constitutes an important linguistic bridge between the two testaments, as Melvin Peters acknowledges, "[The Septuagint] provides the context in which many of the lexical and theological concepts in the New Testament can best be explained."[32] Significantly, *proskuneō* is the predominant term used in the Septuagint to translate the Hebrew ḥwh; meaning "to bow (down)," "to make/do obeisance," or "to pay homage," ḥwh is the word most commonly translated "to worship" in the Old Testament.[33] Unlike *proskuneō*, there is nothing in the etymology or early usage of ḥwh that as much as hints at kissing. The correspondence between them (semantic overlap) lies in the area of meaning that encompasses bowing down, doing obeisance, offering respect. It is this usage that carries forward

---

30. *NIDNTT* 2, 875.

31. Cf. *TDNT* 6, 759.

32. Peters, "Septuagint," in *ABD* 5, 1103. The precise date and origins of the Septuagint are unclear. The issues are usefully summarised in ibid., 1093ff.

33. In 162 out of 173 of its occurrences, ḥwh is translated by *proskuneō* in the Septuagint. For a detailed discussion of the use of *proskuneō* in the Septuagint, and in other Jewish sources, see Greeven, *TDNT* 6, 760–63. He offers marginally different numbers (164 of 171 instances), but the strength of the correspondence is clear. Cf. *NIDNTT* 2, 876–77. A substantive study of ḥwh, and its usage, can be found in Fretheim, *hawah*, in *NIDOTTE* 2, 42–4. Fretheim also notes that *proskuneō* is the regular translation of ḥwh in the Septuagint. On both terms, and their congruence, see also, Peterson, *Engaging with God*, 57–63.

into the New Testament.³⁴ In 1 Kings 19:18 *proskuneō* is used in the Septuagint to translate the Hebrew *nāshaq*, "to kiss." The passage speaks of those "whose knees have not bowed down to Baal and whose mouths have not kissed him." Although this refers to the practice of kissing the deity, the concept is found in, at most, only two other places in the Old Testament (Ps 2:12[?]; Hos 13:2), and *proskuneō* is not used in either.³⁵ This is the exception that proves the rule. One vestige of the past (if that is what it is), set against all other occurrences in both Septuagint and New Testament, as well as the contemporary non-biblical literature, is not sufficient to construct an argument that *proskuneō* generally maintained any association with kissing.³⁶ There are four other verses in the Septuagint in which *proskuneō* and "kiss" occur together (Exod 18:7; 1 Sam 20:41; 2 Sam 14:33; 15:5), but in every case *proskuneō* carries the sense of bowing down or prostration, whilst a different verb (*phileō* in Exod 18:7, and *kataphileō* in the other verses) is used to convey the action of kissing. If anything, this favors the argument that a change of usage has essentially taken place by the time the Septuagint was produced, three hundred years or so before the writing of the New Testament.

In the New Testament, *proskuneō*, whilst it can be used for one (or more) person's response to another (e.g., Matt 18:26; Rev 3:9), is primarily employed when a divine being is the object. The inner attitude that corresponds to the outward, physical gesture of bowing down, or prostrating oneself, is that of giving honor, showing respect, or expressing submission. Indeed, the word invariably signifies this inner attitude, whether or not an actual physical gesture is involved.³⁷ When God is the object

---

34. Cf. Nützel, "The use of *proskuneo* in the NT is based on that of the OT, with a stronger concentration of the meaning in the direction of worship" (*EDNT* 3, 175).

35. 1 Kgs 19:18 and Hos 13:2 are both references are to idol worship. Ps 2:12 is unique, if it is construed as a reference to kissing the deity (though this is disputed by many; see, e.g., Goldingay, *Psalms*, 93–94), in that the worship involved is of the one true God.

36. There really are no adequate grounds for the surprising assertion found in *TDNT* 6 that the one use of *proskuneō* to translate *nashaq* "shows that the element of kissing, including cultic kissing, was still present in the Greek world at the time of the LXX" (761). Interestingly, a footnote indicates that this comment was by Bertram, not Greeven, the author of the article. Equally, no great weight should be given to the one solitary place where, idiosyncratically, *kataphileō* (to kiss) is used to translate ḥwh (1 Kgs 2:19).

37. Contrast this with Due (see fn. 8) and with Ross (see fn. 10). Space constraints preclude a more comprehensive examination of the relevant data. For details, substan-

of the response, *proskuneō* is regularly translated "worship."[38] As already noted, this is the most common word for worship in the New Testament. The fact that its Hebrew counterpart, ḥwh, is the most frequent worship word in the Old Testament means that in both testaments—and it is vital to grasp this, if we are to have a genuinely biblical view of worship—there is a common perspective on what worship is.[39] Worship entails a response to God which includes bowing before him, figuratively, if not literally, and honoring him in a spirit of reverence and submission.[40]

And not a kiss in sight. The kiss that may originally have been the reason for the word's form is, in the biblical usage of *proskuneō*, no longer part of its field of reference; neither does it figure in its meaning. To persist, therefore, as so many do, in asserting that *proskuneō* means "to kiss (towards)" is both unhelpful and misleading. It is, in short, a myth.

CONCLUSION: DOES IT MATTER?

So, we have exposed a myth. The question is, "Does it really matter?" There are a number of important reasons why this is not mere pedantry. First, a general point. The text of Scripture, and therefore its language, demands to be taken seriously ("correctly handled," as Paul puts it in 2 Tim 2:15) if our goal is to fathom its meaning, rather than impose our own meaning on it. Failure in this can lead to all kinds of error.[41]

---

tiating the above summary, see Greeven, *TDNT* 6, 763–65; Nützel, *EDNT* 3, 174–75; Schönweiss and Brown, *NIDNTT* 2, 877–78. See, further, the illuminating essay by Karen Jobes, "Distinguishing the Meaning of Greek Verbs in the Semantic Domain for Worship," in which she analyses the various verbs used for worship in the New Testament, showing areas of overlap and divergence of meaning.

38. It is a moot point as to whether, in some Gospel passages, at least, when Jesus is the object, worship is intended or not. Translations differ. Important as this is, it is not significant for our present purposes. To pursue this issue, see the reading referenced in the previous footnote.

39. *Proskuneō* is, of course, only one of several words used for worship in the Bible. It does not, therefore, tell us everything. However, its frequency does give it a particular importance. Whilst the two testaments differ significantly in the forms and expressions of worship that they depict, they are uniform in their understanding of what it is, its essence. For an overview of the biblical words for worship, which highlights the unity between the testaments, see Jack, "Understanding Worship," 85–94.

40. The element of submission is emphasised strongly by Jobes, "Distinguishing the Meaning" 207, 211, and Peterson, *Engaging with God*, 63, 73.

41. For examples, sometimes with serious consequences, see Carson, *Exegetical Fallacies*.

Second, in this particular case, the myth surrounding *proskuneō*—that it has something to do with kissing—is all too often used to support views of worship that cannot legitimately be derived from the use of this term. True, in some instances, nothing is made of the "kiss," as in some of the examples noted earlier. What, then, is the point? Since the association is erroneous, as we have demonstrated, a concept is introduced that has neither relevance nor validity, and that, conversely, has the potential to be misleading. Worse still, in other instances, significance *is* attached to the "kiss." Usually, this involves some move from "kiss" to "intimacy," and, at times, beyond. Peter Craig-Wilde's fantasy, with its intimacy and eroticism, is an example of outrageous excess, built on the seemingly innocuous error of misconstruing a biblical word. Not all are guilty of such excess, of course. Graham Kendrick, for example, more temperately suggests that *proskuneō* "gives us a beautiful picture of worship as we approach the King of kings and Lord of lords; with open face, eye to eye, our hearts full of love and thanks, our wills set firmly to obey him, enjoying an intimacy and a mutual affection that the watching angels find astounding."[42]

Attractive though this picture of worship may be, it most certainly is not to be derived from the word *proskuneō*. For one thing, if you are bowing down, you are hardly eye to eye! More seriously, the word simply does not signify "intimacy" or "mutual affection." Insofar as these are legitimate facets of our worship, they are not to be derived from this term. Even when, in its pre-biblical usage, *proskuneō* may, in some contexts, have denoted an act of kissing, the kiss was not one of intimacy. Quite the reverse. It involved kissing the ground, feet, or the hem of a garment. It was an act of homage. A kiss, but not as we know it.[43] The truth is that at no point in *proskuneō*'s history has intimacy been part of its semantic domain.

So much for what *proskuneō* does not mean. The final reason the identifying of this myth matters is a positive one; namely, it opens up the way to a truer appreciation of a biblical understanding of worship. In the persistent current debates about worship, usually centered on matters of style and practice, one fundamental question is frequently neglected.

---

42. Kendrick, *Worship*, 23–24.

43. The closest contemporary parallel, though not common these days, might perhaps be bowing to kiss the hand of someone to whom one is presented—a courtesy, not an intimacy.

What is worship? More specifically, what is the biblical understanding of worship? A key starting point in answering this question is the biblical vocabulary for worship.[44] Whilst only one of several terms, *proskuneō*, important for its frequency of use, emphasizes that worship has to do with honoring God, submitting to him (with or without the corresponding gesture of bowing down, or prostration). As Karen Jobes concludes, "the prevalence in the New Testament of *proskuneō* . . . to refer to Christian worship indicates that Christian worship centers on submission to God's authority."[45] This, far more than intimacy, is a dominant aspect of biblical worship, yet it is not a major theme, if present at all, in much contemporary talk about worship, or in its expression. Here is a serious challenge to the "me-centered," consumerist-orientated, performance-driven worship (whether contemporary or traditional in its style) that too easily finds a place in our worship services and gatherings. Grasping the correct meaning of *proskuneō* affords a much-needed perspective, and, where necessary, a corrective, that biblically faithful worship entails responding appropriately to God; offering a humble response that, irrespective of form, rightly honors him for who he is and submits in obedience to his authority. This is transformational worship. This is what it means, in part, at least, to worship in spirit and in truth.[46]

---

44. And it is only a starting point, albeit a significant one. The task of constructing a biblical understanding (theology) of worship involves considerably more. See the works by Due, Ross, and Peterson referred to above.

45. Jobes, "Distinguishing the Meaning," 211.

46. Cf. John 4:23–24, where the verb for "worship" is *proskuneō*.

7

On the Mountain

Worship as Community Experience in Matthew

Stephen Haar

INTRODUCTION

The Gospel of Matthew comes first to mind when people want to answer questions about the biblical foundations of mission in the New Testament. The reason is simple. Matthew's Gospel opens and closes with the theme of mission: the sending of a promised Savior named "God with us" (1:23) and the sending of disciples to proclaim this Savior who promises to be "with you always" (28:16–20).

The Gospel of Matthew often comes to mind when people investigate the biblical foundations for church and ministry. The reason is simple. Matthew alone uses the term *ekklēsia*, the common word used by Greek-speaking Jews for the congregation of the people of God. Indeed, Matthew arguably provides "a discipling manual, a handbook of Jesus' life and teaching"[1] that is instructive for ministry and life together as a Jewish-Christian community engaged in Gentile mission.

But few people turn to the Gospel of Matthew when considering the theme of worship in the New Testament, despite the clear structural, linguistic, and theological significance given to worship in Matthew. As the curtain rises on Matthew's narrative visitors from the East appear on the scene: they come to worship the newborn king of the Jews. As the

1. Keener, *Commentary*, 51.

curtain falls on the final scene, disciples gather to worship the risen Jesus before being sent out to make disciples of all nations (28:17–20). More than six decades ago, George Dunbar Kilpatrick suggested the language of Matthew's Gospel reflects a liturgical purpose, but his has been an almost solitary voice.[2] No major work on worship in Matthew has been published to date.[3]

There are thirteen examples of worship in Matthew.[4] The writer also mentions two occasions when worship does not take place (2:8; 4:9), and three times when Jesus teaches about worship (4:10; 5:16; 15:8–9). In addition there are many reported instances of prayer,[5] fasting,[6] blessing,[7] and thanksgiving,[8] offering,[9] vows,[10] feasts,[11] observances,[12] and singing[13]—actions normally associated with worship.

This essay does not attempt to provide a comprehensive treatment of the theme of worship in Matthew. Instead, it is an attempt to join the stimulating discussion on the relationship between worship and human community arising from challenges posed by the emerging church movement and by popular demands for a return to "biblical worship."[14] What contribution might a first-century writing bring to a twenty-first-century question? First, I will highlight the importance of language in

2. Kilpatrick, *The origins*, 72–100.

3. Some important literature on worship in the New Testament includes: Bradshaw, *The Search*; Cullmann, *Early Christian*; Delling, *Worship*; Hahn, *The Worship*; Martin, *Worship*; Moule, *Worship*. For two recent brief treatments of worship in Matthew, see Peterson, *Engaging with God*; Powell, *God with us*.

4. Matt 2:11; 8:2; 9:8, 18; 11:25; 14:33; 15:25, 31; 18:26; 20:20; 21:16; 28:9, 17.

5. Matt 5:44; 6:5–13; 7:7–11; 9:38; 14:23; 18:19; 19:13, 22; 24:20; 26:36–44.

6. Matt 4:2; 6:16–18; 9:14–17.

7. Matt 14:19; 26:26.

8. Matt 15:36; 26:27.

9. Matt 5:23; 6:2–4; 8:4; 23:18, 19, 23.

10. Matt 5:33–37; 23:16–22.

11. Matt 26:17–19.

12. Matt 12:1–12; 24:20; 28:1.

13. Matt 26:30.

14. Gibbs and Bolger, *Emerging Churches*. Emerging churches identify themselves as communities that practice the way of Jesus within postmodern cultures. Typically they live highly communal lives, welcome strangers, serve with generosity, participate as producers, create as created beings, lead as a body, and take part in spiritual activities. Strangely, perhaps, they claim that community is not found in worship; instead, people who discover community in shared experiences then meet in worship.

Matthew's understanding of worship. Second, I will draw attention to the setting for worship in Matthew. Third, I will discuss how mountains are a feature unique to Matthew's narrative as a place of gathering for Jesus and his community: the disciples and the crowds. Next, I will consider clues in Matthew's text to the life setting of Matthew's community, and propose how an understanding of this social location leads to a greater appreciation of the meaning of Matthew's text. Finally, I will offer some comments on how Matthew's Gospel presents both a challenge and gift for today's discussion on worship and community.

THE LANGUAGE OF WORSHIP

The use of language is an important key to Matthew's understanding of worship. Matthew uses eight Greek terms that are generally translated as "worship"; yet, clearly, *proskuneō* is Matthew's favorite.[15] Apart from the book of Revelation, Matthew uses the word more than any other New Testament writing. Further, none of the thirteen occurrences of this word in Matthew is found in Mark, and only two have parallels in Luke (Luke 4:7, 8).

The history of the meaning of the word *proskuneō* is uncertain and debated.[16] It is a compound word comprising the preposition *pros* (towards) and the verb *kuneō* (to kiss). In early Greek literature it was used in reference to various oriental customs involving both partial and total bodily gestures of respect and supplication directed towards someone of higher social status; including bending, bowing, casting oneself on the ground, and the kissing either of feet or the hem of clothing or the ground.[17] Kneeling and prostration were also common worship practices before certain sacred objects or at sacred places in seeking favor from the gods.[18]

In the Septuagint, *proskuneō* encompasses a similar range of meaning as found in extra-biblical Greek; including bowing down or bending over to show respect, especially as an expression of service, gratitude, or supplication (e.g., Gen 23:7; Ruth 2:10; 1 Sam 20:41; 2 Sam 14:4; 16:4).

---

15. Matt 21:16, *aionos*; 5:16; 6:2; 9:8; 15:31, *doxazō*; 14:19; 21:9; 23:29; 25:34; 26:26, *eulogeō*; 15:36; 26:27, *eucharisteō*; 11:25, *exomologeō*; 4:10, *latreuō*; 15:9, *sebō*; 2:2, 8, 11; 4:9,10; 8:2; 9:18; 14:33; 15:25; 18:26; 20:20; 28:9, 17, *proskuneō*.

16. Gruber, *Aspects of Non-verbal Communication*, 244.

17. Greeven, "*proskuneō*," in *TDNT*, 758–59; Homer *Iliad* 6, 474; *Odyssey* 23, 208.

18. Aeschylus, *Prometheus* 936; *Agamemnon* 1068; Plato *Republic* 451a.

In the law of Moses worshippers are commanded to "bend over" before the Lord when offering their first fruits at the sanctuary, as an expression of gratitude and submission to God (Deut 26:1–11). David and the whole assembly prostrate themselves before the Lord with praise and thanksgiving when presenting gifts for the building of the temple. The same posture is adopted by people who encounter the grace and power of God, in answered prayers, assurances of forgiveness, or promises of victory (e.g., Gen 24:52; Exod 34:8; 1 Chron 16:9; Ps 28:9; 95:9; 138:2; Job 1:20–21). When people prostrate themselves before angels, rulers, and prophets this is a demonstration of belief that these beings were God's agents in some way (e.g., Gen 18:2; 19:1; 37:9; Exod 18:7; 1 Sam 28:14; 2 Kgs 2:15). The later avoidance of the term *proskuneō* by Josephus and Philo, in reference to Jewish worship, reflects a growing distinction being made in popular usage between the worship practices of non-Jews and worship offered to the God of Israel.[19]

Matthew's distinctive understanding of worship is highlighted by continuities and discontinuities with the use of the term *proskuneō* in the Septuagint. What is new in Matthew, and other New Testament writings, is that people bow in worship before Jesus in ways previously reserved for the worship of God.

The word *proskuneō* first appears in Matthew's story of the Magi (2:1–12). These representative worshippers from the Gentile world fall down and worship the one born king of the Jews (*pesontes prosekunēsan autō*). At a basic level, the language of Matthew 2:2 reports their actions as homage paid to royalty. Yet, when read in the context of Matthew's story of a divine messenger announcing to Joseph in a dream (1:20–23) that the child will be called Immanuel, God with us, it is equally clear that the evangelist intends the implied reader to attach greater significance to the actions of the Magi. Their actions introduce an unfolding theme in Matthew about the divine sonship of Jesus, to whom all nations should bow the knee. Matthew's narrative about Jesus the Christ is bracketed by opening and closing scenes set in the context of worship. During the time of his ministry, people with human needs approach Jesus asking for life and health. At a deeper, spiritual level people recognize him as "God with us" and the risen Son of God.[20] David Peterson correctly observes, "Matthew's presentation of Christ is designed to elicit such worship.

19. Greeven, "*proskuneō*," 762.
20. Matt 14:33; 16:16; 27:56; 28:9, 17.

Disciples continue in the worship of Christ as they confess him, obey his teaching, proclaim his heavenly rule, and bring others to acknowledge him too."[21]

The clearly physical nature of worship implied by Matthew's preference for the word *proskuneō* is intensified by the use of companion verbs like "to fall down" (*piptein*) before the one worshipped (2:11; 4:9; 18:26), "to fall face down" (17:39, *epesen epi prosōpon autou*), "to kneel" (17:14, *gonupetein*), "to grasp hold of" (*kratein*) Jesus' feet (28:9). This phraseology is not something that Matthew simply inherits from his sources. In Synoptic parallels there are instances when Mark and Luke report a change in the physical posture of petitioners who approach Jesus, whereas Matthew does not mention those details.[22] Instead, Matthew characteristically mentions how they worship (*proskuneō*) Jesus, while Mark and Luke do not. Matthew's focus in these narratives is not on the attitude and posture of the worshipper, as Powell claims, but on the person and the presence of the one worshipped.[23]

THE SETTING OF WORSHIP

The setting or location is another important key to understanding worship in Matthew. The place for instruction of the disciples in Mark is the house; it stands in contrast to the synagogue and temple. The place of worship in Luke-Acts is the temple. Worship in Matthew, however, generally occurs out-of-doors; or, more precisely, outside of Jerusalem.[24] It is true that Matthew records one occasion of worship in the temple (21:16), and the Magi are reported to have entered the house to worship the infant Jesus (2:11), yet the geography of worship is demonstrably in Galilee and often on a mountain.

Already in the infancy narrative, Matthew alerts the reader to the importance of Galilee for his presentation of the life and work of Jesus. The family of Jesus is warned in a dream (2:22) not to return to Judea after the death of Herod, but to settle in the district of Galilee. The repeated use of scriptural citations in the story of Jesus' birth (2:6, 15, 18, 22) and in the story of his relocation from Nazareth to Capernaum at the

---

21. Peterson, *Engaging with God*, 87.
22. Matt 8:2; 9:18; 15:25; Mark 1:40; 5:22; 7:25; Luke 5:12; 8:41
23. Powell, *God with Us*, 46.
24. Matt 8:2; 9:8; 11:25; 15:25; 28:9.

beginning of his public ministry (4:12–14) underscore Matthew's claim that these events happened in accordance with God's purpose. In this way the reader is persuaded that Nazareth, Galilee, and Capernaum are the divinely appointed theaters of ministry for Jesus the Messiah.

There is widespread agreement that Matthew carefully structures his material both at the macro- and micro-level. The five major discourses in Matthew, first suggested by B. W. Bacon, each conclude with the phrase "when Jesus had finished saying (all) these things" (7:28; 11:1; 13:53; 19:1; 26:1). Four of these five discourses clearly have a Galilean setting, and, in contrast to Mark, the transition from Galilee to Judea is recorded more deliberately by Matthew, "When Jesus had finished saying these things, he left Galilee and went through the region of Judea beyond the Jordan" (19:1; cf. Mark 10:1).

Yet, Matthew gives mixed messages about the structure of his Gospel. Readers can discern different divisions and patterns depending on which cues they choose to highlight. Kingsbury points to three verses that might also be taken as major division indicators (1:1; 4:17; 16:21).[25] The first announces the beginning of Jesus' ministry. The second and third share the same opening formula, introducing discrete sections of teaching and powerful works by Jesus: "From that time, Jesus began to . . ." Matthew also uses literary techniques such as repetition (e.g., 5:21, 27, 31, 33, 38, 43), the ordering of stories or blocks of teaching in groups of three (e.g., Matt 6:1–18), and the use of inclusion. Matthew adopted repetition from his sources, such as two feedings of the crowds and two demands for signs; but, he also created his own doublets, such as the tree and its fruit (7:15–20; 12:33–35), the healing of two blind people (9:27–31; 20:29–34), and the summary of Jesus' ministry among the crowds (4:23; 9:35). Matthew repeats what is important to him. The same is true of inclusions. Smaller and larger blocks of material are framed by *inclusio*; the most identified being the name "Immanuel" for Jesus (1:23) and the promise of the risen Lord to be "with you always" (28:20), which frames the entire Gospel. This characteristic structuring of smaller units of material in Matthew needs greater attention by interpreters; certainly when considering Matthew's understanding of worship.

At important points Matthew reminds the reader about the Galilean setting of his story (4:23–25; 15:29; 17:22), and, significantly for Matthew, two of these occurrences share matching narrative sum-

---

25. Kingsbury, *Matthew*, 15–16.

maries that prepare for two mountain episodes. The literary connection between a mountain scene at the beginning of Matthew's Galilean section and one at the end, which is beside the Sea of Galilee, should not be overlooked by the reader; especially since Matthew's summaries indicate this structure is intentional.

Detailed comparative study[26] of the significance of mountains and related patterns of thought in ancient world cultures documents how mountains were considered to be places where the divine might be encountered. Due to their prominence and height mountains were places where heaven and earth were linked together.[27] Yet, while mountains are a persistent image that signifies many different things in the Bible, there is little emphasis placed on height. Beginning with the Garden of Eden[28] and culminating with John's vision of the meeting together of heaven and earth that breaks the boundaries of space and time (Rev 21:10), mountains are closely connected with sacrifice, covenants and worship: being the location for key encounters with God in redemptive history.[29] "The sacredness of Old Testament mountains rests on historical events in which Yahweh in his freedom came to bind Israel to himself as his people. As physical localizations of the relationship between Yahweh and his people, the sacred mountains of the Old Testament can almost accurately be described as covenant mountains."[30]

Mountains are not sacred due to any intrinsic cosmological or geological features, but because of the presence of God.[31]

Worship is something made possible by the presence of God. This is a fundamental biblical perspective. Significant in this regard is the Old Testament teaching about God drawing near to his chosen people so that they might draw near to him. The New Testament witnesses to the fulfillment of these ideas in the person and work of Jesus Christ.

---

26. Clifford, *Cosmic Mountain*, 2–25.

27. Ryken et al., *Dictionary of Biblical Imagery*, 574.

28. While not readily apparent in the text of Genesis, the mountain location of the Garden of Eden is a metaphorical reference in Ezek 28:13–15.

29. Gen 8:4; 9:8–17; 22:1–18; Exod 19–20; Josh 8:30–35; 2 Sam 7:8–13; Isa 56:7; 65:25; Zech 8:3; Matt 21:1; 28:16; Rom 11:26; Rev 14:1.

30. Donaldson, *Jesus*, 50.

31. Moses encounters God on the top of Sinai not because its peak was in heaven, but because God comes (descends) to the mountain (Exod 19:9–15).

CROWDS AND COMMUNITY

Many scholars have noted that mountains feature prominently in Matthew as significant sites for the life and ministry of Jesus.[32] Most commentators characterize these mountain scenes as places of revelation. However, more recently, Terence Donaldson's stimulating, detailed tradition-historical study of six Matthean mountain narratives has argued for conclusions that run counter to the consensus of scholarly opinion. Donaldson concluded that Matthew's chain of mountain scenes was deliberately linked together to form a literary and theological pattern, encompassing central Matthean themes—ecclesiology, Christology, and salvation history—and climaxes in the final scene of the Great Commission.[33] "The mountain" in Matthew functions not as a "place of revelation" but as an eschatological site—the place where the messianic community is created, where Jesus' role as the obedient and enthroned Son is manifested, and where, as a result, a new period in salvation history is begun.[34]

> [T]he mountain motif in Matthew serves to focus characteristic Matthean themes in the areas of Christology, ecclesiology and salvation history. The Christological theme of the nature of true sonship and the path of obedience that the Son must follow to receive sovereignty is set out principally in the Temptation and Transfiguration Narratives and brought to culmination in the closing scene—though the authority of Jesus is also in view in the Sermon on the Mount (cf. Matt 7:28–29). The ecclesiological theme of the gathering of the eschatological community and its constitution as the Church is developed in the Sermon, in the second feeding miracle, and ultimately in the final commissioning passage—though the community is also in view in the command to "hear him" in Matthew 17:5. These two themes together

---

32. Albright and Mann, *Matthew*, 32; Grundmann, *Das Evangelium*, 102; Filson, *Commentary*, 75; Kingsbury, *Matthew*, 56–58; Lange, *Das Erscheinen*, 392–445; Livio, "La signification," 13–20.

33. Donaldson, *Jesus*, 203–11.

34. The use of the articular but unspecified *eis to oros* is not unique to Matthew (Mark 3:13 parallel Luke 6:12; Mark 6:46 parallel Matt 14:23; Matt 5:1; 15:29; 28:16; Luke 9:28; John 6:3, 15). Foerster, "*oros*," in *TDNT5*, 475–87. The noun *oros* can refer to a more broadly defined geographical area such as a "mountain range," "desert," or "field," and can be translated "into the hill country." However, while this is a possible translation, the Synoptics typically refer to the "hill country" by the plural *eis ta orē* (Matt 18:12; 24:16; Mark 5:5; 13:14; Luke 21:21; cf. Heb 11:38; Rev 6:15, 16).

form the basis for Matthew's development of salvation history, in that the vindication of the Son ushers in an age of fulfillment in which the Church finds its existence.[35]

The mountain in Matthew is a place of gathering for Jesus and his community: the disciples and the crowds. In fact, the phrase *eis to oros* bears all the characteristics of an early Christian toponym; a highly stylized term that grew out of common belief and witness that a mountain setting was characteristic of the ministry of Jesus.[36] Twice Jesus is said to go up on the mountain *eis to oros* in the company of his disciples and the crowds (5:1; 15:29). These occurrences, one at both the beginning and end of Matthew's narrative concerning Jesus' Galilean ministry, demarcate what might be termed a geo-theological *inclusio*. Certainly, the textual repetition in 4:23 and 9:35, together with evident common features between 4:23–5:1 and 15:29–31, confirm Matthew's use of literary *inclusio*. Then, in 28:16, the disciples go up on a mountain in Galilee, to which Jesus is said to have directed them. Matthew also locates Jesus *eis to oros* in 14:23. On this occasion, however, Jesus is on the mountain alone; a striking exception to the mountain scenes in Matthew. This appears to be a traditional reference preserved from Matthew's sources without any obvious editorial efforts to make it comply with his mountain motif. Evidently Matthew did not see this as a contradiction. Perhaps this is because the story (14:22–33) is not confined to a mountain location. A more significant and compelling explanation, as indicated by the account of Jesus walking on the water, is that the story focus is Christological rather than ecclesiological or eschatological.

The presence of crowds with Jesus is a unique feature of Matthew's mountain scenes. According to Matthew, the crowds gather around Jesus (4:25; 8:1, 18; 9:36; 13:2; 14:13; 15:30; 19:2; 20:29) to hear his teaching and to glorify God (9:8; 15:31); and they recognize Jesus as Messiah (12:23; 21:9–11). Jesus speaks of them as a ripe harvest and the disciples are sent out on a mission among them (9:37–10:1).[37]

---

35. Donaldson, *Jesus*, 196.

36. Examples of other early Christian toponyms that find no mention outside the New Testament include: Gethsemane, Golgotha, the Sea of Galilee. See Notley, "The Sea," 183–88.

37. The noun *ochlos* occurs 175 times in the New Testament. Matthew uses the word fifty times, Mark thirty-eight, Luke forty-one, John twenty, Acts twenty-two, and Revelation four times.

Matthew 4:23—5:1

The crowds are first mentioned in special material provided by Matthew (4:23–25) to introduce the first major teaching discourse of Jesus (chs 5–7) and narrative about the messianic ministry of Jesus (chs 8–9). After stories about Jesus' birth and childhood—intended to present Jesus as the one in whom God's promises are fulfilled (1:18–25) and the one whom nations eagerly anticipate (4:12–16)—Matthew takes up material found in Mark, from the ministry of John the Baptist through accounts of Jesus' baptism, temptation, commencement of public ministry, and calling of disciples. Indeed, in chapters 3–4 and 12–28, Matthew follows Mark's sequence of material exactly, often using identical words. This only serves to highlight the theological significance for Matthew of additional material found in chapters 5–11. Certainly the repetition of Matthew's introductory summary (4:23) in a concluding summary (9:35) confirms its structural significance. In this way Matthew isolates a section of the gospel to focus on the messianic ministry of Jesus among the crowds.

In contrast to Mark, where the mountain appears to be a place where Jesus goes with his disciples to escape the crowds (Mark 3:13 *anabainei eis to oros*), in Matthew a large crowd follows Jesus from Galilee and is present with the disciples when Jesus teaches on the mountain (Matt 5:1, *idōv de tous ochlous*). In Mark 3:13–16, the mountain is the setting for the calling of the Twelve, from among the nation of Israel, who form the foundation members of the eschatological community: "Follow me, and I will make you become fishers of men" (Mark 1:17). In preparation for the Sermon on the Mount, Matthew constructs a summary statement of ministry in Galilee (4:23–25), including the gathering of great crowds around Jesus (4:25). This introduction climaxes as Jesus ascends and begins to teach. In Matthew, however, the Sermon on the Mount is not meant to be read simply as a collection of sayings by Jesus: a Christian Torah delivered by a new Moses.[38] Instead, this gathering of people to Jesus on a mountain is given as evidence in fulfillment of end-time expectations, prophesied by Isaiah: "Land of Zebulun, land of Naphtali, on the road by the sea, across the Jordan, Galilee of the Gentiles—the people who sat in darkness have seen a great light, and for those who sat in the region and shadow of death light has dawned" (Matt 4:15–16).

---

38. Davies, *The Setting*, 25–108.

The crowds are portrayed as a major objective of Jesus' ministry in Galilee. They are invited to join the new community called into existence by Jesus the Messiah. However, unlike the disciples, to whom the secrets of the kingdom of heaven have been revealed (13:10, 16–17), the crowds are not yet portrayed as real followers of Jesus. Even so, they are enthusiastic about Jesus, recognizing a difference between his teaching and the scribes (7:28). They call Jesus a prophet, saying on more than one occasion that never has anything like this been seen in Israel.[39] They are present with the disciples when Jesus challenges and censures the Scribes and Pharisees.[40] Jesus accuses these authorities of having neglected, even abused, the crowds leaving them "harassed" and "like sheep without a shepherd" (9:36); opening the possibility of them becoming "lost sheep" (10:6; 15:14). For Jesus to announce that his mission is to be directed toward them is an affront to cultural and religious sensitivities.[41] Matthew's use of the term "Israel" when Jesus speaks to the crowds (8:10; 9:33; 10:6, 23; 15:24) shows that his interest is theological rather than merely geographical. As Jesus engages the crowds in Galilee "healing every disease and every affliction" he fulfills the servant prophecy of Isaiah (42:1–4; cf. Matt 12:18–21); demonstrating by word and action that a broader definition of Israel is emerging.

Matthew 15:29–31

Before turning his narrative attention toward Jerusalem, in 15:29–31 Matthew reports another mountain-top gathering of crowds around Jesus. Matthew reminds readers of his Galilean framework by providing a final summary statement of Jesus' work among the crowds that mirrors an introductory statement placed at the beginning of the Galilean ministry (4:23–5:1).[42] Significantly, this summary stands at the center of an apparent Matthean intercalation. In this way Matthew highlights his

---

39. Matt 9:8; 12:23; 15:31; 21:8–11, 46; 22:23.

40. Matt 9:18; 12:22–23; 15:1–10; 21:10–17, 23–27; 22:23–33; 23:1–39.

41. Ezra 9:1–2; 10:2, 11; Neh 10:20–31; m. *Aboth* 2:6; 5:10; m. *Hagigah* 2:7 and others. The "people of the land" (ʿam hā ʾāreṣ) in late biblical and rabbinic literature were those who did not, or could not, observe the written and oral law to the level expected by those who set the standard for religious piety and practice of the day. The people of the land were considered by the Pharisees as being no better than Gentiles. Cf. Oppenheimer, "Am Ha-Arez," 834–36.

42. Note also the regular appearance of similar summaries in Matt 9:35–38; 11:1, 4–6; 12:15–21.

juxtaposition of two stories: the worshipful approach of the Canaanite woman (15:21–28) and the crowds who gather around Jesus and glorify God (15:32–38). The questioning exchange between the woman and Jesus over bread, and who it is that should be fed, finds its resolution in the feeding that follows. The crowds are the lost sheep of Israel. They come to Jesus and he feeds them.

The summary recollection of Jesus' healing ministry among the crowds underlines Matthew's understanding that the mighty actions of Jesus are evidence of his messianic identity and the inbreaking of the kingdom of God (4:23; 9:35; 10:7; 11:4–5; 12:28). The feeding of four thousand in a desert place with seven loaves and a few fish is further confirmation that this gathering of disciples and the crowds with Jesus on the mountain is to be understood as an eschatological event.[43]

One of the central features of Jewish expectation in the Old Testament and Second-Temple period was that a great gathering of Israel would come to the holy mountain of God where they would be created anew as the people of God.[44] Some later rabbinic and Jewish-Christian references identify the site of this banquet as mount Zion.[45] A frequent metaphor in the Old Testament is that of sheep and shepherd and of Israel as a scattered and leaderless flock. The prophets envision an age of fulfillment when the scattered flock will be gathered to the mountain of God and be fed.[46] This gathering of God's scattered flock was anticipated as the first act in an end of age drama that also included a procession of nations to worship on God's mountain in a rebuilt, glorious temple; and, to join in a messianic feast.[47]

---

43. It is possible that the number seven had special significance for early Christians. The book of Revelation has seven letters to the churches. The number seven here could be representative of the new community of Jesus, including the lost sheep of Israel and all the people of God in the diaspora. Seven was a significant symbolical number in Jewish thought. The menorah, or lampstand, had seven arms, and was a common symbol of Judaism.

44. Isa 35:10; Tob 14:4–6; *1 Enoch* 90:28–36; *Pss Sol* 17:28–35; *Jub* 1:15–17; *1 Bar* 5:1–9; *2 Bar* 40:1–4; *4 Ezra* 13:25–36.

45. Ex R. 25:8; Num R. 13:2; Pesik R. 41:5; 5 Ezra 1:38–48.

46. Jer 31:10–14; Ezek 34:14, 16–27.

47. *2 Bar* 4:2–4; *Adam and Eve* 29:1–10; Ex R. 15:21; Lev R 24:4; Cant R. 7:5; Midr Ps 14:6; 36:6; Isa 2:2–4; 25:6–10a; Tob 13:7–18; *1 Bar* 5:1–9; *Ps Sol* 17:28–35; *1 Enoch* 90:28–36; *Sib Or* 3:652–731, 772–95.

The implied reader of Matthew's carefully crafted stories in 4:23–5:1 and 15:29–31 cannot be left in any doubt that Matthew understands these events in terms of eschatological fulfillment. In Matthew, the feeding of Israel by Jesus on the mountain heralds the coming salvation of the nations is near; it points forward to the mountain-top conclusion of the Gospel where the risen Lord commands his disciples to gather all nations (*panta ta ethnē*) into his community. However, it is neither the mountain setting, nor a restored temple, but the presence of Christ that makes this an eschatological event. In effect, Matthew is claiming there is no longer any need for the temple. It is not in the temple that people find the fulfillment of the promised "God-with-us," but in Jesus. In Jesus people find something greater than the temple (12:6).[48] Those who gather to Jesus, find in him the fulfillment of all the hopes of mount Zion and the heavenly Jerusalem. In this way, Matthew anticipates what the letter to the Hebrews says about the location and focus of acceptable worship in the new community of Jesus. "You have not come to something that can be touched, a blazing fire, and darkness, and gloom, and a tempest, and the sound of a trumpet, and a voice whose words made the hearers beg that not another word be spoken to them . . . But you have come to mount Zion and to the city of the living God, the heavenly Jerusalem . . . and to Jesus, the mediator of a new covenant" (Heb 12:18–24).

Matthew 28:16–20

It is no accident that Matthew chooses a mountain setting for the end of his Gospel. There is widespread agreement among scholars that the form and content of 28:16–20 are carefully written in accordance with key themes developed throughout Matthew's narrative, such as Christology, ecclesiology, and eschatology. It follows in such a context that neither should Matthew's choice of setting be dismissed as an incidental geographical reference. The awkward transition between 28:15 and 28:16 is a definite clue that the writer wanted to close his narrative with a mountain scene. Indeed, the final verse confirms this.

The appearance of the phrase *sunteleia tou aiōnos* in both 24:3 and 28:20 provides a direct literary link between Matthew's final two mountain scenes. Matthew brackets the events of the passion, death and resurrection of Jesus with two mountain stories in order to highlight

---

48. In John 4:19–26 Jesus appears as the replacement for both Mt. Gerazim and Jerusalem.

the universal sovereignty and presence of the risen Lord Jesus with his people. The life of the called and commissioned community of Jesus, between the cross and close of the age, is determined by the presence of the risen Lord rather than any terrors of apocalyptic future, or threat of judgment. The theme of the presence of the Lord introduced in 1:23 and repeated throughout Matthew's narrative, including stories of people gathering around Jesus on the mountain, is most completely and finally described in Matthew's closing scene with the risen Lord's promise to be present with his people until the end of the age.[49]

In 28:16–20 the risen Lord provides more than a mission command. Included with the imperative to "Go!" is an invitation to "Come!" Matthew's understanding of the purpose of the new community of Jesus, the church, is reflected in a combination of terms: *mathēteusate, baptizontes, didaskontes*, and *eneteilamēn*. Jesus commands the disciples to invite the nations to join their community and learn the ways of a disciple. This command is eschatologically based, as Jewish end-time expectations looked to the gathering of God's scattered people followed by the nations in procession to mount Zion. However, in Matthew the gathering point for the new people of God is not mount Zion but the risen Lord. Among the Synoptic Gospels, only Matthew draws a direct contrast between Jesus and the temple in Jerusalem, with the inference that religious focus had passed from one to the other (12:6). "It is Christ who has replaced Zion as the center of eschatological fulfillment, and the mountain motif in Matthew acts as a vehicle by which Zion expectations are transferred to Christ."[50] The Gospel concludes with the picture of an infant Church mountain-top gathering with the risen Christ standing at the center.

WORSHIP AND THE MATTHEAN COMMUNITY

Reconstructing the life setting of Matthew and his implied community of readers is a challenging task. The slim evidence external to the Gospel is late and relatively untrustworthy.[51] The interpreter, therefore, needs to proceed intuitively, inferring the life situation from internal evidence, attempting to discern which clues in the text point to the evangelist's

---

49. Matt 17:17; 18:20; 26:29.

50. Donaldson, *Jesus on the Mountain*, 184.

51. Eusebius, *H.E.* 3.24.6; 3.39.25–26; 6.25.3-4; Irenaeus, *Adv. Haer.* 3.1.1; Epiphanius, *Pan.* 29.9.4.

situation as opposed to those elements belonging to common tradition, and deciding how much significance to give to these clues.

Debate over the life setting of Matthew's community arises from tension created between a number of characteristics of his Gospel that evidence, on the one hand, a Jewish-Christian milieu—emphases on Old Testament fulfillment (1:22–23; 2:15, 17–18, 23; 4:14–11; 8:17; 12:17–21; 13:35; 21:4–5; 27:9–10), on the enduring validity of the law (5:17–20; 23:1–3), on the exclusiveness of the mission of Jesus and the Twelve (10:5–6; 15:24), on unexplained Jewish practices (15:2; 19:3)—and emphases, on the other hand, that exhibit a Gentile-Christian context; for example, interest in a universal mission (4:15; 10:18; 12:21; 13:38; 24:14; 28:19–20), a focus on mission to the Gentiles (2:1, 13–15; 4:13–15; 8:5–13; 15:21–28; 24:9–14), censure of Jewish religious authorities (chapter 23), reference to *their* synagogues (4:23) and *their* scribes (7:29), and a number of replacement references (8:5–13; 20:1–16; 21:28–45; 22:1–14).

Clues about Matthew's community can be discovered from the text itself. Yet equally important for identifying Matthew's location and for having a richer appreciation of the meaning of the Matthean text is to read the text from the perspective of social, economic, political and religious realities in first century Palestine under Roman colonial rule. The reception history of the Gospel of Matthew also provides valuable information about its historical location.[52]

Four decades ago, Odil Steck proposed the following hypothesis about the life setting of Matthew's Gospel.[53] Jewish Christians forced out of Palestine by the Jewish War, whose own traditions were collected in the Sayings source, joined the Gentile Christian communities in Syria, whose book was the Gospel of Mark. More recent proposals for the social location of Matthew's Gospel argue for a post-war text.[54] The period after 70 CE, that is after the destruction of Jerusalem, was a watershed period during which the minority Jewish-Christian sect faced some fundamental decisions. Judaism at the time viewed Christians as dissenters and deserters from the synagogue. The choice facing Jewish-Christians was either gradual integration into the Gentile-influenced Christian

---

52. Köhler, *Die Rezeption*.

53. Steck, *Israel*, 310–11.

54. Meier, "Antioch," 12–86; Luz, *Matthew 1–7*, 93; Overman, *Matthew's Gospel and Formative Judaism*, 16–19; Saldarini, "Gospel of Matthew, 39"; Duling and Perrin, *New Testament*, 329–33; Sim, *Social World*, 31–40; Carter, *Matthew*, 36–37.

community—a choice that presented the risk of gradual loss of identity—or, the decision needed to be made to retain separate group identity; positioned between Gentile Christians and Pharisaic synagogue. "[T]he evangelist's community partook of two worlds, the Jewish and the Christian. Although they saw their Christianity as the true fulfillment of Judaism, they also were very conscious that they had broken with their unbelieving brothers and sisters. They were struggling to define and defend a Jewish Christianity to the Jews on the one hand and to realize their unity with Gentile Christians on the other. This twofold challenge explains some of the basic tension encountered in the Gospel."[55]

THE LANGUAGE OF WORSHIP

Our examination of the language of worship in Matthew, together with our detailing of the structural and theological importance of setting, particularly mountain settings, for Matthew's understanding of worship, is not inconsistent with scholarly proposals about the social location of Matthew's community. Indeed, the identified conflict with a resurgent Pharisaism, in the wake of the destruction of the temple and the demise of the Jerusalem priesthood, provides a vital contextual clue for our understanding Matthew's out-of-doors setting for worship.[56] Further, Matthew's use of the verb *sunagō* to describe the crowds being gathered around Jesus reflects a possible reaction to those who insisted on a domestic location for worship.[57] Reference to Matthew's community as

---

55. Hagner, "The *Sitz im Leben*," 49–50.

56. Hayes and Mandell, *The Jewish People*, 210. "With the destruction of the Temple, the animal sacrifice cult came to an end in Jerusalem. Along with the loss of the Temple, the priestly guilds lost occupational usefulness and prominence. Worship became concentrated in the services of the synagogue, devoid of sacrifice. Many ritual demands of the scriptures were spiritualised and sublimated so as to be obeyed without being observed. Ordinary life was reinterpreted to replicate aspects of Temple service—charity and good deeds were understood as sacrifice and the table in the home replaced the altar. The teacher-rabbi replaced the priest as the religious authority and interpreter of the will and word of God."

57. When used of persons, the verb *sunagō* can mean to bring or call together, assemble (Matt 22:10); to show hospitality take in, invite in (Matt 25:35); or in the passive sense, to assemble, come together, be gathered together (Matt 18:20). The noun *sunagōgē* refers to a formal meeting for worship (Acts 13:43); specifically of Jews meeting together (Acts 9:2), the place of gathering (Matt 4:23).

ekklēsia in 16:18 provides even more evidence of Matthew's differentiation, this time by title rather than language or location.[58]

Details in Matthew's narrative provide insight into aspects of worship life in his community.[59] There is the practice of baptism and the formation of disciples (28:16–20). The narrative in Matthew (over against Mark 14:22–23) evidences a transformation of the last supper or Passover meal into a celebration of the Lord's Supper for the "forgiveness of sins" (26:26–28). Other worship elements include the Lord's Prayer (6:9–13), requests to Jesus for help that reflect language familiar in later Christian liturgy (*kuriē eleēson*, 17:15; 20:30–31). Emerging forms of leadership and ministry are reflected both in reference to "prophets, sages, and scribes" (23:34) and by the prohibition of titles such as "rabbi," "father," "master" (23:7–10) in preference of the role of "servant," or "minister" (*diakonos*, 23:11).

Evidence in the wider context of the New Testament indicates that from its earliest beginnings there was in the Christian church an intrinsic link between worship and community. Jesus came preaching the kingdom of God and early Christian life and worship was seen as an embodiment of God's reign of justice and peace. The life of early Christian communities was shaped and empowered by imitation and worship of Jesus. In other words, they worshipped how they lived, and lived how they worshipped. The montage of the apostolic age provided by the writer of Luke-Acts details community meetings enjoying table fellowship, being one in heart and soul, holding all possessions in common.[60] It is not unreasonable to assume similar characteristics for Matthew's community. Certainly the record of history is that, in the absence of shrines, temples, and public feast days, early Christians continued to meet and celebrate in private homes (Acts 2:4; 1 Cor 16:19; Col 4:15; Phlm 1:2; 1 Pet 2:5; 2 John 1:10) public buildings (Acts 20:7) and open spaces (Acts 16:3; 27:35). Some defended their lack of altars and shrines by arguing that God's temple was the whole world and couldn't be enclosed in a building made by human hands (Acts 7:48; cf. 2 Sam 7:6).

---

58. Whereas Jewish-Christians adopted the Greek word *ekklēsia* for their communities, other Jews embraced the term synagogue for theirs. This tension is reflected, as noted above, in references to "their synagogues" and the "synagogue of the hypocrites."

59. This is investigated more fully in Hultgren, "Liturgy," 659–73.

60. Acts 2:42–47; 4:32–35.

The nature of worship as community experience in Matthew is brought into sharper focus as reader and interpreter alike recognize the Gospel story is presented on two levels. At an immediate level Matthew narrates the past story of Jesus. On another level, he interweaves the story of his own community with the religious history of Israel. In so doing Matthew proclaims the Lord's presence in his own community's history to encourage people facing radical political, cultural, and religious changes in the aftermath of the disruptive, destructive, and era-defining events of 70 CE. Matthew invites new perspective and hope in proclaiming the good news of "God with us." For "[t]he past story of the one who is present with his community as a living Lord can never be only a story of the past."[61]

In Matthew, we can discern an emerging reinterpretation of Jewish end-time hopes concerning a gathering and recreation of God's people in a new temple on mount Zion. Matthew claims the presence of Jesus on the mountain—not the mountain itself, nor the temple, nor the city of Jerusalem—qualifies as an eschatological event and gathering point for the people of God. The focus and foundation of the *ekklēsia*, the congregation of the people of God, is Jesus Christ. Matthew's community and other early Christian communities of the New Testament era identified holy space wherever Christ is or has been. They personalized holy space in Christ, and because of this Christo-centricity they declared their "freedom from space and attachment to spaces"[62]—remembering the promise of Jesus, ". . . where two or three are gathered in my name, I am there among them" (Matt 18:20).

WORSHIP AND THE FUTURE OF COMMUNITY

The church today lives in the best of years; lives in the worst of years. Not 89 CE, or 1789 CE, but 2009 CE. Not Jerusalem, or the Paris and London of Dickens' *Tale of Two Cities,* but the struggle between global city and local community. Not the end of royal rule and the modern birth of a real republic, but the end of the optimistic individualism of modernism and the postmodern birth of pessimistic pluralism. Pluralism promotes the diversity of cultural traditions and the associated necessity of different estimations of truth representing those communities. What this

---

61. Luz, *Studies*, 17.
62. Davies, *The Gospel*, 367.

exactly means for the global and local community has been explored in recent decades by philosophers, political scientists, sociologists, and cultural theorists. Yet, there remains little consensus on how to understand the nature of this epochal culture shift.

The existing church—the pluriform expression of historic Christian churches—is not immune to the radical challenges of postmodernism. Like the early Matthean community, it is faced with questions of identity and the necessity of change. Many observe the increasing divide between the church and its surrounding culture and believe the very existence of the church is under threat. Others, however, consider the emerging culture offers unexpected opportunity for the church to rediscover its past and to escape the malaise of its present.

History witnesses that it is impossible for the church to worship outside or apart from its cultural context, and the existing church is no exception to this reality as contemporary culture continues its own metamorphosis. So what possible contribution might Matthew's writing to a first century community in cultural transition bring to twenty-first century Christian communities seeking to understand the dynamics of a postmodern world and how the gospel is incarnated and articulated into this context? Matthew's Gospel provides both gift and challenge to the debate involving the existing church and emerging church movement[63] over the relationship between worship and human community, and popular demands for a return to "biblical worship."

Matthew's Gospel provides a challenge to the existing church in its captivity to epistemological assumptions of the modern age that have resulted in what sociologist Robert Bellah once called the "culture of separation;" the consignment of the church to the periphery of public conversation that in the same process reduced faith to an intellectual as-

---

63. The emerging church movement involves the house church movement, simple church movements, and churches that may not even have a "worship service." It is correct to refer to an emergent church movement rather than "the emergent church" since churches that embrace this label present a vast diversity in style, organization, theology, and ministry practices. Andrew Jones, considered a credible voice for the movement, makes this comment in an early blog: "I have tried to define [the emergent church movement] and have failed miserably. My apologies. It may be of some console for you to know that no one else has succeed in defining it, and some of us have been at it a long time. Maybe that is okay. People in the emerging culture do not really want or need such a definition. And some of us are hesitant to give one, because behind the practices and models of emerging church lies a radically different mindset, value system, and worldview" (Weblog post "Emerging Church Definition 1.0").

sent given to a set of theological propositions and the individualization of worship.[64]

Matthew's emphasis on the physical nature of worship, implied in his preference for the verb *proskuneō*, is a reminder that God cares about physical things and involves the physical in worship. God created a tabernacle with detailed instructions and Solomon built a temple that was a worship site for all kinds of rituals and physicality. The healing ministry of Jesus to the poor and broken (Matt 11:4–5) was a sign of the presence of the kingdom of God: God embracing the physical, touching the physical, transforming the physical. Matthew's report about the involvement of the whole self in the act of worship, then, is not so much a comment on posture as an essential personal worship response, as it is a Christological clue. A number of psalms celebrate the promise that the nations will one day come and bow down before the Lord (Ps 22:27, 29; 86:9). The prophets announced the pilgrimage of nations to mount Zion (e.g., Isa 2:1–3; 27:12–13; 66:23). Matthew likewise paints a picture of Jesus as the one to whom "every knee should bow."[65] In this, Matthew's Gospel offers a gift to the church today facing questions of identity and the necessity of change: a reminder that acceptable worship begins with the action and approach of God. As Jesus gathers the crowds to himself, they recognize his true identity in word and action. Then people, in the presence of Immanuel—the one named "God with us"—respond with their whole being as they are gathered into the new community of God. In this *ekklēsia* Jesus Christ is the focus of worship; and, the foundation for all experience of Christian community.

Worship in the emerging church movement has a greater emphasis on the physical. The use of practices like the lighting of candles, standing for prayer, anointing with oil, and frequent use of the Lord's Supper, on the one hand, reclaim ancient practices, but, on the other hand, represent a postmodern protest to engage the whole person in worship, not just the intellect. Emergent worship aims to "immerse the worshipper in a sensually rich environment that is designed to draw out an openness to the incoming of God."[66]

Matthew does not deliver a sacred tradition from Jesus about forms of worship, but in narrating how Jesus in his earthly mission gathered

---

64. Bellah, *Habits*, 334.
65. Cf. Isa 45:22–23; Phil 2:10.
66. Morgenthaler, "Emergent Church," 224.

people around himself, feeding and caring for them, the Gospel provides more than enough clues for the church today reflecting on the relationship between worship and life, worship, and human community. A. G. Hebert, the Anglican liturgical leader, once wrote,

> To worship God in church is not a substitute for the service of God in daily life: rather, it is that which makes the service of God possible by bring the things of daily life into the light of eternity. And so the Christian redemption is not merely individual but social, so the normal type of Christian worship is not the individual's meditation, but the common worship of the Body, when members are met together to learn the meaning of the common life which is in Him.[67]

In contrast to the cultic celebrations of the Graeco-Roman world, which were governed by strict customs about social status, class, age, and gender, early Christian communities largely ignored these divisions. Women, children, and slaves were all welcome to participate in the same worship unless they were excluded because of some public sin or disciplinary action. We read Paul's angry reaction when it was reported to him that there were divisions between rich and poor within the community at Corinth. Evidently, people were being excluded from the communal meal and dining area, perhaps even being provided inferior meal, and were only included in the celebration of the Lord's Supper. Paul concluded that the Corinthians were not eating a true holy meal. They were eating and drinking to their own judgment by injustice shown to the poor in the body of Christ (1 Cor 11:17–22).

Caring for the disadvantaged in the community was evidence of faith in God (1 John 3:16–18) and as important as participation in worship itself (Matt 12:7–12). In early Christian communities those who were charged with the distribution of community resources were evidently the same people who presided over community meals (Acts 6:1–2). Interestingly, the terms the church later adopted for its life of public worship—*leitourgia, diakonia, offere, oblation, eulogia*—were originally words of service for particular social concerns, but later employed for cultic purposes as well.[68]

Matthew's record of Jesus' special concern for the poor, for the "people of the land" (ʿam hā ʾāreṣ), is a challenge to the existing church

---

67. Hebert, *Liturgy*, 160.
68. Pecklers, *Worship*, 166.

to reclaim the social dimension of membership in the body of Christ. As Christians follow the law of Christ and live a life of worship they learn to recognize their living connection to the creation, their community with the homeless, elderly, marginalized, abused, and forgotten people of society.

The emerging church movement challenges the existing church by saying that the way a person lives is more important than what they believe; and, that a passionate, servant life is the best apologetic for the way of Jesus. Emerging people love to quote the word of Jesus recorded in Matthew, "You will know them by their fruits" (Matt 7:20). The kingdom way of life was demonstrated by Jesus not by way of power and status but by way of love and suffering, in order to create a new community where the fruit of the Spirit overcomes the powers of the world and fallen human nature. The heart of the emerging church's concern with social justice is a conviction that anyone who thinks a Christian can withdraw from society, locking themselves away from the world in holy huddles waiting for heaven to come soon, are being unfaithful to the calling and commission of Jesus Christ.

The Gospel of Matthew presents worship as community experience: the new people God gathered around Jesus Christ. In gathering around Jesus—indoors and outdoors—this new community participates in the saving work of God and is impelled toward the community of the world. Further, in community worship, those who gather around Jesus provide a social model for the world, inasmuch as they practice the key characteristic of Christian living: love and mutual submission (Matt 5:19; 25:35–40; cf. Eph 2:8–10; 5:21).

8

Time and Location

Aspects of Realized Eschatology, Paul, and Our Worship

Michael Parsons

INTRODUCTION

THE APOSTLE PAUL'S VIEW of what it is for Christians to worship God is clearly much broader than "worship" as it is generally defined by most of us in the twenty-first century. Without restricting it merely to "what happens in church" Paul allows for the whole of life (including what happens in church) to be designated as "worship"—that is, he allows for worship to be both ecclesial and extra-ecclesial in nature. David Peterson speaks of this breadth when he alludes to "Paul's revolutionary use of [the] terminology of worship with reference to a Christ-centered, gospel-serving, life-orientation."[1] We see this clearly, for example, in the way the apostle takes the words from the cultic setting to the wider life of every believer and of the Christian community in Romans 12:1–2.[2] "I appeal to you therefore, brothers [and sisters], by the mercies of God, to present your bodies (*sōmata*) as a living sacrifice, holy and acceptable to God, which is your reasonable worship (*logikēn latreian*). Do not be conformed to this age (*tō aiōni toutō*), but be transformed by the renew-

---

1. Peterson, *Engaging with God*, 219. Hart, *Truth Aflame*, 500, says, "In the broadest sense worship is *any* proper response to the revelation of our Triune God," (emphasis added).

2. See Jewett, *Romans*, 727; Esler, *Conflict and Identity*, 310–12.

ing of your minds (*nous*), so that you may discern what is the will of God—what is good and acceptable and perfect."

Here Paul is appealing for those of us who know Christ and the mercies (*oiktirmōn*: plural) which have been shown by God through him to render service and obedience with our whole being. We might note, perhaps, that Paul is connecting his application (imperative) to his theology (indicative) here.[3] He has shown previously God's character in his saving work—closely aligned to the idea of "mercy": kindness (2:4), patience (9:22; 11:22), love (5:5; 8:35, 39), and grace (1:7; 3:24; 4:16; 5:2, 20, 21; 6:1, 14, 15, 17; 11:5, 6), for example, and although the words *oikirein*, *eleos*, and *eleein* are absent from chapters 1–10 the mercy of God is never far from Paul's mind. This is clear thematically as he outlines God's faithfulness to Jew and Gentile (chaps. 1–3) and that despite their sin (e.g., 3:9, etc.); justification by faith and life in Christ (chaps. 4–7), and life by the Spirit (chap. 8). However, it is correct to say that "mercy" is the particular keynote of chapters 9–11 (e.g., 9:15, 16, 18, 23; 10:12, 13, 20, 21; 11:22, 31, 32) as Paul reaches the climax of his teaching on the gospel of God's righteousness (announced at 1:17). That, then, is the basis on which the apostle motivates the believers to offer themselves to God in worship—that is, by presenting our bodies, "ourselves as a totality" in self-giving action to the Lord's service in gratitude for his mercy.[4] At this point James Dunn speaks of "whole person commitment lived out in daily existence," whilst Charles Talbot mentions our "total self given to God."[5] Given the context, it is clear that our giving of ourselves should be done in a voluntary and enthusiastic way before God; not as Bowen

---

3. See Parsons, "Being Precedes Act," 217–47; particularly, 233–37.

4. Peterson, *Engaging with God*, 178. Peterson is right to emphasize that we worship God both because of who he is and because of his grace (mercies) towards us (221). There seems to be no textual reason for suggesting that only our physical bodies are in view here; contrary to Murray, *Romans*, 110, for example. This does not fit well into vv. 3–8, nor 9–21, which exhort to attitude (vv. 3, 9–12, 15–16) as well as to action (vv. 6–8, 13, 17, 20, 21).

5. Dunn, *Romans 9–16*, 710, quoted by Volf, "Worship," 203–11; Talbot, *Romans*, 285, respectively. Hart, *Truth Aflame*, 503, reflects on Rom 12:1–2, saying, "Worship is also a *service* or *ministry* to the Lord. We offer our total bodily lives as a consecrated sacrifice to God . . . This encompasses our total daily life as well as our personal and corporate times of worship. It is both an *inward* ('spiritual') and a *rational* ('reasonable') worship," (emphasis original).

suggests, "because of God's mercy towards us, *we owe him a duty*." This appears entirely to miss the point.[6]

Peterson says that when we read the following chapters of Romans (12–15) in the light of Romans 12:1-2, as a kind of sub-heading, it is clear that "*acceptable worship* involves effective ministry to one another within the body of Christ, maintaining love and forgiveness towards those outside the Christian community, expressing right relationships with ruling authorities, living expectantly in the light of Christ's imminent return, and demonstrating love especially towards those with different opinions within the congregation of Christ's people."[7]

The apostle wants our whole lives to be consecrated to the Lord in worshipful service, and his desire highlights the importance of every sphere of our lives as worship-oriented opportunities to serve God and to bring him glory. Likewise, Talbot defines appropriate worship as "proper behavior in church and society," as "a liturgy of life," and, later, as "a liturgy of righteous living," concluding that "the true worship for which the apostle called embraces the whole of believers' lives from day to day."[8] Similarly, Miroslav Volf concludes that because Christian worship consists both as service to God and in joyful praise of God, "There is no space in which worship should not take place, no time when it should not occur, and no activity through which it should not happen."[9] By implication, this underlines the importance of home, the work place, school, college, leisure time, and church as places and times in which we are to worship God with our whole being—for worship in these situations is an acknowledgement of God who has created us, who gives us life, and who has redeemed us in his Son, Jesus Christ.

Nevertheless, this text might imply more than that for, as Robert Jewett points out, Paul's only other use of priestly language in the letter is at Romans 15:16 in the context of the conversion of the Gentiles.[10] Here Paul speaks of the obligation or mandate that binds him to his

---

6. Bowen, *Romans*, 154 (emphasis added). See also, Evans, "Romans 12:1-2," 9.

7. Peterson, *Engaging with God*, 178 (emphasis original). Moo, *Encountering the Book of Romans*, 176, also suggests that Rom 12:1-2 stands as a kind of heading for Rom 12:1—15:13; as does Cousar, *Letters of Paul*, 146. See also, Glad, "Paul and Adaptability," 35–36.

8. Talbot, *Romans*, 284, 285, respectively.

9. Miroslav Volf, "Worship," 204.

10. Jewett, *Romans*, 729. See also, his comments on Rom 15:16 (907).

mission, or, rather, to God's mission (*missio Dei*).[11] The apostle speaks of his ministry as "the priestly service of the Gospel of God (*hierourgein to euanggelion*—sacred duty of proclaiming the Gospel), so that the offering (*prosphora*) of the Gentiles may be acceptable." Therefore, we might ask whether at Romans 12:1–2 the apostle is implying the possibility that our worship, broadly conceived as inside and *outside* of the church assembly, has missional implications.[12] Perhaps this is so.

PAUL AND ESCHATOLOGY

Though I am aware that on a close reading of Paul's letters it is clear that no single focal point or center should be isolated from the rest (Christology, soteriology, pneumatology, eschatology, ecclesiology, and such like), and certainly not at their expense, it remains true that, as the apostle sees it, the Christian life is embraced by eschatology.[13] That is because for Paul the distinguishing character of Christian life is that it is an eschatological existence.[14] To put this from the reverse angle, as it were, the apostle does not consider eschatology as merely a subject *in* his theology, but rather a vital, permeating, and controlling framework or matrix to his theology of salvation in Jesus Christ. Therefore, an understanding of eschatology in Paul is absolutely vital to an understanding of his theology and its implications.

Of course, though the word "eschatology" is generally recognized as descriptive of "the last events" (death, resurrection, tribulation, judgment, and the like), this is a very limiting way in which to conceive of it, for it implies much more than that. Those future happenings, which we sometimes term the "last events," are merely *determinative* members in a whole series of events—including the Christ-event itself and beyond. That is, they are decisive to our understanding of the rest; they reveal meaning and significance to the whole. Because this is the case, it al-

---

11. Chae, *Paul as Apostle*, 46, 264, reminds us of this duty as integral to the apostle's calling. See also, Paillard, *In Praise of the Inexpressible*.

12. See chap. 3 of the present volume for an Old Testament perspective on this aspect of worship.

13. See the recent essay on this by Porter, "Is there a Center?" 1–19; particularly, 6–12. For some of the suggestions for a center in Paul's theology see 8–10. See also, Cousar, *Letters of Paul*, 76–86.

14. Giesen, "Eschatology in Philippians," 245, speaks of "Paul's entire existence [as] eschatologically orientated." See also, Chamblin, *Paul and the Self*, 158.

lows for a tensional-unity between the present and the future, often now referred to as "the already" and the "not yet." So for Paul we live our lives of "acceptable service" (inside *and* outside of church assembly) between the polarities of what has already been accomplished in Christ and what has yet to be fully realized by God's continuing redemptive activity.

To a large extent the tension is determined by the presence of the Holy Spirit as the divine eschatological gift and, thus, by the pneumatic nature of the new creation (see 2 Cor 5:17; Gal 6:15; Col 3:10; cf. Eph 2:10). That is, it is the presence of the Spirit of God that so concretely brings together what we have become in Christ with the juxtaposed impulse to live as those who have not yet become what Christ would have us to be (see Phil 3:12—4:1). The eschatological tension in the reality of the Holy Spirit's presence in believers and within the church community is implied, for example, in the three Pauline images of the Spirit as the down payment (*arrabōn*—see 2 Cor 1:22; 5:5; Eph 1:14), the first-fruits (*aparchē*—see Rom 8:23), and the seal (*sphragis*—see 2 Cor 1:22; Eph 1:13–14; 4:30).[15] These Pauline images forcefully indicate that with the Spirit the power and life of the new age is already realized. It has already broken in and in such a way as to enable believers to live through the present age in the power of the new and coming age.

Of course, there are implied in this state of affairs important repercussions for Paul's teaching. The redemption already accomplished in and by Christ, given through the work of the Spirit, impels believers to godliness in the present age while the salvation-not-yet-attained demands a future-orientated, moral exertion on the part of the believer. That is, the present is determined by both the past and the future. As Paul understands it, the Christian should be concerned with a manner of life consonant with and demanded by eschatological reality (present and promised) within the contemporary and largely antagonistic world. Believers are eschatological beings (in Christ, no less than a new creation: *kainē ktisis*—2 Cor 5:17; Gal 6:15) and our life and worship should demonstrate this fundamental and gracious change even now.

---

15. See Harris, *Raised Immortal*, 143–44, 148–49; Ziesler, *Pauline Christianity*, 70; Bertone, "Function of the Spirit," 75–97. Minear, *Images of the Church*, is still seminal in the area of Pauline imagery. See 112–13; and, generally, chap. 4, "The New Creation," 105–35. Wright, *Paul*, 146, concludes that the Spirit is "a gift from God's future, the gift which guarantees that future."

In this context it is interesting to note that often the apostle Paul adopts the concept of dualism when he speaks of our present, eschatologically-determined existence in Christ. He does so because while believers have been taken into the eschatological realm by Christ, and through the Spirit, they remain in the world and the apostle wishes to indicate something of that tensional experience in his pastoral theology and exhortation. There is in the Pauline correspondence, therefore, that which I am going to term "horizontal dualism" and also that which may be called "vertical dualism." Briefly and simply put, the former phrase ("horizontal dualism") refers to the time-framework in which the age to come has already pervaded the present age—a time-framework, in other words, in which both ages co-exist. The latter phrase ("vertical dualism") has to do with the believer's location, the Pauline concept of "the heavenlies" in terms of which believers somehow simultaneously exist in the heavenly realm with Jesus Christ whilst living in the world.

Given that Paul's understanding of worship is all-inclusive, embracing as it does the whole of our lives, it is clear from the fact that those lives are eschatologically-defined that believers are to give themselves in "acceptable worship" (Rom 12:1–2) in a context that is fraught with tension—both moral and spiritual. In light of this, the purpose of this short essay is threefold: that is, to explore the meaning and implications of Paul's realized eschatology in these images of the believer's time and location in Christ, to set our worship (broadly understood) into the eschatological context that they suggest, and to reflect on some of the implications that arise.

Horizontal Dualism: The Two Ages

The teaching of the two ages was a characteristic of apocalyptic Judaism (see, for example, 2 Esd 4:2; 6:9; 7:13) and most New Testament scholars seem to agree, in general, that Paul accepted this two-age structure, taking over the perspective of Jewish apocalyptic and adapting it in light of the momentous Christ-event.[16] That is, as Timothy George puts it, "For Paul . . . the death and resurrection of Jesus has radically punctuated

---

16. See Cousar, *Letters of Paul*, 96–97; George, *Galatians*, 87. Note, though, that Wright, *Paul*, 135–53, speaks of this but insists that the apostle "re-imagined" aspects of the apocalyptic. One influential scholar who does not accept the two-age interpretation is Esler, *Conflict and Identity*, 310.

this traditional time line."[17] We can discern this, perhaps, in Ephesians 1:21; 2:2–3; Galatians 1:4; 1 Corinthians 2:6–7; 2 Corinthians 4:4, and in similar texts.[18]

In a significant work from the nineteenth century on Pauline eschatology, Geerhardus Vos, for example, demonstrates a modified acceptance of this view.[19] He points out that the Old Testament looked forward to the coming Messiah as the one great future eschatological event (seen in the repeated prophetic phrase, "the Day of the Lord" and such like)[20] and, consequently, that it saw "this age" and "the age to come" as simply terms of chronological succession and significance. In other words, Vos indicates that the Old Testament scheme saw "this age" coming to an abrupt halt as the Messiah is revealed, at which time the "new age" would begin—the one following the other.

However, Vos draws the conclusion that the New Testament writers complicate the picture because they discern that with the coming of Messiah Jesus the old scheme is too simple to elucidate the actual event. Therefore, New Testament writers divide the event (designated "the Day of the Lord") into two stages; that is, the present Messianic age and the consummated future state. However, importantly, the New Testament finds the age to come anticipated already in the present age because of the eschatological event of Christ. The Messianic appearance now begins to unfold itself into two successive epochs; as Vos concludes, "the age to come was perceived to bear in its womb another age to come."[21] The previous simple chronological scheme is no longer adequate to account for the present, rather more complex, eschatological reality brought in by Christ. Therefore, the old scheme is now modified by New Testament

---

17. George, *Galatians*, 87. Similarly, Schrage, *Ethics of the New Testament*, 181, says, "Jesus' cross and resurrection are understood as epochal eschatological events making salvation a present reality." Schrage prioritizes Pauline Christology, and allows for the importance of eschatology only within that. See also, Hayes, *Moral Vision*, 19–27.

18. The subject of those letters which should be included in a study of Pauline theology is one which is clearly too complex to be dealt with in this short essay. I am assuming that it is *at least* possible that Paul wrote the contested letters, and that they have the same canonical "weight" as the rest. On this complex subject, see Collins, *Letters that Paul Did Not Write*; Neumann, *Authenticity of the Pauline Epistles*; Porter, *Pauline Canon*. See also, Rowland, "Apocalyptic Vision," 220–29.

19. See Vos, *Pauline Eschatology*, 1–40.

20. See Kreitzer, *Jesus and God*, 125–28, where he shows that Paul shifted the reference from God to Christ in his description of the "Day of the Lord."

21. Vos, *Pauline Eschatology*, 36.

writers who present the resurrection of Christ as the definitive event.[22] Now, in the new scheme, at his resurrection this present age continues, but the future age is already realized *in principle* in heaven and in the lives of Christ's followers. (Of course, the future age will only be *fully* realized after the second coming of Christ.) According to Vos, therefore, the New Testament believer lives in this present world and, *in principle*, in the world to come at the same time.[23] It might be noted, though, that Vos does not hold that the co-existence of the two temporal ages is possible. He says, for instance, that "the two sequences of time are mutually exclusive. So long as one age lasts, no other can supervene."[24]

In what has become one of the seminal studies on the subject, Andrew Lincoln acknowledges his debt to Vos' work, but suggests that this last point is the weakness of the former scholar's construction.[25] Lincoln suggests that it is much more likely that Paul accepted dualism even within the age-structure of his theology—he refers to Romans 12:2; 1 Corinthians 1:20; 2:6; 3:18; 10:11; 2 Corinthians 4:4; Galatians 1:4; and, Ephesians 2:2, 7. He asserts that the dualism between "this age" and the "age to come" is redemptive-historically produced, connected as it is with Christ's death and resurrection with which the new age dawned.[26] According to Lincoln, this gives the period between the resurrection and the *parousia* a peculiar complexion in that it is characterized by the concurrence, the co-existence of the two ages; and, in view of the ethically qualified antithesis between them, the conflict between the two ages.

In an early, significant essay, "The Time of Hope in the New Testament," Paul Minear seems to spell this out well.[27] He writes, "There is a process that moves forward from the past into the present; there is also a process that moves backward proleptically from the future into the past. The New Testament treats the first as particularly characteristic of the age that is passing away; the second as characteristic of the age that comes."[28] That is, there is a past-present continuum ("this age") and a future-present continuum ("the new age"). On the one hand, the

---

22. Ibid., 38.
23. See also, Vos, "Eschatological Aspect," 25–58; particularly, 91, 115.
24. Vos, *Pauline Eschatology*, 37.
25. Lincoln, *Paradise Now*, 171.
26. Ibid., 71, 172–73, 178, 186.
27. Minear, "Time of Hope," 337–61.
28. Ibid., 346.

former is intrinsically characterized by "passingness;" on the other hand, the latter is characterized by "comingness."

The eschatological concept formulated here comes out strikingly, perhaps, in Paul's use of the words *kosmos* and *aiōn*. The two words essentially correspond together in the apostle's writing; but, whereas *kosmos* primarily has a spatial reference, *aiōn* has a temporal one. *Kosmos* denotes several things in Paul's writing, but it is the use of the word in its sense of humanity viewed in relationship to God (*coram Deo*) that is of particular importance here.[29] In this sense, of course, *kosmos* has a moral connotation referring to the world at variance with God, accountable (Rom 3:19), and condemned under his judgment (Rom 3:6; 1 Cor 6:2; 11:32). In this way *kosmos* is a term of intensity whose primary significance is ethical or qualitative—for instance, the apostle says to the Galatians that it is this "world" that has been crucified to him. The word *kosmos* in this context means everything outside of Christ, and in that sense it is contrasted to the cross of Christ in which Paul legitimately seeks his glory and puts his trust: "May I never boast of anything except the cross of our Lord Jesus Christ, by which the world has been crucified to me, and I to the world" (Gal 6:14). The term "crucified" (perfect indicative passive of *stauroō*) points to the absolute nature of the contrast—it is an act of finality by which the world is now dead as far as Paul is concerned (cf. Phil 3:7–8).

We notice too that Paul continually draws a similarly sharp distinction between the sphere of the believers' existence and the *kosmos*. For instance, he says that believers are those who "have not received the spirit of the world but the Spirit who is from God" (1 Cor 2:12); neither are they going to be condemned with the world (1 Cor 11:32). He also reminds those at Colossae that once they "were alienated from God;" indeed, they were enemies (Col 1:21), just as the world still remains. But now they have been rescued by grace and translated into a different sphere altogether (Col 1:13). Nonetheless, Paul says that for now believers are to remain within the "crooked and depraved generation" (Phil 2:15).

The word *aiōn* has similar implications. The only explicit reference to the two-age structure in Pauline theology seems to be Ephesians 1:21,

---

29. See Sasse, *kosmos*, 867–98. He notes that there are 157 occurrences of the word in the New Testament, of which 46 are in Paul's writing. See also, Bultmann, *Theology*, 254–59.

where he speaks of "the present age" and "the age to come."[30] Marcus Barth states that the "main contrast elaborated upon in Ephesians is that between the *past* period of division, sin, hiddenness, darkness, and the *present* time of peace, sanctification, revelation, light." He cites, as examples, Ephesians 2:1–10, 11–13; 3:3–5; 4:17–24; 5:8.[31] Nevertheless, implicit references appear to run through the apostle's writing. In Galatians 1:4, for example, Paul outlines the consequence of Christ's death as that of rescuing believers "from the present evil age (*ek ou aiōnos tou enestōtos ponērou*)." Here, again, Paul is writing about the evil-dominated age, not the material world. Because Christ has already entered the resurrection age and believers share in the risen life of Christ, they are, here and now, extracted from "the present evil age."[32] In 1 Corinthians 1:20 the apostle asks, "Where is the philosopher of this age? (*tou aiōnos toutou*)"—an age evidently sinful and alienated from God.[33] In his second letter to the Corinthians (2 Cor 4:4) Paul mentions "the god of this age (*ho theos tou aiōnos*)," by which he probably means Satan.[34]

Enough has been said, perhaps, to show the aptness of Herman Ridderbos' remark that both *kosmos* and *aiōn* "constitute the description of the totality of unredeemed life dominated by sin outside Christ."[35] He speaks of it further as the "human situation qualified by sin," concluding that "to belong to the world means to be a sinner, to participate in sin and to experience judgment on sin."[36] Consequently, some of the primary characteristics of the present age or world can be outlined as follows.

---

30. It has been suggested that Paul's statement in 1 Cor 10:11 (that his generation is comprised of those "on whom the fulfillment of the ages has come") indicates the overlap of the two ages. For example, in the influential *TDNT*, Michel states, "In a surprising way visible only to faith the end of the old aeon and the dawn of the new has come upon the community" (3:625). However, Barrett, *First Epistle to the Corinthians*, 227, is probably correct in saying that the phrase is to be understood as suggesting that the particular age of history has been completed. He paraphrases the clause as follows: "Who are confronted by the end of these past ages of history."

31. Barth, *Ephesians*, 1.155 (original emphasis).

32. See also, 1 Cor 6:11.

33. Here, the phrase is virtually synonymous with "of the world (*tou kosmou*)" and with "the world (*ho kosmos*)" of v. 21. The implication is found again in 1 Cor 2:6, 8; 3:18.

34. See, for comparison, John 12:31; 14:30; 16:11. Reference could be made to Eph 2:2; Rom 12:2.

35. Ridderbos, *Paul*, 91.

36. Ibid., 93.

- It is transitory. It is passing away, coming to nothing (1 Cor 2:6; 7:31).[37] Here, *aiōn* primarily suggests a time that is passing away, not the *quantity* of time, but the transitory *quality* of time.
- It is evil (Gal 1:4; Eph 5:15).
- It is dominated by sin and death (Rom 3:9; Gal 3:22; cf. Rom 5:12; 6:12, 14; 7:11, 14; 8:10).
- It is the domain of Satan and of demonic forces—powers alien to God (1 Cor 2:6; 15:24; Rom 1:20; 8:38; 2 Cor 4:4; Gal 4:3; Eph 2:2; 6:12).
- It is the home of hollow philosophy and deceit (Col 2:8, 20).
- It is alienated from God (Eph 1:21), and being without God, it is consequently without hope (Eph 2:12; 1 Thess 4:13).
- It is condemned by God (1 Cor 11:32), and it is under God's wrath (Eph 2:3).
- It is a realm of suffering (Rom 8:18). Carl Hoch says that "The present age is a time of affliction and a time when death is operative."[38]

Given these characteristics, it is not surprising that the apostle epitomizes the realm of the present age or world in the striking image "the kingdom of darkness" and contrasts it acutely with the kingdom of the Son whom God loves (Col 1:13).

Clearly, the present age or world is that sphere to which the *ekklēsia* (the believing community) emphatically does *not* belong (1 Cor 5:10; Phil 2:15; cf. 1 Cor 7:32–33; Col 2:20). Believers, then, do not belong to the world but, nevertheless, we do live in it. There is, therefore, an inevitable tension set up in Paul's own experience and in his theology. Terence Callan speaks of this as follows. "Christians live partly in the new age that has already begun to appear and partly in the old age that has not yet completely ended. They need to be aware that they themselves have not arrived at the fullness of salvation, and they need to beware lest the old age determine their thought and action rather than the new age that has dawned."[39]

---

37. In 1 Cor 7:31 *schema* should be taken as meaning "essence," not "form."
38. Hoch, *All Things New*, 156.
39. Callan, *Dying and Rising*, 111.

In Ephesians, for example, there is a continual contrast between what believers once were ("of the world") and what they are now "in Christ." Barth remarks, significantly, "Only one thing is clear: the transitoriness, deceptiveness, and the adversity of the time in which the saints live does not excuse the people of God from using every opportunity and tackling each task they are given."[40]

Indeed, Paul's own testimony within this context is that he conducted himself "in the world (*anestraphēmen en tō kosmō*)" and especially in his relations with the Corinthians "in the holiness and sincerity that are from God" (2 Cor 1:12). It is in such a way that Paul wishes the Philippians to live. He admonishes them, "Do everything without complaining or arguing, so that you may be blameless and pure, children of God without fault in a crooked and depraved generation, in which you shine like stars in the universe" (Phil 2:14–15).

Vertical Dualism

The apostle's framework of "vertical dualism" appears, for example, in his references to "the heavenlies." In Lincoln's major study of this subject the author shows that, for Paul, "heaven and earth, though distinct aspects of reality, formed one structure, one created cosmos" and that this fact has a bearing on the believer's life in the present.[41] This is evidenced as the apostle relates his charismatic experience (2 Cor 12) and signifies thereby that "the paradise of the end-time . . . is conceived of as already existing in heaven now." This is also importantly seen as Paul indicates in Ephesians 6 that the believer's existence is a present battle related to the context of "the heavenlies."[42]

"The Heavenlies"

Galatians 4:26 is an interesting and significant verse in this context. Here Paul contrasts "the present city of Jerusalem" with the "Jerusalem that

---

40. Barth, *Ephesians*, 2.578–79.
41. See Lincoln, *Paradise Now*, 191–92.
42. Ibid., 80–82, 164. Lincoln cites 1 Thess 5:8; Rom 13:12; 2 Cor 6:7; 10:4. He cross-references to Dan 10:13, 20; Test Abr 7:3; Rev 9:11; 19:11–21; 1 QH 11, 16. The distinctive feature of Paul's understanding is that the believer is said to be involved now, "fighting from a position of victory having been seated with Christ in the heavenlies" (165). See also, Chamblin, *Paul and the Self*, 176–79, for a balanced view of this subject.

is above."[43] However, there is an issue of interpretation regarding this image. Some scholars identify "Jerusalem that is above" with the church, noting that "above" is the equivalent of "spiritual" or "from above." Some, less specifically, see here a reference to the community of the new covenant, whilst still others equate the phrase with the new age that began with Christ.[44] However, it seems probably more likely that Paul means to signify the *principle* of heavenly life—"an order which is now being realized and the benefits of which are now being experienced by the believer."[45] Believers have their birth from her, she is above, and with her comes freedom. In other words, the heavenly dimension of the Christian has a dynamic and determinative effect on their life.

This idea is present also in Ephesians where the concept of "the heavenlies" is most pervasive. Believers are said to be "blessed in the heavenly realms (*en tois epouranios*) with every spiritual blessing in Christ" (Eph 1:3).[46] This probably denotes the sphere lying beyond the world of our senses, the place of the throne of Christ (Eph 1:20-21; cf. Col 3:1). It is here, in principle, that believers now dwell (Eph 2:5-6). In this context Maile, for example, speaks of "the heavenlies" as "the spiritual sphere in which God, Christ and the powers of darkness and the believer exist together, and as well as sharing Christ's reign and receiving the blessings of salvation the believer is involved in spiritual warfare."[47] The relationship between Christ, believers and "the heavenlies" touched upon in Ephesians 2:5-6 is again apparent in Colossians 3:1-3. Having died with Christ believers have been raised with him, not only to newness of life, but also to experience the principle of eschatological life now hidden with Christ in God in "the heavenlies."[48] From this short passage

43. The concept of the New Jerusalem was prominent in Jewish apocalypticism—see, for example, Isa 2:54; 10-14; Ezek 40-48; Zech 12-14; Tob 13:9; *Jub* 4:26; *2 Baruch*; *4 Ezra*. See also, Heb 12:22; 13:14; Rev 3:12; 21:2—22:5; but Paul evidently includes the Gentiles.

44. George, *Galatians*, 343, simply equates the contrast between the two Jerusalems with the fact that believers have entered the new age, and are really citizens of another commonwealth (Phil 3:21).

45. Betz, *Galatians*, 247. For Betz "the present Jerusalem" signifies the sphere of the flesh (*sarx*), the world, law, sin, death, and "the Jerusalem that is above" signifies that of the Spirit (*pneuma*), God, Christ, spirit, the benefits of salvation.

46. Barth, *Ephesians*, 2:78, though admitting that the text reads "in the heavenlies," nevertheless, prefers to translate it as "with full spiritual blessing of the heavens."

47. Maile, "Heaven," 382.

48. On the subject of dying and rising with Christ see the short but excellent treatment by Lewis, *Glory of Christ*, 384-87.

four important ideas emerge: (a) the believer's link with the heavenly world is vital and exists here and now; (b) for the believer, the unseen world is centered in the Lord Jesus Christ; indeed, the heavenly life of the believer is and remains totally bound to Christ; (c) the connection to Christ and to "the heavenlies" will be fully manifested at the second coming of Christ; and, (d) this relationship that believers sustain to heaven must be determinative of their present lives.

Heavenly-Mindedness

The basic text in respect of the relationship between "the heavenlies" and the believer is probably Philippians 3:20 where Paul asserts that "Our citizenship is in heaven." The *New International Version* translation of this phrase ("citizenship") is not the best at this point. Lincoln posits the idea of "state" or "commonwealth" which certainly seems in line with the intention of Paul's statement.[49] Lincoln comments on the fact that Philippi was a Roman colony with the Roman form of constitutional government, Roman coinage, speaking Latin, and so on. In other words, Philippi reflected Rome in practically every way. For believers in that city, then, the image implies that "their state and constitutive government is in heaven and [that] they are to reflect this rule in every respect."[50] Therefore the believer's heavenly *politeuma* ("state" or "commonwealth") is determinative of their existence here and now. Here, then, "Paul affirms a 'realized eschatology' in the sense that the source of the life the believer now enjoys, its determinative power, is in heaven."[51] In contrast to those whose "destiny is destruction" (Phil 3:19) and whose minds

---

49. Lincoln, *Paradise Now*, 220 n. 62. See also, Lambrecht, "Our Commonwealth," 309–15, who comments that the translation of *politeuma* as "commonwealth" is inadequate. He suggests "homeland" or even "fatherland." However, many commentators, including Silva, *Philippians*, 214 n. 66, disregard this possibility. See also, Fowl, *Philippians*, 173–74.

50. Lincoln, *Paradise Now*, 100, see also, 131. Surely, Paul is asking more than that they should have the same pride that they have in their Roman citizenship in their Christianity. This, rather weak conclusion, is from Williams, *Paul's Metaphors*, 150.

51. Lincoln, *Paradise Now*, 101. We might note that Giesen, "Eschatology," 261–67, objects to Lincoln's interpretation: "In that case, the Christians are understood as heavenly citizens in the world that would underline both their being alien to all earthly things and their belonging to the heavenly world. The state is rather primarily subject to the exercise of power regulated by its constitution. The life of the true Christian is, therefore, destined by a power in heaven, namely by the exalted Christ" (262). However, this appears not to materially alter the conclusion that believers' lives are determined from above, the heavenly realm in which Christ dwells.

are on earthly things, believers set their minds on the source of their life—heaven, from whence Christ will come to fit them for that place by transforming their lowly bodies to be like his glorious one. Paul asserts that, therefore, we "eagerly await (*apekdechometha*) a Savior from there" (Phil 3:20).

Heavenly-mindedness and earthly-mindedness are again set in opposition in the third chapter of Paul's letter to the Colossians. However, as Dunn says, Paul is here primarily trying to reflect on the Christian's change of perspective, not on a change of ontology.[52] The apostle tells them which way to focus, given their identification with the risen Christ. The following points may be briefly noticed: (a) Paul uses the spatial concept ("things above") to contrast the believer's heavenly-mindedness with earthly-mindedness ("not on earthly things").[53] They are to look "upward" towards the place where Christ is. (b) Again, the centrality of Christ is clear and important. It is because they "have been raised with Christ" (v. 1) and because their lives are "now hidden with Christ in God" (v. 3) that they are to be heavenly-minded. (c) Paul teaches that the whole direction of the believer's life is to be towards things above. The present tense of *sēteō* (to seek) indicates that what is called for is a continual and habitual action, and that of *phroneō* (to think) signifies the present orientation of the whole of one's life—"ourselves as a totality."[54] (d) Importantly, we need to note that the ethical consequences of this are outlined from verse 5 onwards. Lincoln underlines this point, saying, "For Paul having a transcendent point of reference, setting one's mind on the one who is above, was therefore no escape from issues of social concern but was the very thing which should motivate believers" in that area.[55] Lincoln's conclusion on Paul's use of "the heavenlies" is perceptive. He says that "The life of heaven is to be worked out on earth by the believer (Col 3:1f.). The paradox of the situation, however, is that this heavenly life and power are to be displayed in the midst of a state of humiliation (cf. Phil 3:20 with 2:5–11) and through decaying earthly bodies that are still part of the present evil age (cf. 2 Cor 5:12)."[56]

---

52. Dunn, *Colossians*, 203. See 202–7. See also, Melik, *Philippians*, 143–44.
53. See O'Brien, *Colossians*, 160.
54. Peterson, *Engaging with God*, 178.
55. Lincoln, *Paradise Now*, 130.
56. Ibid., 187–88.

REFLECTIONS

It will be helpful briefly to summarize what has been said. First, we might simply underline that the apostle Paul speaks of worship as broadly conceived, embracing, as it does, the whole of a Christian's life and every context in which we find ourselves, for in every circumstance and situation Christians face the challenge of acknowledging the Lord who has shown such amazing mercy in Christ and to serve him in faithfulness.[57] That self-sacrifice is what the apostle considers to be authentic worship—"a fitting response to grace received."[58] Integral to this worship is non-conformity to this age (or world); together with what might well be a gradual transformation by the renewing of our minds (Rom 12:2). Therefore, times of praise in the midst of that daily challenge—prayers, devotions, church services, home group gatherings, and the like—become *heightened* moments of acknowledgement, worship, and self-giving.

Second, Paul assures us that our life as Christians, as those who have died and been raised *with* Christ and those who are *in* Christ, is eschatological—it partakes of and is defined by eschatological newness.[59] That is, "Through initiation into Christ and his community, believers participate in, but also anticipate, the benefits and reality of the life of the resurrection."[60] Because of Jesus' resurrection, and the coming of the Holy Spirit we have *new* life, we are a *new* creation; we live in the *new* age and are participants of a *new* location. The presence of the Spirit assures us that we already experience the new age in the present, but also that we will experience it fully in the future. This centralizes the Holy Spirit in our experience for he brings future blessings now, with the impulse to live as those determined by "things above," together with the enablement necessary to live as worshippers of a holy God. That is, believers possess the present enabling power of the eschatological Spirit that makes

---

57. Dawn, *Reaching Out*, 80, rightly asserts that "the point of worship is to recognize that God alone matters."

58. Jewett, *Romans*, 724. He continues, "In response to mercy received, believers are here [i.e., Rom 12:1–2] called to respond with ethical worship involving nonconformity with the present evil age and transformation of the mind, expressing the restoration of righteousness that Christ provides." Dawn, *Reaching Out*, 106, says that "all that happens in life is our worshipful response to God and God's revelation."

59. Hay, "Paul's Understanding," 45–76 (56), underlines our connection with Christ: "For Paul all Christians are by definition persons of faith and persons who live in Christ." See also, Callan, *Dying and Rising*, 108–14.

60. Thompson, *Colossians*, 69.

worship, faithfulness, and godliness possible in a fallen world. And, the major task of the church as vanguard of the new age, "alive to God in Christ Jesus" (Rom 6:11) and walking "in newness of life" (Rom 6:4), is to live in faithfulness to Christ.[61]

Third, as we have observed, embedded in this and as a corollary to it is the fact that Christians are taken from the present world or age which is at variance with God, alienated, and condemned. "There is therefore a tension in Christian experience between the earthly and the heavenly, the present and the future." Maile points out that "the believer lives in this world while belonging to another, in this age while anticipating the age to come."[62] This is part of the reason that causes Volf to assert the following. "Worship can never be an event taking place simply between the naked soul and its God. It must always include active striving to bring the eschatological new creation to bear on this world through proclamation of the good news, nurture of the community of faith and socio-economic action . . . Fellowship with God is not possible without cooperation with God in the world."[63]

This, then, is the present context in which we are challenged to embody the gospel, to worship the Lord with our whole beings in self-sacrifice and total commitment.

Certain things follow. For instance, if our lives are determined by eschatological reality, as Paul suggests, and if we live already as citizens of a new world and age having the eschatological Spirit central to our lives and experience, then what we do in worship—both narrowly conceived and broadly considered—should anticipate what the Lord will accomplish through Jesus Christ, his Son, and what he is *already* accomplishing in and through the community of faith.[64] That is, both our moral life before God and our praise should be understood in the light of the eschatologically-charged situation. Notice how Volf brings together both aspects of worship as he argues this point.

---

61. See Cousar, *Letters of Paul*, 140–42.

62. Maile, "Heaven," 383. Ziesler, *Pauline Christianity*, 70, speaks of believers, corporately, as "A people of the future living in the present world." See also, 120–22.

63. Volf, "Worship," 207–8, 208, respectively. See Rom 6:13, 22; Phil 2:12-13; Eph 2:10; Gal 5:25.

64. See Zizioulas, *Lectures*, 135–39, where he speaks of the church as the image of the future. He says, "The Church is the image or icon of the kingdom of God . . . The Church depicts the end time in history" (136).

> As Christians worship God in adoration and action they anticipate the conditions of this world as God's new creation. Through action they anticipate a world in which Satan will no longer "deceive the nations," a world in which God will "wipe away every tear" from the eyes of God's people, a world in which peace will reign between human beings and nature. Through their adoration they anticipate the enjoyment of God in the new creation where they will communally dwell in the triune God and the triune God will dwell among them. (Rev 21–22)[65]

So the church, even in its present foretaste of eschatological reality, begins to expect, to anticipate the marvelous works of God in Christ and, according to Don Saliers, our worshipping lives in every circumstance and situation—socially, politically, and individually—become the testing place of those very expectations. Saliers suggests that as we pray together in community we are not, therefore, simply recalling the past Christ-event, but that prayer itself "bespeaks and enacts the impossible possibility of the future becoming present." He continues, "The present outpouring of the Spirit that brings all things to memory about the whole history of God's passion for the suffering, groaning creation, is a crisis in time, for the Spirit enables us to remember what has not yet come to be in history."[66]

Therefore, we must not accept Paul's thoughts on the new age or "the heavenlies" simply as abstract theological constructs in his eschatological understanding. We need to recognize, as Saliers points out here, that the eschatological presence of the Spirit is "a crisis in time," for it forces us daily to make a choice to oppose the life of one model ("this age") and to emulate the life of the other ("the age to come"); to continue in sin or to be part of a radically alternative society; to follow the dictates of this present world or to be authentic followers and disciples of Jesus Christ, to continue to put self first or to worship the living God as he deserves.

Finally, the apostle's eschatological understanding that we have briefly outlined in this chapter should alert us to the fact that we must

---

65. Ibid., 208. He continues, "When we adore God, we worship God by enjoying God's presence and by celebrating God's mighty deeds of liberation. When we are involved in the world, we worship God be announcing God's liberation, and we cooperate with God by the power of the Spirit through loving action." Saliers, *Worship as Theology*, 225, speaks of "an awakened sense of . . . *telos* (the future aims of our world) [as being] indispensible to the worship of God."

66. Ibid., 68.

not mistake membership in the heavenly state, or of the new age (in contrast to the present evil age), as merely "otherworldliness." Peter O'Brien argues that to realize the eschatological (or heavenly) nature of the church must *not* result in envisaging it without earthly dimensions. "On the contrary," he says, "throughout Ephesians [for example] it is clear that believers, both individually and corporately, have responsibilities to Christ as Lord in a whole range of earthly spheres."[67] Later, he explains, "No area of personal existence stands outside [Christ's] control; and so the life ruled from above where Christ is reigning turns out to be a life in marriage, parenthood, and everyday work."[68] Perhaps that is part of the reason for Paul's insistence that worship is looked upon in the broadest possible way embracing as it does the whole of our lives (Rom 12:1–2). In our inherent fragility and weakness we have divine enablement to *live out* our worship in and for the benefit of the present age. The church as heavenly entity meets together to worship (in its restricted aspect of praise, reading Scripture, prayer, preaching, and so on) in order to bring glory to the God who initiates that worship through the Spirit, and in order to renew its sense of identity and its call to a new way of life. Then, the goal of that worship is to give a clear vision of the reign of God, to be a missional community drawing others into the presence and grace of Jesus Christ.[69] It is interesting that Marva Dawn says that "The Christian community, to be a genuine gift to the postmodern world, must deliberately be an alternative society of trust and embodied faithfulness . . . In the Christian community, people left homeless by the postmodern ethos can find a home . . . The godless can find the true God."[70]

Similarly, Tom Wright, suggests the same, saying that "despite the misplaced enthusiasm of some, post-modernity does not give us a new home, a place to stay."[71] But the Christian community, authentically

---

67. O'Brien, "Church," 110.

68. Ibid., 118.

69. See Dawn, *Royal "Waste" of Time*, 333–44. Cousar, *Letters of Paul*, 149, is right to emphasize the communal aspect of worship: "Individuals, having listened and talked and having been nurtured in the life of the new age, have to make their own decisions, but they do so not as soloists but as members of a chorus."

70. Dawn, *Royal "Waste" of Time*, 55, 56, respectively.

71. Wright, *Paul*, 172. Mercer, "Postmodernity and Rationality," 336, says, "God, the Holy Trinity, is community, and in that community of love we find our identity in the postmodern sea of shifting images and personal fragmentation . . . If we cannot demonstrably love one another, then we might as well pack up." See also, Corney, "Have you got the right address?"

worshipping the Lord in adoration and in life *does* offer a new home. According to Paul's theology, the Christian community is Spirit-filled, it is God's redeemed humanity, a new model of what it means to be human, a community living in the power of the new age, an eschatological people utterly devoted to the worship of its gracious God.

PART TWO

Worship and Practice

9

The Trinity and Lament

Robin Parry

INTRODUCTION: LAMENTING THE LOSS OF LAMENT

When was the last time that you heard a prayer in church that reflected this?

> But I, O LORD, cry out to you; in the morning my prayer comes before you. O LORD, why do you cast me off? Why do you hide your face from me? Wretched and close to death from my youth up, I suffer terrors; I am desperate. Your wrath has swept over me; your dread assaults destroy me. They surround me like a flood all day long; from all sides they close in on me. You have caused friend and neighbor to shun me; my companions are in darkness. (Ps 88:13–18)

Or this:

> How long, O LORD? Will you forget me forever? How long will you hide your face from me? How long must I bear pain in my soul, and have sorrow in my heart all day long? How long shall my enemy be exalted over me? (Ps 13:1–2)

About a third of the Psalms in the book of Psalms are prayers of lament—both individuals lamenting and the whole community lamenting—and yet somehow many Christians feel distinctly uncomfortable with the idea of such spirituality. How could we pray to God like the Psalmist? "Rouse yourself! Why do you sleep, O Lord?" (Ps 44:23). "Why,

O LORD, do you stand far off? Why do you hide yourself in times of trouble?" (Ps 10:1).

Surely to speak to God in such ways is ungrateful and irreverent! Surely the faithful should be rejoicing in the Spirit, even in affliction, so how can grief be a Christian response? And yet there in the Bible stands this vast collection of prayers—not simply in the book of Psalms but throughout the Old Testament—that gnaw away at our fixed-grin spirituality. Something is missing in public Christian worship and that something is honesty.

Do not misunderstand me—we Christians often find these "irreverent" prayers very helpful when they are used *in private* but we would not usually wish to be heard speaking in those ways in public. And even though, if asked directly, we may say, "Of course, lament is a good thing," we still often feel rather uncomfortable about it. If we are honest we often feel somewhat ambivalent about sadness. Thus, some pastors, such as Rick Warren, have a policy of never using songs that reflect sadness.[1] Cheerful worship is compulsory.[2] My point is not that we ought to purge joy from worship. God forbid! It is simply that we need to recall that there is "a *time* to weep and a *time* to laugh, a *time* to mourn and a *time* to dance" (Eccl 3:4, emphasis added).

The loss of lament in Christian spirituality is, or so I want to suggest, a costly loss. Given that public worship plays a significant role in shaping the contours of the relationship with God of individual Christians we are possibly failing to enable each other to handle tragedy and pain

---

1. Warren, *Purpose Driven Church*, 286–87. Rick Muchow, the Pastor of Magnification at Warren's Saddleback Church explains the logic: "When pastor Rick Warren talks about [not using] songs in a minor key, he is addressing the issue of how music makes you feel. One of our principles at Saddleback is to keep the music and the message upbeat for the seeker-sensitive audience. Some songs in minor keys are very slow and dark. Not all songs in minor keys fit into that category ... It's not so much about the key of the song as how the song makes people feel, and many minor key songs make people feel sad and hopeless. It's about not using sad songs for evangelism in either a major or a minor key. As you know, pastor Rick speaks to a wide audience ... He aims to make the services a celebration of the resurrection rather than a memorial service ... Everything boils down to how the song makes you feel" (http://legacy.pastors.com/RWMT/article.asp?ID=149&ArtID=6506).

2. I appreciate that there are some real practical problems with knowing how to integrate lament into ordinary public worship—not least because on a normal day lots of people won't be feeling like lamenting. It is my plea is that we, at least, give some thought to how it might be done. Even asking the question would be a good start.

with honesty and integrity.³ The lack of prayers and songs of lament is potentially depriving Christians of a language with which to make sense of, and to express, sorrow. There is a danger of modeling only joyful prayer in communal worship—encouraging grieving people to pull themselves together and join in the joyful worship of the community when this sometimes amounts for them to little more than telling lies in musical form.

So let me deal with a couple of common Christian concerns about lament.

A Concern that Lament Is Hope-less

After the resurrection we have solid grounds for hope so how can resurrection hope exist alongside the hopelessness of lament? This is a good question, but biblical lament does *not* lack hope. As Jamie Grant observes,

> For the Christian, neither hope in Christ nor certainty of ultimate divine resolution to our problems in any way denies the human need for lament. Lament is not based on the psalmist's lack of future hope; lament is grounded in the psalmist's *present* experience of life with God in the world. Lament is intrinsic to humanity living in relationship with God in his good *but fallen* world . . . The knowledge that everything will be alright does not change the fact that, in our humanity, we need to respond before God to those present realities that are not alright.⁴

The Psalmist asks, "Why?" and "How long?" but neither of those questions need indicate a lack of hope for an ultimate salvation. After the death of his son in a climbing accident, Nicholas Wolterstorff wrote,

> Elements of the gospel which I had always thought would console did not. They did something else, something important, but not that. It did not console me to be reminded of the hope of resurrection. If I had forgotten that hope, then it would indeed have brought light into my life to be reminded of it. But I did not think of death as a bottomless pit. I did not grieve as one who has no hope. Yet Eric is gone, *here* and *now* he is gone; *now* I cannot talk with him, *now* I cannot see him, *now* I cannot hug him, *now* I cannot hear of his plans for the future. *That* is my sor-

---

3. Parry, *Worshipping Trinity*, 8–16.
4. Grant, "Psalm 44," 10–11 (original emphasis).

row. A friend said, "Remember, he's in good hands." I was deeply moved. But that reality does not put Eric back in my hands. That's my grief. For that grief, what consolation can there be other than having him back?[5]

So Christian hope for the future can co-exist with lament *precisely because* deliverance and consolation lie in the future and our present experience can be dark.

A Concern that Lament Is Irreverent

At times those praying come out and directly complain about God and this, we fear, is irreverent. But in the book of Job it was the friends, those who spoke all the theologically sound words, who God rebuked. And it was Job, the man who had spent a long time criticizing God very openly, that God said had spoken rightly about him or *to* him (the Hebrew in Job 42:7 could be translated either way). Job feared God and the fear of God is compatible with honest lament. God was saying that when Job brought his pain in prayer *he spoke rightly*. There will be times in which psalms of individual and communal lament will be the appropriate way of relating to the Lord honestly.

Whilst we may see lament as an act of unbelief this is not the case. Lament is not a severing of relationship with God but takes place precisely *within* that relationship.

> The lament is the response of one who cares enough to take the meaningless before God. This is an act of faith. To take our honest questions to God is not an act of defamation towards the character of God, but an act of affirmation. Why are there wrongs in this in-between time? Why are they so severe? How long must we endure? These are the cries within the context of faith-struggle in this in-between time. And if Christians can muster at least as much faith as the Old Testament Psalmist and Prophets, then the release of such questions finds its form in the lament.[6]

Lament gives voice to our sorrow, our pain, our grief, our anger. The sense of powerlessness and the loss of one's voice are intrinsic to many kinds of suffering and lament counters that. It gives the powerless and broken ones their speech back.

---

5. Wolterstorff, *Lament for a Son*, 31 (original emphasis).
6. Resner, "Lament," 131.

Lament, however, is not simply the voicing of sorrow but is also a prayer for salvation—a yearning for a future different from the present that rises up within the depths of our being. Lament is simultaneously sorrow, yearning, and intercession.

So lament is one important biblical mode of engaging with God when the lights go out. It is not a rejection of God but an act of clinging to God for dear life when there is nowhere else to go. However, it is my contention that a *Christian* understanding of the place and practice of lament will be enhanced once it is incorporated within a full-orbed Trinitarian theological vision of God.

LAMENT AND THE TRINITY

In Christian theology all of the Father's engagement with creation is mediated through the Son and in the Spirit. God created and sustains the world through his Word and his Spirit. When God acts in the world he does so through his Word and his Spirit. When creation responds to this God it must come to the Father, through the mediation of the Son, by the enabling of the Spirit.

One of the great insights of Trinitarian theology is that all worship and prayer is not merely a human response to God but is, in the words of a Matt Redman song, a "gifted response."[7] That is to say, the response that we make to God in worship is a response that is enabled by God.[8] This has implications for how we think about the human activity of lamenting. We should conceive of our lamentation as being offered to the Father, through and with Jesus, in the power of the Holy Spirit.

It is clear in all biblical laments that the one to whom the lament is offered is Yahweh, the God of Israel. And Yahweh, in this context, is the God and Father of our Lord Jesus Christ.[9] Lament is not merely the

---

7. Redman, "Gifted Response."
8. See Torrance, *Worship*; Parry, *Worshipping Trinity*; Ngien, *Gifted Response*.
9. I say "in *this* context" because the New Testament sometimes uses Yahweh texts to refer to the Father, sometimes to the Son and, at least once, to the Spirit. See Marshall, "Do Christians Worship?" 231–64. Marshall writes, "If Israel's God is the Trinity, and makes himself available to the world as such in the unfolding of these particular events, then we should expect the depiction of all this in the New Testament and Christian worship to use terms referring to the God of Israel in fluid ways. Sometimes they will refer to the Father, sometimes to the Son, and sometimes to the Spirit . . . But they will refer exclusively to none of the three . . . The lack of referential fixity in Christian discourse about the God of Israel teaches us, in other words, that the Father is the God

expression of pain but is first and foremost a *plea* directed towards God the Father.

The Sorrow of the Father

How is God related to our pain? An interesting place to begin thinking about *that* is the book of Jeremiah. The book is mostly given over to warnings of coming judgment from God. But how does God "feel" about the suffering that such punishment would bring? There are three passages in the book (Jer 4:19-21; 8:18—9:2; 14:17-18) when the line between Jeremiah's words and God's words blur. The prophet speaks his own sentiments but also speaks God's. Here is one such passage:

> My joy is gone; grief is upon me; my heart is sick within me. Behold the cry of the daughter of my people from the length and breadth of the land:
> "Is the LORD not in Zion? Is her King not in her?"
> Why have they provoked me to anger with their carved images and with their foreign idols?
> "The harvest is past, the summer is ended, and we are not saved."
> For the wound of the daughter of my people is my heart wounded; I mourn, and dismay has taken hold on me. Is there no balm in Gilead? Is there no physician there? Why then has the health of the daughter of my people not been restored? Oh that my head were waters, and my eyes a fountain of tears, that I might weep day and night for the slain of the daughter of my people! (Jer 8:18—9:1)

Who speaks here? Jeremiah? God? Yes.[10] I believe that God does "suffer" in his divine being, when his people suffer.[11] He is "grieved" to

---

of Israel, the Son is the God of Israel, and the Holy Spirit is the God of Israel, yet there are not three gods of Israel, but one God of Israel" (258).

10. See Fretheim, *Suffering of God*, 156-59; McConville, *Judgment and Promise*, 65-67.

11. See Fretheim, *Suffering of God*; Torrance, "Does God Suffer?" 345-68. Torrance resists the attempt to exclude suffering from God on the basis of definitions of what God *must* be like that are formed in advance of God's self-revelation. But he also resists the move towards saying that God is, in his essence, love and so if creatures suffer God *must* suffer with them. Torrance argues that God chooses to share in our suffering through a free (though not arbitrary) gracious act of love. I agree with Torrance's first move but am not convinced by his second as I have never seen the theological value in elevating the divine will over the divine nature in matters such as this. It is true that

see them in pain even if he himself has inflicted it. This is reflected in Rabbinic Jewish writing on Lamentations. *Lamentations Rabbah* pictures the following scene in heaven.

> At that moment the Holy One, blessed be he, wept, saying, "Woe is me! What have I done! I have brought my Presence to dwell below on account of the Israelites, and now that they have sinned, I have gone back to my earlier dwelling. Heaven forefend that I now become a joke to the nations and an object of ridicule among the people." . . . When the Holy One, blessed be he, saw the house of the sanctuary, he said, "This is certainly my house, and this is my resting place, and the enemies have come and done whatever they pleased with it!" At that moment the Holy One, blessed be he, wept, saying, "Woe is me for my house! O children of mine—where are you? O priests of mine—where are you? O you that love me—where are you? What shall I do for you? I warned you but you did not repent."[12]

Such is the love of the Father. However, a full-blown Christian theology must go further. Trinitarian theology would lead us to see a double movement in lament. First, there is a movement from the Father towards creation, through the Son and in the Spirit. Second, there is a movement from creation towards the Father, through the Son and in the Spirit. In Christ God moves "downwards" towards humanity and humanity moves "upwards" towards God.

Perhaps we see the downwards movement in the lamenting of Jesus over Jerusalem. As he approached and saw the city he wept over it and lamented the spiritual blindness that would lead to its inevitable destruction (Luke 19:41–44; cf. Matt 23:37–39; Luke 13:34–35). Is this not the lament of the Father expressed to his creatures through the Son, in the Spirit? Do we not see something of the "passion" of the Father here in the passion of the Son? Of course, we must beware of imagining that God is just like us and should remain reverently agnostic about what it

---

the triune God does not *need* the world in order to be love. Creation is not a *necessary* act on God's part. It is, nevertheless, a *fitting* act for the self-giving God. Once God has chosen to create, then, given that God *is* love, he will love his creation. For God not to love his creation would be for God to fail to be God—impossible! And whilst divine love for creation is not necessarily suffering love it seems to me that *if* creation suffers *then* the divine lover will experience something *analogous to* suffering love. I maintain that God *cannot* be indifferent to the suffering of his creatures.

12. *Lamentations Rabbah* XXIV.ii.1.I–2.C–D. The reference system is that of Jacob Neusner.

is like for *God* to "suffer" in his divinity. Nevertheless, we should not shy away from using the bold language of emotion which the biblical writers had no hesitations about using of God.[13]

Lamenting through the Son

But, whatever it means for God to "suffer" in sympathetic love, in Christ something radically different happens: God suffered *in the flesh*. That is to say that *the Logos was the divine subject of the human suffering of Jesus*. In Christ *God* experienced human suffering, not simply as a divine sympathizer who stands beside us but *as a human who suffers with, as, and for us*. This is beyond mere divine sympathy and places God in shocking proximity to our broken condition.

When considering lament in terms of Christ's role as the-creature-before-the-Creator—the upward movement of lament from creation to the Father, through the Son and in the Spirit—the holy of holies for our reflections must be Golgotha. At the place of the skull we find a complaint psalm on the lips of Christ—"My God, my God, why have you forsaken me?" (Ps 22:1). It is important to appreciate that this Psalm was not incidental to the crucifixion narratives but was fundamental (in Matthew, Mark and John at least) in shaping them.[14] We must also bear in mind that Mark's passion narrative alludes not merely to Psalm 22

---

13. It seems to me that *absolute* impassibility would represent an imperfection in God not a perfection. Arguably the Church Fathers did not teach *absolute* impassibility, see Gavrilyuk, *Suffering of the Impassible God*. See, also, Scrutton, "Emotion in Augustine," 169–77. The primary concern of the Fathers was to maintain that God was not subject to *irrational* and *sinful* passions and, also, to defend *divine transcendence* against those who presume that God's love or anger, say, are simply a magnified version of what humans experience. One can make such theologically protective moves without resorting to the extreme and unbiblical stance of *absolute* impassibility.

14. This is evidenced by the fact that there are numerous allusions to Psalm 22 in the passion narratives and not merely the quotation of 22:1 found on Jesus' lips. The use of this psalm in the early church for interpreting the story of Jesus is also testified to by the linking of the praise section in Heb 2:12 (Ps 22:22) to the solidarity in which the human Christ stands with us. (On the significance of Heb 2:12 for a Trinitarian theology of worship see Man, *Proclamation and Praise*.) Heb 5:7 also seems to have Ps 22:1–2 and 24 in mind when the author writes, "During the days of Jesus' life on earth, he offered up prayers and petitions with loud cries and tears to the one who could save him from death, and he was heard because of his reverent submission." If Psalm 22:24 is in mind here then this would directly link the praise section at the end of the Psalm with the resurrection—a very natural hermeneutical move for those who have made the connection between the suffering of the psalmist and the suffering of Christ.

but to various other lament psalms.[15] Richard Bauckham explores the implications of this:

> Through allusions to other psalms of lament Mark places Jesus' dying words in the context not only of Psalm 22 as a whole but also of the psalms of lament in general, of which there are about forty in the Psalter. It is not merely that Psalm 22 was read by Mark and other early Christians as a messianic psalm that prophesied the sufferings and subsequent vindication of the Messiah, though this doubtless was the case. It is also that, in relating the passion and death of Jesus to the psalms of lament in general, Mark relates the passion and death of Jesus to the situation of all who wrote and used those psalms, those who cried out to God from the desperate situations those psalms describe. Since these psalms were in constant use, Mark could not have regarded them as *exclusively* messianic, i.e., as referring to experience unique to the Messiah. On the contrary, a messianic reading of them would have to be *inclusively* messianic, i.e., referring to the way in which the experience of the Messiah gathers up into itself the experiences of all whose sufferings find expression in those psalms.[16]

In his Messianic role Jesus partakes in the covenant curses that a disobedient Israel has brought upon itself. Compare the exilic sufferings of Daughter Zion (a personification of Jerusalem) in Lamentations 1 with those of Christ. Jesus' suffering runs in parallel to Jerusalem's in numerous ways as he plays out his role as her representative. Like Jerusalem tears were upon his cheeks as he prayed alone in the garden (Lam 1:2a). Like Jerusalem he knew betrayal by his "friends" who left him to suffer alone (Lam 1:2b). Like Jerusalem Jesus was beaten, stripped naked, publicly humiliated, and afflicted (Lam 1:8–10). Like Jerusalem he was reduced from a high and noble status to dust (Lam 1:1, 7). Like Jerusalem he bore the divine curse for covenant disobedience (Lam 1:3, 5; Gal 3:13). Like Jerusalem he was violently attacked by a pagan occupying force (Lam 1:10, 15). Like Jerusalem he felt abandoned by Yahweh in the face of these pagan military oppressors (Lam 1:9b, 11b, 20). Like Jerusalem he was mocked and despised by those who looked

---

15. Bauckham, "God's Self-Identification," 255, lists the following allusions to lament psalms: Mark 14:18/Ps 41:10; Mark 14:34/Pss 42:5, 11; 43:5; Mark 14:55/Ps 37:32(?); Mark 14:57/Pss 27:12; 35:11; 69:4; Mark 15:24/Ps 22:18; Mark 15:29/Ps 22:7; Mark 15:30–31/Ps 22:8(?); Mark 15:32/Pss 22:6; 69:9; Mark 15:34/Ps 22:1; Mark 15:36/Ps 69:21; Mark 15:40/Ps 38:11.

16. Bauckham, "God's Self-Identification," 256 (original emphasis).

on at his destruction (Lam 1:7d, 21). The suffering Christ embodies the sufferings of his city and his people depicted in the moving lament of Lamentations 1.

We should note that Jesus' experience of alienation from God was not simply an inner feeling of despair but the *concrete reality* of suffering injustice, betrayal, torture, and defeat at the hands of those who worship false gods. "It is somewhat misleading to say—of the psalmist or of Jesus echoing his words—that he *feels* forsaken by God as though this were an understandable mistake. What Jesus experiences is the concrete fact that he has been left to suffer and die. God has, in this sense, abandoned him, not merely in psychological experience but in the form of the concrete situation that Jesus experiences."[17]

And he yells out to Yahweh from the depths of his being. Christ lamenting in our place![18] Here *our* alienation from God is taken up within the very humanity of God himself. This is God "abandoned" by God; our human experience of God-forsakenness relocated within the being of God.

> The ["division"] in God [at the cross] must contain the whole uproar of history within itself. Men must be able to recognize rejection, the curse and final nothingness in it. The cross stands between the Father and the Son in all the harshness of its forsakenness. If one describes the life of God within the Trinity as the "history of God" (Hegel), this history of God contains within itself the whole abyss of godforsakenness, absolute death and the non-God ... All human history, however much it may be determined by guilt and death, is taken up into this "history of God," i.e. into the Trinity ... There is no suffering which in this history of God is not God's suffering; no death which has not been God's death in the history of Golgotha.[19]

God does not simply suffer in sympathy with us—*in Christ* God the Son suffers in our place *as one of us*. God knows what it is like to be a powerless human victim.

Returning to Jesus' use of Psalm 22, we need to note the "contradiction" between Psalm 22:1–2 (ET) and 22:24 (ET)

---

17. Bauckham, "God's Self-Identification," 257.

18. On Christ's representative and vicarious ministry see Torrance, "Christ in our Place" and "Prayer and the Priesthood of Christ." See also Torrance, *Incarnation*.

19. Moltmann, *Crucified God*, 245, (emphasis added).

> My God, my God, why have you forsaken me? Why are you so far from saving me, so far from the words of my groaning? O my God, I cry out by day, but you do not answer, by night, and am not silent. (22:1–2)

> For he has not despised or disdained the suffering of the afflicted one; he has not hidden his face from him but has listened to his cry for help. (22:24)

This suggests that the Psalmist's perception of the situation has changed. He is in terrible suffering having been abandoned by God (22:1–8, 12–18). He calls to Yahweh for salvation (22:9–11, 19–21) and *then*, perhaps after receiving some salvation oracle from the priest, takes on an attitude of confidence that God has heard him and will deliver him (22:22–31). The same pattern is seen in the story of Jesus on the cross. Mark 15:25 sees Jesus on the cross from the third hour (about 9AM). From the sixth hours (12PM) until the ninth hour (3PM) an ominous darkness descends over the land (Mark 15:33; Matt 27:45; Luke 23:44). During this period of six hours Jesus has been experiencing the suffering of the righteous individual in the Psalms. At about 3PM Jesus cried out in a loud voice, "My God, my God! Why have you forsaken me?" When groping around for words to express the feelings of grief at his "abandonment" by the God whom he had worshipped from birth it is no surprise that these words came to mind. Jesus was saturated in the scriptures of Israel and cannot have missed the parallels between his predicament and that of the psalmist.

It is interesting that the cry of dereliction comes not long before Jesus dies. This is not a period of doubt he went through near the beginning of his time on the cross and quickly got over. This was a simmering, growing grief held back in dignified silence until he can hold in no longer. For Matthew and Mark it is the last thing they record Jesus saying before his crying out in a loud voice and dying.

Luke and John record more positive last words ("Father, into your hands I commit my spirit," Luke 23:46; "It is finished," John 19:30). Whilst we need to respect the different emphases of the different gospels it is perfectly possible to imagine Jesus drawing hope and inspiration in the midst of his despair from the ultimate deliverance experienced by the psalmist with whom he has so identified himself. But even if we use Psalm 22 to hold together the dark words of Jesus recorded in Matthew and Mark with the positive, final words in Luke and John we must emphasize that (a) the darkness of his suffering expressed in the cry of dereliction was not a momentary doubt but a growing and prolonged anguish, (b) the darkness experienced was not some Scripture-quoting ritual done for show but a genuine expression of how Jesus felt,[20] (c) Jesus was not *abandoning* God in this prayer (for the psalmist, as for Jesus, God is still "*my* God," the one to whom they turn for deliverance. This is grief expressed *within* a covenant relationship with God) and (d) that the positive change in Jesus' final moments may well have been influenced by the end of Psalm 22.[21]

Now where does this story place the Christian vis-à-vis the laments of Israel? Jesus himself takes the prayer tradition of complaint against Yahweh upon his own lips.[22] Jesus prays the lament *as his own prayer*. He stood as Israel's Messianic representative suffering *and lamenting* with his people Israel. He stood as the Adamic representative of the whole of humanity suffering *and lamenting* with those broken upon the wheel of life. This must, for the Christian, legitimate Israel's worship tradition of lament.

But the situation is more complex for the Christian than this might suggest. On the following Sunday Jesus was raised from the dead and at that point the praise section at the end of Psalm 22 was more fitting for the situation. Lament is appropriate on the cross but not by the empty tomb. So where do Christians stand now in relation to the cross and its cry of dereliction and the resurrection with its song of joy? Is lament appropriate this side of Easter?

Matthew Boulton has helpfully suggested a way of linking Jesus' use of Psalm 22 to the inaugurated eschatology of the New Testament. He maintains that in Psalm 22 there is a negation of the God of glory but a clinging to God's promise of salvation. In Boulton's view the Psalm does not end with salvation but with a vow to praise in light of the *promise of a future salvation*. The vow to praise is "an eschatological form of speech, a present trace of a future event, a foretaste, both present and absent,

---

20. As already noted Jesus' forsakenness was *more than* a psychological experience on his part but it was not *less than* one.

21. But we must note that the coming resurrection does not obliterate the darkness of the cross. In fact, it serves to highlight the depth of that darkness. On this see Lewis, *Between Cross & Resurrection*.

22. The lament Psalm 69 was also seen as speaking in the voice of Jesus (see Rom 15:3; John 2:17).

'already' and 'not yet' in play."[23] Jesus' use of the psalm, liturgically commemorated in Holy Week, has implications for the pattern of Christian worship itself.

> Jesus' citation of Psalm 22 fashion's Easter's "hallelujah"—and with it all proper Christian praise—into an eschatological act, a gesture at once indicating decisive divine victory ("He is risen!") and the ongoing facts of crisis and suffering, which is to say, the fact that divine victory if nonetheless forthcoming, nonetheless "not yet." . . . Christian praise is properly eschatological praise, jubilant insofar as it witnesses to divine victory and deliverance, anguished insofar as it witnesses to creation's ongoing need of the same.[24]

Lament serves as a complaint against God but also as a turning towards and clinging to the divine promise thus reconfiguring praise as an "impossible" revival of hope in the midst of darkness. "Christian doxology is properly offered by way of cruciform lament, continually reworked into Easter's "hallelujah" by way of human anguish and indignation, which is to say, continually reworked into eschatological praise by way of unabashed Christian lamentation."[25]

In a similar way, Barth suggestively claims that the act of hope in Christ is a "comforted despair," something that stands in contrast to non-Christian forms of optimism and pessimism.[26]

But, I suggest, Christ does not simply mediate our lament in his suffering upon the cross. As the book of Hebrews explains, Jesus stands now as our High Priest, as man-for-God in the presence of the Father. In this priestly role he intercedes for us as our representative. He fulfils this role as one who understands our pain and sorrows—our brother made like us in every way. It seems to me theologically plausible to suggest that Christ's ongoing prayers to his Father include laments and as such he can mediate our own laments to the Father. In this way we know that God hears our cries *because we know that he hears Jesus' cries.*

But I spoke of the lament in the Trinity so what of the Spirit?

---

23. Boulton, "Forsaking God," 70.
24. Ibid., 74–75.
25. Ibid., 78.
26. Barth, *CD*, IV.1, 633, 636. See McDowell, "Mend Your Speech a Little."

Lament in the Spirit

Romans 8:18–30 helps us to get some insight into the Spirit and a certain mode of lament. I offer the two diagrams reproduced at the end of this chapter as a way to clarify the logic of the text. Paul draws a parallel between Jesus' suffering, the suffering of Christians, and the suffering of the whole created order (Rom 8:17–25). Indeed, Paul's underlying theology is one which sees an intimate relationship between humanity, Israel, Christ, and the Church. Israel represents all humanity before God—it is a microcosm of humanity. Jesus, as the Messiah of Israel, represents the whole people of Israel—he is Israel in microcosm. In Romans 8 Paul's focus is on Christ, Church, and Creation. I only mention humanity as a whole and Israel in particular because it helps us begin to imagine how Paul's teaching might begin to have wider implications than those he brings out in this context.

First of all notice that the story of Christ, the Church, and Creation run in parallel—suffering then glory, death then life. Jesus was crucified, died, was buried, and *then* was raised from the dead by God through the Spirit (Rom 8:11). Paul is saying that the story of believers will be like Christ's. Currently we are in our mortal bodies and we suffer with Jesus. We shall die. But then we shall be raised by God through the same Spirit that he raised Christ. Paul speaks of this future as one in which the very glory of God himself is revealed in us. It is a resurrection to immortality; it is our adoption as sons—that is, children and heirs of God.

In the same way the story of the whole created order is one of frustration and slavery to death and decay followed by liberation and participating in the freedom of the children of God.[27] In other words, when God resurrects his people he will then resurrect the whole creation. And Paul pictures both the creation and the Church (and, by implication, Jesus himself on the cross) as currently "groaning." We'll come back to that.

So the story of the church and of creation is darkness now but light to come—a story *already* played out in the life of Jesus. So Paul can write that "our present sufferings are not worth comparing with the glory that will be revealed in us" (Rom 8:18). And Paul knew some serious sufferings and times of real despair (2 Cor 1:8–9; 11). It is *this* man who says that "our present sufferings are not worth comparing with the glory that

---

27. For contemporary theological reflections on this theme in light of Darwinism and ecological concerns see Southgate, *Groaning of Creation*.

will be revealed in us." That future is what enabled him to face the present darkness. Paul, who, for the joy set before him, endured the shame and suffering. But we need to see that for Paul this eager expectation of God's new days existed alongside the present experience of grief and sorrow. This is where the groaning comes in. The groaning is three things at once.

First, it is an expression of sorrow, pain, and frustration at the current state of affairs. In this respect it is something like a lament. It is like moan from the depths of our being—a painful awareness that all is not as it should be. Second, it is simultaneously a groan of expectation for a better future. Paul describes it as "groaning as in the pains of childbirth"—notice how that image blends pain with an expectation of, and longing for, new life. He speaks of us "groaning eagerly as we wait eagerly for our adoption as sons" (cf. 2 Cor 5:2–4).

The idea of lament as an expression of grief and expectation is well put by Nicholas Wolterstorff in his comments on Matthew 5:4—"Blessed are those who mourn, for they will be comforted." Who are the mourners? "The Mourners are those who have caught a glimpse of God's new day, who ache with all their being for that day's coming, and who break out into tears when confronted by its absence . . . The mourners are aching visionaries."[28]

Aching visionaries who simply refuse to accept the current state of affairs. Here we also glimpse something of the way in which the Spirit moves the people of God into action, even rage, *against* injustice and *for* love in his gathering up of the people of God into the responsive and creative action of lament. It is what John Swinton refers to as "raging with compassion."[29]

Third, it is intercession. We have already spoken of how the Old Testament laments serve as expressions of sorrow and also as prayers for salvation. Well, this deep primal moaning of which Paul speaks is also an expression of grief and simultaneously a prayer to God for new creation. It is at this point that Paul introduces the Holy Spirit. The Spirit himself groans. In sorrow for the present darkness? Yes. In hope for a better future? Yes. But, most critically, in intercession for that new future. The Holy Spirit is praying for the Church. The Holy Spirit knows the Father's

---

28. Wolterstorff, *Lament for a Son*, 85–86.

29. Swinton, *Raging with Compassion*. My thanks to Jason Goroncy for this observation on the active role of Spirit-inspired lament against injustice.

will and purposes fully. We do not. So when the Spirit prays for us he is praying in perfect accord with God's cosmic purposes—his ultimate purposes for the whole created order.

Earlier we reflected christologically on the sufferings of Jerusalem in Lamentations 1. I would now like to reflect on them pneumatologically. In the light of Romans 8 I suggest that the Spirit of God participates in Jerusalem's sorrows. The Spirit groans with all those who groan as they yearn for liberation. Jerusalem groans at her humiliation and turns away her face from onlookers (Lam 1:8c), just as her priests groan at the cessation of temple festivals (1:4b) and her people groan as they search for food (1:11a). This groaning in Lamentations 1 looks back (mourning what is lost), looks around (expressing despair at the current situation) and looks forward (yearning for a reversal of the calamity). So also the Spirit, participating in the groaning of creation, groans as he looks back and looks around seeing a shattered world but he also groans like a woman in childbirth looking forward, bringing to birth a new creation. The Spirit's groaning, whilst a participation in creation's groaning, also transforms it. It is a hope-infused groaning that looks to the future with confidence. The Spirit can enable our groaning to become participation in his groaning and in Christ's groaning. That is to say, Spirit-transformed groaning is still an expression of pain at the current situation but it is not an expression of hopelessness.

So the Spirit is groaning with and for us as he seeks to bring us through to resurrection. The Spirit is praying creation into glory. And here is the amazing thing—the Spirit does not simply pray for us—he prays for us *through us*. He makes our own groaning a vehicle for his groaning. And that's good because so often we don't know what we should pray for or how we should pray for it. But the Spirit does and he helps us in our weakness.

How? Many people have struggled to know what phenomena Paul refers to here. Nowhere else does he speak of the Spirit praying in groans. Is this some odd phenomena not mentioned elsewhere? Or is it tongues? Or is it something else? I suggest that we not try to pin it down too tightly as I think it can manifest itself in a range of ways. Sometimes speaking in tongues is a manifestation of the Spirit praying in groans too deep for words through us. Now, this is an unusual and fascinating perspective on tongues. Charismatics usually think of it as a language of joyful praise but why can't it sometimes be the language of lament; speaking in tongues as lamenting in the Spirit? Perhaps Romans 8 surprisingly presents the charismatic gift of glossolalia

> as deep and agonizing groans of human weakness that are changed by the Spirit of God into a cry for redemption, and even a foretaste of this redemption in the here-and-now . . . Rather than tongues being a sign of an escape from this world into heights of glory, they are expressions of strength in weakness, or the capacity to experience the first-fruits of the kingdom-to-come in the midst of our groaning with the suffering creation. They bring to ultimate expression the struggle that is essential to all prayer, namely, trying to put into words what is deeper than words. They express the pain and the joy of this struggle. They are, in the words of Russell Spittler, a "broken language for a broken body until perfection comes."[30]

Finding a language for pain is one of the needs for those afflicted. Here is a pneumatic gift of lament that can play a role parallel to more conventional modes of lament.

Sometimes, I think the Spirit's groaning can manifest itself in a deep primal scream that rises up from the depths of our being. Sometimes the Spirit can pray through us in simple tears. The old spiritual masters used to speak of the "gift of tears"—something one rarely hears of these days. Consider this sentiment from one of the speakers in Lamentations 3.

> My eyes flow with rivers of tears
>   because of the destruction of the daughter of my people.
> My eyes will flow without ceasing,
>   without respite,
> until the LORD from heaven looks down
>   and sees;
> My eyes cause me grief
>   at the fate of all the daughters of my city.
> (Lam 3:48–51, trans. mine)

Also, whilst this is not Paul's main focus, I think that the Spirit can inspire and pray through our conventional laments spoken in normal human languages—"My God, my God, why have you forsaken me?" We are to pray in the Spirit at all times and praying in the Spirit is far

---

30. Macchia, "Groans Too Deep for Words." Macchia, "Sighs Too Deep for Words," 47–73.

more than simply speaking in tongues. Praying in the Spirit is *all* Spirit-inspired prayer *whatever form* it takes.

CONCLUSION

All this puts lament in a whole new light. The Holy Spirit enables us to participate in Christ's lament to the Father. This lament is not the voice of faithless, hopeless, rebels who have given up on God and blaspheme him to his face. It is not the morbid moaning of miserable and weak Christians who need to pull themselves together. It can be a faithful, Spirit-inspired way of engaging with our covenant Lord and in his own feelings towards the world. It allows us to engage God honestly. It enables us to express our pain and to find a voice when we feel weak and powerless. It embodies an aching and a yearning for a different future and a refusal to accept things as they are. It is prayer that God's kingdom comes and his will be done *on earth* as it is in heaven. Perhaps Jesus was right after all—"Blessed are those who mourn for they shall be comforted." God says, "Yes" to those who mourn; "Yes" to those with the courage to admit that things are not alright; "Yes" to those who have given up pretending that they know why God has allowed disaster to fall; "Yes" to the weak and smashed; "Yes" to those who sing a broken hallelujah; "Yes" to those raging with compassion; and "Yes" to the aching visionaries, for they shall see God.

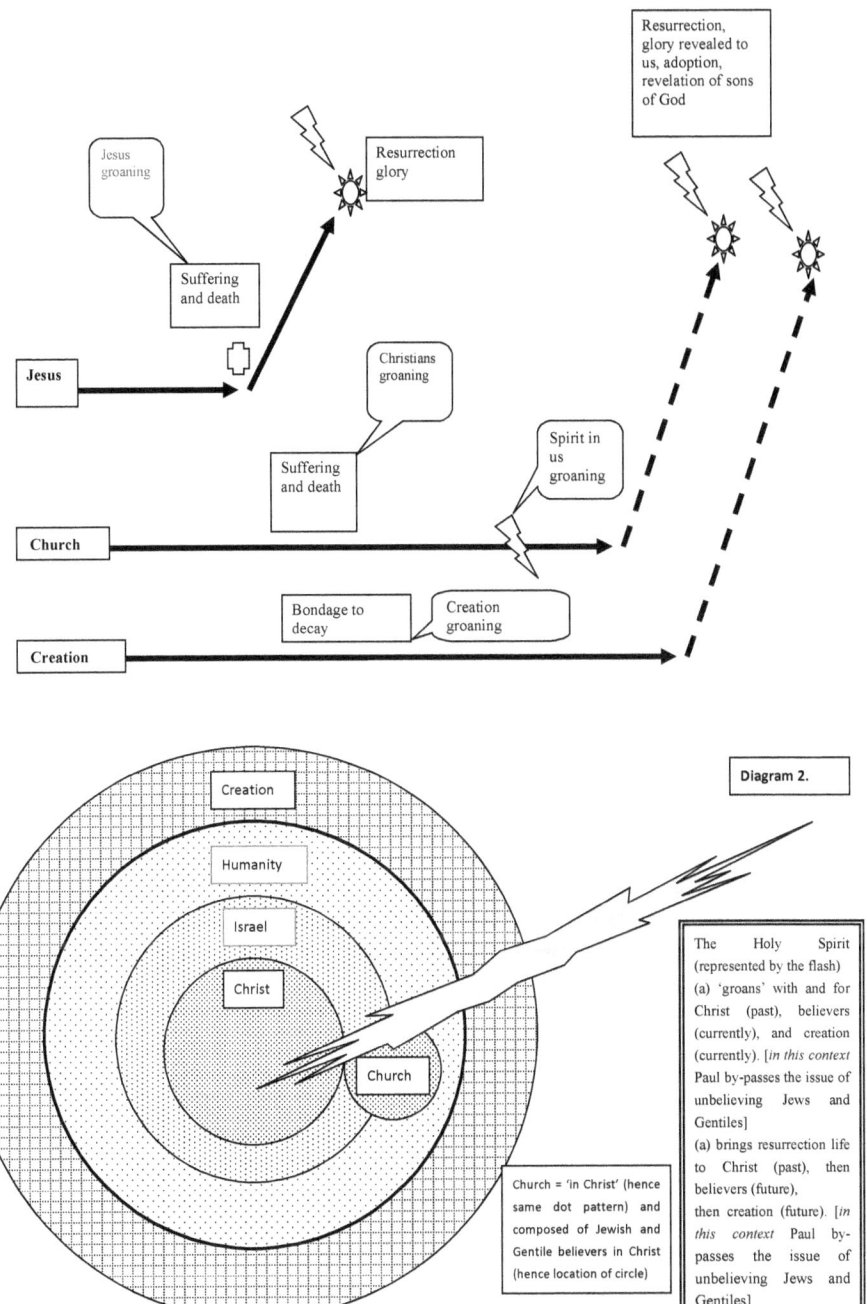

Diagram 2.

10

Art for God or to God through Art?

Angela McCarthy

> Images open the heart and awake the intellect, and, in a marvelous and indescribable manner, engage us to imitate the persons they represent. —*St. John Damascenus*[1]

INTRODUCTION

CHRISTIAN ART HAS BEEN an integral part of faith and worship for almost two millennia. Is that because the human need to express mystery is captured most fully through our creative processes, or is it because the presence of God within us can surface into the conscious realm most effectively through the creation of beauty? While this might be an impossible question to answer, it also could be the vehicle for examining an understanding of the importance of the connection between God and all that is beautiful. Friedhelm Mennekes says that "Art demonstrates spiritual facts such as peace, depth, intensity, and so on. Thus art lends form, colour, tension, and proportion to the invisible. It harnesses awe and leads dawning comprehension to active creativity."[2] Through such creative activity Christians have made visible the reality of God who became incarnate.

Christians are "people of the book" because of the profound degree of sacredness of the Scriptures and the depth of understanding of Christ

---

1. Quoted by Didron, *Christian Iconography*, 3.
2. Mennekes, "Interconnection," 27.

as Logos, the Word of God. However, throughout our history the expression of these texts through visual art has led us to a greater depth of understanding of our image of God.

The richness of Christian art lies in the narratives expressed through visual images but the symbolic language of such images has largely been lost to people of the twenty-first century. Our ability to "read" artworks of previous eras has been eroded and so the capacity of art to draw us to the sacred has been diminished. Even our ability to "read" contemporary works of art is limited if the symbolic language is not understood. So often people will say, "I know what I like" but will be unable to access works of art because of the absence of the symbolic language that is required. Is it also apparent that to approach the sacred through visual art, to develop our connection and understanding of God through creative processes, has become limited by our almost exclusive use of the spoken and written word in our worship practices?

Our current media-focused culture is highly visual with many images used to attract and disturb the viewer so the visual imagery always demands newness. Current forms of street and consumer art in Australia have changed the audience and perception of art in that those who now patronize art are no longer the ecclesial power figures as in the past, but rather, those who are much more closely involved with everyday living and the economic and political processes that determine present realities.

Reading religious art, particularly from different eras, requires a specific visual language which is not always utilized in modern images. Why should we bother? What will the inclusion of art works contribute to our sense of the sacred? Will we find God in art, or will our artistic expression draw us toward God? This chapter examines the importance of art in religious activities, the tradition of icons, and how our communities can be drawn into the dance of faith as we re-educate ourselves and re-enliven our capacity to respond in faith to art works that will open us to an encounter with the divine.

CHRISTIAN ART

We can see "beauty as revelation, and art as the human mediation that both enables and limits its revelatory power."[3] In Pope John Paul II's letter to artists he refers to the artist as the image of God the Creator.

> None can sense more deeply than you artists, ingenious creators of beauty that you are, something of the pathos with which God at the dawn of creation looked upon the work of his hands. A glimmer of that feeling has shone so often in your eyes when—like the artists of every age—captivated by the hidden power of sounds and words, colours and shapes, you have admired the work of your inspiration, sensing in it some echo of the mystery of creation with which God, the sole creator of all things, has wished in some way to associate you.[4]

Artists themselves engage in the creative process of God in bringing to fruition responses that can only be evoked through the senses. In the ninth century, following the end of iconoclasm, Photios emphasized in one of his sermons that seeing the imagery of Christ makes it easier to accept the truth of his incarnation in the flesh than merely reading the Gospel accounts.

> Christ came to us in the flesh and was carried in the arms of his mother. This is seen and confirmed and proclaimed in pictures, the story is made clear by means of our personal eyewitness and viewers unhesitatingly accept this truth.[5]

Over the centuries Christian art has developed from images adapted from the Greco-Roman culture around the Christian communities, through extraordinary eras of development in theology and technical expression (where the Christian aspects were culturally dominant), to a point in Australian culture where religious art is almost a cultural sideline. Ancient civilizations such as Egypt and Mesopotamia give us rich examples of how they developed an understanding of the divine/human connection and expressed it in artistic forms making the invisible, visible. Christian art, however, comes from a profound shift in the understanding of the presence of God in the world. God became present in the flesh of Jesus Christ, God was no longer invisible. "Jesus of Nazareth

---

3. Viladesau, *Theology and the Arts*, 5.
4. Pope John Paul II, *Letter*.
5. Cormack, *Icons*, 47.

provided a face that one could see, describe, picture, a voice that emerged from an identifiable face."[6] The Christian encounter with Jesus Christ, "God-with-us," is a profoundly personal, and yet, communal experience. "Perhaps today, these same walls cry out to us in vain because of our "poverty," our distancing ourselves from the colour, joy and communion. In our own time, we run the risk of losing the power of communications that can be found in and through images."[7] Religious art in Australia was almost non-existent until the second half of the twentieth century. "The main reason appears to be that we inherited a vacuum from the old world where art had lost its identity when it lost its connection with the things of the spirit."[8] Through most of the history of Christianity, art has been closely woven with the work of the Church in combining the Word with visual artistic expression, "but when the limit of realism had been reached after the end of the seventeenth century, it seemed that all that needed to be said had already been said, and an age of repetition began."[9] In nineteenth century Europe, a period of imitation of the "glories of Romanesque, Gothic and Baroque" was prevalent and this absence of anything new also flowed into the Australian experience.[10] The churches built in Australia were mostly in the style of English Gothic revival. The social reality of Australian congregations was that they were scattered, poor (particularly in the Irish Catholic communities) and therefore unable to commission works of art for the glory of God. Where the Protestant communities avoided visual arts, other than stained glass windows and sculptured lecterns and other objects, the Catholic community was prey to "sentimental realism."[11] Plaster statues abounded and where art had once been the work of artists' hands for God, now they were untouched by human hand. Plastic images, even luminescent, and unimaginably poor, sentimental images filled the need and distracted the faithful.

---

6. Moloney, *Life of Jesus in Icons*, 11.
7. Ibid., 15.
8. Knoor and Knoor, *Religious Art*, 3.
9. Ibid., 3.
10. Ibid.
11. Ibid., 4.

THE CONTEMPORARY EXPERIENCE

Following two world wars and a depression a new language of art was needed to "meet the needs of the spirit in a time of great disturbance. The climate was at last right for resurgence."[12] The Blake Prize was established in Australia in 1951 to offer a platform to encourage art works that were "capable of giving inspiration."[13] While the Blake Prize has not increased the number of liturgically useful paintings, it has encouraged religious art. More recent criticisms of the Prize, however, echo the development of art that is closely allied to social change. Australia is now an intensely pluralistic and secular society. The decision to recognize atheism as a religious construct suffered much criticism and the Christian tag for the Blake Prize is no longer appropriate as other religious groups are represented. "Art works don't only operate within the setting of the gallery, museum, or private home—they also resonate in the big world of ideas and social change and the tacky, sticky worlds of the politics of perception that surrounds debates about refugees, Indigenous Australia or terrorism."[14] The latest Prize (2007) was won by Shirley Purdie, an indigenous artist from Warmun in the East Kimberley, for her *Stations of the Cross*. This ancient Christian theme was set in the landscape of the Bungle Bungle Ranges and it is "a strong visual exploration of a story of passion and suffering that also echoes her communal history and identity.... This unsettling content and form of expression stands in contrast to the often-cheerful reception of Indigenous art that thrives on a decorative spirituality feeding Western hunger for meaning."[15] Purdie's work is local, relevant, and evocative, and expresses something about the last journey of Jesus that resonates with the suffering of her people so it tells us something of who we are and something of our God in a very particular linking of time and place. The Stations of the Cross is a form of worship that dates from the Middle Ages where different aspects of the Passion and Death of Jesus are relived in prayer and meditation. Purdie's work invites worship that links the past and the present, the political and the religious. Art is capable of making these links and expressing meaning that cannot be accessed by text alone.

12. Ibid., 5.
13. Ibid.
14. Pattenden, *What's Art Got to Do with It?*
15. Ibid.

Balan insists that in a unique way art maintains "the image, the idea, and the real." He continues, "It maintains the symbolic. In recent years it has been popular for artists to sever the relationship, rendering the language mute. But humanity needs art only so long as it preserves this relationship. In so doing, art reflects what makes us distinctly human—creations (image) with souls (idea) made in the image of God (reality). And so art continues to be a means of conveying clues in our search for meaning."[16] Instead of using art to assist us in finding meaning and therefore finding God in our reality, post-industrialization has removed the artist from the production of religious artifacts to the point that "mass produced reproductions of Christ have primarily served to devalue the objects and mute their significance."[17] Balan also attests to a further result of this reduction in the creator's touch in that it eliminates the historical progression of the artistic development of Christian imagery which has been in action for two thousand years and it also takes away the artists' action in service to God.[18] This particular direction in Christian imagery is difficult to counteract as the Christian consumer is presented with mass-produced religious, pious goods for purchase.

Contemporary directions were explored by Rosemary Crumlin in mounting the exhibition *Beyond Belief: Modern Art and the Religious Imagination* in the National Art Gallery in Melbourne in 1998. The exhibition involved twentieth century religious art from various countries that explored religious works in a non-linear way. At the beginning of the century, the iconography of religion and spirituality was usually Judaeo-Christian, narrative, and figurative. By the close of the century, the interest is not so much narrative and scriptural as diffusely spiritual, questioning, and focused less on a life after death than on a spirit that swells within the body, the earthy, and—more rarely—society. Such changes can be clearly identified by looking at the shifts in the iconography of the works.[19]

The diversity of images within this collection showed that contemporary artists are seeking to engage with religious themes in a different way. The artists represented in the exhibition were searching for "faithfulness, integrity, and some sort of inner life that does not entail

16. Balan, *Pursuing the Sacred in Art*, http://dappledthings.org/adv06/essayart01.php.
17. Ibid.
18. Ibid.
19. Crumlin, *Beyond Belief*, 9–10.

commitment to ritual or permanence or religion."[20] In a sense the art itself became a symbol, a vessel for sharing what is sacred in a broader sense and tied to social themes and experiences. This mirrors the social aspects of religious practice in contemporary Australian culture where commitment to religious practice is lessening but the desire for spiritual sustenance is evident. Religion has been moved to the sidelines of society and has "become a private matter for individuals to decide whether and to what degree they should be involved."[21]

While our current culture struggles to express what is sacred using the visual language of times past and moves towards forming a new language that can express our deepest meanings, we are left with a need to understand the place of art in our religious practice and what it can offer our communities in worship and personal spiritual development.

DO WE NEED ART?

The question then arises, do we need art? If we base our decision on the hierarchy of human needs then the answer has to be "No," but it is "precisely the unnecessary which makes us human" because "the aesthetic perspective is one that is concerned with human experience at its deepest and widest."[22] Eisner declares that we, as humans, "give simultaneously both a personal and a cultural imprint to what we experience; the relation between the two is inextricable."[23] Our cultural nature is not limited to those things that are new around us. Our cultural nature is truly derived from what has gone before so understanding the richness of our path to the present is critical to the understanding of current experiences of reality.

The mind with which we perceive reality can be described as an "organ of the mind."[24] We experience life, our lived reality and therefore God, with our whole embodied person which is dependent on our senses to bring what we experience to consciousness. What we perceive using our physical senses is filtered personally and culturally as it is processed by our intelligence to bring understanding. What we perceive with our

---

20. Ibid., 11.
21. Bouma, *Australian Soul*, 129.
22. Durker and Smith, "Is Art Necessary?" 27–32.
23. Eisner, *Arts and the Creation of Mind*, 1.
24. Langer, *Philosophy*, 84.

senses is "just as capable of *articulation*, i.e. of complex combination, as words. But the laws that govern this sort of articulation are altogether different from the laws of syntax that govern language. The most radical difference is that *visual forms are not discursive.*"[25] This brings us to the need to have our experience of God not only defined in discursive language but also in visual language. Our experience of God, and our image of God, is greatly enriched by the use of visual language as well as by the texts and spoken words that we use in such a variety of ways.

Early Christians were conscious of the understanding that Jesus of Nazareth was indeed the Son of God. Over the first two centuries of Christianity this doctrine developed and was clearly enunciated at the Council of Nicaea (325 CE) and further confirmed through the Council of Chalcedon (451 CE).[26] Jesus of Nazareth was truly the Son of God so now there was the experience of a physical presence of God on earth. Christians wanted to know what he looked like and so early Christian art provides details from this period. There was no tradition of portraiture of Jesus as there was with other great figures of Antiquity such as Socrates, so the images of Jesus came from "pure projections in the psychological sense; that is, inventions corresponding to what people needed or wanted from him. The enormous variability of images of Christ is one of the immediate consequences of this."[27] An exceptionally important aspect of this development is the recognition that images are not static and they are not neutral. Texts can always be analyzed in a discursive manner but visual art does not behave in the same manner. "Images not only express convictions, they alter feelings and end up justifying convictions."[28] For example, following the adoption of the Christian faith as the official faith of the Roman Empire in the fourth century, the image of Jesus was more commonly seen as a ruler of an empire, as the Pantocrator, dressed in imperial purple in contrast to his image as the Good Shepherd painted on the walls of the catacombs.[29] Our cultural expression of images of Jesus should link us to this history but also express something of the meaning we seek in our own time and place. The most consistent form

---

25. Ibid., 86.
26. McGrath, *Historical Theology*, 33.
27. Mathews, *Clash of the Gods*, 11.
28. Ibid.
29. Kelly, *World of the Early Christians*, 137.

of Christian art has been the icon which culturally was developed in the Eastern Christian communities.

ICONS

The word "icon" comes from the ancient Greek word "*eikon*" which means "likeness, image, representation."[30] This could refer to living images, mirror images, and imaginary forms of images—visions. Today, the term can mean a small symbol on a computer screen, or someone to be greatly admired in the public sphere of life. In the religious sense though, it refers to a religious image that is sacred, particularly in the Eastern Orthodox Christian tradition. Since they present profound theological understandings through symbolic language, it is usual to refer to them as having been written, rather than painted. They are either written onto wooden panels or onto church walls but can also be mosaic or carved from ivory or made with precious metals. The subject matter is usually Christ, the Virgin Mary, angels, apostles, other saints, or scenes depicting the story of their lives.[31] These details are not the most important characteristics. Their religious and spiritual function is of far greater importance. "The pictorial representation is transformed into a holy icon by two elements that lie beyond its material existence and appearance. One is the dynamic relation of the image to the actual person it represents, its prototype. The second entails an equally dynamic relation among the actual person represented, his or her image, and the viewer; that is, among the prototype, the icon, and the faithful who venerates it."[32] The icon therefore, through the image and the deeply spiritual way in which it has been prepared, leads the viewer to enter into a dynamic relationship with the person, or persons, portrayed. "There is the reality of the icon, which is a picture of some bit of this world, so depicted and so constructed as to open the world to the 'energy' of God at work in what is being shown."[33]

For the earliest Christians, Jesus was real, was a man who walked and talked with them and who was also God. "[A]s Man He dwells, taking to Himself a body like the rest; and through His actions done in that

---

30. Kartsonis, "Responding Icon," 58.
31. Ibid., 60.
32. Ibid.
33. Williams, *Ponder These Things*, xv.

body, as it were on their own level, he teaches those who would not learn by other means to know Himself, the word of God, and through Him the Father."[34] The people who pray with icons are therefore led into a dynamic relationship with the person portrayed and experience God in a very personal way.

MEANINGFUL EXPRESSION OF OUR IMAGE OF GOD

Over many years of teaching I have encouraged students to show their image of God through various kinds of media, music, visual art, and text. Often, God is presented as an old man in the clouds which relies on the image of God the Father as the Ancient of Days. There is confusion about how Jesus fits into the picture and students, in both secondary and tertiary education, often refer to "Jesus and God." There is an acute need within our highly visually-oriented, media-driven culture to call on real art to deliver differing Scriptural images of God to extend our perceptions and understanding. The mystery of the Trinity has perplexed theologians and even caused a major schism in Christian history so how can a visual expression of this mystery help us?

An icon that profoundly expresses the Trinity is by Andrei Rublev, painted around 1410.[35] The Trinity is represented by the three angels who "appeared to Abraham by the oaks of Mamre, as he sat at the entrance of his tent in the heat of the day" (Gen 18:1). The three figures fit perfectly into a circle, a symbol of perfection and eternity. All figures have the same face being of the same essence, and are dressed in blue, the symbol for heavenly truth.[36] The interior perspective of the icon is not what we would expect where the vanishing point is somewhere in the distance. In icons the vanishing point is the position of the viewer and so it has a disturbing and yet riveting aspect. We are drawn into the presence of God through the reverse perspective of the image. This echoes Gospel values that insist if one is to be first, one must be last. To receive, one must give. The very center of the icon is the chalice, on a table/altar in which there is roasted lamb. The symbolism of Eucharist is inescapable.

The right hand figure represents the Holy Spirit and while clothed in heavenly blue, also wears green which is the symbol of hope, of spring,

---

34. Athanasius, *On the Incarnation*, ch.3.

35. Cormack, *Icons*, 93.

36. An early and informative study of symbols from iconography is from Jameson, *Sacred and Legendary Art*, 35.

of new life, and particularly immortal life. Behind the Holy Spirit is a mountain, the place where one encounters God. This brings to mind the transfiguration (Matt 17:1–8; Mark 9:2–13; Luke 9:28–36; 2 Pet 1:16–18) where the glory of God was revealed in three figures and the voice of God was heard. For Elijah when he went to Horeb, he heard God speak in the sheer silence (1 Kgs 19:12) as the Spirit speaks in the silence of the heart. The Spirit touches the table, the altar, bringing the reality of God's action into the sacrifice as in the epiclesis preceding the consecration of bread and wine in a Eucharistic celebration.

The central figure is Jesus Christ. Behind Jesus is a tree. While on the narrative level it belongs to the story of Abraham sitting under the oaks of Mamre where he is visited by three angels, in iconography it also represents the tree of life and the tree on which Christ died to bring about the redemption of all humankind. He wears the unifying blue of the heavenly trio, but also a rich, earthy, red-brown garment that anchors him as a real person on earth, while the stripe of gold over his shoulder indicates that the splendor of God's presence is totally within him. The use of gold in icons indicates the splendor of God's presence in all of creation. A nimbus of gold is shown around the heads of those who are of God to show God's presence, and around the head of images of God. Jesus' right hand lies on the table with two fingers extended indicating his dual nature of God and man.

The figure on the left is the Father who has a translucent robe over the blue which indicates that he cannot be seen. He can only be known through the Son who he focuses on while the Son focuses on the Father, and the Spirit focuses on them both. "All things have been handed over to me by my Father; and no one knows the Son except the Father, and no one knows the Father except the Son and anyone to whom the Son chooses to reveal him" (Matt 11:27). The Father holds a staff showing authority over all of Creation and behind him there is a house which refers to John 14:2, "In my Father's house there are many dwelling-places. If it were not so, would I have told you that I go to prepare a place for you?" Every gesture, direction of gaze, and aspect of the icon holds meaning and the most open aspect of the icon is that facing the prayerful viewer. The invitation is to join in the sacred meal, to become part of this divine group, to become part of God's life here on earth.

As the icon invites the community to enter into the life of the divine, so too do other symbols, ritual actions, and the use of Scriptural text in proclamation and homiletics. "However crucial the verbal dimensions of celebration, including catechesis, instruction, and reflection, there is also need for a rich symbolic communication to bring people emotionally and intellectually into a mystery in which words are inadequate."[37] The use of art and music provide such symbolic communication. The human response is enriched as song engages us in different levels of sensory experience that can help us access the nature of God, to enter into the mystery. "Many religious experiences are inextricably aesthetic—few, indeed, could be called purely spiritual or intellectually theological."[38] Where the concentration of effort is limited to intellectual responses it is very easy for barrenness to creep in and overwhelm the spirit.

A PASTORAL ACTION IN COMMUNITY

So what can an interest and budding understanding of icons offer a community in a pastoral sense? Without access to real icons and their liturgical function, I looked for a way in which those in my classes and interested members of our community could be drawn into prayerful recognition and spiritual action. I have now used the following process in post-graduate theology and religious education classes as well as for our parish community and the wider community. In the tertiary education classes the students were required to write their own icon in silence for one hour each day during the intensive units which lasted for a week. A brief understanding of icons was explored, the icon to be copied was explained and the materials made available. Sacred music accompanied the action which was begun in prayer, but otherwise there was silence and stillness. In the Eastern Orthodox tradition one cannot write a "new" icon. "Likenesses are sanctioned and authenticated by tradition and passed down in unbroken chains from teacher to pupil."[39] Each is carefully prescribed by the theology of the Church and where a new one is required for a recent saint, then "prayer and spiritual enlightenment are necessary in order to create a likeness."[40]

In the community and parish settings, the process was centered on Lent (four weekly sessions) and Advent (three weekly sessions) with

---

37. Viladesau, *Theology and the Arts*, 3.
38. Ibid., 2.
39. Freeland, "Foreword," 5.
40. Ibid.

each session focusing for the first half hour on the Gospel of the week and an understanding of icons. Digital presentations of various icons made it a visual feast since there are many images available on the World Wide Web. The materials were made available (acrylic paints, a board with the black outline glued onto it, brushes) and the final hour was devoted to the action of writing, preceded by prayer. Participants later spoke of deeply moving experiences as they interacted with the image and allowed their own response to become visible. The technique required that the gold paint be applied first (for traditional icon writing gold leaf is often used). Gold represents the splendor of God, the presence of God in time, the uncreated light of God's presence, so immediately there was a sensory interaction between the gold and the participant.[41] Color has a strong capacity to alter our state of mind through its sensory impact and when working in a protected environment without any communication with other people, the color is given space and time to work. Different symbolic attributes of colors were introduced to the participants in the explanation of the particular icon chosen for the sessions. However, the participants were given the opportunity to change the colors (except for the gold). Upon reflection at the completion of the sessions, it became obvious that any change of color was deeply related to the spiritual expression of the particular person and they were amazed at how their choice strongly resonated with the traditional symbolism of the color chosen.

Traditional icons require a great deal of preparation with the careful selection of wood that is not damaged and that will not warp. If they are large they have strengthening sections placed on the back to prevent warping. A linen piece is fixed to the painting surface (if required) and many layers of gesso are applied and sanded before paint can be applied. The gold leaf background is applied first and then many layers of paint are applied thinly over time, accompanied by prayer. The paint is usually mixed using egg tempera but ancient icons also used encaustic where thin layers of heated wax were mixed with the pigments for application to the panel. Prayer and fasting are necessary in the tradition of writing icons. Fasting need not be the denial of what we enjoy but can be in the manner of Isaiah 58:5–9 where fasting is strongly connected to just actions. "Fasting from self-centred and self-serving ideas and actions is

---

41. Pearson, *A Brush with God*, 28.

a far greater and more difficult sacrifice than simply depriving ourselves of small luxuries."[42]

The traditional methods were greatly adapted for the community and class sessions that I directed but the spiritual effect was not in doubt. At the conclusion of each session we sat in silence and viewed our work for a few minutes and then participants left quietly. The response was always one of wonder and awe at the presence of God in this action. Even the students who were surprised at being asked to work in this way were amazed at how centered and prayerful they became and how the interaction with the subject of the icon became powerful in relationship. The quality of painting and representation was not important and there was, of course, a large diversity among each group, but it was not an issue. The result was an image that will always provoke personal prayer among the participants even if they choose not to have it on display. "Insofar as 'pastoral' theology enters into the study of the communication of the message" this proved to be an effective way of pastorally extending the gospel of the season and the capacity to engage in a prayerful action that required different and imaginative skills in the participants.[43] As in St Anselm's classic statement that theology is "faith seeking understanding," a level of engagement in faith was present, time was spent seeking the heart of the gospel, and then reaching an understanding that is different to previous ideas, making visible to the participant what was previously invisible.

CONCLUSION

Extending our capacity to make visible that which is invisible brings us to a deep and rich encounter with God. Visual art, as well as other creative arts, can assist us personally and communally so that we move together, as in a dance, towards a deeper understanding of faith. The experience of religious activities that only encompasses the written and spoken word can become arid and unwelcoming but with the inclusion of the creative, Godly, part of ourselves we can enliven and re-educate ourselves once more to be in awe of the sacredness of our existence.

---

42. Ibid., 12.
43. Viladesau, *Theology and the Arts*, 4.

11

Worship as Information, Formation, and Transformation

Nancy Ault

INTRODUCTION

Evelyn Underhill's book *Worship* begins as follows. "Worship, in all its grades and kinds, is the response of the creature to the Eternal: nor need we limit this definition to the human sphere. There is a sense in which we may think of the whole life of the Universe, seen and unseen, conscious and unconscious, as an act of worship, glorifying its Origin, Sustainer, and End."[1] First and foremost, public worship in all its forms is a human response of praise to the Eternal. However, this response is made by particular communities in specific times and places. Although the Eternal may be the focus and *raison d'être* of worship, there are many dynamics present and these can be investigated through theological, ritual, and communication studies to name a few.

One of the dimensions inherent in worship is education. Whether we are aware of it or not, when we gather to worship we become participant learners. We are being educated in and through our liturgical praxis. Yet for many Christians, public worship is in a state of flux, surrounded by controversy or entangled in post-modern fragmentation or commercialization. Consequently attention on the Eternal may be lost and in the attempt to make services relevant and meaningful, even replaced by a focus on the worshipper.

---

1. Underhill, *Worship*, 3.

The challenge for liturgical praxis in western, post-modern countries is to keep awareness centered upon the Eternal—transcendent and immanent—at a time when social-cultural forces may be impelling worshippers towards patterns more familiar amongst self-help or empowerment groups. A number of the shifts and nuances associated with such changes, for better or for worse, may be discerned through what is conveyed in and through public worship. As a way of beginning an exploration into some of the dynamics present in liturgy, its educational aspect, particularly with respect to participative learning, sustainable education, and communication will be examined. However, before beginning, an explanation about the usage of the words "worship" and "liturgy" is required.

Worship and Liturgy

When Christians appropriated the Greek word *leitourgia*, it was used to refer to any office or service performed for the public.[2] In the New Testament *leitourgia* is applied to both secular offices and Christ's priestly offering. Through Christian usage, *leitourgia* gradually came to be applied to public worship. Although the word "worship" is frequently used to signify a public service, it has a much wider meaning. Worship encompasses all of our lives because our relationship to God cannot be compartmentalized.[3] Hence it could be argued that liturgy represents the ordered and corporate worship of Christian communities whereas worship represents a way of life, the awe and adoration offered to God in our daily lives. However for the purpose of this essay, the words "liturgy" and "worship" are used interchangeably, mindful that many Christian communities do not consider their services of worship liturgical.

Worship and Education

When we gather to publicly worship God, we are more than worshippers. We become participant learners. Our services of worship teach us about our faith, how to live as Christians, and how to engage in the wider world with transformed minds and hearts. As students, our learning can be seen through two different paradigms. The human mind can be likened to a computer in which learning is formal, individualistic, and linked

---

2. Chupungco, "Definition of Liturgy," 3.
3. Forrester et al., *Encounter with God*, 3.

to internal psychological processes. Alternatively and complementary to this learning paradigm, the human mind can be likened to a text and thinking compared to textual interpretation.[4] In this metaphor, learning is developmental, social, mediated, and located in meaningful action.[5] Although both paradigms of learning are present in worship, it is the latter which particularly shapes us as participant learners.

By means of worship, people engage with a specific Christian tradition characterized by its language, stories, rituals, symbols, and customs. To move from simple facts about their faith to intuitive understanding within their faith, worshippers need to go beneath the surface motions of worship and become deeply immersed in their Christian tradition as this is mediated via liturgical praxis. In varying degrees, through this process, they may incorporate more and more of the tradition into their horizon of meaning.[6] Hence by liturgical participation, worshippers are shaped and grow in their faith. With this growth, there may be an increased freedom and flexibility that enables them to effectively negotiate the contingencies associated with their environment, integrating their knowledge and experience as they do so.[7]

As participant learners, worshippers are located in multiple systems extending from the worship environment to the wider world. All of these systems interconnect and influence each other. Public worship is not an isolated phenomenon. According to Fagerberg, the liturgy is "theology in action" by which he means that theology emerges in and through the process of worship.[8] Given the social nature of worship, the emerging and operant theologies may be wide ranging and quite different from one community to another depending on a number of conditions including the historical-cultural milieu in which the community is immersed. In one context, there may be an emphasis on the worshippers as individuals in an I-Thou relationship with Jesus, whereas in another, the stress may be on the worshippers as the corporate Body of Christ. Worship is part of a hermeneutic cycle where such factors as the predominating operative theology, the community and its systems, and individual and corporate experience may be reflected upon. This

---

4. Hermans, *Participatory Learning*, 271.
5. Ibid., 275–80.
6. Gadamer, *Truth and Method*, 302.
7. Hermans, *Participatory Learning*, 278.
8. Fagerberg, *What is Liturgical Theology?* 15.

reflection can subsequently influence worship which in turn shapes theology, the community, and experience.

Participant learning through liturgical praxis, is related to more than just content, the facts of the Good News of God's saving grace in Jesus Christ. Learning includes all the dimensions of a living Christian tradition such as the use and interpretation of symbols, gestures, body language, and space.[9] As participant learners, we assimilate consciously and unconsciously the *Zeitgeist* of our tradition. Through this tradition we construct our own worldview and tell our personal stories using its language, images, and narratives.[10]

Because of the incarnation of God in Jesus Christ, Christianity is an embodied religion. So too, Christian worship is mediated through form, time, and space. Hermans observes that "the origin and meaning of religious practices are to be found in socio-historically situated activities in which individuals engage either marginally (as novices) or in more focal roles (as experts)."[11] If worship is not seen to be relevant and applicable to people's daily lives, to connect to the socio-historical context, then there can be a tendency to disengage. When this alienation occurs, learning may be constructed negatively over and against what is perceived. Therefore, it is imperative that worship connects with the heart (emotions), the mind (intellect), and the body of worshippers if it is to remain meaningful.[12]

Public worship by its nature is rooted in multiple contexts that are rich in associated meaning and activity. When we participate in worship, we are learners. We have no choice. Some of what we learn will be explicit and intentional but much will be unintentional and unconscious. Therefore it is important that we are aware of the educational dimension inherent in worship. Otherwise our liturgical praxis may be characterized by contradictions and fragmented thoughts and actions.

What we learn, how we learn, and the depth at which we learn will contribute positively or negatively to our growth towards Christian maturity as individuals and communities. In his book *Sustainable Education. Re-visioning Learning and Change*, Stephen Sterling describes three orders of learning. The first order of learning refers to the transfer

9. Hermans, *Participatory Learning*, 291, 293.
10. Ibid., 290.
11. Ibid., 296.
12. Ibid., 276–78.

of information; the second order deals with formative processes; and the third order is associated with transformational change.[13] Each of these categories provides a different focal point and set of questions which may be used to analyze and reflect upon liturgical praxis. However, before looking more closely at the educational dimensions of worship in terms of information, formation, and transformation, it is important to consider the modes of communication that are operant in each of these orders of learning.

WORSHIP AS COMMUNICATION

For early Christians, exegesis of Scripture was pre-eminently the way of encountering the mystery of God in Jesus Christ. The reading and singing of Scripture formed a central part of their worship and hence, the liturgy also came to be recognized as a place of engagement with God. In worship we stand at the edge of God's mystery where God calls to us and we respond both corporately and as individual members of the Body of Christ. Evelyn Underhill's definition suggests that the dynamics of worship are unidirectional. However, worship has been likened to a "ritual form of communication."[14] Therefore, liturgical space becomes the liminal space of encounter and communication. Furthermore, as a form of communication, worship is sustained through the relationships engendered.[15] Encounter, communication, and relationship characterize the participatory learning that occurs in worship.

Communication occurs when some sort of effect or response is elicited. It is a complex circular process involving both verbal and non-verbal components. Additionally, it may be both intentional and unintentional. In public worship, the liturgical leadership may intend to convey God's word of grace but this message can be subverted by other elements present in the form and presentation of the service and/or within the worshippers, themselves. For both the sender of a message (liturgical leader) and the receiver (worshipper), the whole person is involved and hence, communication is influenced by the person's physical, emotional, and intellectual states as well as by the environmental factors. Although a message can be conveyed through all or any of a

---

13. Sterling, *Sustainable Education*, 11.
14. Rosier, "The Spirit and Power of the Liturgy," 397.
15. Hermans, *Participatory Learning*, 210.

person's senses of hearing, seeing, feeling, tasting, and smelling, it may not be equally available to each worshipper. Consequently, worshippers may disengage from the liturgy. For example, a person may spend the sermon doing a word-search on the pew sheet simply because he or she can't hear what is being said. The communication that occurs in public worship is multidimensional.

It might be supposed that the liturgical leadership and the participants are separate entities, with one being the conveyor of the message and the other being the receiver. However, communication occurs only in relation to both. According to Chris Hermans, "Communication assumes an utterance, someone else's response to it, and a relation between the two. These three elements should not be disjoined. There is not such thing as a 'floating' utterance directed to no-one, nor a response from nowhere. Utterance and response cannot be conceived of except in relation to each other."[16] In worship, the presence of God in Jesus Christ is presupposed. Therefore, added to the interactions between leadership and participants is the dynamic of God's utterance and the response of all worshippers (leaders and participants). Hence, many relational layers are woven together in public worship.

Verbal communication through reading Scripture, preaching, praying, and singing forms an important component of worship. However, the very transcendence, immanence, mystery of God stretches language. At this point we discover that we come "to the absolute end of ourselves and touch the beginning of the radically Other."[17] We have crossed that linguistic boundary where "language signals its fundamental limitation."[18] Metaphorical language (where we use one thing to speak of another), images, signs, and symbols become the vehicles through which insights into the Eternal are communicated.

Although meaning may be conveyed through the linguistic play with language and artifacts, it is highly subjective and susceptible to social-political-cultural factors. Therefore, if metaphorical language, images, signs, and symbols are to live, each generation needs to pass an understanding of their meaning to succeeding generations. With respect to the Eucharistic elements of bread and wine and the vessels used to contain them, Foley writes that "they are sacred because they mediate

16. Ibid., 227.
17. Nolan, *Now Through a Glass Darkly*, 2.
18. Ibid.

presence to the assembly. And it is in the hands of the assembly that they belong."[19] Collectively, we construct and reconstruct the shared images and symbols used in worship to convey God's word of grace to us. Metaphorical language (and associated images, signs, and symbols) is vulnerable to context and consequently, both outsiders and insiders can be alienated from God's word of grace through misunderstanding or incomprehension.

Non-verbal communication plays a significant and often overlooked part in worship. A worship leader racing up the central isle of a church, placing his or her briefcase on the communion table and launching into a hearty "Good morning" conveys a different message from a worship leader who is part of a procession of people who sedately walk down the central isle and reverently place the Bible, bread, and wine on the communion table. How things are said or sung and who does this; how people move and the gestures they make; and how space is arranged and used all communicate non-verbally to worshippers.

One of the conditions of participant learning is that learning is located in meaningful action. The sign/word/symbolic-act is "basically an act of communication."[20] Moreover, such acts can be performative in that through them something is held to be true or to have happened.[21] An example of such a performative act occurs in the Baptism where through the word-act, "I baptize you in the name of" and sign/symbolic-act such as immersion in water, a person is incorporated into the Body of Christ. Worship is a communication-act that occurs via word, sign, symbol, and action, and through which the world can be transformed into another reality.[22]

Worship provides a space for communication between God and the gathered community and between the individual worshippers themselves. This communication is shaped by both time and place. Although the focus is upon God, through participation in worship and what is communicated therein, worshipers become learners. As will be seen in the following, their learning may be informative, formative, and transformative.

---

19. Foley, *From Age to Age*, 173.
20. Young, "Sacrament, Sign, and Unity," 100.
21. Swinburne, *Revelation*, 26.
22. See Driver, *Liberating Rites*.

WORSHIP AS INFORMATION

Worship can be studied through the lens of first-order learning. Here worship answers fundamental questions such as, Who is God? Who is Jesus Christ? What is the Good News? In this first category of learning, learning is generally considered passive. As a participant learner in worship, a person could be considered like a vessel into which information is explicitly or implicitly poured. When worship is analyzed with attention to first-order learning, the concern is with the transmission of the facts of faith. Whether a Christian tradition considers itself as liturgical or not, through the enactment of corporate worship, people are educated as believers. The practice of corporate worship has an epistemological function of which we need to be aware.

Intentional catechizing began as part of the liturgy in the form of preaching the gospel to newly-converted catechumens. The focus was on conveying the good news concerning the life, death, and resurrection of Jesus of Nazareth and what it meant to live a Christian life in response to God's self-revelation. In this catechistical element of liturgy, Jesus was seen to be the teacher. In his *Pedagogue*, Clement of Alexandria writes of Jesus: "Educator of the little ones, an Educator who does not simply follow behind, but who leads the way, for his aim is to improve the soul, not just to instruct it; to guide to a life of virtue, not merely one of knowledge."[23] Here the facts of the faith and the formation of life within the faith are not separated. This highlights the problem of analysis. Although the three categories of learning inherent in worship may be examined separately, in reality they are intertwined and form a composite.

The Shema begins with the words, "Hear, O Israel" (Deut 6:4). We learn about our faith through hearing Scripture read and sermons preached. Furthermore, we also hear through the prayers we say, the hymns and songs that we sing and any other readings that may be used in our services. Wood has highlighted the importance of hymns when he suggests that "the heart of our theology lies in our hymns. They are our sung creeds: they often set forth what we believe and practice more sharply and freshly than either our prayers or our sermons."[24] Many different theologies can be communicated verbally in a single service of

---

23. Sloyan, "Religious Education," 7.
24. Wood, *Contending for the Faith*, 181.

worship. The liturgical leadership may intend to communicate one message through the reading and interpretation of Scripture but this message may be subverted through the hymns and prayers. Consequently, rather than informing us about the nature of God, about Jesus Christ, and about Christian community, we could be unintentionally educated in contradictory messages and fragmented theologies.

The teaching dimension found in worship is not limited to what is heard. God's call to us and our response to God is enacted bodily through all our senses. As depicted through Scripture music, art, architecture, dance, and drama can be found in Jewish worship. In addition to the aural arts, public worship utilizes a range of mediums including the visual arts such as stained glass windows, banners, and paintings to name a few; the kinesthetic arts of movement and dance; and the arts of architecture and artifacts. According to Sloyan, with the declaration of Christianity as the official language of the empire by Theodosius I in 380, worship was a "feast for every sense."[25]

The use or not of the different arts creates and sustains a symbolic landscape representative of both the Christian tradition and the worshipping community. In pre-Reformation, western churches visual and performative arts were important. For example, paintings, sculptures, and stained glass windows were non-verbal ways of conveying God's history. They were the books that the unlettered could read. With the Reformation and increasing literacy amongst worshippers, a shift in worship occurred from the visual to the aural and word based arts. Such a shift may have conveyed a non-verbal message and it could be asked if worshippers in the Reformed traditions were implicitly taught to value the mind above the body, the intellect above the emotions. Some people believe that what is seen or what is heard influences their souls.[26] This belief illustrates the complexity of sensory-based communication as both informative and formative.

It has been said that entering a church is "a metaphor for entering into a shared world of symbolic narratives and meanings."[27] In the most minimalist Christian worship symbols and metaphors will be present through the gospel stories even if the community's own symbols, metaphors, and rites are not recognized and named. In traditions which

---

25. Sloyan, "Symbols of God's Presence," 308.
26. Wood, *Contending for the Faith*, 176.
27. Kieckhefer, *Theology in Stone*, 135.

claim to be non-liturgical, ritual is present through expectations about the order of worship and the way different parts of the service will be enacted. Sloyan claims that

> We are by nature incurably drawn to ritual in the realms of both the sacred and the profane. In either, it will be good ritual or bad ritual; there is no third option. That is because the way we use the senses in public prayer is of the greatest importance. There is at our disposal the book of the world. There are the movements, the postures of the human body, and there are the arts, verbal, visual, and aural, so many avenues of sense, not to impede the word of God but to be given life and meaning by that word. Such is the oldest principle of Christian worship.[28]

In this "shared world" worship is like a text with worshippers learning to interpret this text according to their Christian tradition. Ritual, whether intentional or accidental, will be informative, teaching worshippers not only about God and Jesus Christ but also about the "book of the world."

William Seth Adams in "An Apology for Variable Liturgical Space" observes that the form and shape of the places in which we worship and the arrangement of objects in these spaces reflect the community which gathers to offer public worship.[29] Concretely and symbolically the spaces/places of worship communicate. For example, in the Byzantine tradition, to participate in the liturgy was to participate in the worship of heaven. Therefore, the church building was seen as "a point of junction between heaven and earth—symbolized by the round expanse of the dome, sometimes adorned with stars, and the square nave on which it rests, standing for the earth with its four corners."[30] Although liturgical space, design, and use may convey biblical and theological insights into the nature of God, it can also communicate a Christian understanding about the order of the world. Along with the basilica, the vesture and ceremonies surrounding the emperor were also adopted and adapted in worship and together conveyed to the worshippers the hierarchal nature of reality and their place in it. The order of space, who has the right to move through this space and to where, all non-verbally and implicitly teach worshippers about God, Jesus Christ, and Christian community.

---

28. Sloyan, "Symbols of God's Presence," 319–20.
29. Adams, "An Apology," 239.
30. Kieckhefer, *Theology in Stone*, 150.

When we gather to worship, we enter a "shared world" characterized by space and time, verbal and non-verbal communication, literal and symbolic meaning. We are embodied in the world and in our worship. As participative learners, it is to be hoped that the word of God that is conveyed will give life and meaning to this embodiment. In the first category of learning, we learn the facts of our faith through our senses. However, it is not enough to know about our faith. We are called to be disciples and this entails living the faith. This brings us to the second order of learning in worship, that of formation.

WORSHIP AS FORMATION

Worship can be examined through the lens of formation. Here, some of the fundamental questions that are addressed include, How do we live our lives as Christians? What is the relationship between God, self, others, and the world? In the educational environment, when we move to a second order of learning, reflection is introduced. At this level, discussion, negotiation, and self initiated/generated exploration occurs; questions are encouraged, concepts are explored, and imagination and intuition are nurtured. This learning style introduces a greater degree of flexibility and creativity because the horizon of our awareness is extended. Two dimensions of second-order or formational learning may be observed in worship. First, worship can be considered as theological reflection in action, a movement from the facts of faith to the dialogue between these facts and life experience with the subsequent distillation of reflective insight into liturgical praxis and living. Second, within and through the dynamics of worship, participants may learn to discern the movements of the Spirit collectively, personally, and in the world. Participation in public worship can be a formational activity in Christian life and ethics.

As with first-order learning, what is conveyed to worshippers about the nature of Christian life and ethics can be explicit as in preaching or implicit as in the arrangement and use of space. Similarly, learning can occur at both the conscious and unconscious levels of awareness. Albeit not the prime focus of worship, as participant learners, the potential for development, the social dimension of worship, the contextual mediation of knowledge through the tradition and meaningful action are important elements within the formative process.

Earlier when examining the role of the environment in participatory learning, it was suggested that worship is part of a reflective hermeneutic cycle involving the interplay between worship and context. The distillation of Christian insights into the praxis of worship demonstrates theological reflection in action as each community brings their story into dialogue with God's story. There is mutual interaction between worship, belief, and experience with each contributing to the other. Debra Murphy claims that "the intimate connection between knowledge and action, between learning and bodily practice, is to recognize that, for Christians, worship is the site at which our formation and education are initiated and completed (insofar as they can ever be complete). What we do, how we act, in the liturgical assembly shapes us in particular and powerful ways and is both formative of identity and catechetical in the most basic sense."[31] Worship, however it is enacted through language, symbols, music, movement, aesthetics, and space or the lack thereof is formative. Through the communication-relational dynamics inherent in worship, we are influenced as individuals and as communities. In our worship is our becoming the Body of Christ.

As a gathered community, worshippers form the Body of Christ in a particular time and place which will influence the way worship is conducted, its symbols, metaphors, and rituals. As Catherine Bell observes, "[R]itual acts must be understood within a semantic framework whereby the significance of an action is dependent upon its place and relationship within a context of all other ways of acting: what it echoes, what it inverts, what it alludes to, what it denies."[32] Therefore within our liturgies what is included and what is excluded, what is emphasized and what is ignored, and what is celebrated and what is denigrated will theologically inform the community. This is important because as John D. Zizioulas observes in *Being as Communion: Studies in Personhood and the Church*: "[T]he Word of God does not dwell in the human mind as rational knowledge or in the human soul as a mystical inner experience, but as communion within a community. And it is most important to note that in this way of understanding Christ as truth, Christ Himself becomes revealed as truth not in a community, but as a community."[33] Christ is the heart of Christian worship and as participant learners we are formed in Christ. And here is a challenge to our public services of worship. Whose community is being formed? This brings to the fore is-

31. Murphy, "Worship as Catechesis," 324–25.
32. Bell, *Ritual Theory*, 220.
33. Zizioulas, *Being as Communion*, 21.

sues of power and order as they are disclosed through the leadership, language, and the use of space.

Liturgical praxis does not escape human group dynamics. Communities have their distinct power dynamics. According to Jeanne Halgren Kilde, "within church spaces, God, clergy, and laity meet and negotiate their respective relationships. Consequently, the meanings associated with church architecture are often about power and authority."[34] Operating within liturgical space, Kilde identifies power associated with God, social power linked with influence and authority structures, and personal power.[35] Throughout most of Christendom, liturgical praxis has demonstrated a hierarchical social order in which a select few men have dominated and other men and women have been marginalized. Reflecting on contemporary worship and formation in Christian life, it might be asked if worshippers are being formed in the mode of Christ's subversiveness, reinforced in a particular *status quo* or even recreated in a past political structure. As Walter Brueggemann suggests, our liturgical praxis could be challenged with the question of whether it demonstrates "the practice of a counter life through counter speech."[36]

Good intentions do not create good worship or an ethical life. Hauerwas and Willimon write that "You begin by singing some sappy sentimental hymn, then you pray some pointless prayer, and the next thing you know you have murdered your best friend."[37] In public worship, we are given an exemplar of ethical integrity in the person of Christ. Our worship models a conception of Christian life and relationships within that life. Additionally, we learn the language with which we can articulate an ethic of justice and care. Through our liturgical praxis, we may be explicitly (or implicitly) challenged to reorder our lives. On the other hand, we may be formed in an ethic of sweet sentimentality.

The encounter and relationship with God in Jesus Christ defines and colors liturgical praxis as a "ritual form of communication."[38] Within second-order learning, there is openness and exploration and in worship this may be associated with discerning the movements of the Spirit of God both within the individual worshipper's heart and within the

---

34. Kilde, *When Church Became Theatre*, 10.
35. Ibid.
36. Brueggemann, *Finally Comes the Poet*, 3.
37. Quoted in Wood, *Contending for the Faith*, 174.
38. Rosier, "Spirit and Power of the Liturgy," 397.

gathered community. John T. Chirban claims that "[the] implications of spiritual discernment are far-reaching for a vital and viable Christian life. In fact, the quality of spiritual discernment in the Church may serve as a barometer of the health of the Church. So, we ask, who and where are the discerners today?"[39] As part of the process of communication, discernment presupposes active and intentional listening, waiting in silence for the other to speak. Discernment is found in the relational space between utterance and response and without such spaces, however they are created, the worshipping community may be swept along on a tide of words, emotions, and actions whose formative power could be the re-creation of frenetic secular activity in a religious setting. In liturgical discernment, worshippers seek to see, to hear, and to understand and perceive Christ's "new way."[40]

Worship is public prayer. In prayer, according to Bishop Theophan the Recluse, "the principal thing is to stand before God with the mind in the heart, and to go on standing before Him unceasingly day and night, until the end of life."[41] In worship we become contemplatives, standing before God in prayer with "the mind in the heart" and this leads to the final lens through which we may view worship, the transformative lens.

WORSHIP AS TRANSFORMATION

When we come to examine worship through the third lens we move into the realm of transformation. From an educational perspective, Sterling argues that if education is to be sustainable there needs to be a movement from transmissive and first-order learning to transformational or third-order learning. Whereas first-order learning concerns information transfer within an accepted worldview, third-order learning requires a change in our perceptions, conceptions, and actions. We "need to 'see' differently if we are to know and act differently."[42] Liturgically, the challenge is our on-going conversion and transformation into the likeness of Christ (2 Cor 3:18) and the concomitant question, Do we allow the transforming power of the Spirit into our worship and into our lives?

---

39. Chirban, "Spiritual Discernment," 36.
40. Ibid.
41. Kallistos of Diokleia, *Power of the Name*, 1.
42. Sterling, *Sustainable Education*, 52.

As Evelyn Underhill points out, worship is first and foremost about the Eternal. Yet as participant learners we are engaged in a conversation with this God who is both transcendent and immanent. Whereas information about God can be communicated and Christian life can be modeled, transformational moments are a gift from God. To be open to the movements of the Spirit liturgically, we need to "stand before God with the mind in the heart"—a state which favors neither intellectualism nor emotionalism.[43] In worship we are summoned into a space of awareness, a space where the movements of the Spirit may be discerned between utterance and response. Moreover, we are invited to allow our own lives as individuals and as a gathered community to resonate and move in harmony with the Spirit of God.[44]

As participant learners, we bring the whole of our lives to the act of public worship and as such, draw upon our individual and corporate experiences, knowledge, intuition, and understanding. If we are "to 'see' differently," then, as participant learners, our worship may challenge us to shift and change in our worldviews.[45] Frank Senn distinguished two functions in rituals: first, rituals maintain continuity with the past, and second, rituals facilitate change.[46] God speaks a word of self-disclosure and in our encounter with God in Jesus Christ, we are changed—remade—God's speech-act in us. In this way, worship becomes a communication-act of transformation.

As Christians, we do not live in a spiritual vacuum—how we live our lives and what we proclaim and do have consequences outside of public worship. If we make the conceptual shift that Sterling envisions, we become more than just participant learners, we become activists, called to take responsible action in the world. The information about our faith that we learn through verbal and non-verbal communication, consciously and unconsciously; the experiences we gain from practicing the model of Christian life that is communicated in and through worship; and the insights of faith that we are given, when integrated grow into wisdom. In other words, the shifts that occur as we grow in the Body of Christ, lead to "wisdom in action."[47]

43. Kallistos of Diokleia, *Power of the Name*, 1.
44. Principe, "Toward Defining Spirituality," 130.
45. Sterling, *Sustainable Education*, 52.
46. Senn, *Christian Liturgy*, 8.
47. Sterling, *Sustainable Education*, 53.

Although will-power, focused attention, and concerted effort may achieve many goals in the world, in worship, transformational learning requires another dimension that is demonstrated in Gregory of Nyssa's writings. He uses the word *epectasis* to describe the movement of the soul deeper and deeper into the mystery of God. The soul is represented by the Bride in the Canticle of Canticles. Each movement is compared to stripping off a garment. However, once one garment is removed the soul discovers that there is yet another garment—"even after that complete stripping of herself she still finds something further to remove."[48] Gregory of Nyssa presents a process of continual growth where at each stage the soul learns to see, to know, and to act differently—"grace endlessly creates new eyes to look upon ever new suns."[49] As vision is expanded, reality is seen with greater clarity. Furthermore, every ending is a new beginning in an ongoing transformation "from glory to glory" (2 Cor 3:18).

As participant learners, it is possible to learn about our faith and to be formed in Christian living. However to be transformed, we are invited to move deeper and deeper into the mystery of God; to be drawn into an astounding love affair, an affair of profound passion in which the mind and the heart are equal partners in the presence of God. In *Where the Wasteland Ends*, Theodore Roszak captures a vision that is applicable to understanding the dynamics of worship as transformation.

> Unless the eye catch fire
> The God will not be seen.
> Unless the ear catch fire
> The God will not be heard.
> Unless the tongue catch fire
> The God will not be named.
> Unless the heart catch fire
> The God will not be loved.
> Unless the mind catch fire
> The God will not be known.[50]

In worship, we are invited into a relational communication-act where God's love—revealed in the life, death, resurrection, and ascension of Jesus Christ—outpoured through the Spirit, transforms our lives. The

---

48. Daniélou, *From Glory to Glory*, 60.
49. Ibid., 64.
50. Roszak, *Where the Wasteland Ends*, 296.

movement of love need not be one way. God's love may be returned through the many dimensions of human love and self-emptying actions that take place in our different life settings. In and through worship, we are caught up into the great exchange of love between God and creation.

CONCLUSION

In worship we are participant learners. There is interplay between worship and the cultural, historical, and social context in which it takes place. Directly and indirectly, intentionally and unintentionally, worship with its language, symbols, music, movement, aesthetics, space, and ritual forms or the lack thereof, teaches and informs us, shapes and forms us, and changes and transforms us. Ultimately, in simplicity, humility, and compassion our lives are caught up into the reckless, foolhardy *kenotic* love of God and at the end of our services of worship, we are sent out into the world to be bearers of this love.

12

Pastoral Rituals and Life-cycle Themes in Family and Individual Worship[1]

ALAN NIVEN

THERE ARE THREE CENTRAL themes that guide the content of this chapter—the observation and integration of the ritual patterns of our own life, the development of ritual processes in a pastoral-theological context, and, the practice of ritual.

OBSERVE AND INTEGRATE THE RITUAL PATTERNS OF YOUR LIFE

From beginning to end the rituals of our lives shape each hour, each day, each year. Everyone leads a ritualized life. Rituals are repeated patterns of meaningful acts. If you are mindful of your actions, you will see the ritual patterns. If you see the patterns, you may understand them. If you understand them, you may enrich them. In this way, the habits of a lifetime become sacred. Is this so?[2]

I observe my mid-life journey of faith through the lens of Easter themes. It is a lens that has developed and guided my pastoral formation as I have responded to the reality of the practical signs and living symbols of death and resurrection that I experience in myself and others. Nowadays it is difficult to define an actual age bracket and say "that's

---

1. An earlier version of this chapter appeared in MacKinlay, *Ageing*. It was based on a presentation to the Third National Conference on Ageing and Spirituality (2007) hosted by the Centre for Ageing and Pastoral Studies, Charles Sturt University, Canberra, Australia.

2. Fulghum, *From Beginning to End*, vi.

mid-life" or "that's where senior life begins," but there are some pivotal moments and inner-life activities that are common to this passage of the life-cycle. I consider the predictable and ordinary, celebratory or sad occasions that I and my circle of contemporaries have witnessed over the last decade—the silver wedding anniversaries of friends and the golden anniversaries of parents; the funerals of parents, favorite uncles, aunts, mentors, and key figures from childhood and adolescence; the twenty-first parties of our children and their friends. The engagements of our children and their friends remind us of our own distant celebrations; the act of helping married or partnered children move into new homes or watching the little arrivals will trigger strong memories; our parents wave their final farewell to the family home; memorial or remembrance services bring many poignant reminders of mortality. One of the early texts on the so-called "sandwich generation" indicates that life consists of tiny points of connection that form stories that "hold meaning only because of how someone hung them together . . . We do well to frame them—either literally, or by prayer, tears, stories, litanies of remembrance. Such mementos matter a lot, especially when shared with loved ones."[3]

Each celebration and ritual sketches my dying to former patterns of living and points to my rising to new ways of being. The drive home or solitary moments in the garden are often filled with thoughts that are alternately sad and joyful, yet also convey the sense of a God who journeys with us. This is an experience that is both strangely disturbing and comforting in its dual promise of struggle and hope.

An Easter-like theme emerges: "Very truly I tell you, unless a seed falls into the earth and dies, it remains just a single grain; but if it dies, it bears much fruit" (John 12:24 NRSV). Christian tradition suggests that relinquishing some aspect of my being provides one way of reframing loss, change, and transition as a pathway to new and richer experiences. When we pay attention to our own small deaths such moments may help us to identify long-held regret over our mistakes and tugs of discomfort at our sins of omission. One look in the mirror simultaneously reveals the brushstrokes of the years and again we confront our mortality. Questions begin to form. How will we live reflectively and engage new insights? How will we deal with the ripples from the past composed of the myriad triumphs and failures, neglected celebrations and accumulated grief from forgotten corners of our lives? The predictable and

---

3. Gibson and Gibson, *Sandwich Generation*, 33.

continual appearance of these seed-moments offers fruitful times of reflection and self-awareness.

One common factor becomes apparent. These moments are usually accompanied by some form of ritual and in addition to "the specific rituals of religious groups." it is important to affirm that "rituals form an important aspect of life within any community."[4] The diversity, richness, and human dimension of our individual, family, and community rituals may deepen our self-understanding and sensitivity to our own frameworks of existence, or to our faith and spiritual life. Such themes are shared with all humanity but for those of us who work in the caring professions, this reflection can also train us in the art of being open to ritual-making where the purpose of a ritual is to "be cathartic, a way of releasing tension or pain . . . to invoke the presence of divinity or . . . to bridge the gulf between the human and physical world and the world of spirit and the unseen."[5] Psychiatrist and family researcher Jerry Lewis suggests that if "one wants to know what is central to a family's sense of its self, it may be best provided by a knowledge of the family rituals."[6] Lewis affirms the insights of anthropology explored later in this chapter through the lens of pastoral theology.[7]

The spiritual journey of mid-life, indeed the formation of pastoral carers, echoes Easter themes as we integrate the struggle, mercy, and grace of the journey of the Divine, (for some it is the cycle and mystery of nature) alongside our humanity. Transition through the stages of the life-cycle should prepare us for the tasks of later life where death and life confront us more clearly. Deeper growth emerges as we explore with others the spiritual dimensions of pastoral mutuality where we can "join [a] person in seeking revelation and believing that a way will open up that is not yet clearly seen."[8] Our insights and discoveries develop in community, in pastoral engagements, in conversation with peers and mentors, or in robust exploration with supervisors or spiritual directors. Our experience of grief and reflection upon ritual is often the bridge to great self-discovery. Evelyn and James Whitehead write that sadness,

---

4. MacKinlay, *Spiritual Growth*, 137.

5. Northcott, "New Age Rites," 191.

6. Lewis, *Monkey-Rope*, 141.

7. For an early introduction see van Gennep, *Rites of Passage*. For a later discussion see Turner, *Ritual Process*.

8. Wicks and Rodgerson, *Companions in Hope*, 60.

grief, and ordinary (rather than clinical) depression can alert us that something has become intolerable. Such passages of loss and seasons of regret "invite us to re-examine our life; [their] misery motivates us to face a challenge or a loss we have been avoiding; it can ready us for mature grieving and change."[9]

Mid-life and the later years prepare us for an appreciation of life and death in which the integration of losses and the celebration of new understanding emerge as a major theme. Reflection upon accumulated loss, the extending journey through the life-cycle, and the challenges of integrating these experiences are very much a part of preparing to care for others. Teaching in a context of pastoral formation, practical theology, and theological field education leads me to observe in twenty, thirty and forty year olds similar, though less extensive, patterns of growth and reflection to the ones that I experience in my fifties. I am very conscious of the relevance of Wilfred McSherry's statement that the spirituality of identity, vocation, and reflection "is not a separate entity that can be turned on or off at the touch of a switch because it is continually present, whether we are conscious of this or not."[10] McSherry argues that by "fostering our own spiritual awareness we will be more focused and receptive to those who may have a spiritual concern" and hopefully, self-awareness generated through "reflection, critical analysis and appraisal of oneself and experiences" can then add maturity and compassion to our service of others.[11] The same integrated outcome can be true of our ritual awareness. Fulghum concludes, "If you are mindful of your actions, you will see the ritual patterns. If you see the patterns you may understand them. If you understand them, you may enrich them."[12]

This chapter seeks to encourage pastoral carers to become more conscious of the role of ritual in their own lives if they wish to use or develop ritual in their care for others. Evan Imber-Black and Janine Roberts evaluate ritual from the perspective of research into family therapy.[13] They ask the following questions.

---

9. Whitehead and Whitehead, *Seasons of Strength*, 7.
10. McSherry, *Making Sense of Spirituality*, 89.
11. Ibid., 164.
12. Fulghum, *From Beginning to End*, vi.
13. Imber-Black and Roberts, *Rituals for our Time*, 57–78.

- How will we affirm our rituals or identify where some crisis has interrupted sustaining rituals?
- How will we find the energy and courage to assert what gives us life and remove frozen rituals or challenge the obligatory rituals that oppress and diminish our sense of self?
- What rituals are fresh and new and what has disappeared that we mourn or feel angry about?

If I can engage emotionally and cognitively in a review of the rituals in my own life (often with a supervisor or spiritual director) then my pastoral practice and sensitivity will be enhanced accordingly. Imber-Black and Roberts suggest we start with ourselves. "Whether the ritual style in your life now is minimized, interrupted, rigid, obligatory, imbalanced, or flexible, or some combination of these styles across various categories of rituals, you can examine your rituals and determine if they are meeting your relationship needs, or whether you want to try changing some of the patterns."[14]

This chapter argues that our use of ritual in a pastoral context and our ability to explore the needs of others in a sensitive and creative way is strongly linked to our own capacity for reflection. It may not matter a great deal whether we simply use a single Prayer Book and the same denominational resources all the time or create an eclectic *pot-pourri* from a variety of traditions or caring disciplines, religious or otherwise. However, it does matter what pastoral skills and sensitivities, professional safeguards and sound ritual theory we use to develop ritual and worship responses to the multiple pastoral issues presented by those we minister *to* and *with*.

DEVELOP AN AWARENESS OF RITUAL PROCESS

My early and ongoing formation in pastoral care owes much to writers who explore the theological and socio-political implications of ritual.[15] Some writers engage the pastoral and theological application.[16] Others

14. Imber-Black and Roberts, *Rituals for our Times*, 75.

15. Consider the eschatological dimensions of worship and ritual in Moltmann, *Church in the Power of the Spirit*, 261–75. For a pastoral approach to the Christian sacraments as the performance of freedom see Driver, *Magic of Ritual*, 195–222.

16. For a ritual response to communities and individuals experiencing a number of challenges from divorce to disability see Ramshaw, *Ritual and Pastoral Care*. For

develop creative and inclusive rituals, prayers, and responses.[17] These writers and others have been my companions in pastoral/theological conversation in response to the challenge of the suggestion that people are seeking to reinstate ritual as a source of spiritual identity, or collective action and belonging, and of personal and social transformation; or have taken up many of the functions and characteristics of ritual as it operated in primal, pre-modern cultures and re-engaged it with the quest for individual meaning and psychological well-being in the flux and mêlée of social and cultural life which represent the experience of modernity; or create rituals which reflect the smorgasbord character of the religious ideology and the symbol structure of the New Age, drawing upon many different spiritual paths and religious systems.[18]

Ministers, pastoral carers, and chaplains commonly use counseling/listening skills and theological reflection in order to adjust the style, content, form, and metaphors of a particular ritual to meet the needs, culture, context, and wishes of the person or family. There has been for many years a greater willingness to move beyond the traditional, pre-constructed religious rituals of various prayer books while still valuing them as a core resource characterized by great beauty of form, theological insight, transcendent wisdom, and literary grace. Over twenty years ago, Ramshaw identified the shifting nexus between formal, communal ritual and an individualized pastoral creativity. The "conflict many people see between ritual and an empathic response to individual needs has often been created by poor pastoral practice."[19] This can lead religious practitioners either to actively oppress and dis-empower others or neglectfully ignore deeper needs and the search for meaning and spiritual insight. In a seminary, one of the goals of pastoral formation is to impart to students an understanding of reflective practice that "involves both listening and praying, empathy and ritual" and thus to ensure that the false dichotomy between Ramshaw's "ritualists" and "counselors" may dissolve.[20]

---

another early text on Church-based practice with clear pastoral/liturgical themes see Willimon, *Worship as Pastoral Care*. A sound integration of pastoral theology, biblical narrative, and ritual is developed in Anderson and Foley, *Mighty Stories*.

17. Morley, *All Desires Known*; Ward and Wilde, *Human Rites*; Abbott, *Sparks of the Cosmos*; Goulart, *God Has No Religion*.

18. Northcott, "New Age Rites," 195–96.

19. Ramshaw, *Ritual and Pastoral Care*, 55.

20. Ibid., 56.

As a new pastor/counselor in the late 1970s I appreciated William Willimon's cautionary note from C. S. Lewis who wrote that our call was to "feed my sheep" not "run experiments on my rats."[21] With this warning in mind a number of foundational guidelines explicate ritual theory but within pastoral practice the section that follows considers Moltmann's theology of eschatological hope in the context of ritual and worship.[22] It also affirms Stephen Pattison's assertion that pastoral care as a discipline should not be relegated "to an ancillary, almost optional and unconsidered, place in ecclesial practice and academic theology."[23]

DEVELOP A FACILITY WITH THE PRACTICE OF RITUAL

I have developed a pastoral *checklist* that originates in a dialogue between theology and the social sciences and also incorporates the insights of pastoral theology and ritual theory.

- Historical continuity (Security).
- Indicative character (Meaning).
- Ritual frameworks incorporate social significance (Belonging).
- The "human" purposes of ritual.
- The reality of pastoral power.
- Practical guidelines.

Historical Continuity (Security)

Rituals serve as a buffer to the impact of the apparent speed and crisis of change and provide a sense of security when everything else seems to be disrupted or unstable. For many residents in an aged care facility there is a predictable comfort in the regular visits of trusted persons, the volunteer who reads letters or a favorite book every Wednesday, and a quiet prayer or blessing offered at the end of a weekly service of worship. Observation of anniversaries, seasons, birthdays, and times of remembrance helps to regulate the rhythm of life and anticipate a moment when the ritual will be enacted once more. As the past is engaged and brought into the present moment the participant in worship or ritual

---

21. Willimon, *Worship as Pastoral Care*, 17.
22. Moltmann, *Church in the Power of the Spirit*, 261–75.
23. Pattison, "Is Pastoral Care Dead?" 7–10.

often experiences a sense of ordering this future dimension that in turn becomes what I would describe as a midwife to hope.

Betty, frail and terminally ill, describes two rituals that sustain her—one obviously religious, the other a habit of a lifetime. "My favorite magazine has arrived and Jean will be here soon to do the crossword with me. She writes the words in for me. I'm not enjoying the treatment at the moment but Jean and my crossword get me through."

MacKinlay highlights the value of ritual in an "environment of aged care."[24] She affirms what Friedman describes as the concept of "orienting anchor" in phases of distress or transition.[25] I have observed that people are often grateful for the "anchor" effect of either religious or long-term personal and social ritual as the emotional storms rage in a crisis. The implication of "orienting" suggests that effective or accurately-located ritual will enable a person to take a compass reading with a view to continuing their journey towards a yet-to-be-experienced horizon. Betty told me about another important ritual. "Our little worship service on a Friday is something I'd hate to miss. Even when I'm too sick to go I know they're praying for me. One day I won't be there at all, you know what I mean. That's ok, it's what is supposed to happen—taxes and death. They'll still be there."

Betty has identified two important rituals that sustain her in the present; one social, the other religious, but both deeply spiritual because they are linked to Betty's identity, sense of wellbeing, and awareness of hope. She has also linked the traditions that have been a part of her life in the past (historical continuity) with her inner sense of peace about an unknown future. There is an element of personal commitment to the two rituals that have sustained her for many years. Her frailty has invited others in to share these special moments but the essence of future-ordering hope continues to be expressed in each ritual. Betty's experience seems to indicate that a personal belief system and accompanying "values and attitudes can bring hope in . . . the future or, from a religious perspective such as life everlasting, enabl[e] individuals to draw strength from their convictions and commitment."[26] Repetition is neither meaningless nor boring. Betty's present is linked to her past and her future seems ordered—the rhythm of ritual has done its job. Effective carers

---

24. MacKinlay, *Spiritual Growth*, 137.
25. Friedman, "Anchor amidst Anomie," 135.
26. McSherry, *Making Sense of Spirituality*, 56.

will observe and take note and they will respect all meaning-making and liberating rituals, be they social or religious.

Indicative Character (Meaning)

Ritual therefore "invites us to remembrance, to hope, or to a new page in life" that may even be prompted by our anticipated death, and through this process, continually serves to affirm and reaffirm meaning.[27] Relevance in the present emerges because the ritual becomes the symbol that points beyond itself. However, the ritual must be interpreted within the culture and family system to which it belongs or from which it develops. "What we have grown up with is both familiar and will be the vehicle of meaning for us. To be deprived of this may be particularly distressing."[28]

In effective pastoral care the partner-disciplines of psychology and family studies reinforce the need to engage people in pastoral conversation prior to exploration of the use of ritual, whether pre-constructed or yet to be created. "Taking some time to tell stories about previous rituals is another way to draw people into the process of ritual reflection, and ultimately broader participation."[29] It is neither appropriate nor advisable to assume that a ritual approach is desired by all people but I need to be informed and guided by peoples' stories and open to all possibilities or the end result may be more about *my* meaning rather than the resident's or parishioner's meaning. Consider the ritual of prayer. Ramshaw's description of the tension that exists for the pastoral carer is helpful. "The split between "ritualists" and "counselors" has gone so deep that, at the other extreme from the unempathic ritualist, one finds the [carer] who listens and listens and never prays. This may be appropriate in some situations . . . but as a constant strategy it can be just as much a means of avoidance as unasked-for ritualizing."[30]

I suspect that clergy or chaplains in the past may have felt that the task of ritual-making belonged exclusively to them and perhaps they even believed that discussion on the topic might be too much for the resident or parishioner. In reality, Betty became my instructor in her

---

27. Moltmann, *Church in the Power of the Spirit*, 263.
28. MacKinlay, *Spiritual Growth*, 136.
29. Imber-Black and Roberts, *Rituals for Our Times*, 294.
30. Ramshaw, *Ritual and Pastoral Care*, 56.

world of meaning, symbol, and ritual as together we prepared a small service in which she would hand over her rings (wedding and engagement) to her two daughters.

Betty is 89. Her husband died many years ago and until her fall she lived independently. She has two daughters nearby and one son interstate. The daughters provide excellent care through visiting and companionship. Betty wants to sell her house and find a permanent home that suits her level of health. Complicating illnesses have developed and Betty's doctor has indicated that Betty may not "get through." One daughter is realistic but the other keeps insisting that mum will one day go home. For Betty, each day becomes a difficult journey of adjusting to the two perspectives of her daughters. Her honest talks with her doctor have revealed to her what she suspected. She is failing rapidly and her doctor is talking in terms of months. One daughter refuses to acknowledge this and the other, who accepts the situation and talks to her mother about it, is becoming more frustrated as the days go by.

Betty talks to you as her pastoral carer. She wants to pass her rings on to her daughters hoping that the meaning will be apparent for the one who is struggling. She asks you to pray as she does this. You have taken this conversation on to the point where she sees the value of a small service or ritual. Betty has a realistic, practical and firm faith. She attends the chapel service when she can and she misses her local church. The daughters do not express their faith overtly or attend church but they own, respect, value, and support their mother's faith. Betty wants you to "run" the service and says, "You'll know what to do. I've thought about it a lot since we talked and I'm so worried about my daughter. I think it will help her. You know I'll be saying goodbye, don't you, and this is the only way I can?"

This scenario prompts a number of questions.

- How do I negotiate the power I have been given? How do I best use Betty's trust?
- How will I involve the daughters as we work on the service? If the "planning time that precedes a ritual can be as important as the ritual itself" how do I work with the obvious love and intimacy that already exists for these three women? [31]

---

31. Imber-Black and Roberts, *Rituals for Our Times*, 83.

- No matter how much trust I have been given, to what extent is the pastoral carer always a *welcome stranger* who is invited to walk on the holy ground of peoples' stories?

- Should I seek to confront the issues directly or will I run with the mother's less confrontational approach, let the ritual do its work and then see what develops?

- All rituals need some sort of statement of purpose. What is the purpose of this ritual and who will articulate this? If ritual is the symbol that points beyond itself what is the meaning that "becomes present in an accentuated way?"[32]

A Ritual Framework Incorporates Social Significance

Friedman's "orienting anchor" also owes much to a sense of participation that is enhanced by the reduction of isolation and the building of community. Moltmann affirms that every ritual "stands in a framework of social coherences and also establishes social coherences" and thus changes in our role and identity can be delineated.[33] In other words, as people observe our rituals they see who we are or are becoming, our identity and character is expressed and our belief systems are portrayed. In ritual "all take their parts in a collective dance or drama—it involves an inner consent and an outer submission to the forms and rhythms of the rite . . . Ritual also involves the breaking of the usual boundaries and hierarchies of social life—what Victor Turner calls the liminal moment where identities are fused and social status is temporarily abrogated."[34]

Driver draws upon the anthropological work of Van Gennep and Turner and locates the three phases to this process—separation, liminality, and reincorporation—within a context of community (*communitas*) and relationship.[35]

Separation. Symbolic behavior signifies the detachment of the individual or group from the wider group. In a wedding a couple separates from their family of origin and their parents in particular, often with some gesture of recognition that the moment is symbolic of *leaving and*

32. Moltmann, *Church in the Power of the Spirit*, 264.
33. Ibid.
34. Northcott, "New Age Rites," 191.
35. Driver, *Magic of Ritual*, 157–65.

cleaving. A young scout, prior to his investiture, will cross a symbolic river to stand apart from the pack. The worker recently made redundant is invited to come forward to receive a gift from his peers after clearing his tools from his locker. Each week, Betty comes out from the daily life of her aged care community to join a small group of fellow-worshippers for one hour of sacred time.

Liminality. During this phase the characteristics of the subject are ambiguous because participants are in a process of change or transition. People stand on the threshold (Latin—*limen*) of a new role, identity or, in Betty's daughter's case, a new understanding of her relationship with her mother. During the ritual we have left the past and we do not yet have the attributes, insights, or awareness of our future state. The bride and groom in a wedding service pause in that pre-celebratory space before they are announced to be husband and wife. The scout has not yet stepped back to rejoin his awaiting peers and enact among them his new privileges. The worker stands before his peers as he prepares to leave his workplace, acknowledges the gift as a parting symbol of what they have shared together and speaks a few words about what he may see as the future.

At the pivotal point in our ritual of the two rings (as they were taken off and handed over) Betty's daughter began to cry. The whole experience in her mother's hospital room had seemed what she described as "surreal" (or liminal) until that moment when the meaning dawned. These insights had been frozen in denial and now conspired with the movements of the ritual to create an atmosphere where she felt "something was about to happen." The "something" was the arrival of a truth where her tears of present and anticipatory grief were met by the embrace of her mother and sister as they comforted her. The daughter now has the task of moving on from this liminal point and choosing to live in her new state of being.

Reincorporation. After the consummation of the rite of passage or ritual, the person is redefined in a new state with fresh rights and obligations. Identified and introduced as husband and wife the couple walk forward to be greeted, welcomed, and accepted into their community in a new role. The scout rejoins his peers and exercises his new status. The newly-retired worker moves on, conscious that he no longer belongs to the group and leaves as a member of society with a different role. Betty's daughter begins to live in a world where she is confronted with the reality that her mother will not be present in the same ways she has known.

What is the significance of our own story for our reflective practice? As we stand at the liminal, transitional, feeling-filled, and intense moment between separation and reincorporation at many points in our lives (often crisis points and rites of passage) we are at our most individuated because we are unsure to whom we belong, who we are, or how we will cope. Hopefully, our reflection will lead us to deal more wisely and sensitively with those in our care whenever we remember in glimpses of mutuality the vulnerability, fragility, and paradox of those moments.

The "Human" Purposes of Ritual

I often ask this question when supervising: "How do the rituals in your life work for you?" The discussion will then be based on a number of themes as we focus on rituals that address relating, changing, healing, believing, and celebrating.[36] I then invite the student to identify and explore key issues where their own experience can enrich their practice.

Relating. Rituals provide an opportunity to shape, express, and maintain relationships. We then discuss together the major life-cycle shifts and identify what rituals worked or didn't work.

Changing. During transitions we use rituals to create and indicate for ourselves and others the changes we are accepting or grappling with. I invite the student to identify the emotional, spiritual, and practical support they received and ask them to apply the insights to a case study from their own practice.

Healing. Rituals can facilitate the recovery process after loss, times of trauma, or relationship breakdown. I invite the student to write a story of some form of healing they have experienced and describe the people, places, times, and seasons before identifying any ritual or liturgical aspects. In the case of chaplains or pastoral carers, theological reflection will lead us to consider biblical and theological insights and resources.

Believing. Rituals express and give voice to life-beliefs even as we explore the meaning of that belief. "One of the functions of ritual is to mark the pathways for morality to follow."[37] I invite reflection on the meaning for them of rituals such as prayer, blessings, anointing, listening

---

36. Imber-Black and Roberts, *Rituals for Our Times*, 26–56.
37. Driver, *Magic of Ritual*, 33.

as faithful companioning, presence, silence, touch, the sacred, or communion. Fulghum notes, "If you are mindful of your actions, you will see the ritual patterns... In this way, the habits of a lifetime become sacred."[38] I ask the student to write-up a ritual they have used and to identify the contours and shapes of belief.

Celebrating. Rituals provide an opportunity to affirm and recognize with joy and thanksgiving all aspects of our lives. It is satisfying when supervisees begin to apprehend dimensions of thanksgiving in the simple rituals of sleeping and waking, restored health, a walk with the dog, a meal on the table, employment, or even a completed assignment! Shopping, mowing the lawn, hospital visiting, tending plants, reading, or writing become the *stuff* of ritual that enables us to celebrate who we are. I have observed that this discipline enables carers to develop rituals that flow naturally and unselfconsciously out of the ordinary. Whether the pastoral carer uses a Prayer Book or a Poetry Book, a pre-constructed ritual or a collaborative gem, the people they care for will dwell comfortably in the meaning and flow of the ritual.

The Reality of Pastoral Power

There is often a power crisis as we develop skills in communication in ritual-making. Habermas' concept of communicative competence challenges ritual makers to embody the following dynamics.[39]

- Offer each person a roughly equal opportunity to speak and contribute. How often does this happen when someone approaches a minister, a priest, a pastoral carer, or a celebrant?

- Demonstrate a balanced subject/object role during the dynamics of interaction. This is seen in the ability to influence events such as choice of ritual, decisions on time and place and as to whether or not the various parties are free to participate or not. Consider some of the rituals that you have developed or participated in. Have they incorporated the hallmarks of a collaborative exercise?

- Demonstrate a symmetry of complementary modes; for example, speaking and listening, questioning and answering, conceal-

---

38. Fulghum, *From Beginning to End*, vi.
39. Habermas, *Communication*, 57–58.

ing and revealing. This will indicate whether or not people even connect with us as human beings. How mutual is the encounter and who has control?

- The same rules and norms apply to all participants and no participant has any privileged position. We can only speak of each person being valued for their unique contribution to the process. There is nothing wrong with one person having more experience, education, or expertise, but are the dynamics expressive of values we cherish such as equality, shalom, freedom of expression, or justice-making?

What happened for Betty? She began by saying, "You'll know what to do." The process concluded with Betty choosing the readings and prayers from selections I brought, organizing a private space with the nurse, ordering afternoon tea for us all, and deciding exactly how she would hand over the rings and what she would say. She asked for comment on some aspects of grief and asked me to open with a statement of purpose that we drew up together. I closed with a prayer and a blessing as mother and daughters held hands with each other. I was very conscious of being a privileged guest.

EXCURSUS: A CASE-STUDY IN SHARING POWER

Consider the dynamics of the following case-study where another face of power becomes apparent—the hierarchy of care-*givers* that sometimes inhibits the community of care-*giving*.

I received a phone call from a nurse (Paul) in an aged-care facility. He explained that James was dying and asked me to come and pray. He had known James for a number of years and James had asked him to ensure that prayers would be offered at the end of his life. However, no minister was available and his remaining family lived interstate. Upon arrival I saw that James had placed a screen around the bed. A table was laid with a white cloth, a lit candle, an open Bible, and flowers. Classical music played softly. James' hair was neatly combed. His breathing was erratic and the doctor had just left. Paul was extremely fond of his elderly patient and when I arrived he explained the context again and quietly prepared to withdraw. I asked if he would like to stay. He nodded, drew the curtains and waited. I began to open the books I had brought and invited him to read one of the passages of Scripture. He paused and then nodded so I also indicated one of the prayers that focused on God's continuing care for James beyond death. "Is that ok?" he asked. "If you would like to," I replied. We shared the ritual. Paul read Scripture, prayed, and assisted me in a simple service as James quietly took his final breaths.

I believe our companionship created a sense of community that also embraced James. I wondered about other occasions when through busyness, insecurity, insensitivity, or tiredness I may have lost the opportunity to express Turner's twin concepts of *liminality* and *communitas*.[40] These concepts describe moments when ritual serves to diffuse hierarchy, equalize power, create unity, and level social structure.

REFLECTION AND PRACTICAL GUIDELINES

Consider these questions: How would I describe my role? Who should be the facilitator of the ritual? How often do those with pastoral power assume the compliance of others without really thinking? How does the role of the "expert" impoverish the care we offer? What cultural issues collude with the way we use power? I could ask many more questions but Driver sums up my thoughts. "Ritual is the license we give one another and our spirituality to don bright colours and move in circles and claim this moment as *kairos*. Only where there is death does ritual cease. Without it we literally die."[41]

The following guidelines incorporate pastoral insights from the perspective of a practitioner.[42]

1. Discuss the key issue with all parties and just "imagine" for a while what a ritual response might entail.

2. Think of others who could perform or participate in the ritual. While respecting the role of appropriate "experts" remember that life-experience or special relationships may be qualifications we sometimes overlook.

3. Allow the stories and metaphors of each person to be offered and valued. Within this context enable those involved to work collaboratively with you in the design of the ritual. Do not force your religious presuppositions on others but remember that it

---

40. Turner, *Ritual Process*, 42.
41. Driver, *Magic of Ritual*, 9.
42. For deeper application see Mitchell, "Ritual in Pastoral Care," 68–77.

is ok for you to express your spiritual values. It may end up that you enable a person to be more true to their beliefs by *not* having a chaplain or pastor.

4. You may give guidance on the form of the ritual or worship event but it is good to enable and resource others as they develop, draft, and design the content.

5. Remember that a ritual may have many different and significant meanings for each participant. A similar issue may occur for other parties but meaning is not necessarily transferable.

6. For those whose practice on a one-on-one basis leads to the use of ritual it is important to be cautious. Community rituals or those involving a number of people have fewer inherent risks and more checks and balances.

7. The reality of pastoral boundaries and incidents of abuse have challenged the ministry of touch but careful practice and rituals such as anointing or blessing are valuable resources.

8. As I have already noted there has been a greater willingness to move beyond the traditional, pre-constructed religious rituals we might find in a Prayer Book. However, we must still value them as a core resource characterized by great beauty of form, theological insight, transcendent wisdom, and literary grace.

CONCLUSION

I leave the final words to Robert Fulghum's *Propositions on Ritual*.

- To be human is to be religious.
- To be religious is to be mindful.
- To be mindful is to pay attention.
- To pay attention is to sanctify existence.
- Rituals are one way in which attention is paid.
- Rituals arise from the ages and stages of life.
- Rituals transform the ordinary into the holy.
- Rituals may be public, private or secret.
- Rituals may be spontaneous or arranged.

- Rituals are constantly evolving and reforming.
- Rituals create sacred time.
- Sacred time is the dwelling place of the eternal.
- Haste and ambition are the adversaries of sacred time. Is this so?[43]

---

43. Fulghum, *From Beginning to End*, 20.

13

Rhythm and Worship

In Search of Pachelbel

Travis R. Fitch

INTRODUCTION

There is good reason why Pachelbel's *Canon in D Major* has, over the last 300 years, accompanied countless brides on their wedding day. More than merely providing the listener with a grounded sense of tonality, Pachelbel's *Canon* beautifully exemplifies the principal of how an undergirding, steady, and repetitive rhythm attractively offers a platform on which a simple motif can come to life. What is more, such a principal is not solely reserved to the confines of music. Consider how intricately the filaments of rhythm are woven into the tapestry of creation. To some degree, life is both held together by and reinvigorated within a rhythmic framework—a rhythm that can be neither controlled nor mastered but instead should be thoughtfully entered into.

It is tragic, despite such obvious embedding of rhythm within creation by the Creator, how little rhythm is actually present within the lives of the Creator's image-bearers. Certainly, there have been frequent occasions I have rushed around trying to be in three places at once, called back "Too busy!" to someone's request, or exhaustedly used the phrase, "I could do with an extra day in the week!"[1] Such frenzied images sound

---

1. It is ironic that I found myself beating my steering wheel with intensifying frustration at the road works that obstructed my journey to the contemplative New Norcia Monastery from where I am writing. Perhaps if I had not tried to fit so many things in

more like a depiction of when the earth was "welter and waste" than the Creator's beautiful handiwork![2]

In this essay I hope to do more than simply draw attention to the striking relationship between rhythm and worship—as if this relationship were some kind of tourist attraction. My aim is twofold: first, to demonstrate that a *God-centered life-cadence* (rhythm) is imperative to *living in alignment with who God is and how God orders things to be* (worship); and, second, to reflect on practical wisdom regarding rhythmic worship that has proven helpful in the development of my own evolving God-centered life-cadence. After surveying the biblical and theological foundation that both demonstrates the relationship between rhythm and worship and offers a framework of thinking when considering a *God-centered life-cadence*, the chapter concludes with an exploration of some of the practical workings associated with the concept of rhythmic worship. These will be organized under four broad categories with which to think when considering the rhythmical life of a worshipper—rhythmic reflection, rhythmic relationships, rhythmic recognition, and rhythmic regeneration.

THE GOD OF RHYTHMIC WORSHIP

Scripture's first page, more precisely its first 34 verses, contains the story of creation. A feature easily obscured, unless the passage is vocalized, is the way the account is arranged around a rhythm of repetitive phrasing.

- An introductory word of announcement, "God said" (Gen 1:3, 6, 9, 11, 14, 20, 24, 26)

- A creative word of command, "Let there be" (Gen 1:3, 6, 9, 11, 14–15, 20, 24, 26)

- A summary word of accomplishment, "And it was so" (Gen 1:3, 7, 9, 11, 15, 24, 30)

- A descriptive word of naming or blessing, "God called" or "God blessed" (Gen 1:5, 8, 10, 22, 28–30)

- An evaluative word of approval, "God saw that it was good" (Gen 1:4, 10, 12, 18, 21, 25, 31)

---

before I left I would not have been in the position where I ended up frantically rushing so as to become contemplative!

2. Gen 1:2; translated by Alter, *Five Books of Moses*, 17.

- A concluding word of temporal framework, "It was evening and it was morning, day" (Gen 1:5, 8, 13, 19, 23, 31).[3]

Perhaps it was mere instinctive knowledge of repetition's efficacy in pedagogy that has something to do with rhythm's presence in the Creation account. Given that it is woven throughout the fabric of our origin-narrative, each time we come to read of our beginnings, perhaps we should also consider the importance of rhythm in our existence.

Moving on from Genesis and specifically when observing Yahweh's relationship with the freshly rescued people of Israel, one cannot help but notice the rhythmic worship practice God imbeds into the composition of Israel's new existence. For example, the Jewish feast *Pesach* (Passover—introduced in Lev 23) is, according to Deuteronomy 16:1–3, to be observed annually for the rest of the Israelites' lives as it commemorates the night God rescued Israel out of the oppressive hands of the Egyptians.

Shabbat (Sabbath) is perhaps the most striking of all the rhythms that God sets into Israel's life-song and this, perhaps, is because of its frequency; Israel was to observe the weekly *Shabbat*, the seven-yearly *Shabbat*, and the seven-times-seven-yearly *Shabbat* (Jubilee).[4] *Shabbat* primarily recalls the story and implications of God's Creation-work and the rescue of Israel from slavery in Egypt. With Exodus 20:8–11 tying *Shabbat* to the Creation story, worshippers rhythmically acknowledge that they are to work for six days and rest for one because that is what God did. The maintenance of this *Shabbat* ritual ensured that Israel was engaging in a multilayered perpetual reminder; namely, that they were created to live as God orders things to be; that they were to live as God's image-bearers and were to reflect to the surrounding nations what God is like; and that, by resting, they were to acknowledge that they were the creat*ed* not the Creat*or* and so were contingent on God's life-sustaining and benevolent provision. The last of these implications is a wonderfully freeing invitation to remember that I am not God—only God is God. In his commentary on Deuteronomy, Christopher Wright intimates as much, saying, "We have seen the primary human failing is toward idolatry—giving ultimate value and worship to that which is not God. Alienated from God as the source of our fulfillment and rest, we endow

---

3. Adapted from Hartley, "Genesis: Primeval Prologue," 18.
4. Lev 25.

work and the whole economic enterprise with a significance beyond its God-given role."[5]

The *Shabbat* rhythm thus becomes a safeguard whereby we are reminded that we are, as Paul critiques humanity, to worship the Creator and not the created (Rom 1:25).

In the precursor to Israel's covenant renewal at Moab, Deuteronomy 5:12–15 connects *Shabbat* to God's rescue of Israel from slavery. Brueggemann's insights on this passage are worth noting at this point as *Shabbat* goes beyond the act of remembrance and becomes a statement of resistance. "As long ago as Egypt and as recently as Babylon, Israelites were pressured into the production necessities of the empire. Work stoppage is not only a great act of trust in YHWH, but it is a daring act of refusal. Israel refuses because to be defined by production (and consumption) entails the loss of the very freedom given in the Exodus."[6]

We must also bear in mind that the slavery of being defined by production and consumption is actually not by the oppressive brute force of an Empirical army, but by their seductive illusions and fantasies—what Sine describes as the alluring apparitions of affluence that appear above Boom Town's horizon.[7]

The *Divine Office* is the series of fixed-hour times of prayer that trace back to the Rule of St. Benedict. For St. Benedict of Nursia (ca 480–547 CE) this call to prayer was the distant echo of the Jewish voices who spoke of rhythmic praise of God. "The prophet says: Seven times a day have I praised you (Ps 119:164). We will fulfil this sacred number of seven if we satisfy our obligations of services at Lauds, Prime, Terce, Sext, None, Vespers and Compline, for it was of these hours during the day that he said: Seven times a day have I praised you (Ps 119:164)."[8]

Together with this call to seven-fold prayer and praise, the Hebrew Bible appears to demarcate specific times of daily *communal* worship and creedal-type recitals. The *Shema*, a prayer adapted from three sections of Torah (Deut 6:4–9; 11:13–21; Num 15:37–41), was and is recited by Jews

---

5. Wright, *Deuteronomy*, 74.

6. Brueggemann, *Deuteronomy*, 73.

7. Aroney-Sine and Sine, *Living on Purpose*, 35–38. In light of this, *Shabbat* stands in the distance critiquing my own Western Australian community's push to allow for full Sunday-trading in the retail sector and simultaneously offers an answer to the question, How will we, as the community of God (not just individuals), refuse to be defined by such obsession and greed, and all of its harmful effects?

8. Fry, *Rules of St. Benedict*, 44.

at the beginning and end of the day and is intended to bring worshippers back to the foundational truth that they were created to engage every fiber of their being in loving God. The Jewish custom of practicing three fixed prayer-times a day reaches back to the age of Daniel and perhaps even the days of the psalmists.[9] To the question of how these worship rhythms would have impacted on the life of Jesus, McKnight suggests, "It would have been nearly impossible for Jesus to have been a Jew in the first century, at least a pious Jew, and not to have participated in Israel's sacred prayer rhythm of praying with the community of faith."[10]

It is debatable whether Jesus was dedicated to the fixed hours of Temple prayer and worship. Nevertheless, we must pay attention to Jesus' own life-cadence.[11] Along with the prolific nature of his restorative ministry, for Jesus, there is regular retreat into prayerful solitude. In Mark's Gospel we witness Jesus' response to an extraordinary day of ministry that would leave most people attempting to access their full annual-leave entitlements twice over. What is Jesus' next course of action after an occasion requiring such immense levels of emotional and physical output? Mark tells us that "in the morning, while it was still very dark, he [Jesus] got up and went out to a deserted place, and there he prayed" (Mark 1:35). This example is just one of a number of times where Jesus demonstrates two fundamental elements to the worshipful life. It has been aptly described as Jesus' "two-step dance of life"—receiving from the Father, responding to the world; receiving from the Father, responding to the world.[12] This rhythm is not only adopted by Jesus but is also taught to his disciples as orthopraxy, or right practice, they too should embrace. Progressing through Mark 6, and following Jesus' sending out of the disciples on a ministry exercise (Mark 6:6b–13), we encounter the disciples upon their return with what may well have been adrenalin-charged reports of the miracles that took place. As if to recognize this pace as unsustainable, Jesus responds by saying, "Come away to a deserted place all by yourselves and rest a while" (Mark 6:31).

---

9. Ps 55:17 describes the worshipper crying out to God in the morning, at noon, and at night, while Daniel would "get down on his knees three times a day to pray to his God and praise him" (Dan 6:10).

10. McKnight, *Praying*, 32.

11. We notice, though, that Acts 3:1 appears to depict the disciples continuing this worship-rhythm.

12. See Mark 7:24; Luke 9:28, and Matt 26:36. The phrase is attributed to Sheridan Voysey.

As people who bear God's image and as followers of Jesus, the evidence of rhythm and of rhythmic worship leaves us with the sober challenge to examine whether our lives currently reflect the engaging beauty found in the steadiness, repetition, *and* developing motif of Pachelbel's *Canon in D Major*.

The following may be described as my search for Pachelbel; however, it is far more profound than a musical analogy. Worshipping God, in its fullest sense, is the offering of our whole lives so as to live as God orders things to be; in fact when we live in such a way, it is as though we reverberate with God's perfect intentions for us.[13] Furthermore, if rhythm is intrinsic to creation and is part of the Creator's overflow then the pursuit of a rhythmic existence is a crucial element to worshipping God. Put another way, if the best possible way to live is the way God orders things to be (worship), and if God orders things rhythmically, then embracing a God-centered rhythmic existence is a core component to truly living.

However, one further point should be noted and we will do so by considering the jubilee rhythm as mentioned earlier. In the broadest sense, the jubilee was an occasion that saw the return of land to its original owners and the release of people who had sold themselves into slavery in order to make ends meet. When unpacking the intricacies and implications of jubilee, Wright highlights the holistic missional nature of jubilee as not only possessing obvious socioeconomic ramifications but also containing "inner spiritual and theological motivation."[14] "To apply the jubilee model, then, requires that people obey the sovereignty of God, trust the providence of God, know the story of the redeeming action of God, experience personally the sacrificial atonement provided by God, practice God's justice and put their hope in God's promise for future. Now if we summon people to do these things, what are we engaging in? Surely these are the very fundamentals of evangelism."[15]

While Wright isn't suggesting that jubilee was evangelistic in the contemporary sense, the point is that this rhythm was to be embraced partly because it spoke powerfully of the God whom Israel worshipped. When Israel worshipped God by means of the *Shabbat* rhythm they uniquely heralded to the surrounding nations that Yahweh was creator,

---

13. Rom 12:1–2.
14. Wright, *Mission*, 299.
15. Ibid.

sustainer, sovereign, and rescuer. For Christians this same responsibility and opportunity to reveal the God whom we worship is wrapped up in God's intentions for humanity. From the beginning of creation (Gen 1:26) to the commissioning of Israel (Exod 19:5–6); from the New Testament to today (2 Cor 3:18; 1 John 3:2), God has always intended that men and women reflect the magnificence of God as seen in the face of Christ (2 Cor 4:4–5).

How does this take place? Tom Wright explains that revealing God is made possible for us because of the presence of God's Holy Spirit in our lives. He says that "the Spirit is given so that we ordinary mortals can become, in a measure, what Jesus himself was: part of God's future arriving in the present; *a place where heaven and earth meet.*"[16] While I wholeheartedly agree with Wright, I would also want to add that if we are to be the intersection of the realm and reign of God in a rebellious world and in so doing display a life of full-scale worship, then we must embrace rhythm. If rhythm is missing, then in some ways we could further conclude that our representation of God on earth is deficient. That is, it is upon the skeleton of rhythm that the flesh of God-worship and God-imaging best comes to life.

AN OVERVIEW OF THE GOD-CENTERED LIFE-CADENCE

The following rhythm has been developed to maintain a healthy life within the context of our ministry, or work, or family, and ultimately because I believe it is a crucial element to whole-life worship and true image-bearing. Its outer framework is somewhat Hebraic in nature in that it consists of daily rhythm, weekly rhythm, monthly rhythm, and yearly rhythm. Its inner workings are a mixture of Jewish traditions (*Shabbat* and *Shavuot*); Christian traditions (the *Divine Office* and *Lent*); biblical instruction, and common sense. One dominant ingredient worth highlighting common to every component is that of *intentionality*. Developing rhythm alone proves insufficient for the productive life-cadence; for even procrastination, for example, could be approached rhythmically. Therefore, it is important that we approach the life-cadence and its components intentionally for the sake of both sustainability and fruitfulness. As we will see, intentionality within a worshipper's life-cadence means continually bearing in mind questions such as "How might I be mindful

---

16. Wright, *Simply Christian*, 124 (emphasis added).

of God in this activity or moment of rest?" and "What would it mean to reflect God in this activity or moment of rest?"

A caveat is required at this point for those of us who are human. Establishing a God-centered life-cadence is well and fine so long as we recognize we will regularly find ourselves out of sync with one or more of its aspects. Yaconelli's candor refreshingly offers us hope. In presenting one of his "non-principles" for spiritual growth he writes,

> For years I believed it when people told me, "You either love God or you don't," "You are either committed or you aren't," "Give God 100 per cent!" Sounds very spiritual, but the truth is there is no such thing as 100 per cent commitment . . . I am a morning person, so I wake up with a fairly high commitment level—say 73 per cent. Then I go to work and my commitment level drops to 45 per cent; I get a pay rise and my commitment level shoots up to 92 per cent; my wife and I have a row and it drops to 9 per cent; and then *Baywatch* comes on television and I'm up to 80 per cent again (just kidding). Every day my commitment level moves up and down like a boat in rough seas, and my overall commitment might average out to 57 per cent for the entire day. We *strive* for 100 percent, we *want* to give 100 per cent (sometimes), we *wish* we could give 100 per cent, but life isn't quite so simple.[17]

It is essential that we are honest about our frailty as humans and our dependency on God's grace. Therefore, when our worship becomes distorted and our lives feel out of sync with God's order, we simply and humbly ask God to help us and realign us and then we thankfully re-enter the groove.

UNPACKING THE GOD-CENTERED LIFE-CADENCE

For the purpose of this chapter, the abbreviated version of the God-Centered life-cadence that my wife and I have developed will be unpacked using the four categories of rhythmic reflection, rhythmic relationships, rhythmic recognition, and rhythmic regeneration.

Rhythmic reflection

Through rhythmic reflection we endeavor to be transformed by an encounter shaped by the risen Christ; it is here that we engage in what Paul describes as the setting of our hearts and minds on things above and not

---

17. Yaconelli, *Messy Spirituality*, 116–17 (original emphasis).

on earthly things (Col 3:1–2). We bring ourselves before God with the attitude of the Psalmist who says, "Search me, God and know my heart, probe me and know my mind. And see if a vexing way be in me, and lead me on the eternal way."[18] We seek to know and hear from God what it means to live in alignment with how God orders things to be.

The various praxes associated with prayerful contemplation are infused with what are imperative to transformative reflection—namely, silence and solitude. For Dom John Main, a Benedictine monk, silence and solitude are of utmost value, understanding them as "a path into the reality of the universe, where God is in charge and we are not, where we can be flooded by God's love."[19] In an essay taken from his book *Moments of Christ*, Main writes,

> Now to tread the spiritual path we must learn to be silent. What is required of us is a journey into profound silence. Part of the problem of the weakening of religion in our times is that religion uses words for its prayers and rituals, but those words have to be charged with meaning and they must be charged with sufficient meaning to move our hearts, to set us out in new directions and to change our lives. They can only be charged with this degree of meaning if they spring from spirit, and spirit requires silence.[20]

Main is right to insist that the moving of our hearts and the changing of our lives comes through willingness to enter silence because silence is the language of the Spirit. God's Spirit resides in us in silence, so in order to hear what the Spirit is saying we must enter that silence. Meeting God in the silence is no more clearly seen than in the life of Elijah. Fearing the death-threats of Jezebel, Elijah makes a painstaking journey, albeit one assisted by God, to the mountain called Horeb. Upon Elijah's arrival a conversation ensues between Elijah and God in which Elijah expresses his grave fears, to which God responds by telling Elijah to go out on the mountain and experience God's presence as he passes by. How will the Lord pass by? Will the experience be like that of the post-exodus gathering that stood at the perimeter of this very mountain and witnessed the noise, and thunder, and extreme heat connected to the manifestation of God's presence?[21] For Elijah, there *is* a strong wind,

18. Ps 139:23–24; translated by Alter, *Book of Psalms*, 483.
19. Foster and Griffin, *Spiritual Classics*, 155.
20. Quoted in Ibid., 156.
21. Exod 19.

the mountain *does* shake violently and fire *also* breaks out. However, we are told that the Lord is not in any of these. Where is the Lord? God is to be known by Elijah in the "sound of sheer silence" (1 Kgs 19:13). In the midst of our own noisy existence, where busyness and the information-overload fed through media and Internet perpetually badgers us, silent and prayerful reflection work to bring us back to what is most important in life and to what it means to be God's image-bearers and wholehearted worshippers.

Interfacing with solitude and silence are the components of ritual and liturgy. The *Shema* illustrates how ritual and liturgy play a crucial part in rhythmic worship. The *Shema*, a twice-daily Hebrew prayer most likely recited by Jesus, reminds the worshipper to love God with all of their lēbāb (heart, mind, will), their nepheš (soul, life, inner-being, emotion), and their mᵉʾōd (might, strength). In other words, we are to engage our whole being in worshipping God. What better way to approach and conclude each day's activities than with a liturgical reminder (a *Shema*) that expresses to God the desire to live in full alignment with who God is and what he is doing in the world? While we may not pray the original *Shema* twice daily, organising our lives around fixed hours of prayerful reflection and utilising invaluable resources like *The Divine Hours*[22] or *The Little Book of Hours*[23] to supplement these times will not only lead to our own transformation but something of God will inevitably permeate our relationships, our workplaces, and our areas of ministry as we become more like Christ and reflect God's image.

The ritual aspect, and by this I am specifically thinking of the fixed-hour nature of rhythmic reflection, enables us to enter each period of the day with renewed focus. My mobile phone sounds an alarm in the early morning, calling me to prayer so that I might greet not only the day thankfully but my wife and three children lovingly; at 12:30 pm preparing me for the second half of the day, where my intentional God-worship often starts to wane; and at 7:30pm calling my wife and I to commit the evening's activities to God.

There are numerous other colors to bring to the canvas of rhythmic reflection—reflective Bible reading and journaling, for example. In his helpful theological reflection aid, *Making Life Decisions: Journey of*

---

22. In *The Divine Hours*, Phyllis Tickle provides a liturgy for four fixed-hour prayer times and covers each day of the year.

23. Community of Jesus, *Little Book of Hours*.

Discernment, Pound grounds each of his forty reflections in an extended period of silent meditation fuelled by a portion of Scripture, and encourages the worshipper to sit "with the Scripture echoing in your mind" and to "spend a significant time listening to what the Spirit of God is saying to you" followed by writing down any subsequent and meaningful reflections.[24] It is in this reflective process that I have begun to experience a deeper satisfaction in prayer through learning to articulate aspects of life that have often remained wordless. One practice that eventuated from experimenting with these different approaches in rhythmic reflection has been the regular composing of prayers that are fired by passages of Scripture relating to the various seasons and experiences of life or by inspirational writings.

Rhythmic reflection guards against the hollow practice of only coming to the Bible on Sunday, or if there is a Bible-study to lead, or a sermon to preach. It enables us to function in a less distracted and reactionary manner; and, in doing this, it fires our God-worship in the key area where our love of God is revealed—in our relationships.

Rhythmic Relationships

How does one maintain *relational* health and how does a rhythmical approach to our relationships further energize our worship? The litmus test of our God-worship is the quality of the relationships we hold. Jesus, when answering the question of which commandment in the law holds greatest weight, joins the "Great Commandments" from Deuteronomy 6:5 and Leviticus 19:18 by saying that the second is just like the first. In other words our worship of God is inextricably linked with our love of others. The apostle Paul infers the same in Colossians 5 where he precedes his exhortation to "walk by the Spirit" (worship) by quoting Leviticus 19:18 concluding that "the entire law is fulfilled in keeping this one command." The implication is that the authenticity of our God-worship is measured by the quality of our love (Gal 5:14).

This poses a challenge to the *Facebook*™ populace. *Facebook*™, the internet relationship-playground, promulgates that it will help you "connect and share with the people in your life."[25] In my two-week *Facebook*™ experiment I managed to accumulate twenty-four "friends" within a

---

24. Pound, *Making Life Decisions*.
25. http://www.facebook.com/.

matter of days and a further twenty-five requests to be a "friend" shortly thereafter. Between updating my "status" and maintaining contact with my twenty-five newfound "friends," as well as my regular life offline, it occurred to me that even the most concerted participation in *Facebook*™, while leaving me amused and entertained, would hardly result in deeper connection and sharing with others. To a number of my "friends" who have 500 more "friends" than me, my question is this, "Where do you find the time to be a friend to 550 people?" A generation that seems to search for connection and sharing appears to be sadly and cheaply satisfied.[26]

The sentiment of God's intention for our relationships with others has been beautifully captured by Alter's rendering of Genesis 2:18: "And the Lord God said, 'It is not good for the human to be alone, I shall make a *sustainer beside him.*'"[27] Willard and Johnson identify the "sustainer beside us" as a crucial participant within the process of our spiritual maturation. For Willard and Johnson the sustainers are multiple and not singular and the act of sustaining is to be reciprocated. They describe this sustenance as the "reciprocal rootedness" in others, maintaining that "stable, healthy living requires the assurance of others being *for* us" and that "if this assurance of others being *for* us is not there, we are but walking wounded."[28] Reflecting on who is *for* us, as well as who we will in turn be *for*, reminds us that our relational health is not determined by how many people we have around us but by the depth and quality of the relationships in which we are rooted. Rhythmic and intentional interaction with the people who make up this group is what the sphere of rhythmic relationships is all about.

The questions of "Who is *for* me?" and "Who am I *for*?" should perhaps be first asked within the context of the relationships we hold closest—for some it is the family into which we were born while for others it is the family birthed through us. The regular consideration of these questions acknowledges that merely being at home for considerable periods of time does not necessarily guarantee that my time will be utilized well or that my family will receive the best of me. In order to be *for* my

---

26. Personal observation leads me to suspect a tragic amount of time is being wasted on an exercise that, while brimming in popularity, is lacking in actual relational nourishment. Jesus had twelve close friends and, of those twelve, three enjoyed a distinctive level of intimacy with Jesus.

27. Alter, *Five Books of Moses*, 21–22 (emphasis added).

28. Willard and Johnson, *Renovation of the Heart*.

wife and children I must deliberately consider the question "What do they most need from me right now?" Furthermore, Willard and Johnson remind us that this is a reciprocal process and so it is equally important that I consider *and communicate* how they can in turn be *for* me—what I need from them.

From a practical perspective, engaging in rhythmic relationships involves both spontaneity and premeditation; with the latter inspiring the former. The foundational aspect to developing rhythmic relationships, that is relationships that intentionally express and inspire the love and character of Christ, is the creation and maintenance of a biblically grounded mission-statement or what has also been called "a philosophy of ministry."[29] In consideration of the rhythmic relationships sphere, this process enables us to assess the degree to which our relationships reflect what we believe they should and to identify the enriching activities crucial to our worship of God as it is expressed within the context of our key relationships; whether we are married or single, living with our parents or away from them. As our beliefs and purpose are articulated and honed, and as relational observations are made, we may discover the need to invest more intentionally into some relationships and withdraw from others; we may discover the need for a spiritual director or mentor with whom we will regularly meet; and we may well discover that a sizeable reordering of life and reconnection with significant others needs to take place.

Such connection should not only be thought of on an individual level—*me* in my marriage, *me* with my children, or *me* in my friendships. While Genesis 2 insists the inhumanness of an isolated individual, I would argue that this is equally applicable in marriage. While marriage sees the two become one and experience deep companionship with each other, this new "one" should guard against the virulency of isolation. Winner's insightful critique on society's individualistic tendencies, from a Jewish perspective, is extremely helpful in highlighting the importance of guarding one's marriage from the abyss of isolation. Of the Jewish wedding traditions that Winner mentions, the parties after

29. I am indebted to lectures by David Michie through whom I first encountered this process. It involves answering three questions on belief, purpose, and practice, with each question being built upon its antecedent. The questions are (1) "What do I/we believe: about God, life, worship, relationships, money, sex, Jesus, the Bible, rest, children, etc." (2) "What do I/we principally want my/our life to be about?" (3) "How will I/we practically go about this over the coming year?" See appendix.

the wedding night are most striking. Winner points out the absence of an immediate honeymoon. "Instead of honeymooning, the newlyweds attend seven nights of parties in their honour. These parties are called the *sheva brachot*, after the 'seven blessings' recited at each post-wedding bash. Intended to distract husband and wife from one another's sexual charms, these parties can range from a casual pizza get-together to the most formal champagne and caviar."[30]

What is the point of these parties? Winner says that they are designed to push married couples into their community because "marriage, after all is not just a change in individual circumstances. The husband and wife will relate differently to one another, to be sure, but they will also engage the community differently," and marriage, Winner rightly notes, "is a group-project." In light of this, our personal rhythm includes monthly get-togethers with another married couple where we candidly and respectfully reflect upon both the strengths and growth-areas of our marriages. We engage in these intentional conversations as participants in God's goal for our lives: that we would love God with our whole being, love others in a way that reflects God's love for us and our love for God, and that we might be transformed into the Lord's image "with ever-increasing glory" (2 Cor 3:18).

Rhythmic Recognition

The third sphere of the God-centered life-cadence involves rhythmic recognition. As evidenced in the Psalms, grateful recognition or thanksgiving for who God is and what God has done is an essential element of worship—"It is good to give thanks to the LORD, to sing praises to your name, O Most High" (Ps 92:1). This being the case, we will use the "thanksgiving" psalm as the basis for this aspect of a worshipper's rhythmical existence. McCann's list of the typical thanksgiving-psalm elements offers a helpful framework in which to think when approaching rhythmic recognition.

- Expressions of praise and gratitude to God
- Description of the trouble or distress from which the psalmist has been delivered
- Testimony to others concerning God's saving deeds

---

30. Winner, *Mudhouse Sabbath*, 128.

- Exhortation to others to join in praising God and acknowledging his ways.[31]

These four characteristics are not merely qualities of a thanksgiving song, but they are the essence of thanksgiving itself—whether expressed in song or feast. The Jewish festival of *Shavuot* (literally "weeks") has its origins in Leviticus 23:15–21, according to which *Shavuot* occurred on the fiftieth day, or seven weeks after the "wave offering" (vss 9–14) that acknowledged the first sheaf of Israel's harvest. Most succinctly *Shavuot* was a day of thanksgiving for the early harvest and a worshipful gesture that was "made in order to refer and relate all of life to the character and action of Yahweh, the one who is known in festival as giver and transformer of life."[32] Later this feast would come to be known as *Pentecost* (literally "fiftieth") by Greek-speaking Jews because it was celebrated on the fiftieth day from the Sabbath beginning the Passover.[33] Interestingly, after the destruction of the Second Temple in 70 CE, modern Jewish observance continued to remember God's provision only with the added tradition of recognizing *Shavuot* as the day Yahweh gave the law to Moses at Sinai.[34] It was on the day of *Shavuot*, or *Pentecost*, that God sent the promised Holy Spirit to fill the followers of Jesus—the birthday of the Christian Church (Acts 2:1).

Given the nature of thanksgiving, there is a correlation between McCann's four elements of the thanksgiving-psalm and the nature of this particular thanksgiving feast and its various focal points. Along with the obvious grounds for the expression of praise and gratitude to God in *Shavuot*, specifically God's sustaining of life, such expression is importantly connected to previous distress from which the worshipper has been delivered—through the wide-angle lens of Jewish memory it is slavery in Egypt prior to the exodus and Passover that forms this distress, while for Christians it is the distress of being the captives of sin and death from which God has rescued us. When considering the last two of McCann's elements we should note the missional overtones of the feast as those "outside" the celebration are brought in.[35] God's closing remarks

---

31. McCann, "Book of Psalms," 647.
32. Brueggemann, *Worship*, 12.
33. Freeman, "Feasts," 367.
34. Kasdan, *God's Appointed Times*, 51–52.
35. Brueggemann, *Worship*, 13. We must also bear in mind Christopher Wright's caution to not perceive Israel's worship acts as evangelistic in the contemporary sense.

in relation to *Shavuot* and the associated harvest instruct Israel to care for the poor and the resident foreigners. While not stated here specifically, God elsewhere reasons that Israel should care for those who have pressing needs because that is precisely what God did for Israel when they were slaves in Egypt.[36] Therefore, the care being expressed to those with pressing needs becomes an extension of God's benevolence where those on the "outside" are welcomed into God's loving provision.

For those of us who view Pentecost through a Christian lens this poses a challenge. What would it look like to vibrantly and creatively memorialize our God-providence story in a way that articulates not only gratitude, but the distress from which we have been rescued and the way in which that has been achieved? Furthermore, how might we do this in a way that the recipients of this thanksgiving are not only fellow journeyers but those who remain in the distress of being captive to sin and death? Some might retort, "That's easy! Our church service or weekly gathering does that!" and others may add that our everyday lives should express this very disposition. Both of these are true, but there is more to it. The point of rhythmic recognition is that we build intentional recurring occasions of thanksgiving into our existence. Let me offer two examples of how this may take place.

First, rather than relying on the local church to lead us through remembering Pentecost, we might consider hosting an annual traditional *Shavuot* meal where, with friends, we creatively recognize the origin and developments of *Shavuot* and so give thanks for God's life-sustaining provision. Such a feast would also emphasize the significance of the Holy Spirit being sent at Pentecost; this significance is beautifully summarized by Clark Pinnock. "[A]t Pentecost the church received the Spirit and became the historical continuation of Jesus' anointing as the Christ. The One baptized in water and Spirit now baptizes the disciples. He transferred Spirit to them so that his actions could continue through their agency."[37]

What a profound and critical reality for us, as disciples of Jesus, to remember!

---

36. While Exod 22:21 and 23:9 demonstrate something of God's rationale behind the care for the needs of foreigners, it is Lev 19:34 that offers possibly the most striking, saying: "The alien who resides with you shall be to you as the citizen among you; you shall love the alien as yourself, for you were aliens in the land of Egypt: I am the LORD your God."

37. Pinnock, *Flame of Love*, 118.

Second, periodically invite friends, Christian or not, to some form of aid-dinner party. While you may not choose these words, the invitation would inform them that part of the purpose of the dinner is to consider how we might pool some of our resources to relieve people in the distress of impoverishment and starvation. The "why?" question may be answered at the party as the host speaks of how they were once in distress, but God.

These are two of a number of ways to worship through rhythmic recognition.[38] Regardless of how we choose to engage in this sphere, the goal is to order our lives around thanksgiving in order that gratitude may be our primary posture before God.[39]

Rhythmic Regeneration

The final sphere of the God-centered life-cadence, rhythmic regeneration, houses those deliberate occasions where rest, recreation, or physical fitness takes place. Despite the vast number of Christian leadership books on the market, few have addressed the topic of recreation. The closest could be Hybels' *Courageous Leadership* which touches briefly on what it means to work at a sustainable pace.[40] Personal observation leads me to the conclusion that the absence of rhythmical fun in our lives results in the loss of both our ability to laugh and our sense of humanity and, tragically, it produces people who continually focus on their next allotment of annual leave rather than enjoying and engaging with the task at hand.[41]

In his practical guide to physical, mental, and spiritual health, Rediger emphasizes the importance of recognizing ourselves as "whole-beings"—body, mind, and spirit.[42] That these three elements of our being are interrelated means that our neglect of one will impact on the others. While there are obvious areas of crossover, the first three spheres of the God-centered life-cadence have predominantly pertained to the areas of our mind and spirit. With the *Shema* beckoning us to worship God with

---

38. My own life-cadence includes *Lent* and the *Stations of the Cross* together with these.

39. McCann, "Book of Psalms," 647.

40. Hybel, *Courageous Leadership*, chap. 9.

41. Sadly, all too often, even when that annual leave does arrive, the possibility for fun is often missed as most of the leave-time is spent just beginning to unravel.

42. Rediger, *Fit to Be a Pastor*, 64.

our whole-being, rhythmic regeneration takes into account the role of physicality in our worship.

There are two levels on which physical well-being impacts the life of a worshipper—that which we express directly *to* God and that which we express *about* God. When we care for our bodies by eating healthily, exercising regularly, and resting effectively we show our appreciation to God for the bodies he has created and entrusted to us; not to mention the physiological affect that diet, exercise, and restful fun have upon our functionality and, therefore, our ability to engage with God and others.[43] Rhythmic regeneration also has missional implications in that caring for our physical well-being bears witness to the God whom we worship. When Paul affirms the physical body (1 Cor 6:12–20), Blomberg highlights the wider implications of this as Paul's approach "counteracts those forms of dualism which allege that the material world, including our human bodies, is irredeemable."[44] While Paul's determination in this passage is to demonstrate the abhorrent spiritual implications of sexual sin, Blomberg rightly widens the consequential scope of the argument when he points out the full salvific nature of the gospel. "Christians must always guard against a truncated gospel that seeks to save souls but not bodies or that is unconcerned for the stewardship of the earth. To the extent that the kingdom is inaugurated, we must begin to model even in this life the priorities of care for our bodies and our planet that we will be able to perfect in the life to come."[45]

It can therefore be said that rhythmic regeneration plays a part in our telling of the good news of what God is doing in the world. To neglect this sphere of life is to present a distorted version of the gospel which is not really gospel at all.

---

43. See Needels et al., "Power up your brain." This exposé on research pertaining to the prevention of Alzheimer's disease points out that "exercise boosts circulation, including blood flow to the brain, which uses a full 25 percent of the oxygen that enters our lungs. It also bolsters brain-nurturing chemicals and reduces stress, which has been shown to damage the brain. Physical activity can also ease depression, which slows thinking and may precede the onset of Alzheimer's. For similar reasons, relaxation techniques such as yoga and meditation are often recommended, as is avoiding smoking and not consuming too much alcohol, though research indicates that moderate drinking may help reduce stress" (50–51). They go on to point out that a sense of purpose and fun is a proven contributory factor to overall well-being and functionality.

44. Blomberg, *1 Corinthians*, 128.

45. Ibid.

Rhythmic regeneration involves the deliberate and recurring setting aside of time for planned holidays, fun with friends, regular exercise, or simply doing nothing. It should be noted that when these activities are understood through the lens of rhythmic regeneration they become infused with the same sacred ingredients of what we might call *Shabbat*-theology. Therefore, swimming laps at the pool each morning has a substantially greater rationale to it than merely keeping fit as rhythmic regeneration interprets that activity to be expressing something both *to* God and *about* God. If the underlying principles of *Shabbat* permeate the activities within rhythmic regeneration then it makes sense to make the observance of *Shabbat* the preeminent event in this regenerating sphere.

Kasdan, a Messianic Jew, understandably advocates for a more traditional adoption of *Shabbat* practice by "Messianic Jews and Messianic Gentiles" in his guide to understanding and celebrating the biblical holidays.[46] For Kasdan, this involves the traditional *Shabbat* times of late Friday afternoon until Saturday sunset, the opening blessings and closing service of *Havdalah* ("separated"), and the traditional meals and liturgies associated with *Shabbat*. While Kasdan's view is not shared here on this particular point, he is right when he says that "as with all the feasts, the most important element is the spirit in which we observe the holy days."[47] Therefore what should be imbibed of *Shabbat* is the desire to rhythmically stop, and rest, and worship the Creator. Whether it is through self-composed liturgies that remind us of the origins of *Shabbat*, a festive meal of home-made pizzas, a recurring familiar activity or place to go in order that we might simply *be* or play together, the incorporation of a worship time with others, or candles that symbolize God's presence and Jesus as Light of the World; *Shabbat* can and should be colorful, creative, and enthusiastic so as to act out the rest we will one day know in full (Heb 4:9–11).

CONCLUSION

Through a God-centered life-cadence we discover something that the ancients knew thousands of years ago—to stay connected with who God is, what God is doing, and what it means to be God's people we must

---

46. Kasdan, *God's Appointed Times*, 9.
47. Ibid.

embed into our days, weeks, months, and year deliberate rhythms of remembrance, reflection, and regeneration. The crucial component to a life-cadence is intentionality. It is not difficult to fill our lives with activity, even rhythmic activity, and much of that activity could be, at its core, very valuable. The key to seeing the full benefit come to bear in our lives comes down to our intentionality prior to and inside those rhythmic actions. Equally thrilling is the knowledge that through a God-centered life-cadence we are opened up to discover our part in an evolving *magnum opus* of worship more splendid than the likes of Pachelbel ever dreamed or imagined and all because we will be continuously contemplating the Great Composer's intentions for our life's song.

APPENDIX

The invaluable process of developing a personal mission statement involves answering three questions with each question being built upon its antecedent. The questions are, What do I/we believe: about God, life, worship, relationships, money, sex, Jesus, the Bible, rest, children, etc, (beliefs); What do I/we principally want my/our life to be about? (purpose); How will I/we practically go about this over the coming year? (practice). The following demonstrates how these questions might be answered. It is worth bearing in mind that this is by no means exhaustive.

We believe that:

- Our greatest joy comes from knowing, delighting in, and reflecting God. We continually wrestle to embrace this truth.

- We can know and experience God through God's written Word, through Jesus, and by the power of God's Holy Spirit. Intentional rhythmic, prayerful reflection plays a crucial part in this happening.

- There is no better way to live than the way God orders things to be, as demonstrated by Jesus. It is the way of the humble servant, of generosity, of acceptance, and of forgiveness; it is the way of praying for our enemies, of mercy, and it is the way walked by *shalom*-makers even through suffering and to death—Jesus said, "Take up your cross and follow me."

As a result of what we believe, we aim:

- To have a home that is open and inviting to people from all walks of life, where we can meet physical, emotional, and spiritual needs in a way that shows what God is like
- To laugh with those who laugh and weep with those who weep
- To love others more than our own comfort
- To be committed to pursuing justice and *shalom* on earth in the midst of injustice
- To become more aware of where we contribute to suffering in the world.

We will do this by:

- Focusing on the theme of humility, as demonstrated by Christ
- By speaking less and listening more—specifically listening to what people *aren't* saying; asking questions from an interested, curious, reflecting heart
- Learning more each week about social and environmental issues here and around the world
- Sponsoring, corresponding with, and praying for our *Compassion* children.

14

In Praise of Worship

The Trinitarian Nature of Christian Devotion

MICHAEL O'NEIL

INTRODUCTION

CHRISTIAN WORSHIP IS IN crisis today, according to Reformed Evangelical theologian Donald Bloesch. Having lost a sense of divine transcendence, traditional worship has become formalistic, while contemporary worship has become "gnostic and secular." Worse yet is the worship of those groups who having discarded traditional forms of theology and worship, have re-conceptualized God and whose worship thus lies under the specter of idolatry.[1] "If there is anything that characterizes modern worship," asserts Bloesch, "it is the loss of the sacred."[2] For Bloesch, genuine Christian worship is grounded in the unity of *logos* and *pneuma*, a creative response to God's gracious act of condescension in Jesus Christ, taking the form of praise, proclamation, recollection, and prayer, originating in the work of the Holy Spirit and aimed at the glory of God.[3] Of these elements, evangelical proclamation is primary. As such, Bloesch insists that the pulpit should be centrally located in the

---

1. Bloesch, *Church*, 129–30.
2. Ibid., 116; see also 35–38.
3. Ibid., 118–22.

front of the sanctuary with a table below to indicate "the subordination of the sacrament to the Word."[4]

In a similar vein Simon Chan worries that many Evangelical churches have abandoned the liturgical heritage of the church, and have ceased trusting in and following what the Spirit is doing in the church, choosing rather to "dumb down" their practices of worship, adopting marketing techniques and cultural practices to draw a crowd.[5] For Chan, this is a critical misstep since there can be "no separation between the liturgy and the church. *To be church is to be the worshipping community making a normative response to the revelation of the triune God.*"[6] While less strident in his language than Bloesch, Chan is actually more radical, claiming not only that worship is constitutive of the church, but that *that* worship is a *normative response* to revelation. Therefore, Chan insists that "true worship must reflect the reality of who God is. That is, whatever the liturgical forms may be, they must conform to certain theological norms."[7] For Chan, the criterion of true worship is its "correspondence to the work of the triune God, which reveals who the triune God is . . . 'Liturgy above all, is the work of the Trinity in its *execution* and *content*.'"[8]

Although both Bloesch and Chan write from an Evangelical perspective and share deep concern for the state of contemporary practice in Evangelical worship, their fundamental theological commitments continue to bring them into conflict regarding the theology and practice of worship. Chan is critical of Bloesch's description of worship as "creative response" to God's self-revelation, finding in this description the suggestion that worship is largely a human construct, "something worshippers could do creatively rather than 'pathically' by letting revelation shape their response."[9] He accuses Bloesch of an abiding rationalism because of his elevation of the Word *preached* above the sacrament,

---

4. Ibid., 143; see 133.
5. Chan, *Liturgical Theology*, 16, 39.
6. Ibid., 42 (original emphasis).
7. Ibid., 57.
8. Ibid., 58–59 (original emphasis). Chan is citing Kilmartin, *Systematic Theology*, 102.
9. Ibid., 13. Chan here utilizes Hütter, *Suffering Divine Things*, where theology is "pathos" in the sense that it is not simply a human construction, but always a response to the prior *poiesis* or construction of the Spirit.

and of allowing a pragmatic rather than theological rationale dictate the frequency of Eucharistic celebration.[10] Although Bloesch does not interact with Chan, it is clear that on theological grounds he would also criticize the manner in which Chan construes the worship of the church, for Chan's Eucharistic ecclesiology views the church as a kind of continuing incarnation, a "divine-humanity because of its organic unity with its Head, Christ."[11] This conception of the church extends the uniqueness of the Incarnate into the life and being of the church such that Chan can argue that

> if the church is the living body of Christ ontologically linked to the Head, then tradition is the life of the "embodied Christ" through time ... the extension of the Truth, the progressive actualizing of the Truth through time until it reaches its eschatological fulfillment.[12]

It is this mode of ecclesial ontology that allows Chan to argue for normative forms of worship in the church. But Bloesch rejects this variety of ecclesial ontology as an "ecclesiology from above" preferring to maintain a sharper distinction between Christ and the church, and thus allowing greater scope for "creativity" in the worship practices of the church.[13]

10. Ibid., 13.
11. Ibid., 23.
12. Ibid., 31.
13. Bloesch, *Church*, 75. Two observations should be noted. First, to be fair, Chan does acknowledge that "we must not so conceive of the church's identity with Christ as to deny that the church is also *not* Christ but distinct from Christ" (see Chan, *Liturgical Theology*, 28, 170, original emphasis), but his stress falls so consistently and firmly on identity (with either Christ or the Spirit) that the notion of distinction is attenuated at best. The issue at stake is Christological rather than simply ecclesiological, and concerns the nature of the relation between deity and humanity in the one person, Jesus Christ. Karl Barth clearly saw that the Chalcedonian formula that applied to the two natures in Jesus Christ must also be applied by analogy in the sphere of ecclesiology. That is, the unity between Christ and the church is strictly, irreversibly and one-sidedly a unity of *grace* (rather than an "organic" unity), with the distinction between the two carefully maintained in such a way that there is no confusion, change, division, or separation with respect to the two natures, "the distinction of natures being in no way annulled by the union." For an excellent treatment of Barth's ecclesiology see Bender, *Karl Barth's Christological Ecclesiology*. In this respect, Bloesch's position is to be preferred. Second, while Bloesch's position does allow more space for "creativity" in the worship ministry of the church, like Chan, he would argue strongly that worship practices should be shaped theologically. Further, it is evident that the space for creativity that Bloesch

This very brief engagement with two theologians who share similar concerns about the theology and practice of worship in Evangelical churches reveals immediately the depths of the disagreement that swirls around this topic. If the field of engagement were broadened to include other theologians and practitioners, including advocates of contemporary and other forms of worship practice, the extent of disagreement would quickly escalate. If that is the case, is there really any hope that such differences can be resolved or transcended, or is the church fated as it were, to an ineluctable plurality of worship forms, styles, and practices, in which our best hope is simply to understand and appreciate the other as best we can?

From Bloesch and Chan we may correctly learn that worship *per se*, is not an independent theological subject matter. That is, questions about the nature and practices of worship must be located and treated more broadly in theological discussion about the nature of the church, and ultimately in theological reflection on the nature and mission of the triune God, for it is only in this embracing context that we can begin to understand *what* worship is, and only then what *function* and *forms* it may have in the life of the gathered community of God's people. Further, examination of Bloesch and Chan's work shows that matters of theological method, interpretation, tradition, and even aesthetics cannot be ignored in this discussion, but also play a role in formulating an appropriate theology of worship to inform our development of practice. It is evident that a short essay could never adequately treat this breadth of material. This essay, therefore, will investigate the nature and theological location of worship in an attempt to provide a Trinitarian framework for the practice of contemporary worship in an Evangelical setting.

THE THEOLOGICAL LOCATION OF WORSHIP

Simon Chan correctly notes that it is impossible to develop a sound theology of worship without a proper understanding of the connection between worship and the church.[14] Even more fundamentally, a sound theology of worship requires a proper understanding of the relation between the church and creation. Chan argues that the church is the

---

would allow remains strictly circumscribed, so much so that many Evangelicals would find his proposals far too restrictive and conservative.

14. Chan, *Liturgical Theology*, 41.

expression of God's ultimate purpose itself, and not simply an interim instrument to accomplish God's greater purposes in creation.[15] That is, "the church precedes creation in that it is what God has in view from all eternity and creation is the means by which God fulfils his eternal purpose in time. The church does not exist in order to fix a broken creation; rather, creation exists to realize the church."[16]

To say this is to insist that the church is an end in itself and exists for God's sake, and thus its *raison d'être* derives not from the world but from the purposes of the electing God. This means that the primary task of the church is defined in terms of its being rather than its activity. Or to state the matter differently, the activity of the church arises from what the church *is*—a people chosen and called into existence by the saving work of God to be his people in fellowship with God. The first task of the church, therefore, is simply to be the church. In this way, the church's role vis-à-vis the world is paradigmatic before it is instrumental. The church exists not simply as the vanguard of the new creation or the vehicle of God's redemptive purpose for the world. Rather, the people of God enlivened by the Spirit and incorporated into Christ exist as the living expression of God's ultimate purpose for humanity generally. Failure to recognize this fosters the tendency to view the church as simply one of any number of entities whose legitimacy is to be determined solely on their ability to serve some higher, over-arching goal, usually established by secular reason. Relevance to the world then becomes the main criterion by which the church defines its *raison d'être*.[17] When the church embraces the logic of this position its worship becomes instrumental toward an assumed greater end such as personal or social wellbeing. We worship because of some desired outcome other than simply fellowship with God.[18]

---

15. Ibid., 21.

16. Ibid., 23. It is worth noting that Chan's ontology of the church has been decisively influenced by Robert Jenson. In this statement we hear echoes of Barth mediated through Jenson, who observes that in the work of Stanley Hauerwas, "what we are reading is a genial twist on the systematics of Karl Barth, one that puts the actual church where that shifty 'covenant' was: the creation is the outer ground of the church and the church is the inner ground of the creation" (see Jenson, "Hauerwas Project," 285–95, 293).

17. Ibid., 26.

18. See Willimon, *Pastor*, 75.

WORSHIP IN THE SPHERE OF GRACE

Consideration of the theological location of worship amongst those "enlivened by the Spirit and incorporated into Christ as God's people" has a further crucial implication: worship is necessarily set within a Trinitarian context. A number of key New Testament texts bear witness to the Trinitarian fellowship into which Christian believers are called, though perhaps none more so than the seminal words of Jesus. "But an hour is coming, and now is, when the true worshipers shall worship the Father in spirit and truth; for such people the Father seeks to be His worshipers. God is spirit, and those who worship Him must worship in spirit and truth."[19]

Many commentators on John's gospel claim that the phrase "worship in spirit and truth" should be understood in Christological and pneumatological terms.[20] That is, the Father seeks true worshippers, those whose worship is in accordance with the redemptive revelation given in Christ, and empowered by the Spirit. Of course, the marvelous truth implicit in these words is not just that the Father *seeks* these worshippers, but also that the hour has "now come" in Christ whereby the Father's desire shall be realized in the gracious activity of the Holy Spirit.

That worship is necessarily set within a Trinitarian context has three primary characteristics. First, authentic Christian devotion worships God in accordance with his self-revelation as Father, Son, and Holy Spirit. It is this divine identity revealed in the mystery of salvation that sets Christian worship apart from other forms of religious worship.[21] It is sadly true that much contemporary worship is deficient in this respect. A recent study of popular contemporary worship music by Robin Parry found that only five songs from a catalogue of 362 songs published between 1999 and 2004 were fully Trinitarian in the sense that they re-

---

19. See John 4:23–24. Other important New Testament texts include Matt 28:19; 2 Cor 13:14; and especially Eph 2:18.

20. See, for example, Barrett, *Gospel according to St John*, 199–200; Beasley-Murray, *John*, 62; Burge, *John*, 147; Keener, *John*, 615–16; Ridderbos, *John*, 163–64; Tasker, *John*, 77. Of course, not all commentators are convinced that *en pneumati kai aletheia* has a Christological and pneumatological referent. Leon Morris, for example, argues that while "in truth" refers to "the divine reality as revealed in Jesus," the phrase "in spirit" does "not likely" refer to the Holy Spirit, but to the human spirit, that is, a person should worship in "complete sincerity" (see Morris, *John*, 296, 270–71). See also, Kelly and Moloney, *Experiencing God*, 102–4.

21. Chan, *Liturgical Worship*, 58.

ferred to the three persons of the Trinity substantially or in terms of overt Trinitarian syntax. Thirty-two songs might be classified as "binitarian," addressing two of the three persons. 140 songs referred to only one person of the Trinity—115 to the Son. 185 songs, or 51.1% of the catalogue, referred simply to "You Lord."[22] Parry is careful to note that this is more a failure to elucidate the Trinitarian dimensions of the God we worship than a problem of violating Trinitarian faith.[23] Nonetheless, such paucity of Trinitarian emphasis in contemporary worship cannot help but have a deleterious effect on the faith and spirituality of believers in these environments.[24] Parry argues that "Christian worship should seek to bring God's church into a dynamic encounter with the Christian God—the Holy Trinity. Such worship will ceaselessly and effortlessly move back and forth between the three-ness of God and the unity of God. It will shift focus from the Father to Son to Spirit and back again in a restless celebration of divine love and mystery."[25]

The second characteristic of the Trinitarian context of worship is that Christian worship is Trinitarian in terms of *experience* and not just content. The wonder of Christian worship is not only that believers are given a gracious unveiling of the triune being of God, but being incorporated into Christ entails participation in the divine life itself. Tom Smail characterizes the intra-Trinitarian life as a fellowship of mutual self-giving in which the Father eternally gives himself to the Son in an intensity of self-giving that brings forth the Spirit as the personalized expression of the Father's love for the Son, and which is reciprocated in the Son's self-giving to the Father through the same Spirit: "The mutual self-giving of the Father and Son in the Spirit is of the very essence of the life of God."[26] The triune life is a ceaseless celebration and outpouring of divine love between the three persons of the Godhead, which has overflowed to include all those who respond to God's self-giving love now directed toward humanity in the coming of Jesus Christ. Christian worship is our "participation in the worship that takes place unceasingly in the life of God."[27]

22. Parry, *Worshipping Trinity*, 139–44.
23. Ibid., 133.
24. See Begbie, "Spirituality of Renewal Music," 227–39, 228.
25. Parry, *Worshipping Trinity*, 185.
26. Smail, *Giving Gift*, 157–63, 200.
27. Buxton, *Dancing*, 119.

The most wonderful aspect of this participation in the divine life is its mutuality as a "double movement of grace, which is the heart of the 'dialogue' between God and humanity in worship . . . grounded in the very perichoretic being of God."[28] God the Father pours out his love toward us, giving his very self to us through the Son and in the Spirit, and by so doing calls forth an answering response of love and self-giving from his people inspired and empowered by the same Spirit and corresponding to the loving self-giving of the Son to the Father.[29] Torrance employs the delightful metaphor of a hug to illustrate this double movement of grace.

> When we hug somebody whom we love there is a double movement. We give ourselves to the beloved, and in the same act by putting our arms around the other, we draw that person close to our heart! That is a parable of the double movement of grace, the God-humanward and the human-Godward movement in the priesthood of Christ and the ministry of the Spirit. In his "two hands"—God our Father in grace gives himself to us as God. But in Jesus Christ, the Word made flesh, and in the Spirit we are led to the Father by the intercessions of Christ and the intercessions of the Spirit. We are lifted up by "the everlasting arms."[30]

In the act of worship God lifts us up out of ourselves to participate in the very life of communion for which we were created.[31]

The final characteristic of the Trinitarian context of worship is that our worship is itself a gift *from* the triune God rather than a self-generated gift or work that believers offer *to* God. Torrance suggests that there is "no more urgent need in our churches today than to recover the Trinitarian nature of grace—that it is by grace alone, through the gift of Jesus Christ in the Spirit that we can enter into and live a life of communion with God our Father."[32]

For Torrance, worship is a participation in the Son's communion with the Father. As a faithful high priest, Jesus Christ offered to God the worship and praise we failed to offer. By his life of perfect love and obedience he has glorified God and has offered for us and in our place

---

28. Torrance, *Worship*, 21.
29. See Smail, *Giving Gift*, 199; and Chan, *Liturgical Theology*, 59–60.
30. Torrance, *Worship*, 57.
31. Ibid., 9.
32. Ibid., 49.

true worship of God. Because his humanity is vicarious and representative humanity, Jesus Christ has in reality borne *us* in his death and resurrection, and has presented *us* in himself to the Father as God's dear children. We are welcomed by the Father as those accepted *in* the Beloved. Further, our participation in the *Incarnate's* worship of the Father is likewise a participation in the *eternal* Son's communion with the Father—a relationship which is at once *internal* to the Godhead and *externally* extended to humanity through grace.[33] Christian worship is, therefore, "our liturgical amen to the worship of Christ," a participation in *his* vicarious life of worship and intercession.[34] Christians worship *in* Christ as well as *through* Christ, offering themselves to the Father "in the name of Christ because he has already in our name made the one true offering to the Father."[35]

Worship, then, is not simply a human activity, or simply a human response to the grace of God. It *is* human response to grace, but a response which arises from, is enabled by, and participates in the primary human response to divine grace made by Jesus Christ. As such, even our worship is a gift of grace that God gives to us, rather than something we do to draw near to God, or to bring him near to us. God has already drawn near to us in Christ, and by so doing has taken us up into fellowship with himself in the Son's vicarious humanity.

An implication of this is that God's people are freed from a performance mentality when it comes to worship, for even our imperfect attempts at worship are gathered up by our high priest, converted in him into worship acceptable to God, and presented to the Father on our behalf![36] Worship which thus occurs in the sphere of grace is not only liberated from the pressure to "do it right," but is also freed to develop creative or contextual forms of worship. Nevertheless, worship remains an "ordinance of grace," a "covenanted way of response" to God. Whenever worship loses this sense of being grounded in divine grace, it becomes "a rebellious, idolatrous form of self-expression and self-assertion."[37] Thus, our worship is "worship in truth" to the extent that it acknowledges and

---

33. Ibid., 20.

34. Ibid., 2–3. See, also, Torrance's description of Jesus' high priestly mediatorial ministry in ibid., 37–38.

35. Ibid., 40.

36. Buxton, *Dancing*, 120, 128.

37. Torrance, *Worship*, 52, 97.

celebrates this grace grounded in the saving and high priestly activity of Jesus Christ.

WORSHIP *IN VIA*

We have noted that the Father seeks worshippers who will worship him in spirit and in truth. Our deliberations concerning worship in the sphere of grace were an attempt to explicate what it means to worship God in truth; that is, in accordance with his self-disclosure as the triune God of grace. In this section we will explore what it means to worship God "in spirit" specifically addressing the role of the Holy Spirit in Christian worship.

A careful reading of Torrance's work shows that he has a clear sense of the role of the Holy Spirit in Christian worship. Through the Spirit, *God* meets us in worship, summoning us to respond in faith, obedience, and thanksgiving. The Spirit also helps us in the frailty, weakness, and unworthiness of our response by "lifting us up to Christ who, in his ascended *humanity*, is our God-given Response, the leader of our worship, the pioneer of our faith, our advocate and High Priest, who through the eternal Spirit presents us with himself to the Father."[38]

The work of the Spirit is to seal the heart of the believer with the "benefits" of Christ—forgiveness, sanctification, and sonship—and to summon them to say *Amen* in faith to the unilateral covenant of grace made by God in Jesus Christ.[39] The Spirit realizes Christian participation in the suffering of Christ by bringing the work of Christ to our remembrance, interpreting the meaning of his passion to us, and lifting our hearts and minds in the *sursum corda*, making us participants in Christ's communion with the Father.[40] In short, the Spirit "lifts us out of any narcissistic preoccupation with ourselves to find our true humanity and dignity in Jesus Christ, in a life centered in others, in communion

---

38. Ibid., 77 (original emphasis).

39. Ibid., 66.

40. Ibid., 75–76. Muller notes that the *sursum corda* ("Lift up [your] hearts") has a particular significance in Reformed liturgy, the tradition in which Torrance writes, "as an explanation of the union between the participant in the Lord's Supper and the resurrected Christ." Reformed theology argues for the "operation of the Spirit that joins together by grace the uplifted heart of the believer and the person of Christ with all his benefits." See Muller, *Dictionary*, 292–93.

with Jesus Christ and one another, in a loving concern for the humanity of all."[41]

Torrance's vision of Christian worship as a renewed humanity in communion with God is certainly majestic. Yet in many ways it also appears to be more noetic or even mystical than experiential. Further, despite the evident work of the Spirit in worship as noted above, his treatment of worship is clearly focused more on the person and work of Christ than the Spirit, so that the Spirit's work is at times subsumed into the work of Christ. For example, Torrance suggests that "it is not so much we who remind ourselves of [Christ's sufferings], but Jesus Christ who brings his passion to our remembrance through the Holy Spirit, as our ever-living and ever-present Lord ... Christ ... by his Spirit, lifts us up as we present our memorials before God."[42]

Note that Christ is the acting subject of the believers' participation in his own communion with the Father, with the result that the Spirit is instrumental rather than agential in his work amongst believers. Further, this attempt to understand worship as the gracious activity of *God* also seems to diminish worship as a *human* activity. But worship is surely a conjunction of divine *and* human work, the former calling forth and enabling the latter. Fergusson correctly warns against viewing worship as "an intra-Trinitarian transaction that takes place over our heads, unrelated to the practices of the visible, empirical congregations to which we belong."[43]

Several New Testament scholars argue that "worship in spirit" (John 4:23-4) refers to worship "dynamically animated by God's Holy Spirit."[44] Keener insists that "John here refers to worship empowered by the Spirit ... [who mediates] the presence of God more effectively than the temple had ... The preposition *en* retains its locative sense ... but the sense of the locative in Greek more naturally overlaps with the instrumental than in English, and in early Christian teaching 'worship in the Spirit' seems to have coincided with 'worship (empowered) by the Spirit.'"[45]

Keener suggests that early Jewish Christians would interpret "in spirit" in terms of inspiration, that is, the Spirit as a prophetic or charis-

---

41. Torrance, *Worship*, 97.
42. Ibid., 75.
43. Fergusson, "Theology of Worship," 367-80; 374-75.
44. Burge, *John*, 147.
45. Keener, *John*, 615-16.

matic presence, without whom genuine worship would be impossible.[46] In an extraordinary essay, "Cry for Liberty in the Church's Worship," Ernst Käsemann asserts that "experience of the Spirit is the real hallmark of post-Easter Christianity."[47] In his exegesis of Romans 8:26–27 Käsemann maintains that "the spirit enters the service of worship in a way which is positively objective compared with our own spiritual experiences, and does so by no means wordlessly but with the cries of the enthusiasts."[48] This view of the Spirit's role in worship retains a mystical, or perhaps better, ecstatic dimension in a manner similar to that of Torrance. But whereas the mystic dimension of the Spirit's role in worship in Torrance's view appears more noetic, this understanding of the Spirit's role in worship is more experiential.

There can be no question but that the worship practices of the Pentecostal and Charismatic movements of the twentieth century have forced the church to reconsider its understanding of the Spirit's role in worship. For all the—not insignificant—problems associated with Pentecostal and Charismatic worship, it remains the case that Christian worship has been changed dramatically in many sectors of the church as a direct result of the *experience* of the Spirit in worship.[49] Tom Smail speaks of the immediacy, intimacy, freedom, spontaneity, inner and personal reality, directness, depth, and joy in the near presence of God that the Holy Spirit has inspired through the Charismatic renewal.[50] Smail rejects the criticism that Charismatics have been carried into "vague mystic ecstasies without Christian content." Instead, while "singing in the Spirit" may indeed bypass normal rational faculties, nevertheless

---

46. Ibid., 616, 618. In his earlier work, *Spirit in the Gospels*, Keener notes, "That God is to be worshiped 'in Spirit' could well be taken to mean ecstatic worship . . . This fits our clearest NT pictures of worship."

47. Käsemann, *Perspectives*, 122.

48. Ibid., 129–30. See also Gordon Fee's comment on the nature of the "groaning" (Rom 8:26) in *God's Empowering Presence*, 575–86.

49. For a sympathetic yet honest appraisal of Pentecostal worship see Hudson, "Worship," 177–203. Amongst other things Hudson lists triumphalism, individualism, gimmicks and fads, sectarian withdrawal from culture, and the idolatry of the novel as major dangers confronting Pentecostal and Charismatic worship (see 194–201). For ease of expression, I will henceforth refer to Pentecostals and Charismatics with the single term "Charismatic." This is not to deny or diminish the historical, theological or ecclesiastical distinctions between the two movements. See also, Begbie, "Spirituality" 234–38.

50. Smail, "In Spirit and in Truth," 95–103, 95, 96, 101.

> It reminds us that alongside the praise of the renewed mind there is the praise of the renewed heart that, when it is being evoked by the Spirit, expresses not simply our superficial feelings, but engages the deep primal emotions at the hidden center of our being in our self-offering to the living God . . . From our experiences of such worship we are left in little doubt that it is the Holy Spirit who in these special times and ways has drawn us so deeply and engrossingly into the praiseful worship of the Father and the Son . . . We recognize the same Spirit who was at work in the New Testament churches at work in us.[51]

It is this shift from the cognitive to the experiential which is perhaps the distinctive feature of Charismatic worship in relation to the broader Christian tradition, and both its greatest strength as well as source of potential harm. Hudson notes that with the advent of Charismatic worship, the concept of worship changed from the idea that worship simply expressed the truth of what God had done, to an understanding that it could express the believer's relationship to the Father in ways that were distinctly personal and intimate.[52] What is true of Black Pentecostalism, specifically, may be predicated of Charismatic worship generally: "Worship is expressed through the filter of experience much more than through theology."[53] Unfortunately, the danger of unbridled subjectivity is evidenced in much Charismatic worship. The correct response to this danger, however, is not to forsake subjectivity in worship, but to anchor the subjective experience of worship in the objective truths of revelation—worship in Spirit *and* truth. By reminding ourselves who God is and what he has accomplished for us in Christ we may, like the Samaritan woman, be drawn "out of ourselves" so that our worship becomes genuine response to the objective reality of God, rather than simply an echo of our own hearts.[54]

To speak of *experience* in worship is to acknowledge what many Christians believe, that in the activity of worship they encounter, or are encountered by, the presence of the living God. What differs amongst the various traditions of the Christian faith is the precise *locus* of that

---

51. Ibid., 96–97.
52. Hudson, "Worship," 185.
53. Ibid., 186.
54. Buxton, *Dancing*, 130; Kelly and Moloney, *Experiencing God*, 103.

experience or encounter.[55] Although holding to the dual rubric of *Word and Sacrament*, many Protestants typically locate the divine-human encounter in worship in the preaching of the Word. In proclamation, *God* addresses his people in, with, and through the human words of the preacher. Other Christians—Protestants as well as Roman Catholics—locate this encounter in the celebration of the Eucharist. More recently in Charismatic worship, this existential encounter is sought in the presence and activity of the Spirit in the singing of praises, gifts of the Spirit, and practices of personal ministry, in some cases quite apart from both Word and Sacrament. Ralph Martin suggests that worship in early Christianity and especially in the Pauline mission communities had three sides which roughly correspond to the three dimensions enumerated above—the charismatic, the didactic, and the Eucharistic.[56] In light of New Testament practice, then, the question is well asked whether the Spirit is active in only one of these dimensions, or whether he may use any or all of these dimensions to encounter his people. The natural corollary is that churches' orders of service regularly incorporate aspects of each of these dimensions, so that with joyful and prayerful anticipation God's people may look forward to the work of the Spirit amongst them in all of these ways.

To approach worship in this manner requires openness to the freedom of the Spirit who encounters us in sovereign grace, without attempting to *overly* regulate the means in which the Spirit "will" or "must" act.[57] It is inevitable that some form of structure evolves in the worship practices of any congregation, including those most given to spontaneity.[58] Contrary to sentiments sometimes expressed in Charismatic churches, structure and spontaneity are not inimical to one another, and the sovereign Spirit is able to graciously manifest his presence in and through liturgical forms as easily as in more informal contexts. Authentic worship is not measured in terms of outward expression but inner source and motivation, as well as faithfulness to the truth as it has been revealed

---

55. See Fergusson, "Theology of Worship," 373. Fergusson speaks of the "dramatic character of worship" in which God is not simply a passive object or recipient of our worship, but also active subject who encounters his people.

56. Martin, *Worship of God*, 180–84.

57. Such openness to the Spirit's activity will, of course, also recognize his freedom to encounter us *outside* the context of worship as well as within. *The wind blows where it will.*

58. See Hudson, *Worship*, 187–88.

and enacted in Jesus Christ.[59] Tom Smail offers wise counsel suggesting that those responsible for leading congregational worship maintain a creative tension between freedom and framework, focusing now on the one element, now on the other as the situation warrants: "If we are prisoners of the framework, we shall have to rediscover our freedom in the Spirit; if that freedom is in danger of leading us away from Christ into religious self-indulgence or one-sidedness, we shall have to return to the discipline and sobriety that the framework can offer."[60]

Smail insists that there is ultimately no possibility of conflict between the Son and the Spirit, and that the concern of each is that believers and churches find freedom within the framework of the Father's call and purposes. "Charismatic spontaneity and liturgical conformity to the truth of Christ are not enemies, but allies in securing our well-ordered freedom," asserts Smail.[61] Because worship is "in *Spirit*" as well as "in truth," there indeed arises the possibility of "creative response" to the revelation of God in Christ. As such, there is no single or normative manner in which worship is to come to expression within the faith community. As Buxton reminds us, authentic worship reflects our entire humanity in its socio-historical context. "[O]ur bodies and emotions, our minds and our creative energies, all are available to the Spirit who weaves the response of worship amongst the people of God, both spontaneously and through the employment of ritual and liturgy . . . [T]he Spirit seeks to create an authentic tapestry of worship which reflects not only the rich diversity of life within God but also the unique life of each community of faith."[62]

The mention of "the unique life of each community of faith" leads us to the heart and climax of this section. Worship according to the Spirit is worship *in via*, worship "along the way," an act of the eschatological community in its earthly-historical journey toward the fullness of God's kingdom. We have earlier noted Käsemann's contention that the real hallmark of the post-Easter community was experience of the Spirit, particularly as it came to expression in the public worship of the church. Käsemann goes on to argue that what the Corinthian believers presumed were the tongues of angels and hence a sign of their being

---

59. See Buxton, *Dancing*, 132; and Smail, *In Spirit and Truth*, 102.
60. Smail, *In Spirit and Truth*, 102.
61. Ibid., 102–3.
62. Buxton, *Dancing*, 133–34.

caught up into the eschatological or heavenly sphere, were interpreted by Paul as the groanings of the Spirit. "In an unmistakably Pauline paradox the apostle describes as sighs what the church considers and praises as the manifestation of heavenly tongues and thus compares them with the sighs of the creature and the sighing for redemption from bodily temptation which is familiar to every Christian."[63]

The work of the Spirit in this intercessory sighing is not the work of liberating the praying believer from their human weakness in order to raise them above common earthly conditions and experiences, but precisely the opposite. Käsemann contends that the public glossolalia discouraged in 1 Corinthians 14 is encouraged in Romans 8 because of the changed context. In Corinth glossolalia functioned in service of a *theologia gloriae* (theology of glory) while in Romans 8 it functions as solidarity with and intercession for the brokenness of the created order.

> Far from understanding ecstasies, and particularly the speaking with tongues, as a sign that the Christian community has been translated with Christ into heavenly existence (the view taken by the Corinthian enthusiasts), the apostle hears in these things the groans of those who, though called to liberty, still lie tempted and dying and cry to be born again with the new creation. For it is this that appears here as the specific work of the spirit and hence as the hall-mark of Christian worship when it is moved by the spirit.[64]

It is immediately apparent that Käsemann rejects triumphalism in worship as well as any form of liturgy which removes or isolates the church from a deep solidarity between itself and the world: "The cry for liberty must deeply determine the prayer which is pleasing to God, as well as true Christian worship; and solidarity with the world must not be forgotten, in that worship above all."[65] Rather, Christian worship must be "something like the intercession of Christians for the world. Otherwise

---

63. Käsemann, *Perspectives*, 132.

64. Ibid., 134. Note that Käsemann has certainly overstated the distinction between Paul's comments in 1 Cor 14 and Rom 8. See, for example, 1 Cor 14:16–17 where Paul commends the practice of glossolalia saying, "For you are giving thanks well enough." It is evident that the practice does function as inspirited praise as well as intercession, even though Paul seeks to restrict the practice to personal devotion, unless accompanied by the gift of interpretation.

65. Ibid., 137.

it could not be the basis for our daily service, nor prepare for that service and dismiss us to it."[66]

In similar fashion Smail is concerned that a *theologia gloriae* which does not sufficiently wrestle with a *theologia crucis* (theology of the cross) can engender a form of worship that "concentrates too one-sidedly on the triumphs of Easter and Pentecost and does not sufficiently take into account that they can only be reached by way of the cross."[67] Thus worship must make space for confession, repentance, and intercession as well as exuberant praise. Genuine intercession participates in the agony of Gethsemane where, with Christ, we give ourselves in costly prayer on behalf of the afflicted world of which we are a part.[68] Because the church cannot presume on what God may or may not do, it needs to be prepared to minister to the world and worship from within a framework of a *theologia viatorum* (theology of the journey), trusting in and celebrating the work of the cross and participating in its way, while looking forward to and hoping for the *theologia gloriae* of an Easter and Pentecost faith.[69]

CONCLUSION: IN PRAISE OF WORSHIP

Much more might be said about the wonder of worship, that marvelous gift of grace given to the church by which it is called to participate in the divine life and mission. Barth writes that Christian worship is "the most important, momentous and majestic thing which can possibly take place on earth, because its primary content is not the work of man but the work of the Holy Spirit and consequently the work of faith."[70]

In worship the church is encountered by the triune God, being lifted out of itself by the Spirit and made to participate in the Son's communion with the Father. In worship we find our true and deepest humanity. In worship our lives are re-narrated in accordance with the truth, the revelation of God's saving intent set forth and accomplished in Christ. In worship we are trained in the knowledge of God, nurtured in the love and grace of God, and co-opted into the ongoing work of God. In worship we bear witness to the world of the love and grace of the Father given to hu-

---

66. Ibid., 136.
67. Smail, *In Spirit and in Truth*, 97–98.
68. Ibid., 100. See also, Hudson, *Worship*, 200.
69. Hudson, *Worship*, 203.
70. Barth, *Knowledge of God*, 198.

manity in Jesus Christ. In worship we experience the gracious hospitality of God and are prepared to share the riches we receive with others. In worship our own needs are set within the overarching story of the gospel, and are borne to God in prayer. In worship we find ourselves moved by the Spirit into deeper solidarity with the world, and are primed and sent by the same Spirit into the world as agents of reconciliation, service, and healing. In worship we are formed as the community of the Spirit, journeying in the way of Christ and his cross toward the eschatological kingdom of the Father in which we even now participate though only to a limited degree. In worship we respond in adoring love to the One who has first loved us, for "worship is a way of being in love."[71]

---

71. Willimon, *Pastor*, 75.

15

Worship and the Quest for Justice

Brian S. Harris

INTRODUCTION

Our local newspaper recently reported the findings of a survey on the most unpopular inventions. While I can't confirm the rigor of the research methods used or dogmatically affirm the survey's findings, I was intrigued by the outcome. Religion was rated the tenth least popular invention, with mobile phones claiming the number one spot. My initial instinct was to think that respondents were probably not thinking of Christianity when they spoke of religion. After all, Christians can claim credit for many of the positive social advances made in the last 2000 years. While multiple social factors are invariably at work in societal evolution, it is not fair to explore the abolition of slavery, the protection of the rights of women and children, the development of the welfare state, or the shift in focus from retributive to restorative justice, without repeatedly referring to the Christian faith that motivated and inspired most of those who championed these causes. And they represent a small selection of an impressive array of humanitarian achievements.[1]

It would, however, be simplistic to assume the argument could be closed by referring to some of the more satisfying outcomes resulting from the interface between the Christ story and human his-

---

1. For a fuller, though very accessible account, see Schmidt, *Under the Influence*. Another very simple, but thought provoking introduction to the topic is found in Andrews, *People of Compassion*.

tory.² There is also a shadow side. There have been many times in the history of the church when it has been supportive of a right wing agenda, which on occasion has revealed itself in racism, sexism, homophobia, militarism, ecological and economic exploitation, cultural insensitivity, and more beside.³

Even if not actively supporting exploitation, faith can easily wear unattractive masks.⁴ There is faith as escapism. I still remember the parents of an early girlfriend informing me that they had declined membership of their voluntary pension scheme because Jesus would return long before their retirement. I backed out of that relationship fast! They spent their money on trivia and trinkets, while engaging in endless debate about the exact timetable of Christ's return. They looked forward to the future God had for them, but ignored the gift he has already given. It never struck them that *today* should be enjoyed and that it confers great responsibility.

Then there is faith as the status quo. This mask bears no resemblance to what is required to be an authentic Christ-follower, but nonetheless for many people things are good provided they've been around for more than twenty years. Nostalgia, rather than a commitment to a daring faith agenda, is the driver. Onlookers fail to find it inspiring. There is also faith as smugness and self-righteousness. While most have renounced the wagging finger, the image of Christians as people who see themselves as morally superior to lesser mortals and who "tut-tut" at the folly of unbelievers, persists.

This alerts us to an important truth. Faith can spark life's loftiest journeys but paradoxically, it can also accompany and bolster its most misguided and tragic detours. Dawkins and Hitchens are just two of a

---

2. While it can be argued that we should distinguish between the Christ story and the history of the churches founded as a result of that story, in practice this is difficult to do. However, it is true that the Christ story could (and probably should) serve as the filter to determine the faithfulness or otherwise of the churches formed to their mandate to serve as Christ's body on earth.

3. So, for example, Wallis, *Call to Conversion*, 25 (speaking of the mixed legacy of Evangelicalism), laments, "Evangelicals in this century have a history of going along with the culture on the big issues and taking their stand on the smaller issues. That has been one of the serious problems of evangelical religion. Today, many evangelicals no longer just acquiesce to the culture on the larger economic and political issues, but actively promote the culture's worst values on these matters."

4. The following three paragraphs are a slightly modified form of part of a brief newspaper article I wrote in 2007—"When Faith is the Problem."

growing number of popular writers who have alerted us to the potentially poisonous harvest resulting from religion.[5]

Because of the potentially abusive nature of faith it is important to highlight some of the warning signs that it is at risk of proving toxic. While an exhaustive list is beyond the scope of this essay, danger signals include an insistence on unquestioning faith, or faith as compulsion instead of faith as invitation, or where there is legalism without love, or any form of faith that aims for power and control and attempts to justify the unjustifiable in the name of God.

What can be said about religion in general can also be said of religious worship. While expressions of worship vary greatly, they can serve as a transforming power for good or as instruments of oppression and injustice. At the extreme end, religious worship has sometimes included human sacrifice. Peter Berger's volume, *Pyramids of Sacrifice*, documents all too chillingly the unacceptable sacrifices made to placate the gods, all in the quest of a utopian tomorrow.[6]

Thus alerted to the potential shadow side of worship, I would like to shift the focus to ways in which worship can accompany the quest for justice. This chapter explores the theme under three broad headings, worship and the quest for justice for the self; worship and the quest for justice for the neighbor, and third, worship and the quest for justice for the planet, concluding with some thoughts on worship as a doxology of hope.

WORSHIP AND THE QUEST FOR JUSTICE FOR THE SELF

Simon Chan has reminded us of St Bernard's outline of four stages of love for God. He writes, "For St Bernard, growth in the spiritual life is growth in love. One may begin with love of self for self's sake, proceed to love of God for self's sake, advance to love of God for God's sake and finally end in love of self for God's sake."[7] It is significant that both the opening and closing stages revolve around love of self, though the intent of that love has morphed from love of self for self's sake in stage one to love of self for God's sake in stage four.

---

5. Dawkins, *God Delusion*; Hitchens, *God is Not Great*.

6. Berger's work suggests that whereas in the past calls for sacrifice came in a religious guise, parallel calls for political sacrifice are now made with the assurance that the sacrifice of today will lead to a utopian future—Berger, *Pyramids*.

7. Chan, *Spiritual Theology*, 90.

When worship accompanies the journey of justice for the self it sometimes follows a similar route. At times when the self is crushed, and hope is at best a distant category, worship can provide an anchor for the self, a place for gentle reorientation, an affirmation that we still matter and that even if unknown to others or rejected by others, we are known to God. The one who notes the sparrow's fall, notes our struggles and is not unsympathetic. Those who are older might sing the C. Austin Miles hymn which speaks of coming "to the garden alone, while the dew is still on the roses" and finding that in that garden "He walks with me, and He talks with me, and He tells me I am His own."[8]

This very private version of faith extols the God-encounter as an escape for the self. Worship is a cozy conversation between Jesus and me. While this can verge on a suffocating isolationism, there are times when this is a prerequisite for the restoration of the self. It is the self looking out for the self, and clutching on to faith as a means of survival. But St Bernard's version of the spiritual journey is loftier. He envisions a later stage when love for self is channeled for God's glory. Jesus' summary of the two great commandments, recorded in Matthew 22:37–39, require us to love not our neighbor *and* our self, as if the two are separate categories, but to love our neighbor *as* our self. It would appear that healthy self-love accompanies an ability to love the neighbor and to move beyond one's own boundaries.

Without worship, it is difficult to truly love the self. Deprived of a transcendent perspective, the self is constantly reminded of mortality and frailty. As 1 Peter 1:24–25 notes, "All people are like grass, and all their glory is like the flowers of the field; the grass withers and the flowers fall, but the word of the Lord stands forever."[9] By contrast, when we worship we encounter the one in whose image we are made, and are reminded of our remarkable identity as beings called to be *imago Dei*. Without such encounters we are at risk of forgetting our distinctiveness, and of measuring our days in terms of limitation, rather than against the backdrop of the eternal. In the absence of an eternal perspective we succumb to fear and anxiety. By contrast, when guided by hope we find the freedom to confront our demons. In the presence of the one who is the light of the world, the power of such forces dissipates.

---

8. Bock, *Hymns*, 588.

9. 1 Pet 1:24–25, in turn, is quoting from Isa 40:6–8.

Worship accompanies the quest for justice for the self as in genuine worship-encounters we are liberated to abandon false images of the self. Scazzero writes that "The vast majority of us go to our graves without knowing who we are. We unconsciously live someone else's life, or at least someone else's expectations for us. This does violence to ourselves, our relationship with God, and ultimately to others."[10] Earlier he quotes from Augustine's *Confessions*, "How can you draw close to God when you are far from your own self?" and St Teresa of Avila's insight in *The Way of Perfection*, "Almost all problems in the spiritual life stem from lack of self-knowledge."[11]

This leads to the question of which comes first, the liberation of self-knowledge allowing a genuine God-encounter, or meeting with the Divine as a route to self-awareness and healing. Reality is rarely linear. Worship accompanies the quest for justice for the self not by seeking a single transforming encounter, but by creating safe spaces of hopefulness to which the self regularly returns. Though no magic panacea, it is rarely disappointed. Be it in the garden alone, with the dew still on the roses, or in the strange silence that can descend as one chooses to listen for a different voice in the midst of rush hour traffic, or in a mighty cathedral with flickering candles and stained glass beauty compelling one to gaze upwards, the self bowed in adoration and worship finds the courage to abandon the caricatured self and its accompanying idols. Release from bondage to a self defined by performance, possessions, or popularity is gradually gained.[12]

However, there is no true liberation for the self in permanent isolation. Prior to his elevation as Pope Benedict XVI, Joseph Ratzinger located the essence of the church in the arc between the self and the whole, envisioning it as the communion between the human "I" and the divine "Thou" in a universally communal "We."[13] In liberating the self to be most true to the self, healing experiences of worship do not leave the self in isolation. We are *Created for Community*, to cite the title of a work by theologian Stanley Grenz. Worship draws us into community with fellow travelers. We do not journey as separated individuals but as a family of faith. In the cut and thrust of this household, the self enlarges.

10. Scazzero, *Emotionally Healthy Spirituality*, 66.
11. Ibid., 65.
12. Ibid., 74–78.
13. This is discussed in Volf, *After Our Likeness*, 30.

We weep with those who weep, and rejoice with those who rejoice (Rom 12:15). All this is done together with the One who is present where even two or three meet in his name (Matt 18:20). In the words of the Graham Kendrick song we pray as we sing, and invite Jesus to "stand among us, at the meeting of our lives," and to "Join our hearts in unity and take away our fears." [14]

In that unity we discover our name. It is a name that does not disappoint. Like Jacob, now renamed as Israel and limping from his God-encounter, we shuffle away from Peniel, hesitantly but surely directed on the journey of reconciliation. We begin to see in the face of Esau not our enemy, but our brother. In the healing of relationships, our own self finds healing.[15]

WORSHIP AND THE QUEST FOR JUSTICE FOR THE NEIGHBOR

It is sobering to realize that the Bible itself seems cautious about the role of worship. Genesis 4 (in which Cain and Abel present differing offerings to God) is the Bible's first record of an act of worship. However, it leads to the first murder, clearly a less than promising start. There was no temple in the Garden of Eden, and in John's vision of the future he assures us that in the New Jerusalem there will be no temple (Rev 21:22). Much worship in the Bible is deemed to be unacceptable to God, and invariably this verdict is linked to an exploitative lifestyle rather than to a liturgical oversight.[16]

If worship is to accompany the quest for justice for the neighbor, we need to begin in the place of repentance, and recognize that at times it has aided oppression. All genuine *metanoia* (repentance) involves an about-turn in both our thinking and action. Too often the music that has accompanied our acts of worship has been triumphal, justifying a militant stance towards all those who have opted for an alternate view of the world. While the military language of a hymn such as *Onward Christian Soldiers* springs rapidly to mind, it is hardly an isolated instance, nor is this imagery limited to the older hymns of the church. We should filter all our music through a simple grid that asks what kind of world is en-

---

14. Dare, *Praise*, 131.
15. This imagery flows from Genesis 32:22—33:4.
16. For some thoughtful reflections on this see Boulton, "Unholy Rites."

visioned by this music. To the extent that worship is transformative and contributes towards the creation of the world of which it speaks or sings, it is important that the test is not bypassed and a pleasing tune is not allowed to justify flawed theology.

If some worship is actively aggressive, other forms can validate escapism or a placid acceptance of the status quo. Marx's complaint that religion serves as an opiate for the masses has often been cited. One does not have to dig too deeply to discover reasons for his unease. The music of many of the classic African-American Spirituals is a case in point. It is perfectly understandable that those entrapped in slavery and with little hope of liberation in their lifetime would sing soulfully of the sweet chariot that would swing low to carry them home. Indeed, we must guard against a quick condemnation of such music. It might have been escapist, but for some reality is such that the most humane option *is* escapism. It is too easy to pass judgment from a safe and comfortable historical distance.[17] We should, however, question why some, who live in comfortable homes and have great social security, continue to feed on such images. In many contexts such escapism is a flight from responsibility.

Perhaps it is at the level of expectation that we need to begin. When, for example, we invite worshippers to turn their eyes upon Jesus, assuring them that by so doing "the things of earth will grow strangely dim," do we not encourage worship to be viewed as a departure from reality?[18] Is it not more biblical to assert that as we turn our eyes upon Jesus the things of the world come into clearer focus and perspective? Surely genuine worship encounters help our hearts to resonate with the heartbeat of God. They alert us to the *missio Dei*, and give us the courage to accompany God in his work in the world. And they keep us in touch with those who are fellow travelers on the journey, the community of faith to which we have been called. Corporately this group of pilgrims is commissioned to serve as a sign of hopefulness—a city set on a hill that

---

17. It is sometimes maintained that many African American spirituals, including "Swing Low, Sweet Chariot," were coded with instructions to be used by runaway slaves on the "Underground Railroad" (as the informal network of safe homes in which runaway slaves could seek refuge was known). If this theory is true, it would change the sense in which the lyrics are escapist! However, the likelihood of this theory being valid is, at best, slight. See Kelley, "Song, Story."

18. Horrobin and Leavers, *Mission Praise*, 712.

cannot be hidden, or even more daringly, people who are called to be the light of the dark world (Matt 5:14).[19]

How then might our worship facilitate the birth of such a community? Perhaps Martin Luther King's famous *I Have a Dream* speech (August 28, 1963, at the Lincoln Memorial, Washington D.C.) can alert us to the possibilities inherent in our worship. While the reality of the world in which King's dream was birthed was far removed from the world that he envisioned, the act of giving hope-words helped facilitate the creation of a new order. To dream "that one day on the red hills of Georgia, the sons of former slaves and the sons of former slave owners will be able to sit down together at the table of brotherhood" seemed audacious in 1963. However, each improbable dream articulated by King planted seeds of discontent with the status quo. Slowly that discontent has borne fruit. In a similar fashion, worship that focuses on reality as God intends it to be creates the impetus and hunger for such a reality. Portrayal precedes the actual creation. Just as a building exists first in the architect's mind, then in a plan, and then in reality, so a new order is first dreamed, then expressed, and, if the dream and its expression takes root in our hearts, it eventually becomes reality. The apostle Paul dares to dream of a day when all will be reconciled in Christ. His inclusive vision embraces all things in heaven and all things on earth—see, for example Colossians 1:20. When our worship points to such a vision and invites us to believe it and to live in the light of it, it empowers the realization of this new reality. As we affirm and celebrate our hope, we find the strength to live in the light of our hopes, rather than to obsess about the avoidance of our fears. Our worship invites us to be larger. Trivia no longer dominates the agenda. When we live in the light of our faith "we will be able to hew out of the mountain of despair a stone of hope" (Martin Luther King).

Worship that reminds us of the common humanity we share with our neighbors, the goodness of creation, and the reality of a realm beyond our current gaze, enlarges our outrage at prejudice, violence, pettiness, needless poverty, exploitation, and greed. We are invited to be responsive to the work of the Spirit in our lives, a work that produces the fruit of love, joy, peace, patience, kindness, goodness, faithfulness, gentleness, and self-control (Gal 5:22–23). As the Apostle Paul goes on

---

19. It is suggestive to hold the statement, "You are the light of the world" (Matt 5:14), in creative tension with Jesus' claim, "I am the light of the world" (John 8:12).

to note, against such fruit "there is no law" (Gal 5:23). All celebrate the world-transforming power of such virtues.

At times the reality of worship in the local church is vastly different. Rather than revolving around the world-creating significance of the truths we affirm and embrace, worship can degenerate into battles over volume and instruments. The status of the drummer in the local church band usually provides the clue as to the state of affairs. If there is no drummer, or if he is ostracized, then this is a church that has failed to move with the times. Its pews are likely to be filled with those with graying hair. As in Henry Lyte's famous hymn *Abide with Me* change may well be linked with decay, and it is often resisted with great tenacity.[20] The pendulum often swings as far in the opposite direction. The worship team can attain the status of rock stars, and for those who rise to the top, the royalties from their music can be considerable. As the battles rage, victors sometimes embrace their worship style as an opiate that deadens the cry of the vulnerable. Personal taste and selfishness can become all-consuming, and the eschatological vision can be reduced to one that harmonizes with the current status quo. Clearly, when this happens, rather that aiding the quest for justice, worship becomes an accomplice of inertia, or worse, a boost to the power-base of current stake-holders.

We must, therefore, be careful not to assume an automatic connection between worship and the quest for justice. We should carefully consider the worship journey we have embarked upon. If necessary, course corrections should be made. We might ask questions as to who our worship welcomes. It is not enough to hang a sign affirming that all are welcome to join us in our acts of worship. Hospitality and inclusive worship belong together. Genuine hospitality involves being open to seeing the world from the other's perspective and adjusting one's own practice accordingly. There are many practical and simple steps we can take to show our openness to the neighbor. They can be as simple as projecting readings up in different languages, using photographs and images that reflect a delight in diversity, and praying for concerns beyond our immediate neighborhood.[21]

---

20. The last two lines of the second stanza read: "Change and decay in all around I see: O Thou who changest not, abide with me"—Horrobin and Leavers, *Mission Praise*, 4.

21. For ten practical suggestions, see Hawn, "Cross-Cultural Worship."

WORSHIP AND THE QUEST FOR JUSTICE FOR THE PLANET

While Christians have often looked to the stewardship motif of Genesis 1:28–30 to shape their ethical understanding of their responsibility to the environment, an increasing number of theologians are urging that this responsibility be located more widely within the broader biblical meta-narrative, taking into account the sweep of concerns articulated in both the Old and New Testaments and allowing all narratives to be interpreted in the light of Christ.[22] This broader based ethic shows much promise, as the stewardship motif of Genesis 1:28–30 has sometimes been twisted to justify the commodification of the planet, with the environment providing a useful set of resources which are seen to exist for the benefit of the human race. We have ruled over the earth with human comfort and pleasure providing the rationale for our decision-making, only to realize that such selfish short-sightedness serves neither the interests of humanity, nor the planet. Our destiny is intertwined. We long for the day when all things in heaven and on earth are reconciled in Christ (see Col 1:20). How then might our worship strengthen the quest for justice for the planet?

There is much in our tradition to encourage us. The music of the church often celebrates the goodness of creation. Many of our mothers and fathers in the faith approached creation with reverence and awe, spotting in each insect, flower, and tree the fingerprint of God. The second stanza of George Wade Robinson's nineteenth century hymn *Loved with Everlasting Love* asserts that "Heaven above is softer blue" and earth "sweeter green," "since I know, as now I know, I am His and He is mine."[23]

Robinson's sentiments are worth pondering. Genuine love for the Creator is likely to lead to a love for creation. The opening account in Genesis notes that God proclaims each stage of creation to be good. The divine delight in creation should be echoed in our journey through life. We live on a populated planet. Not all its inhabitants are human, but all were spoken into existence by the voice of God.

At a time when humans are increasingly alienated from creation and often spend the bulk of their waking hours in concrete monstrosities with little natural light or air, it is understandable that our relation-

---

22. For a good example of this see Srokosz, "God's Story."
23. Horrobin and Leavers, *Mission Praise*, 452.

ship with nature is fractured. We need to rediscover the spirituality of creation. On Palm Sunday when Jesus was asked to order the crowd to desist from praising him, he confidently asserted that if they fell silent the stones would cry out in praise (Luke 19:39–40). It was not an idle sentiment. A few days later Jesus' death at Calvary is met with jeers and sneers by the majority of human onlookers. Nature proved more sensitive, and the sun refused to shine (Luke 23:44–45). It should come as no surprise. The Psalmist did not hesitate to invite creation to join in the song of praise to God. Psalm 148 is a good example. Each realm is invited to praise the Lord. It is only in verse 11 that humans are invited to join the song. Sun, moon, stars, clouds, sea creatures, lightening, hail, snow, wind, mountains, hills, fruit trees, cedars, wild animals, cattle, small creatures, and birds all receive their invitation before the first human representatives are mentioned. Human worshippers simply join the existing chorus of praise. Draper's reworking of St Francis' hymn *All Creatures of our God and King* reflects a similar trajectory. The burning sun, the silver moon, the rushing wind and clouds, together with flowing water and fire are invited to join in the chorus, "O praise Him, O praise Him, Hallelujah, hallelujah, hallelujah," before any persons are present. Indeed, it is only in the fourth stanza that humans are requested to join the ever swelling ranks of worshippers.[24]

While we should not labor the point, it reminds us that anthropocentric assumptions about worship are neither rooted in scripture nor in the tradition of the church. If we view nature as a fellow worshipper we will be more respectful of her. We will realize that we have much to learn from her, and will steward her well. Often the best way to steward nature will be to leave her alone. Nature exploited or devastated makes quiet the chorus of praise to God. For a worshipping community this is always unacceptable. In protecting and preserving the earth we safeguard nature's cry of adoration to the Creator.

If worship is to strengthen the quest for justice for the planet it will be when worship is holistic. Rosemary Radford Ruether is correct when she asserts that "It is not enough to have a once a year 'earth day' liturgy that focuses specifically on ecological issues or to have an occasional prayer that mentions ecology. There needs to be a total reconceptualization of liturgical theology that integrates the whole creation as the context for the human-divine relationship. Instead of a privatized 'me and

---

24. Horrobin and Leavers, *Mission Praise*, 7.

God' theology, the human being needs to be understood as embedded in community and community in creation."[25]

WORSHIP AS A DOXOLOGY OF HOPE

In worship we embrace our highest hopes and aspirations. Spirit-enlivened worship assures us of the presence and reality of the risen Christ. Worship affirms our eschatological longing and vision. And when, as in the Wesley hymn *Love Divine, All Loves Excelling*, we experience the mystery of being "lost in wonder, love, and praise" we are able to anticipate something of the future God has in store for us.[26] German theologian Jürgen Moltmann has stressed that by looking from the future back to the present we find the courage to anticipate future reality in the present. It is this refrain that comes through in his book, *The Experiment Hope*. At the end of the work he approvingly quotes from a poem of Ingeborg Bachmann that speaks of a reward "for desertion, for bravery in the face of the friend, for betraying all unworthy secrets and the disregard of every command."[27]

This is worship at its best. It gives us the courage to act out our faith. Rather than idle escapism, this kind of worship serves as a doxology of hope. We affirm and delight in the hope we have, not to enable a deadening of the senses to the struggles of the present, but to liberate us to serve as co-workers with God, committed to constructing the reality we long for and which we believe will ultimately be attained. As participants in the *missio Dei* we align ourselves with ultimate reality. Be it the neighbor who is in need, a species in danger of extinction, rain forests which are disappearing, or prejudice which is being rationalized, we, the people of God, follow the example of our incarnated Lord. We stand in the place of those who cannot defend themselves. We are empowered to do so because of the healing and wholeness we have found in Christ. And we know that when we stand in the gap for others, we sing a song of praise that will not be extinguished. And it is thus that in worship we further the quest for justice.

---

25. Ruether, "Ecological Theology," 231.
26. Horrobin and Leavers, *Mission Praise*, 449.
27. Moltmann, *Experiment Hope*, 189–90.

16

The Preacher as Worshipper

Michael J. Quicke

INTRODUCTION

IN A MESSAGE AT Gordon-Conwell Theological Seminary one summer, Gary Parrett told the story of visiting a church in New York in 1985. The service began with twenty minutes of songs shown on an overhead projector screen and accompanied by guitars. Then the pastor walked to the front, announcing, "Now we will begin our worship." Clearly, he saw music as preparation before the real worship event—his sermon. However, revisiting the same church in 1998 Parrett found that the music group had expanded in size and led singing for thirty-five to forty minutes. At its conclusion the worship leader said, "Boy, that was a wonderful time of worship," as though it was now over as they faced the sermon. In thirteen years the situation had reversed—from viewing preaching as worship, to assuming that music is worship.

Of course, neither stance is correct but this story illustrates how in many contemporary, evangelical churches a serious separation has recently occurred between worship on one side and preaching on the other. Too often both seem to concern different sorts of activity, operating in separate boxes. This chapter will briefly illustrate this problem, before addressing two foundational issues—worship definition and theology—in order to provide fresh impetus for preachers to understand and practice their role as worshippers.

And preachers are my main focus because they have major responsibility. Their highly visible public leadership role inevitably influences local churches' understanding and practice of worship. By attention or inattention, by domination or avoidance of responsibility, preachers impact worship for better or worse. They reveal (wittingly or unwittingly) their own convictions about church priorities, by allocations of time and commitment. When a senior pastor thinks little about worship it is unlikely that many in the congregation will think much either. I seek to challenge preachers to be worshippers and thereby to influence the whole church into deeper ways of worship.

A DIVISION BETWEEN PREACHING AND WORSHIP

Two aspects of current church life serve to illustrate how worship has become separated from preaching—the emergence of the role of "worship leaders,"[1] and the respective literatures of worship and preaching.

In many churches "worship leaders" are now a well-established feature. In larger churches with considerable budgets these may be paid roles. Yet, even in smaller churches, when the pastor is more likely to be responsible for both preaching and leading of worship, volunteer musicians and others are increasingly developing roles alongside the preacher, often gaining their own spheres of influence. Regarded as those with particular responsibility for "worship" they frequently work apart from preachers. Indeed, as in the 1998 visit above, preaching is perceived as something different from worship. First, we worship and then the preacher preaches. This division goes deeply into much current practice.

At a recent conference at Gordon-Conwell Theological Seminary (March, 2009), called "Closing the Gap between Preaching and Worship," I was startled by levels of anger expressed by a few pastors. Agreeing that preaching and worship often operate separately, they expressed disturbing depths of frustration and resentment. One told me that worship had been so defined as "music in weekly church services" that some of the worship leaders he dealt with were "stuffed full of pride and very difficult to work with." Believing they had the key role for "worship" they gave

---

1. The description "worship leader" has been strongly criticized by some, including Don Carson. He says, "The notion of a 'worship leader' who leads the 'worship' part of the service is so bizarre, from a New Testament perspective, as to be embarrassing" (*Worship by the Book*, 47).

preachers a hard time. Equally, I know pastors who might be difficult to work with, too! Another leader told me of the church where the worship leaders, after prayerful discussion and careful strategizing, asked the Senior Minister whether he might *not* preach every Sunday so that they could have more time for worship.

I have also heard much frustration from those who lead worship about the lack of care and interest that Senior Ministers (who are generally also the preachers) have in the structure and planning of worship. For some preachers, providing the Scripture text and theme ahead of time seems to be the total sum of their involvement. It is as though they have relegated worship as a lesser matter. Over the last three years, aware of this growing divide between preaching and worship, I have listened to fellow preachers and discovered a range of reasons why they are *not* involved in worship. They have described worship variously in the following ways.

- Less important—lower down on the priority list behind preaching, administration, pastoral care, leadership.
- Burdensome—always seen as an extra to the heavy work load of a conscientious pastor. So delegate if you can!
- A specialist area about which there is considerable ignorance, for you can be trained to preach without any teaching on worship itself.
- Controversial—dividing people rapidly as they assert musical preferences. So best left alone, if possible.
- An enthusiasm, rather like overseas missions, that some people feel very excited about. So leave it to them.
- A personal pain because locally it may be mired in bad relationships between pastors and worship leaders.

All these contribute to relegating worship as some secondary issue to be dealt with separately from preaching.

This separation of roles is aided and abetted by the literature associated with each. For example, my seminary welcome lounge has magazines for browsing. Among them are *Preaching—the professional magazine for preachers*, and *Worship Leader Magazine—more of what you need to lead*. Most visitors pick up one or the other, for there is minimal overlap of content. And prospective students choose either the Master of Divinity course with preaching, or the Master of Arts in Christian Worship. Those studying worship feel no need to take any preaching courses, and vice versa.

Unhappily, much of the guild literature reinforces a professional divide between worship and preaching with minimal reference to each other. For example, Gregory Dix's classic, *The Shape of the Liturgy*, gives space amounting to two out of 764 pages to the role of the sermon.[2] Even when preaching is identified as a key component by worship leaders, it often receives slight attention. In *The Complete Worship Service—Creating a Taste of Heaven on Earth*, Kevin Navarro extols the importance of preaching: "The more I think of my preaching as an act of worship and not merely as an act of exhortation, the more Gospel I will have in my message."[3] Yet, though he claims that preaching is like the main course in a well-prepared meal, it receives only limited attention in his penultimate chapter. Other worship authors warn about how "efforts at liturgical renewal have often minimized the role of preaching . . . Mainline congregations, discouraged by legacies of poor preaching, tend to minimize the sermon by over-stating the place of the sacraments."[4] Further comments about preaching are eye-opening.

> Preaching is not the high point of worship to which all prior actions are meant to point . . . it is not an automatic apex that towers in importance over the Word, the sacrament or the simple singing of a hymn, because, in fact, truth is at stake in all these actions.[5]

> Whenever I worship or speak at a church where the pastor is the focal point, I feel dominated and stifled . . . the pastor is doing everything for me. I'm simply a receiver, a passive recipient of the actions of one other person.[6]

> The Eucharist, not the sermon should be the center of the church life. The religious individuality that produces itself in the pulpit . . . should not be the center of worship. The sermon should serve,

---

2. Mitman, *Worship*, 28.
3. Navarro, *Complete Worship Service*, 37.
4. Hamstra, *Principled Worship*, 49.
5. Best, *Unceasing Worship*, 106.
6. Webber, *Worship is a Verb*, 3.

not dominate, in the church. It should serve the presence of Christ which we celebrate in the Eucharist.[7]

From the other side, few recent homileticians have written about preaching's role in worship. Thomas Troeger's *Preaching and Worship* concerns the interrelationship of culture, preaching, and worship. Deploying a cultural analysis of the five senses he raises important questions for understanding both preaching and worship but does not seek to integrate them theologically. Will Willimon's *A Guide to Preaching and Leading Worship* provides practical checklists and guidelines but does not pursue how preaching may belong as worship. Of course, other writers make sensitive reference to preaching and worship[8] but, all too often, preaching literature colludes in separating worship from preaching as distinctive disciplines.

Reasons for this separation of worship from preaching are complex and many. However, two causes account for much of this division—the failure by preachers and worship leaders to develop adequate worship definitions and worship theology. To these we must now turn.

WORSHIP DEFINITIONS

How people define worship shows its relative value to them. Worship when understood in limited ways is inevitably devalued. Below are some short-hand (though popular) conceptions of worship that do just that.

- *Music Only*. We have already met this definition of worship that labels it *all* about hymns and songs. "Praise and Worship" in some churches expresses the music program on which worship teams spend 99% of their time. Musical ability is the premier gift for a worship leader. When music becomes all in all, not only do music leaders increase in importance, but acts of worship can be dominated by musical styles and preferences.

- *Sunday Services Only*. This labels worship as Sunday services only, restricting it to a limited churchy activity (though I realize worship services occur on other days too!). Of course, most preachers will agree in theory that worship is not restricted to Sunday services but involves everything that we do. Yet, often

---

7. Wolfhart Pannenberg, quoted in Bolsinger, *It Takes a Church*, 102.
8. See, for example, Taylor, *Preaching Life* and Knowles, *We Preach not Ourselves*.

connections between what happens on Sunday and Monday are left unclear. Worship operates in a one-day, one-hour capsule.

- *Liturgics Only.* "Liturgics" (with similarly rather ugly words like "liturgiology," and those who study liturgy—"liturgiologists") can also define worship, and (unfortunately) give the impression that worship properly understood involves superior ecclesiastical art forms, legislating set orders, colors, smells, and bells, specializing in printed prayer books, ritual, formalism, and sacraments.

- *Pragmatics Only.* Some preachers see worship as a practical business of choosing what happens during church services to make them work effectively. This concerns the low-brow end of informal worship practices that views worship as *just organizing* a sequence of hymns, songs, prayers, and offering.

- *Maintenance Only.* Further, some have a profound suspicion that worship is all well and good for helping saints celebrate, but it misses the whole point of being church, which is mission. Spending time on acts of worship for the in-crowd appears self-serving. "That's not where we should be spending our time and money!" they complain.

All of these definitions are faulty, not only because they confine worship to a single issue but, more importantly, they begin from the human point of view—*our* music, *our* worship services, *our* liturgy, *our* pragmatism, or *our* evangelism.

True worship should always begin with God—it is utterly for him, because of his "worthship." He is both the Subject of worship, who reveals himself in Jesus Christ, and is worthy of all honor, glory, and power; but also the Object of worship who calls worshippers to make offering to him. Two key groups of worship words in Scripture summarize these two aspects of worship.

First, God the Subject of worship invites prostration—to bow self down (*shachah* in the Old Testament, and *proskuneō* in the New Testament—literally "kiss the hand toward"). This describes being totally overwhelmed by God's glory, otherness, worthiness: "Come let us bow down in worship, let us kneel before the Lord our Maker; for he is our God" (Ps 95:6). Here is awe, mystery, wonder, and joy. "The time is coming and has now come when true worshipers will *kiss the hand towards the Father in spirit and truth, for they are the kind of worshippers the Father seeks*" (John 4:23). Such an attitude of worship reveals awareness of God's majesty and grandeur, yet because of his grace to us we can approach him through Jesus Christ (Heb 9:15).

Second, worship involves service for God who is also the Object of worship. In the Old Testament the word *'abad* means to labor and to serve, and in the New Testament *latreuo* refers to a state of servitude. Worshippers are not just knocked prostrate before God's greatness, but also set up on their feet to serve him. On trial before Felix, the apostle Paul says, "I admit that I worship (*latreuō*) the God of our fathers, as a follower of the Way" (Acts 24:14). We are brought low in wonder yet also offer ourselves as living sacrifices (Rom 12:1, 2). Awe, mystery, wonder, joy, are joined with offering and service. All these responses and more are due almighty God because of who he is and what he has done. Worship throws us down and throws us forward. As Jesus makes clear, true worship of God is both adoring and obedient love to him, but also loving service of one's neighbor as God's children (Matt 22:37–39).

Worship is not human-centered but God-centered. It is all about God on his terms. Astounded by his grace, Christian believers belong to new creation in Christ (2 Cor 5:17), living with him and for him for eternity. Not for Sundays only, but for Sundays to Saturdays. Not just with sermons, or music, but with our friends, enemies, work, recreation, zip codes, across the world and in heaven. Worship is *God's greatest idea and our highest activity*. It claims center stage and every other position as well. God is number one, reordering everything else in worship sequence. Christian worship is as expansive as *total Christian living in response to God*. Every time you think you have satisfactorily defined worship, another dimension opens up beyond.

So, worship is *not* another aspect or practice of Christian life, jostling alongside doctrine, church, and preaching. Worship is not something humans do on the way to something more important. It's the reason why we are alive in the first place. God made us to worship, to live in harmony, and in obedience to him. Worship embraces all that we are and all that we have—given by God, and returning to him in praise and by worshipful living. It is the foundational, purpose-driven, *integrator* holding everything else together, *everything* that believers think and do.

Its scope embraces all creation, all thinking, all relating, and all living. Nothing lies beyond its scope.

> Worship, in all its grades and kinds, is the response of the creature to the Eternal ... There is a sense in which we may think of the whole life of the Universe, seen and unseen, conscious and unconscious, as an act of worship, glorifying its Origin, Sustainer, and end ... when conscious it is always a subject-object relationship ... an acknowledgment of Transcendence; that is to say, of a Reality independent of the worshipper, which is always more or less deeply colored by mystery and which is there first.[9]

According to Don Carson, "Worship is the proper response of all moral, sentient beings to God, ascribing all honor and worth to their Creator God precisely because he is worthy, delightfully so."[10] Thomas Troeger says that "Worship is all of us for all of God."[11]

When worship is defined more fully by its throw-down, throw-out, love-God, love-neighbor dimensions, it makes a mockery of those short-hand definitions limiting it to music, Sunday services, and views of liturgy. Instead of preachers separating themselves *from* worship, they need to see that worship becomes the primary description of preaching itself. And worship with preaching reaches far beyond organizing weekly services into full-throated living of a new community for God's glory (1 Pet 2:9, 10). Properly understood, worship is so much bigger than either of the tasks undertaken by preachers and worship leaders. Rather, it integrates everything that is significant for all of us to live to God's glory. Worship is not a sideline but the mainline; not a side show but the main show.

THEOLOGY OF WORSHIP

Necessarily underlying this fuller understanding of worship lies a profounder theology. Anyone who has been reading theology in the last twenty years will be aware of resurging interest in the doctrine of the Trinity. The doctrine of the Trinity has undergone dramatic renaissance through the twentieth century. Theological giants like Karl Barth, Karl Rahner, Wolfhart Pannenberg, and Jürgen Moltmann set about rein-

---

9. Underwood, *Worship*, 13.
10. Carson, *Worship*, 26.
11. Troeger, *Preaching*, 21.

vigorating the classic doctrine with a ferment of writing that continues until the present with Leonardo Boff, Catherine Mowry LaCugna, and John Zizioulas. To this fresh thinking many evangelicals have responded thoughtfully and enthusiastically. Much recent work on worship shows sensitive awareness, especially work by Harold Best, Tod E. Bolsinger, Marva Dawn, James B. Torrance, Kevin Navarro, Robin Parry, and Jonathan R. Wilson.[12] For preaching, too, there have been stirrings. Michael Pasquarello II grounds his important book, *Christian Preaching*, entirely in the doctrine of the Trinity.

Many busy pastors may shrug at this news because memories of dry dusty early church councils make the doctrine of the Trinity seem distant and irrelevant. Admittedly, theology can sound dull and complicated—something abstract, complex, and unpractical. But whenever Christian living misses out theology it dumbs down, allowing faulty definitions, and pragmatism to dominate rather than God's revelation. Theology is *speaking meaningfully about God*. Everyone who expresses ideas about God has a theology, whether they admit it or not! What matters is whether theology is scripturally sound or not—whether it is about the *Christian* God. Christian theology is *speaking meaningfully about God in three persons*.

Some treat the doctrine of the Trinity lightly because of the apparent paucity of specific Scripture references, or consider it mere abstract terms and concepts derived from ancient church councils. True, it took the early church nearly four centuries to finally articulate this doctrine. But the Christian God of Scripture *cannot* be understood without the doctrine of the Trinity. Early Christians expressed the doctrine from the very beginning (Matt 28:19; 2 Cor 13:14). The practice of speaking of God as Father, Son, and Holy Spirit is embedded in the New Testament, though working out the profound theological implications of such practice necessarily took some time.

It is way beyond the scope of this chapter to trace how the Nicene-Constantinople Creed (381 CE) defined the eternal relationship between Father and Son, and how two main models for the Trinity developed. The "Immanent Trinity" (sometimes called the "ontological," "psychological," or "individual" model) describes who God is in his oneness, as triune being. And the "Economic Trinity" expresses how God in three persons

---

12. For a helpful overview of Trinitarian literature see Olson and Hall, *Trinity*. Other titles are found elsewhere in these footnotes. See also, Dawn, *Royal "Waste" of Time*.

has revealed himself in the story of creation—in the act of creation itself, and through the events of incarnation, crucifixion, resurrection, and Pentecost. By stressing the relationality and participation of God's three persons in human history it laid foundations for a "Social Trinity" model that was developed later. This understanding of God's continuing involvement with human action has become highly influential today.

One important word associated with this doctrine is *perichoresis* which describes how the persons of the Trinity do not belong as distinct from each other, but that they dwell inside each other, mutually inhering, drawing life from one another, and therefore are only to be experienced because of their relationship to each other (John 10:38; 14:8–11). Because of their mutuality, no divine person acts apart from the others. For example, in creation, though the Father is Creator, Jesus is also involved (John 1:3), as is the Spirit (Ps 104:30).

Such theology has profound implications for worship. In a thoughtful and accessible analysis in *Worship, Community and the Triune God of Grace*, James B. Torrance sharply contrasts what he terms unitarian and Trinitarian practices of worship. Of course, orthodox preachers rigorously reject any association with the formal teaching of Unitarianism—that God is one person only, with unacceptable denial of the divinity of Christ and of the Holy Spirit. However, Torrance demonstrates that ironically such preachers may actually *practice* forms of worship that *are* Unitarian because they are closed to Christ's continuing work and to the Holy Spirit. Too much worship is made by human hands for all too human purposes.

Though oversimplifying much evangelical practice, Torrance contends that the "evangelical experience" so stresses what Jesus did on the cross that it emphasizes his *work* at the expense of his *person*. This makes us more interested in our experience of blessing than in Jesus Christ himself. Human response can therefore be reduced to the sentiment, "Thank you, Lord, for saving me." Indeed, at worst, Jesus may be regarded as the "way in" to a relationship with God rather than the person through whom we *continue* to draw near to God our Father in the communion of the Spirit.

This view misleads believers into thinking that having once responded to Christ's work on the cross their subsequent worship depends totally on human discipline and energy. Worship becomes all our own work reliant upon our energy and imagination. It is "practical unitarianism" that "has no doctrine of the mediator or sole priesthood of Christ, is human-centered, has no proper doctrine of the Holy Spirit . . . [W]e sit in the pew watching the minister 'doing his thing' exhorting us 'to do our thing' until we go home thinking we have done our duty for another week."[13] In contrast with "evangelical experience," Torrance commends a "Trinitarian-Incarnation model." In the diagram below R1 and R2 describe a twofold relationship, resonating with both immanent and economic models of the Trinity. R1 marks the relationship between God and humanity made possible in the person and work of Jesus Christ, while R2 shows the relationship between Christ and the church "that we might participate by the Spirit in Jesus' communion with the Father in a life of intimate communion."[14]

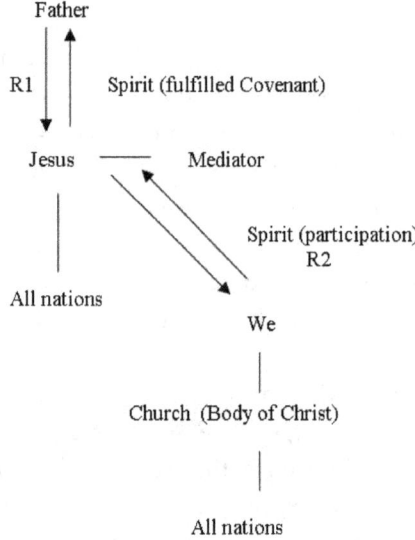

Fig. The Trinitarian, Incarnational Model—adapted from Torrance[15]

13. Torrance, *Worship*, 20.
14. Ibid., 31.
15. Ibid., 30.

This diagram expresses the theological dynamic underlying the all-encompassing view of worship described earlier. *Participation* is central to understanding God's involvement in worship. Defined as the act of taking part, of sharing in something with others as different parties join to work together yet relate to the whole, participation describes the astounding possibilities of Christian worship. Though the three persons of the Trinity belong together in divine community *apart* from creation, they have freely chosen to involve themselves in the human story, graciously enabling humans to participate, join, and share in communion with them. Stunningly, all human response to God, including preaching and worship, may actually participate in fellowship, in joining in, *with* God in three persons. "Worship is not merely something we present to God; it is our participation in the life of God, in the fellowship of the threeness of God."[16]

Instead of "Unitarian worship" closed to Christ's continuing work and to the Holy Spirit, this Trinitarian theology exults not only in Christ's past work but in his continuing intercession and mediation, so that we belong through him with the Father by the Holy Spirit. "Our worship is *with* Christ our brother, *in* Christ our priest, but always *through* Christ our sacrifice whose death for us is the means of our cleansing, renewing, and perfection."[17] See, for example, Ephesians 1:4, 5; 2:18; and Hebrews 2:10–12; 7:25.

Notice in the model that God's action is not one-way (as in practical Unitarianism) but a glorious double movement—expressing the gift of participating through the Spirit in the incarnate Son's communion with the Father (Heb 10:10–14). At its center is not *our* faith or decision-making but the spiritual dynamic double movement: "(a) a God-humanward movement, from (*ek*) the Father, through (*dia*) the Son, in (*en*) the Spirit and (b) a human-Godward movement to the Father through the Son in the Spirit."[18]

Jesus Christ mediates from "above" as well as from "below," enabling believers to participate in double movement: God-humanward from the Father, in the Spirit; but also a human-Godward, moving to the Father in the Spirit. Torrance comments on this. "[The double movement of grace] which is the heart of the "dialogue" between God and humanity in wor-

16. Wilson, *Why Church Matters*, 55.
17. Christopher Cocksworth quoted in Parry, *Worshipping Trinity*, 95.
18. Torrance, *Worship*, 32.

ship is grounded in the very perichoretic being of God, and is fundamental for our understanding of the triune God's relationship with the world in creation, incarnation, and sanctification. What God is toward us in these relationships, he is in his innermost being."[19] By this gracious action God enables us to belong within his fellowship, participate with the Father who gives faith and desire, and draws us through His Son, by his Spirit.

God alone makes worship possible and enables us to participate. Instead of preachers "doing their own thing" exhorting listeners "to do their thing" (to re-quote Torrance), preachers belong within God's double-movement empowerment. The implications of this Trinitarian Incarnational worship model, its relationships, movement, and divine energy, are far-reaching—especially for preachers.

THE PREACHER AS WORSHIPPER

In *360degree Preaching*[20] I proposed a model with a circular dynamic by which the triune God begins and finishes the preaching process. Because God's word "will not return to him void" (Isa 55:10, 11) the preaching process, beginning with God's revelation in Scripture and in Christ, continues by Christ's interceding presence and the Spirit's empowering, to impact hearers for his purpose. Every part of the preaching event is empowered as the triune God speaks through his Word, *and* empowers the preacher, *and* convicts the listeners, *and* transforms the lives of the preacher and the listeners. "The preaching . . . dynamic, found in God, and driven by God, returns to God as individuals and communities are transformed—all within the grace of the Triune God."[21]

However, this double movement dynamic should not be restricted to preaching! In fact, it more appropriately describes how the whole of worship works. Indeed, some worship writers even speak of circular movement. Welton Gaddy specifically envisages worship as beginning in the heights and drawing people in by sheer love. "Giving and receiving form a *circular* pattern between God and the people of God, which defies comprehension and lasts for ever."[22] God's gifts of faith, material

---

19. Ibid., 32.
20. Quicke, *360 Degree Preaching*.
21. Ibid., 49.
22. Gaddy, *Gift of Worship*, xi (emphasis added).

goods, music, and friendship are returned by worshipers through their confession of faith and praise, their tithes and offerings, their music, and their friendship within community. Marva Dawn also emphasizes how worship is a returning corporate gift. "[T]he gifts of worship flow from God the subject and return to God as the object of our reverence... The sermon is not just the gift of the preacher, nor are choral gifts simply the contribution of the choir, but both involve the offering of themselves by all the members of the congregation."[23] Worship moves from God and returns to God by grace. Giving and receiving, calling and responding, initiating and obeying.

It is no surprise that Trinitarian preaching proceeds by exactly the same double-movement of grace that empowers worship. Without diminishing the importance of preaching, we see it falls within this wider dynamic of God's call and response, God's initiating and sustaining, of participating in relationships, movement and power, with God's three persons. Preaching is not a different kind of activity from worship properly understood. It works in the same way, for the same purposes, through the grace of the same empowering triune God. Preaching is not only structurally connected to worship, but everything about it *is* worship. Now preaching is seen to be an element, a vitally important one, within the glorious circular work of God's word of grace returning to him. Preaching is God's prime gift, based upon Scripture, validated through preachers' call and gifting, so that preachers and hearers can respond by giving back their best to God (Eph 4:11–13). Preaching belongs within the rich giving and receiving pattern between God and his people. Consider this carefully crafted definition of preaching by Michael Pasquarello. "Christian preaching is a personally involved participatory and embodied form of graced activity that is the Triune God's gift to the church. This is not subject to human mastery and control, but as an expression of doxological speech is gratefully received and offered back to God through the praise and thanksgiving of the Christian community at worship."[24] The following points might be made in relation to this quotation. "Personally involved" stresses engagement of heart, soul, strength, and mind of preacher and hearers (Luke 10:27). Notice, too, that in Romans 12:1 "offer bodies" involves giving over the whole of ourselves, while "spiritual" can be translated "reasonable" to emphasize

---

23. Dawn, *Reaching Out*, 82.
24. Pasquarello, *Christian Preaching*, 10.

the engagement of mind and heart. "Participatory" resonates with the double-movement as God's three persons actively interact with believers, sharing fellowship with the mutual indwelling of Father, Son, and Holy Spirit. Intentionally, it relates preaching to the economic model of the Trinity where the doctrine of *perichoresis* explains how believers may interact within the Trinity's powerful dynamic, fellowshipping in the life of the Father, Son, and Holy Spirit. This is God's DNA building the church and kingdom.

"Embodied form of graced activity" further describes the nature of worship as expressed in the lives of ordinary people, living out their responsibilities as a new community that is entirely of God's making. "That is the Triune God's gift to the church" highlights how grace comes as gift. Utterly undeserving, we belong together as brothers and sisters only by God's will (John 1:12).

Rather than seeing itself as a special kind of public speaking "subject to human mastery and control," preaching is "an expression of doxological speech" offered to praise God's glory (*doxa*) because its ultimate purpose is to bring glory to the Father. The words "Gratefully received and offered back to God through the praise and thanksgiving of the Christian community at worship" echo how God's grace both gives and receives in our worship. It is all of Him, in three persons, from beginning to end.

What a difference such a definition makes to preachers. Instead of solely preaching *about* God's power, they need to preach *with* God's power; instead of solely focusing on Christ's *past* action, they join in his *continuing* mediation; instead of solely calling for human response *to* Christ, they must invite also responses *with* Him, by the Holy Spirit. And this is true for worship leaders too—not only should they enable worship *to* God, but worship *with* God. Worship is "the gift of participation through the Spirit in the incarnate Son's communion with the Father."[25]

IMPLICATIONS

The implications for preachers are transformative. First, they need to see themselves as *worshippers above all else*. Preachers need to see that their highest calling is to worship. They are worshippers before they are preachers. Loved and called by God's grace they need, as first priority,

---

25. Torrance, *Worship, Community*, 20.

to worship. Christian worship invites us to offer the best of ourselves to God, who gives us life, gifts, faith, and purpose, and has the right to claim every minute of our lives, every relationship we share, and every square inch of our influence. God is the one who calls us from nobodies into being "ambassadors for Christ" (2 Cor 5:20) and locates our obedience to speak his word within the worship of our lives.

Second, they have to see how *preaching itself is worship*. Worshiping preachers see their work as worship; that delivering sermons is offering back to God his revealed word, enabling a whole people to focus their responses in worshipful living, being part of the call and response, the rhythm of being God's people. Preachers themselves are worshippers, not only as they participate in the surrounding elements of singing, praying, communion, but because their preaching itself is a profound act of worship. Preachers do not do something separate from worship when they deliver sermons—they worship when they deliver sermons. Preaching is worship, motivated for the same ends, activated by the same power, offered in the same spirit, as one person enables others to hear and respond to God's fresh word and to live out their part in his story. The more we see worship as participation, the more we value preaching as worship. No longer can we consider preaching as a part of worship, or belonging within worship, but much more boldly—preaching as worship.

Third, preachers must *collaborate* more effectively in preparing acts of worship, since, they can no longer consider their task apart from worship, nor worship leaders see their role apart from preaching. Rather than both "do their own thing," reinforcing the tragic separation of preaching from worship, they belong *together* within the dynamics of the triune God's gracious enabling.

Preachers who belittle worship *miss the whole point*. Not only is their highest calling to be worshipers, but their responsibility to preach is worship through and through. Preachers are worshipers whose sermons are worship. All other descriptions of preaching fall short of God's glory. Today's church needs preachers renewed as worshipers in all that they do, connected vitally with "worship leaders" and the whole community in offering themselves as living sacrifices to God.

Bibliography

Abbott, M. *Sparks of the Cosmos: Rituals for Seasonal Use.* Adelaide: MediaCom, 2006.
Adams, W. S. "An Apology for Variable Liturgical Space." *Worship* 61 (1987) 231–42.
Albright, W. F., and C. S. Mann. *Matthew.* AB 26. New York: Doubleday, 1971.
Allen, L. C. *Ezekiel 1–19.* WBC 28. Dallas: Word, 1994.
Alter, R. *The Book of Psalms: A Translation with Commentary.* New York: Norton, 2007.
———. *The Five Books of Moses: A Translation with Commentary.* London: Norton, 2004.
Anderson, B. W. *Out of the Depths: The Psalms Speak for Us Today.* Philadelphia: Westminster, 1974.
Anderson, H., and E. Foley. *Mighty Stories, Dangerous Ritual.* San Francisco: Jossey-Bass, 1998.
Andrews, D. *People of Compassion.* Blackburn, Vic: TEAR Australia, 2008.
Aroney-Sine, C., and T. Sine. *Living on Purpose: Finding God's Best for Your Life.* Grand Rapids: Baker, 2002.
Ashburn, D. G. "Creation and Torah in Psalm 19." *JBQ* 22 (1994) 241–48.
Athanasius. *On the Incarnation.* Online: www.spurgeon.org.
Bailey Wells, J. *God's Holy People: A Theme in Biblical Theology.* Journal for the Study of the Old Testament Supplement Series 305. Sheffield: Sheffield Academic, 2000.
Balan, D. "Pursuing the Sacred in Art. Dappled Things." (2006). Online: http://dappledthings.org/adv06/essayart01.php.
Barr, J. *The Semantics of Biblical Language.* 1961. Reprinted, Eugene, OR: Wipf & Stock, 2004.
Barrett, C. K. *Church, Ministry and Sacraments in the New Testament.* Exeter, UK: Paternoster, 1985.
———. *A Commentary on the First Epistle to the Corinthians.* London: A. & C. Black, 1968.
———. *The Gospel according to St John: An Introduction with Commentary and Notes on the Greek Text.* London: SPCK, 1967.
Barth, K. *The Knowledge of God and the Service of God according to the Teaching of the Reformation.* 1938. Reprint, Eugene, OR: Wipf & Stock, 2005.
Barth, M. *Ephesians.* 2 vols. AB 34, 34A. Garden City, NY: Doubleday, 1974.
Bartholomew, C. G., and M. W. Goheen. *Drama of Scripture: Finding Our Place in the Biblical Story.* Grand Rapids: Baker, 2004.
———. *Living at the Crossroads: An Introduction to Christian Worldview.* Grand Rapids: Baker, 2008.
Bauckham, R. J. *Bible and Mission: Christian Witness in a Postmodern World.* Grand Rapids: Baker, 2003.

———. "Biblical Theology and the Problems of Monotheism." In *Out of Egypt: Biblical Theology and Biblical Interpretation*, edited by C. Bartholomew et al., 187–232. Grand Rapids: Zondervan, 2004.

———. "God's Self-Identification with the Godforsaken in the Gospel of Mark." In *Jesus and the God of Israel: God Crucified and Other Studies on the New Testament's Christology of Divine Identity*, 254–68. Milton Keynes, UK: Paternoster, 2008.

———. *The Theology of the Book of Revelation*. New Testament Theology. Cambridge: Cambridge University Press, 1993.

Bavinck, J. H. *An Introduction to the Science of Missions*. Translated by D. H. Freeman. Phillipsburgh, NJ: Presbyterian & Reformed Publishing, 1979.

Beasley-Murray, G. R. *John*. 2nd ed. WBC 36. Nashville: Nelson, 1999.

Begbie, J. "The Spirituality of Renewal Music: A Preliminary Exploration." *Anvil* 8 (1991) 227–39.

Bell, C. *Ritual Theory, Ritual Practice*. New York: Oxford University Press, 1992.

Bellah, R. et al. *Habits of the Heart: Individualism and Commitment in American Life*. Berkeley: University of California Press, 1985.

Bender, K. J. *Karl Barth's Christological Ecclesiology*. Aldershot, UK: Ashgate, 2005.

Berger, P. L. *Pyramids of Sacrifice: Political Ethics and Social Change*. New York: Basic, 1974.

Bertone, J. A. "The Function of the Spirit in the Dialectic between God's Soteriological Plan Enacted but not yet Culminated: Romans 8:1–21." *JPT* 15 (1999) 75–97.

Best, E. *A Critical and Exegetical Commentary on Ephesians*. ICC. Edinburgh: T. & T. Clark, 1998.

Best, H. *Unceasing Worship*. Downers Grove, IL: InterVarsity, 2003.

Betz, H. D. *Galatians*. Hermeneia. Philadelphia: Fortress, 1979.

Blauw, J. *The Missionary Nature of the Church: A Survey of the Biblical Theology of Mission*. New York: McGraw-Hill, 1961.

Block, D. I. *The Book of Ezekiel: Chapters 1–24*. NICOT. Grand Rapids: Eerdmans, 1997.

———. *The Book of Ezekiel: Chapters 25–48*. NICOT. Grand Rapids: Eerdmans, 1998.

Bloesch, D. G. *The Church: Sacraments, Worship, Ministry, Mission*. Downers Grove, IL: InterVarsity, 2002.

———. "Whatever Happened to God?" *CT* (February 5, 2001) 54–55.

Blomberg, C. *1 Corinthians: From Biblical Text—to Contemporary Life*. NIV Application Commentary. Grand Rapids: Zondervan, 1994.

Boda, M. "'Declare His Glory among the Nations': The Psalter as Missional Collection." PhD diss., McMaster University, Hamilton, ON, 2006.

Bolsinger, T. E. *It Takes a Church to Raise a Christian*. Grand Rapids: Brazos, 2004.

Bosch, D. J. *Transforming Mission: Paradigm Shifts in Theology of Mission*. Maryknoll, NY: Orbis, 1991.

Boulton, M. M. "Forsaking God: A Theological Argument for Christian Lamentations." *SJT* 55 (2002) 58–78.

———. "Unholy Rites: What's Wrong with Worship?" *ChrCent* 126.2 (2009) 30–33.

Bouma, G. *Australian Soul: Religion and Spirituality in the Twenty-first Century*. Port Melbourne: Cambridge University Press, 2006.

Bouyer, L. "Mysticism. An Essay on the History of the Word." In *Understanding Mysticism*, edited by R. Woods, 42–55. London: Athlone, 1980.

Bowen, R. *Romans*. Vol. 2. London: SCM, 1984.

Bradshaw, P. F. *The Search for the Origins of Christian Worship. Sources and Methods for the Study of Early Liturgy*. London: SPCK, 1992.
Brown, W. P. *Seeing the Psalms: A Theology of Metaphor*. Louisville: Westminster John Knox, 2002.
Brox, N. *Adversus haereses liber III. Gegen die Häresien Buch 3*. FC 8/3. Freiburg: Herder, 1995.
Brueggemann, W. *Deuteronomy* AOTC. Nashville: Abingdon, 2001.
———. *Finally Comes the Poet: Daring Speech for Proclamation*. Minneapolis: Fortress, 1989.
———. *Worship in Ancient Israel: An Essential Guide*. Nashville: Abingdon, 2005.
Bultmann, R. *Theology of the New Testament*. 2 vols. Translated by Kendrick Grobel. 1951–55. Reprinted, Waco, TX: Baylor University Press, 2007.
Burge, G. M. *John*. NIV Application Commentary. Grand Rapids: Zondervan, 2000.
Burkhart, J. E. *Worship*. Philadelphia: Westminster, 1982.
Buxton, G. *Dancing in the Dark: The Privilege of Participating in the Ministry of Christ*. Carlisle, UK: Paternoster, 2001.
Caird, G. B. *The Language and Imagery of the Bible*. London: Duckworth, 1980.
Callan, T. *Dying and Rising with Christ: The Theology of Paul the Apostle*. New York: Paulist, 2006.
Carson, D. A. *Exegetical Fallacies*. Grand Rapids: Baker, 1984.
———, editor. *Worship by the Book*. Grand Rapids: Zondervan, 2002.
Carter, W. *Matthew and the Margins: A Socio-political and Religious Reading*. JSNTSup 204. Sheffield: Sheffield Academic, 2001.
Chae, D. J. S. *Paul as Apostle to the Gentiles: His Apostolic Self-Awareness and Its Influence on the Soteriological Argument in Romans*. Paternoster Biblical and Theological Monographs. Carlisle, UK: Paternoster, 1997.
Chamblin, J. K. *Paul and the Self: Apostolic Teaching for Personal Wholeness*. Grand Rapids: Baker, 1993.
Chan, S. *Liturgical Theology: the Church as Worshipping Community*. Downers Grove, IL: InterVarsity, 2006.
———. *Spiritual Theology: A Systematic Study of the Christian Life*. Downers Grove, IL: InterVarsity, 1998.
Childs, B. S. *Old Testament Theology in a Canonical Context*. London: SCM, 1985.
Chirban, J. T. "Spiritual Discernment and Differential Diagnosis: Interdisciplinary Approaches." In *Personhood: Orthodox Christianity and the Connection between Body, Mind, and Soul*, 35–47. Westport, CT: Bergin & Garvey, 1996.
Christensen, D. L. *Deuteronomy 1:1–21:9*. 2nd ed. WBC 6A. Nashville: Nelson, 2001.
———. "Nations." In *ABD* 4:1037.
Chupungco, A. J. "A Definition of Liturgy." In *Introduction to the Liturgy, Handbook for Liturgical Studies*, 1.3–10. Collegeville, MN: Liturgical, 1997.
Clapp, R. *A Peculiar People: The Church as Culture in a Post-Christian Society*. Downers Grove, IL: InterVarsity, 1996.
Clements, R. E. "Deuteronomy." In *NIB* 2:269–538.
———. *God's Chosen People: A Theological Interpretation of the Book of Deuteronomy*. London: SCM, 1968.
Clifford, R. J. *The Cosmic Mountain in Canaan and the Old Testament*. HSM 4. Cambridge: Harvard University Press, 1972.

Clines, D. J. A. "Tree of Knowledge and the Law of Yahweh, Psalm 19." *VT* 24 (1974) 8–14.

Collins, R. F. *Letters that Paul Did not Write: The Epistle to the Hebrews and the Pauline Pseudepigrapha*. Good News Studies 28. Wilmington, DE: Glazier, 1988.

Comby, J. *How to Read Church History*. Vol. 1. New York: Crossroad, 1993.

Community of Jesus. *The Little Book of Hours: Praying with the Community of Jesus*. Brewster, MA: Paraclete, 2003.

Complete Mission Praise. Compiled by P. Horrobin and G. Leavers. London: Pickering, 1999.

Cooke, G. A. *A Critical and Exegetical Commentary on the Book of Ezekiel*. ICC. Edinburgh: T. & T. Clark, 1936.

Cormack, R. *Icons*. London: British Museum Press, 2007.

Corney, P. "Have You Got the Right Address? Post-Modernism and the Gospel." *Grid* September, 1995.

Cotterell, P., and M. Turner. *Linguistics & Biblical Interpretation*. London: SPCK, 1989.

Cousar, C. B. *The Letters of Paul*. Interpreting Biblical Texts. Nashville: Abingdon, 1996.

Craigie, P. C. *The Book of Deuteronomy*. NICOT. Grand Rapids: Eerdmans, 1976.

———. *Psalms 1–50*. WBC 19. Waco, Texas: Word, 1983.

Craig-Wild, P. *Tools for Transformation: Making Worship Work*. London: Darton, Longman & Todd, 2002.

Crumlin, R. *Beyond Belief: Modern Art and the Religious Imagination*. Melbourne: National Gallery of Victoria, 1998.

Cruse, D. A. *Lexical Semantics*. Cambridge: Cambridge University Press, 1986.

Cullmann, O. *Early Christian Worship*. London: SCM, 1957.

Curtis, E. M. "Man as the Image of God in Genesis in the Light of Ancient Near Eastern Parallels." Ph.D diss., University of Pennsylvania, 1984.

Daniélou, J. *From Glory to Glory: Texts from Gregory of Nyssa's Mystical Writings*. Crestwood, NY: St. Vladimir's Seminary Press, 1979.

Dare, C. *Praise the Lord*. Rondebosch: Scripture Union, 1981.

Darr, K. P. "The Book of Ezekiel." In *NIB* 6:1073–1607.

Davies, J. G. *Worship and Mission*. London: SCM, 1966.

Davies, W. D. *The Gospel and the Land: Early Christianity and Jewish Territorial Doctrine*. Sheffield: JSOT Press, 1974.

———. *The Setting of the Sermon on the Mount*. Cambridge: Cambridge University Press, 1975.

Davis, M. "Atheist Bone Mourned in Church as 'Cultural Christian.'" *Weekend Australian* May 3–4, 2008. Online: http://www.theaustralian.news.com.au/story/0,25197,23637523-5006785,00.html

Dawkins, R. *The God Delusion*. London: Bantam, 2006.

Dawn, M. J. *Reaching Out without Dumbing Down. A Theology of Worship for the Turn-of-the-Century Culture*. Grand Rapids: Eerdmans, 1995.

———. *A Royal "Waste" of Time. The Splendor of Worshipping God and Being Church for the World*. Grand Rapids: Eerdmans, 1999.

———. "Worship to Form a Missional Community." *Direction* 28 (1999) 139–52.

Delling, G. *Worship in the New Testament*. Translated by P. Scott. London: Darton, Longman & Todd, 1962.

Didron, M. *Christian Iconography*. Translated by E. J. Millington. London: Bohn, 1851.

Donaldson, T. L. *Jesus on the Mountain: A Study in Matthean Theology.* JSNTSup 8. Sheffield: JSOT Press, 1985.
Driver, T. F. *Liberating Rites. Understanding the Transformative Power of Ritual.* Boulder, CO: Westview, 1998.
Driver, T. *The Magic of Ritual: Our Need for Liberating Rites that Transform Our Lives and Our Communities.* San Francisco: HarperSanFrancisco, 1991.
Due, N. *Created For Worship.* Fearn, Ross-shire: Mentor, 2005.
Duling, D. C., and N. Perrin. *The New Testament: Proclamation and Parenesis, Myth and History.* New York: Harcourt Brace Jovanovich, 1994.
Dumbrell, W. J. *Covenant and Creation: A Theology of Old Testament Covenants.* Nashville: Nelson, 1984.
———. "The Prospect of the Unconditionality of the Sinaitic Covenant." In *Israel's Apostasy and Restoration: Essays in Honor of Roland K. Harrison*, edited by A. Gileadi. Grand Rapids: Baker, 1988.
Dunn, J. D. G. *The Epistles to the Colossians and to Philemon.* Grand Rapids: Eerdmans, 1996.
———. *The Epistle to the Galatians.* London: A. & C. Black, 1993.
———. *Romans 9-16.* WBC 38B. Dallas: Word, 1988.
———. *Unity and Diversity in the New Testament.* London: SCM, 1977.
———. "Whatever Happened to the Lord's Supper?" *EpRev* 19/1 (1992) 35-48.
Durham, J. I. *Exodus.* WBC 2. Waco, TX: Word, 1987.
Durka, G., and J. Smith. "Is Art Necessary?" *RelEd* 76.1 (1981) 27-32.
Dyrness, W. A. *Themes in Old Testament Theology.* Downers Grove, IL: InterVarsity, 1979.
———. *Visual Faith.* Grand Rapids: Baker Academic, 2001.
Eaton, J. *The Psalms: A Historical and Spiritual Commentary with an Introduction and New Translation.* London: Continuum, 2003.
Eichrodt, W. *Theology of the Old Testament.* Vol. 1. London: SCM, 1961.
Eisner, E. W. *The Arts and the Creation of Mind.* New Haven & London: Yale University Press, 2002.
Esler, P. F. *Conflict and Identity in Romans: The Social Setting of Paul's Letter.* Minneapolis: Fortress, 2003.
Evans, C. "Romans 12:1-2. The True Worship." In *Dimensions de la Vie Chrétienne*, edited by C. K. Barrett et al. Rome: 1979.
Fagerberg, D. W. *What is Liturgical Theology? A Study in Methodology.* Collegeville, MN: Liturgical, 1992.
Farris, S. "The Canticles of Luke's Infancy Narrative; The Appropriation of a Biblical Tradition." In *Into God's Presence*, edited by R. N. Longenecker, 91-112. Grand Rapids: Eerdmans, 2001.
Fee, G. D. *God's Empowering Presence: The Holy Spirit in the Letters of Paul.* Peabody, MA: Hendrickson, 1994.
Ferguson, E. "Spiritual Sacrifice in Early Christianity and its Environment." In *ANRW* II.23:2, edited by W. Haase, 1152-89. Berlin: de Gruyter, 1979.
Fergusson, D. "The Theology of Worship within the Reformed Tradition." In *Loving God with our Minds: the Pastor as Theologian*, edited by M. Welker and C. A. Jarvis, 367-80. Grand Rapids: Eerdmans, 2004.
Feuer, A. C. *Tehillim.* ArtScroll Tanach Series. New York: Mesorah, 1995.

Filson, F. V. *A Commentary on the Gospel according to St. Matthew.* London: A. & C. Black, 1960.

Fishbane, M. *Biblical Text and Texture: A Literary Reading of Selected Texts.* Oxford: Oneworld, 1998.

———. "Transformations of Torah in Biblical and Rabbinic Tradition." *JSRI* 6.18 (2007) 6–15.

Foley, E. *From Age to Age.* Chicago: Liturgy Training Publications, 1991.

Forrester, D. B., et al. *Encounter with God. An Introduction to Christian Worship and Practice.* Edinburgh: T. & T. Clark, 1996.

Foster, R. J., and E. Griffin. *Spiritual Classics: Selected Readings for Individuals and Groups on the Twelve Spiritual Disciplines.* San Francisco: Harper, 2000.

Foster, R. L. "A Plea for New Songs: A Missional/Theological Reflection on Psalm 96." *CurTM* 33 (2006) 285–90.

Fowl, S. E. *Philippians.* Two Horizons New Testament Commentary. Grand Rapids: Eerdmans, 2005.

Frankfort, H. *Kingship and the Gods: A Study of Ancient Near Eastern Religion as the Integration of Society and Nature.* Chicago: University of Chicago Press, 1948.

Freeland, G. "Foreword." In *Icons and Art*, edited by M. Galovic, 5–6. Leichhardt, NSW: Honeysett, 2006.

Freeman, D. "Feasts." In *NBD* 365–67.

Fretheim, T. E. "'Because the Whole Earth is Mine': Theme and Narrative in Exodus." *Int* 50 (1996) 229–39.

———. *The Suffering of God: An Old Testament Perspective.* Overtures to Biblical Theology. Philadelphia: Fortress, 1984.

Friedman, D. A. "An Anchor Amidst Anomie: Ritual and Aging." In *Aging, Spirituality and Religion: A Handbook,* vol. 2, edited by M. A. Kimble and S. H. McFadden. Minneapolis: Fortress, 2003.

Fry, T. *The Rules of St. Benedict in English.* Collegeville, MN: Liturgical, 1981.

Fulghum, R. *From Beginning to End: The Rituals of Our Lives.* New York: Random House, 1995.

Funk R. W. *A Greek Grammar of the New Testament and Other Early Christian Literature.* Chicago: Chicago University Press, 1961.

Gadamer, H.-G. *Truth and Method.* Translated by G. Donald. Marshall, NY: Continuum, 1989.

Gaddy, W. *The Gift of Worship.* Nashville: Broadman, 1992.

Galli, M. "A Deeper Relevance." *CT* (2008) Online: www.christianitytoday.com/ct/2008/may/36.38.html.

Galovic, M. *Icons and Art.* Leichhardt, NSW: Honeysett, 2006.

Gassman, G. "The Church as Sacrament, Sign, and Instrument: The Reception of this Ecclesiological Understanding in Ecumenical Debate." In *Church, Kingdom, World.* Faith and Order Paper; 130, edited by G. Limouris, 1–17. Geneva: World Council of Churches, 1986.

Gavrilyuk, P. *The Suffering of the Impassible God: The Dialectics of Patristic Thought.* Oxford: Oxford University Press, 2004.

George, T. *Galatians.* New American Commentary 30. Nashville: Broadman & Holman, 1994.

Gerstenberger, E. S. *Psalms, with an Introduction to Cultic Poetry.* Forms of the Old Testament Literature. Grand Rapids: Eerdmans, 1988.

Gibbs, E., and R. Bolger. *Emerging Churches: Creating Christian Community in Postmodern Cultures*. Grand Rapids: Baker Academic, 2005.
Gibson, D., and R. Gibson. *The Sandwich Generation*. Grand Rapids: Baker, 1991.
Giesen, H. "Eschatology in Philippians." In *Paul and His Theology*, edited by S. E. Porter, 217–82. Pauline Studies 3. Leiden: Brill, 2006.
Giglio, L. *The Air I Breathe: Worship as a Way of Life*. Eastbourne: Kingsway, 2004.
Glad, C. E. "Paul and Adaptability." In *Paul in the Greco-Roman World*, edited by J. P. Sampley, 17–41. Harrisburg, PA: Trinity, 2003.
Goheen, M. W. "Narrating the World: What Can Church Leaders Do?" *Catalyst* 33.3 (2007). Online: http://catalystresources.org/issues/333Goheen2.htm
Goldingay, J. *Psalms*. Vol. 1, *Psalms 1–41*. Baker Commentary on the Old Testament Wisdom and Psalms. Grand Rapids: Baker, 2006.
Goulart, F. S. *God Has No Religion: Blending Traditions for Prayer*. Notre Dame, IN: Sorin, 2005.
Grant, J. "Psalm 44 and a Christian Spirituality of Lament." Unpublished paper given as the Tyndale Old Testament Lecture, July 2007.
Green, J. B. "Persevering together in prayer: the significance of prayer in the Acts of the Apostles." In *Into God's Presence: Prayer in the New Testament*, edited by R. N. Longenecker, 183–202. McMaster New Testament Studies. Grand Rapids: Eerdmans, 2001.
Greenberg, M. *Ezekiel 1–20*. AB 22. Garden City, NY: Doubleday, 1983.
———. *Ezekiel 21–37*. AB 22A. Garden City, NY: Doubleday, 1997.
Grenz, S. J. *Created for Community: Connecting Christian Belief with Christian Living*. Grand Rapids: Baker, 1998.
Gruber, M. *Aspects of Non-verbal Communication in the Ancient Near East*. Studia Pohl 12/1. Rome: Biblical Institute, 1980.
Gründmann, W. *Das Evangelium nach Matthäus*, THKNT 1. Berlin: Evangelische Verlagsanstalt, 1968.
Guder, D. *Be My Witnesses: The Church's Mission, Message, and Messengers*. Grand Rapids: Eerdmans, 1985.
Habermas, J. *Communication and the Evolution of Society*. Boston: Beacon, 1979.
Hagedorn, A. C. "Placing (a) God: Central Place Theory in Deuteronomy 12 and at Delphi." In *Temple and Worship in Biblical Israel*, edited by John Day, 188–211. Library of Hebrew Bible/Old Testament Studies 422. London: Continuum, 2007.
Hagner, D. A. "The *Sitz im Leben* of the Gospel of Matthew." In *Treasures New and Old: Contributions to Matthean Studies*, edited by D. R. Bauer and M. A. Powell, 27–68. Symposium Series 1. Atlanta: Scholars, 1996.
Hahn, F. *The Worship of the Early Church*. Translated by D. E. Green. Philadelphia: Fortress, 1973.
Hahn, S. "Canon, Cult, and Covenant: Towards a Liturgical Hermeneutic." In *Canon and Biblical Interpretation*, edited by C. Bartholomew et al., 207–35. Scripture and Hermeneutics Series 7. Grand Rapids: Zondervan, 2006.
Halperin, D. J. *The Faces of the Chariot: Early Jewish Response to Ezekiel's Vision*. TSAJ 16. Tübingen: Mohr/Siebeck, 1988.
Hamilton, J. M. *Social Justice and Deuteronomy: The Case of Deuteronomy 15*. SBL Dissertation Series 136. Atlanta: Scholars, 1992.
Hamstra, S. *Principled Worship*. Eugene, OR: Wipf & Stock, 2006.

Harman, A. M. *Deuteronomy: The Commands of a Covenant God*. Fearn: Christian Focus, 2001.

Harris, B. S. "When Faith is the Problem." *The Advocate* (April 2007) 4.

Harris, M. J. *Raised Immortal. Resurrection and Immortality in the New Testament*. Basingstoke, UK: Marshall, Morgan & Scott, 1983.

Harris, R. et al. *Theological Wordbook of the Old Testament*. Chicago: Moody, 1980.

Hart, L. D. *Truth Aflame. A Balanced Theology for Evangelicals and Charismatics*. Nashville: Nelson, 1999.

Hartley, J. E. "Genesis: Primeval Prologue." In *Old Testament Survey: The Message, Form and Background of the Old Testament*, edited by W. S. Lasor et al. Grand Rapids: Eerdmans, 1996.

Hauspie, K. "*Piptōepi prosō mou*: A Set Phrase in Ezekiel?" In *X Congress of the International Organization for Septuagint and Cognate Studies, Oslo 1998*, edited by B. A. Taylor, 513–30. Septuagint and Cognate Studies Series 51. Atlanta: Society of Biblical Literature, 2001.

Hawn, C. M. "Cross-Cultural Worship: Praying Justly." *Clergy Journal* 80.6 (2004) 3–5.

Hay, D. M. "Paul's Understanding of Faith as Participation." In *Paul and His Theology*, edited by S. E. Porter, 45–76. Pauline Studies 3. Leiden: Brill, 2006.

Hayes, J., and S. Mandell. *The Jewish People in Classical Antiquity: From Alexander to Bar Kochba*. Louisville: Westminster John Knox, 1998.

Hays, R. B. *The Moral Vision of the New Testament: A Contemporary Introduction to New Testament Ethics*. San Francisco: HarperCollins, 1996.

Hebert, A. G. *Liturgy and Society: The Function of the Church in the Modern World*. London: Faber & Faber, 1935.

Hedlund, R. *The Mission of the Church in the World: A Biblical Theology*. Grand Rapids: Baker, 1991.

Hermans, C. A. M. *Participatory Learning: Religious Education in a Globalizing Society*. Empirical Studies in Theology 9. Leiden: Brill, 2003.

Hill, A. *Enter His Courts with Praise: Biblical Principles for Worship Renewal*. Eastbourne: Kingsway, 1993.

Himmelfarb, M. *Ascent to Heaven in Jewish and Christian Apocalypses*. Oxford: Oxford University Press, 1993.

Hitchens, C. *God is Not Great: How Religion Poisons Everything*. New York: Twelve, 2007.

Hoch, C. B., Jr. *All Things New: The Significance of Newness for Biblical Theology*. Grand Rapids: Baker, 1995.

Hogg, W. R. "Psalm 22 and Christian Mission." *IRM* 306 (April 1988) 238–46.

Horrobin, P., and G. Leavers. *Mission Praise*. London: Pickering, 1990.

Hudson, D. N. "Worship: Singing a New Song in a Strange Land." In *Pentecostal Perspectives*, edited by K. Warrington, 177–203. Carlisle, UK: Paternoster, 1998.

Hultgren, A. J. "Liturgy and Literature: The Liturgical Factor in Matthew's Literary and Communicative Art." In *Texts and Contexts: Biblical Texts in Their Textual and Situational Contexts: Essays in Honour of Lars Hartman*, edited by T. Fornberg and D. Hellholm, 659–73. Oslo: Scandinavian University Press, 1995.

Huntington, S. *The Clash of Civilizations and the Remaking of World Order*. New York: Simon & Schuster, 1996.

Hütter, R. *Suffering Divine Things: Theology as Church Practice*. Grand Rapids: Eerdmans, 2000.

Imber-Black, E., and J. Roberts. *Rituals for our Time: Celebrating, Healing and Changing Our Lives and Our Relationships*. New York: HarperCollins, 1992.

Jack, C. "Understanding Worship: Part 2." In *The Heart of Worship Files*, edited by M. Redman, 85–94. Eastbourne: Kingsway, 2003.

Jameson, A. *Sacred and Legendary Art*, vol. 1. Boston: Houghton Mifflin, 1895.

Jenson, R. W. "The Hauerwas Project." *ModTheol* 8 (1992) 285–95.

Jeremias, J. *Jesus' Promise to the Nations*. Translated by S. H. Hooke. Studies in Biblical Theology 24. London: SCM, 1958.

Jewett, R. *Romans*. Hermeneia. Minneapolis: Fortress, 2007.

Jewish Publication Society. *[Tanakh] = JPS Hebrew-English Tanakh: The Traditional Hebrew Text and the New JPS Translation* (2nd ed.). Philadelphia: Jewish Publication Society, 1999.

Jobes, K. "Distinguishing the Meaning of Greek Verbs in the Semantic Domain for Worship." In *Biblical Words & Their Meaning: An Introduction to Lexical Semantics* edited by M. Silva, 201–11. Grand Rapids: Zondervan, 1994.

Jones, A. Weblog post "Emerging Church Definition 1.0." February 2, 2004. Online: http://tallskinnykiwi.typepad.com/tallskinnykiwi/2004/02/emerging_church.html

Jones, P. H. "We are *How* We Worship: Corporate Worship as a Matrix for Christian Identity Formation." *Worship* 69.4 (July 1995) 346–60.

Kaiser, W. C., Jr. "Israel's Missionary Call." In *Perspectives on the World Christian Movement: A Reader*, edited by R. D. Winter and S. C. Hawthorne, 25–34. Pasadena, CA: William Carey Library, 1981.

———. *Mission in the Old Testament: Israel as a Light to the Nations*. Grand Rapids: Baker, 2000.

Kalland, E. S. "Deuteronomy." In *EBC* 3:238.

Kallistos of Diokleia. *The Power of the Name*. Oxford: SLG, 1986.

Kartsonis, A. "The Responding Icon." In *Heaven on Earth, Art and the Church of Byzantium*, edited by L. Safran, 58–80. University Park, PA: Pennsylvania State University Press, 2002.

Kasdan, B. *God's Appointed Times: A Practical Guide for Understanding and Celebrating the Biblical Holy Days*. Baltimore: Lederer, 1993.

Käsemann, E. *Perspectives on Paul*. Translated by Magaret Kohl. Philadelphia: Fortress, 1971.

Keener, C. S. *A Commentary on the Gospel of Matthew*. Grand Rapids: Eerdmans, 1999.

———. *The Gospel of John: A Commentary*. Vol. 1. Peabody, MA: Hendrickson, 2003.

———. *The Spirit in the Gospels and Acts: Divine Purity and Power*. Peabody, MA: Hendrickson, 1997.

Kelly, A. J., and F. J. Moloney. *Experiencing God in the Gospel of John*. New York: Paulist, 2003.

Kelly, J. B. "Song, Story, or History. Resisting Claims of a Coded Message in the African American Spiritual 'Follow the Drinking Gourd.'" *JPC* 41.2 (2008) 262–80.

Kelly, J. F. *The World of the Early Christians*. Vol. 1. Message of the Fathers of the Church. Edited by T. Halton. Collegeville, MN: Liturgical, 1997.

Kendrick, G. *Worship*. Eastbourne: Kingsway, 1984.

Kidner, D. *Psalms 1–72: An Introduction and Commentary on Books I and II of the Psalms*. Tyndale Old Testament Commentaries. London: InterVarsity, 1973.

Kieckhefer, R. *Theology in Stone: Church Architecture from Byzantium to Berkeley*. New York: Oxford University Press, 2004.

Kilde, J. H. *When Church Became Theatre: The Transformation of Evangelical Architecture and Worship in Nineteenth-Century America.* New York: Oxford University Press, 2002.

Kilmartin, E. *Systematic Theology of Liturgy.* Kansas City: Sheed & Ward, 1988.

Kilpatrick, G. D. *The Origins of the Gospel according to St Matthew.* Oxford: Clarendon, 1946.

Kimball, D. *The Emerging Church.* Grand Rapids: Zondervan, 2003.

Kingsbury, J. *Matthew: Structure, Christology, Kingdom.* Philadelphia: Fortress, 1975.

Klouda, S. L. "The Dialectical Interplay of Seeing and Hearing in Psalm 19 and Its Connection to Wisdom." *BBR* 10.2 (2000) 181–95.

Knorr, H., and H. Knorr. *Religious Art in Australia.* Croydon, Vic: Longmans, 1967.

Knowles, M. *We Preach not Ourselves.* Grand Rapids: Brazos, 2008.

Köhler, W. D. *Die Rezeption des Matthäusevangeliums in der Zeit vor Irenäus.* Tübingen: Mohr/Siebeck, 1987.

Kowalski, B. *Die Rezeption des Propheten Ezechiel in der Offenbarung des Johannes.* Stuttgart: Katholisches Bibelwerk, 2004.

Kraus, H. *Psalms 1–59: A Commentary.* Translated by Hilton C. Oswald. Continental Commentary. Minneapolis: Augsburg, 1988.

Kraybill, J. N. *Imperial Cult and Commerce in John's Apocalypse.* JSNTSup 132. Sheffield: Sheffield Academic, 1996.

Kreitzer, L. J. *Jesus and God in Paul's Eschatology.* Sheffield: JSOT Press, 1987.

LaGrand, J. *The Earliest Christian Mission to "All Nations" in the Light of Matthew's Gospel.* Grand Rapids: Eerdmans, 1999.

Lake, K. *Eusebius. Ecclesiastical History. Books 1–5,* LCL 153. Cambridge: Harvard University Press, 1926.

Lambrecht, J. "Our Commonwealth Is in Heaven." In *Pauline Studies: Collected Essays,* 309–15. Bibliotheca Ephemeridum theologicarum Lovaniensium 115. Leuven: Leuven University Press, 1994.

Lange, L. *Das Erscheinen des Auferstandenen im Evangelium nach Matthäus.* Forschung zur Bibel 11. Würzburg: Echter-Verlag, 1973.

Langer, S. K. *Philosophy in a New Key.* New York: New American Library, 1951.

Lathrop, G. *Holy Things: A Liturgical Theology.* Minneapolis: Fortress, 1998.

Legrand, L. *Unity and Plurality: Mission in the Bible.* Translated by R. R. Barr. Maryknoll, N.Y.: Orbis, 1990.

Levine, H. J. *Sing Unto God a New Song: A Contemporary Reading of the Psalms.* Indiana Studies in Biblical Literature. Bloomington: Indiana University Press, 1995.

Lewis, A. E. *Between Cross & Resurrection: A Theology of Holy Saturday.* Grand Rapids: Eerdmans, 2001.

Lewis, C. S. *Reflections on the Psalms.* New York: Harcourt, Brace & Jovanovich, 1958.

Lewis, J. *The Monkey Rope: A Psychotherapist's Reflections on Relationships.* New York: Bernel, 1996.

Lewis, P. *The Glory of Christ.* Chicago: Moody, 1997.

Lieb, M. *The Visionary Mode: Biblical Prophecy, Hermeneutics, and Cultural Change.* Ithaca, NY: Cornell University Press, 1991.

Lim, J. "Is Preaching in the Church Still Relevant Today?" *ABJT* 1 (April 2007).

Lincoln, A. T. *Ephesians.* WBC 42. Dallas: Word, 1990.

———. *Paradise Now and Not Yet.* Cambridge: Cambridge University Press, 1981.

Livio, J. B. "La signification théologique de la 'montagne' dans le premier évangelie." *BCPE* 30 (1978) 13-20.

Lohfink, G. *Jesus and Community: The Social Dimension of the Christian Faith.* Translated by J. P. Galvin. Philadelphia: Fortress, 1984.

Longenecker, R. N. "Prayer in the Pauline Letters." In *Into God's Presence*, 203-27. Grand Rapids: Eerdmans, 2001.

Lovas, A. "Mission-Shaped Liturgy." *IRM* 95 (2006) 354-58.

Louw, J. P. *Semantics of New Testament Greek.* Philadelphia: Fortress, 1982.

Luc, A. "A Theology of Ezekiel: God's Name and Israel's History." *JETS* 26 (1983) 137-43.

Luther, M. *Luther's Works.* Vol. 53. Philadelphia: Fortress / Concordia, 1957.

Luz, U. *Matthew 1-7: A Commentary.* Translated by Wilhelm C. Linss. Edinburgh: T. & T. Clark, 1990.

———. *Studies in Matthew.* Translated by Rosemary Selle. Grand Rapids: Eerdmans, 2005.

Lyons, J. *Language and Linguistics: An Introduction.* Cambridge: Cambridge University Press, 1981.

———. *Semantics.* 2 vols. Cambridge: Cambridge University Press, 1977.

Macchia, F. "Groans too Deep for Words", www.apts.edu/ajps/98-2/98-2-macchia.htm.

———. "Sighs Too Deep for Words: Toward a Theology of Glossolalia." *JPTheol* 1.1 (1992) 47-73.

MacKinlay, E. *Ageing, Disability and Spirituality: Addressing the Challenge of Disability in Later Life,* London: Jessica Kingsley, 2008.

———. *Spiritual Growth and Care in the Fourth Age of Life.* London: Jessica Kingsley, 2006.

Maile, J. F. "Heaven, Heavenlies, Paradise." In *DPL* 381-83.

Man, R. *Proclamation and Praise: Hebrews 2:12 and the Christology of Worship.* Eugene: Wipf & Stock, 2007.

Marlowe, W. C. "Music of Missions: Themes of Cross-Cultural Outreach in the Psalms." *Missiology* 26 (1998) 445-56.

Marshall, B. D. "Do Christians Worship the God of Israel?" In *Knowing the Triune God: The Work of the Spirit in the Practices of the Church,* edited by J. J. Bucklet and D. S. Yeago, 231-64. Grand Rapids: Eerdmans, 2001.

Marshall, I. H. "How Far Did the Early Christians Worship God?" *ChM* 99 (1985) 216-29.

Martin, R. P. "Patterns of Worship in New Testament Churches." *JSNT* 37 (1989) 59-85.

———. "Worship." In *DPL*, 982-91.

———. *Worship in the Early Church.* Grand Rapids: Eerdmans, 1992.

———. *The Worship of God: Some Theological, Pastoral, and Practical Reflections.* Grand Rapids: Eerdmans, 1982.

Martin-Achard, R. *A Light to the Nations.* Translated by J. P. Smith. London: Oliver & Boyd, 1962.

Mascarenhas, T. *The Missionary Function of Israel in Psalms 67, 96, and 117.* Lanham, MD: University Press of America, 2005.

Mathews, T. F. *The Clash of the Gods.* Princeton: Princeton University Press, 2003.

Mayes, A. D. H. *Deuteronomy.* New Century Bible. Grand Rapids: Eerdmans, 1979.

Mays, J. L. "The Place of the Torah-Psalms in the Psalter." *JBL* 106 (1987) 3-12.

———, with P. D. Miller, and G. M. Tucker. *Preaching and Teaching the Psalms.* Louisville: Westminster John Knox, 2006.

McCann, J. C., Jr. "The Book of Psalms: Introduction." In *The New Interpreter's Bible* 4:641–82. Nashville: Abingdon, 1996.

McConnell, W. "Worship." In *Dictionary of the Old Testament: Wisdom, Poetry & Writings*, edited by T. Longman and P. Enns, 929–35. Downers Grove, IL: InterVarsity, 2008.

McConville, J. G. *Deuteronomy.* Apollos Old Testament Commentary 5. Leicester, UK: Apollos, 2002.

———. *Judgement and Promise: An Interpretation of the Book of Jeremiah.* Leicester, UK: Apollos, 1993.

McDowell, J. C. "'Mend Your Speech a Little': Reading Karl Barth's *Das Nichtige* through Donald MacKinnon's Tragic Vision." Unpublished paper.

McElhinney, C., and K. Turner. "Wellsprings." (2008). Online: http://www.wellsprings.org.uk.

McGrath, A. E. *Historical Theology.* Malden, MA: Blackwell, 1998.

McKnight, S. *Praying with the Church: Following Jesus Daily, Hourly, Today.* Brewster: Paraclete, 2006.

McSherry, W. *Making Sense of Spirituality in Nursing and Health Care Practice.* London: Jessica Kingsley, 2006.

Meeks, W. A. *The Moral World of the First Christians.* Library of Early Christianity. Philadelphia: Westminster, 1986.

Meier, J. P. "Antioch." In *Antioch and Rome: New Testament Cradles of Catholic Christianity*, edited by R. E. Brown and J. P. Meier, 12–86. New York: Paulist, 1983.

Melik, R. R., Jr. *Philippians, Colossians, Philemon.* New American Commentary 32. Nashville: Broadman, 1991.

Mennekes, F. "Interconnection: Religion and Art." In *Beyond Belief: Modern Art and the Religious Imagination*, edited by R. Crumlin, 25–28. Melbourne: National Gallery of Victoria, 1998.

Mercer, N. "Postmodernity and Rationality: the Final Credits or just a Commercial Break?" In *Mission and Meaning. Essays Presented to Peter Cotterell*, edited by A. Billington et al., 319–38. Carlisle: Paternoster, 1995.

Middleton, J. R. *The Liberating Image: The Imago Dei in Genesis 1.* Grand Rapids: Brazos, 2005.

Millar, J. G. *Now Choose Life: Theology and Ethics in Deuteronomy.* Leicester: Apollos, 1998.

———, and J. G. McConville. *Time and Place in Deuteronomy.* JSOTSup 179. Sheffield: Sheffield Academic, 1994.

Miller, P. D. "'Enthroned on the Praises of Israel': The Praise of God in Old Testament Theology." *Int* 39 (1985) 5–19.

Minear, P. S. *Images of the Church in the New Testament.* London: Lutterworth, 1961.

———. "The Time of Hope in the New Testament." *SJT* (1953) 337–61.

Mitchell, K. R. "Ritual in Pastoral Care." *Journal of Pastoral Care* 43, (1989) 68–77.

Mitman, F. R. *Worship in the Shape of Scripture.* Cleveland: Pilgrim, 2001.

Moloney, F. J. *Life of Jesus in Icons: From The "Bible of Tbilisi."* Strathfield, NSW: St Pauls, 2008.

Moltmann, J. *The Church in the Power of the Spirit: A Contribution to Messianic Ecclesiology.* Translated by M. Kohl. London: SCM, 1977.

———. *The Crucified God: The Cross of Christ as the Foundation and Criticism of Christian Theology.* Translated by R. A. Wilson and J. Bowden. London: SCM, 1974.

———. *The Experiment Hope*. Translated by M. D. Meeks. London: SCM, 1975.
Moo, D. J. *Encountering the Book of Romans. A Theological Exposition*. Grand Rapids: Baker, 2002.
Morgenthaler, S. "Emergent Church." In *Exploring the Worship Spectrum: Six Views*, edited by P. F. M. Zahl and P. Basden, 215–30. Grand Rapids: Zondervan, 2004.
Morley, J. *All Desires Known*. London: Morehouse, 2006.
Morris, L. *The Gospel according to John: The English Text with Introduction, Exposition and Notes*. Grand Rapids: Eerdmans, 1971.
Moule, C. F. D. *Worship in the New Testament*. London: Lutterworth, 1961.
Muller, R. A. *Dictionary of Latin and Greek Theological Terms*. Grand Rapids, Baker: 1985.
Murphy, D. D. "Worship as Catechesis: Knowledge, Desire, and Christian Formation." *TToday* 58 (2001) 321–32.
Murphy, R. E. *Theological Wordbook of the Old Testament*. Chicago: Moody, 1980.
———. "Wisdom and Creation." *JBL* 104 (1985) 3–11. doi: 10.2307/3260589.
Murray, A. T. *Homer. Illiad. Books 1–12*. Translated by W. F. Wyatt. LCL 170. Cambridge: Harvard University Press, 1924.
———. *Homer. Odyssey. Books 13–24*. Translated by A. T. Murray. LCL 105. Cambridge: Harvard University Press, 1919.
Murray, J. *The Epistle to the Romans*. Grand Rapids: Eerdmans, 1965.
Navarro, K. *The Complete Worship Service—Creating a Taste of Heaven on Earth*. Grand Rapids: Baker, 2005.
Needels, T. et al. "Power up Your Brain." *Psych Today* 35.4 (2002) 44–51.
Neumann, K. J. *The Authenticity of the Pauline Epistles in the Light of Stylostatistical Analysis*. Atlanta: Scholars, 1990.
Newbigin, L. *Foolishness to the Greeks: The Gospel and Western Culture*. Grand Rapids: Eerdmans, 1986.
———. "How Shall We Understand Sacraments and Ministry?" Unpublished paper written for Anglican-Reformed International Commission, London, 1983.
Ngien, D. *Gifted Response: The Triune God as the Causative Agency of our Responsive Worship*. Milton Keynes, UK: Paternoster, 2008.
Nissen, J. *New Testament and Mission: Historical and Hermeneutical Perspectives*. 3rd ed. Frankfurt: Lang, 2004.
Nolan, E. P. *Now through a Glass Darkly: Specular Images of Being and Knowing from Virgil to Chaucer*. Ann Arbor: University of Michigan Press, 1990.
Northcott, M. "New Age Rites: The Recovery of Ritual." *The Way* 33.3 (1993) 189–98.
Notley, S. "The Sea of Galilee: Development of an early Christian toponym." *JBL* 128 (2009) 183–88.
O'Brien, P. T. *Colossians, Philemon*. WBC 44. Waco, TX: Word, 1982.
———. "The Church as a Heavenly and Eschatological Entity." In *The Church in the Bible and the World*, edited by D. A. Carson, 88–119. Grand Rapids: Baker, 1987.
Odell, M. S. *Ezekiel*. Smyth & Helwys Bible Commentary. Macon, GA: Smyth & Helwys, 2005.
Olley, J. W. "'Hallowed Be Your Name . . .': Does Ezekiel Speak to Essendon, Eastwood and East Fremantle?" *SPJMS* 35 (2006) 37–43.
———. "'You Are the Light of the World': A Missiological Framework for the Sermon on the Mount." *Mission Studies* XX-1.39 (2003) 9–28.

Olson, D. T. *Deuteronomy and the Death of Moses: A Theological Reading*. Overtures to Biblical Theology. Minneapolis: Fortress, 1994.

Olson, R. E., and C. A. Hall. *The Trinity*. Grand Rapids: Eerdmans, 2002.

Oppenheimer, A. "*Am Ha-Arez*: Second Temple and Mishnah." In *Encyclopedia Judaica*, edited by F. Skolnik, 2:834–36. New York: Keter, 1971–72.

Overman, J. A. *Matthew's Gospel and Formative Judaism: The Social World of the Matthean Community*. Minneapolis: Fortress, 1996.

Oulton, J. E. L. *Eusebius. Ecclesiastical History, Books 6–10*. LCL 265. Cambridge: Harvard University Press, 1932.

Our World Belongs to God. A Contemporary Testimony of the Christian Reformed Church. Grand Rapids: 1985, 2008. Online: http://www.crcna.org/pages/our_world_main.cfm

Paillard, J. *In Praise of the Inexpressible: Paul's Experience of the Divine Mystery*. Peabody, MA: Hendrikson, 2003.

Parry, R. A. *Worshipping Trinity: Coming Back to the Heart of Worship*. Milton Keynes, UK: Paternoster, 2005.

Parsons, M. "Being Precedes Act: Indicative and Imperative in Paul's Writing." In *Understanding Paul's Ethics. Twentieth Century Approaches*, edited by B. S. Rosner, 217–47. Grand Rapids: Eerdmans, 1995.

Pasquarello, M. III. *Christian Preaching—A Trinitarian Theology of Proclamation*. Grand Rapids: Baker Academic, 2006.

Pattenden, R. "What's Art Got to Do with It?" *AAR* (2007). Online: http://www.artreview.com.au/.

Pattison, S. "Is Pastoral Care Dead in a Mission-led Church?" *Practical Theology* 1.1 (2008) 7–10.

Pearson, P. *A Brush with God: An Icon Workbook*. Harrisburg, PA: Morehouse, 2005.

Pecklers, K. F. *Worship: A primer in Christian Ritual*. Collegeville, MN: Liturgical, 2003.

Peters, G. W. *A Biblical Theology of Missions*. Chicago: Moody, 1972.

Peterson, D. *Engaging with God. A Biblical Theology of Worship*. Grand Rapids: Eerdmans, 1992.

———. "Worship in the New Testament." In *Worship: Adoration and Action*, edited by D. A. Carson, 51–91. Grand Rapids: Baker, 1993.

Pierce, T. M. *Enthroned on Our Praise: An Old Testament Theology of Worship*. Nashville: Broadman & Holman, 2007.

Pilavachi, M. *For the Audience of One: The Soul Survivor Guide to Worship*. London: Hodder & Stoughton, 1999.

Pinnock, C. H. *Flame of Love: A Theology of the Holy Spirit*. Downers Grove, IL: Inter-Varsity, 1996.

Piper, J. *Let the Nations Be Glad! The Supremacy of God in Missions*. Grand Rapids: Baker, 1993.

Pope John Paul II. "Letter of His Holiness Pope John Paul II to Artists." (1999). Online: http://www.vatican.va/holy_father/john_paul_ii/letters/documents/hf_jp-ii_let_23041999_artists_en.html.

Porter, S. E. "Is there a Center to Paul's Theology? An Introduction to the Study of Paul and his Theology." In *Paul and His Theology*, 1–19. Pauline Studies 3. Leiden: Brill, 2006.

———. *The Pauline Canon*. Leiden: Brill, 2004.

———. *Verbal Aspect in the Greek New Testament, with Reference to Tense and Mood.* Studies in Biblical Greek. New York: Lang, 1989.
Pound, G. *Making Life Decisions: Journey in Discernment*, 2007. Online: http://makinglifedecisions.blogspot.com/2007/11/copyright-and-download.html
Powell, M. A. *God with Us: A Pastoral Theology of Matthew's Gospel.* Minneapolis: Fortress, 1995.
Principe, W. "Toward Defining Spirituality." *Sciences Religieuses/Studies in Religion* 12 (1983) 127–41.
Psalter Hymnal. Grand Rapids: CRC Publications, 1987.
Quicke, M. J. *360degree Preaching.* Grand Rapids: Baker Academic, 2003.
Rad, G. von. *Deuteronomy.* Translated by D. Barton. London: SCM, 1966.
———. *Old Testament Theology.* 2 vols. Translated by D. M. G. Stalker. New York: Harper & Row, 1962.
Radice, B., *The Letters of the Younger Pliny.* Harmondsworth, UK: Penguin, 1963.
Ramshaw, E. *Ritual and Pastoral Care.* Theology and Pastoral Care Series. Philadelphia: Fortress, 1987.
Rediger, G. L. *Fit to Be a Pastor: A Call to Physical, Mental, and Spiritual Fitness.* Louisville: Westminster John Knox, 2000.
Redman, M. *The Heart of Worship Files.* Eastbourne: Kingsway, 2003.
Resner, A. "Lament: Faith's Response to Loss." *ResQ* 32.3 (1990) 129–42.
Ridderbos, H. *The Gospel of John: A Theological Commentary.* Translated by J. Vriend. Grand Rapids: Eerdmans, 1997.
———. *Paul: An Outline of His Theology.* London: SPCK, 1977.
Robinson, H. W. *Religious Ideas of the Old Testament.* London: Duckworth, 1956.
Rosier, V. "The spirit and power of the liturgy: Understanding liturgical catechesis." *ACR* 83 (2006) 387–405.
Ross, A. P. *Recalling the Hope of Glory: Biblical Worship from the Garden to the New Creation.* Grand Rapids: Kregel, 2006.
Roszak, T. *Where the Wasteland Ends.* Garden City, NY: Doubleday, 1972.
Routledge, R. *Old Testament Theology: A Thematic Approach.* Nottingham: Apollos, 2008.
Rowland, C. "Apocalyptic Vision and the Exaltation of Christ in the Letter to the Colossians." In *The Pauline Writings*, edited by S. E. Porter and C. A. Evans, 220–29. Sheffield: Sheffield Academic, 1995.
Rowley, H. H. *The Biblical Doctrine of Election.* London: Lutterworth, 1950.
Royalty, R. M. *The Streets of Heaven. The Ideology of Wealth in the Apocalypse of John.* Macon, GA: Mercer University Press, 1998.
Ruether, R. R. "Ecological Theology: Roots in Tradition, Liturgical and Ethical Practice for Today." *Dialog* 42.3 (2003) 226–34.
Ryken, L., et al. *Dictionary of Biblical Imagery.* Downers Grove, IL: InterVarsity, 1999.
Safran, L. *Heaven on Earth.* University Park, Penn: Pennsylvania State University Press, 2002.
Saldarini, A. J. "The Gospel of Matthew and Jewish-Christian conflict." In *Social history of the Matthean Community: Cross-disciplinary Approaches*, edited by D. L. Balch, 38–61. Minneapolis: Fortress, 1991.
Saliers, D. E. *Worship as Theology. Foretaste of Glory Divine.* Nashville: Abingdon, 1994.
Sasse, H. "*kosmos.*" In *TDNT* 3:867–98.
Scazzero, P. *Emotionally Healthy Spirituality.* Nashville: Nelson, 2006.

Schattauer, T. *Inside Out: Worship in an Age of Mission*. Minneapolis: Fortress, 1999.

Schmidt, A. J. *Under the Influence. How Christianity Transformed Culture*. Grand Rapids: Zondervan, 2001.

Schmidt, C. J. "Sent and Gathered: A Musical Metaphor for Missional Liturgy." *Word and World* 26.2 (Summer 2006) 121–29.

Schrage, W. *The Ethics of the New Testament*. Edinburgh: T. & T. Clark, 1988.

Scrutton, A. "Emotion in Augustine of Hippo and Thomas Aquinas: A Way Forward in the Im/passibility Debate?" *IJST* 7.2 (2005) 169–77.

Senior, D., and C. Stuhlmueller. *The Biblical Foundations for Mission*. Maryknoll, NY: Orbis, 1983.

Senn, F. C. *Christian Liturgy*. Minneapolis: Fortress, 1997.

Shenk, W. R. *Write the Vision: The Church Renewed*. Valley Forge, PA: Trinity, 1995.

Sherwin, S. "'I Am Against You': Yahweh's Judgment on the Nations and Its Ancient Near Eastern Context." *TB* 54 (2003) 149–60.

Shorey, P. *Plato. Republic, Books 6–10*, LCL 276. Cambridge: Harvard University Press, 1935.

Silva, M. *Biblical Words & Their Meaning: An Introduction to Lexical Semantics*. 2nd ed. Grand Rapids: Zondervan, 1994.

———. *Philippians*. Chicago: Moody, 1988.

Sim, D. *The Social World of the Matthean Community*. Edinburgh: T. & T. Clark, 1998.

Sloyan, G. S. "Religious Education: From Early Christianity to Medieval Times." In *Shaping the Christian Message: Essays in Religious Education*, 3–62. New York: Macmillan, 1958.

———. "Symbols of God's presence to the church: Verbal and nonverbal." *TToday*, 58 (2001) 304–20.

Smail, T. *The Giving Gift: The Holy Spirit in Person*. London: Hodder & Stoughton, 1988.

———. "In Spirit and in Truth: Reflections on Charismatic Worship." In *The Love of Power or the Power of Love: A Careful Assessment of the Problems within the Charismatic and Word-of-Faith Movements*, edited by T. Smail et al., 95–103. Minneapolis: Bethany, 1994.

Smith, R. L. *Old Testament Theology: Its History, Method, and Message*. Nashville: Broadman & Holman, 1993.

Sommerstein, A. H. *Aeschylus. Persians. Seven against Thebes. Suppliants. Prometheus Bound*, volume 1, LCL 145. Cambridge: Harvard University Press, 2009.

———. *Aeschylus. Oresteia: Agamemnon. Libation-bearers. Eumenides*, volume 2, LCL 146. Cambridge: Harvard University Press, 2009.

Southgate, C. *The Groaning of Creation: God, Evolution and the Problem of Evil*. Louisville: Westminster John Knox, 2008.

Srokosz, M. A. "God's Story and the Earth's Story. Grounding Our Concern for the Environment in the Biblical Metanarrative." *Sci Chr Belief* 20.2 (2008) 163–74.

Steck, O. H. *Israel und das gewaltsame Geschick der Propheten*. Neukirchen-Vlyun: Neukirchner Verlag, 1967.

Sterling, S. *Sustainable Education. Re-visioning Learning and Change*, Schumacher Briefings 6. Foxhole, UK: Green Books, 2001.

Swinburne, R. *Revelation: From Metaphor to Analogy*. Oxford: Clarendon, 1992.

Swinton, J. *Raging with Compassion: Pastoral Responses to the Problem of Evil*. Grand Rapids: Eerdmans, 2007.

Talbot, C. H. *Romans*. Macon: Smyth & Helwys, 2002.

Tasker, R. G. V. *The Gospel According to Saint John: An Introduction and Commentary.* Leicester: IVP, 1960.
Taylor, B. B. *The Preaching Life.* Cambridge: Cowley, 1993.
Thompson, J. A. *Deuteronomy: An Introduction and Commentary.* Leicester: IVP, 1974.
Thompson, M. M. *Colossians and Philemon.* Grand Rapids: Eerdmans, 2005.
Tickle, P. *The Divine Hours,* 3 volumes. New York: Doubleday, 2000–2001.
Torrance, A. "Does God Suffer? Incarnation and Impassibility." In *Christ in Our Place: The Humanity of God in Christ for the Reconciliation of the World,* edited by T. Hart and D. Thimell, 345–68. Carlisle: Paternoster, 1989.
Torrance, J. B. *Worship, Community and the Triune God of Grace.* Carlisle: Paternoster, 1996.
Torrance. T. F., et al. *Incarnation: the Person and Life of Christ.* Milton Keynes: Paternoster, 2008.
———. *A Passion for Christ: The Vision that Ignites Ministry.* Edinburgh: Handsel, 1999.
Troeger, T. *Preaching and Worship.* St Louis: Chalice, 2003.
Turner, V. *The Ritual Process.* London: Routledge and Kegan Paul, 1969.
van Gemeren, W. A. *NIDOTTE*, volume 5. Carlisle: Paternoster, 1997.
van Gennep, A. *The Rites of Passage.* Translated by M. B. Vizedom and G. L. Caffee. Chicago: University of Chicago Press, 1908; 1960.
Vicedom, G. F. *The Mission of God: An Introduction to a Theology of Mission.* Translated by G. A. Thiele and D. Hilgendorf. St. Louis: Concordia, 1965.
Viladesau, R. *Theological Aesthetics.* New York: Oxford University Press, 1999.
———. *Theology and the Arts.* New York, Paulist, 2000.
Volf, M. *After Our Likeness. The Church as the Image of the Trinity.* Grand Rapids: Eerdmans, 1998.
———. "Worship as Adoration and Action: Reflections on a Christian Way of Being-in-the-World." In *Worship: Adoration and Action,* edited by D. A. Carson, 203–11. Carlisle: Paternoster / Grand Rapids: Baker, 1993.
Vos, C. J. A. *Theopoetry of the Psalms.* Edinburgh: T. & T. Clark, 2005.
Vos, G. "The Eschatological Aspect of the Pauline Conception of the Spirit." In *Redemptive History and Biblical Interpretation,* edited by R. Gaffin, 25–58. Phillipsburg, NJ: Presbyterian & Reformed Publishing, 1980.
———. *The Pauline Eschatology.* Grand Rapids: Eerdmans, 1972.
Underhill, E. *Worship.* New York: Harper & Brothers, 1937.
Underwood, E. *Worship.* 1962. Reprinted, Eugene, OR: Wipf & Stock, 2002.
Wagner, J. R. "From the Heavens to the Heart: The Dynamics of Psalm 19 as Prayer." *CBQ* 61 (1999) 245–61.
Wallis, J. *The Call to Conversion.* Herts, UK: Lion, 1981.
Walton, J. H. "Deuteronomy: An Exposition of the Spirit of the Law." *GTJ* 8 (1987) 213–25.
Ward, H., and J. Wild. *Human Rites: Worship Resources for an Age of Change.* London: Mowbray, 1995.
Warren, R. *The Purpose Driven Church.* Grand Rapids: Zondervan, 1995.
WCC. *One Baptism: Towards Mutual Recognition of Christian Initiation,* http://www.oikoumene.org/en/resources/documents/wcc-commissions/faith-and-order-commission/ii-worship-and-baptism/one-baptism-towards-mutual-recognition-a-text-in-progress.html.

Webber, R. E. *Worship is a Verb.* Peabody, MA: Hendrickson, 1992.
Webber, R., and P. Kenyon. *A Call to an Ancient Evangelical Future* (2006). Online: http://www.ancientfutureworship.com/afw_wkshps.html
———. "Together in the Jesus Story—An Interview with Bob Webber." *CT* (September 2006). Online: http://www.christianitytoday.com/ct/2006/september/10.54.html
White, J. *A Brief History of Christian Worship.* Nashville: Abingdon, 1993.
Whitehead, E., and J. Whitehead. *Seasons of Strength: New Visions of Adult Christian Maturing.* Winona, MN: St Mary's, 1995.
Wicks, R., and T. Rodgerson. *Companions in Hope.* New York: Paulist, 1998.
Wiersbe, W. W. *Real Worship: Playground, Battleground, or Holy Ground?* Grand Rapids: Baker, 2000.
Willard, D., and J. Johnson. *Renovation of the Heart in Daily Practice. Experiments in Spiritual Transformation.* Colorado Springs: NavPress, 2006.
Williams, D. J. *Paul's Metaphors. Their Context and Character.* Peabody, MA: Hendrickson, 1999.
Williams, F. *The Panarion of Epiphanius of Salamis.* NHS 35. Leiden: Brill, 1987.
Williams, R. *Ponder These Things.* Mulgrave, Victoria: John Garratt, 2002.
Williamson, P. R. "Covenant." In *Dictionary of the Old Testament: Pentateuch*, edited by T. D. Alexander and D. W. Baker, 139–55. Downers Grove, IL: InterVarsity, 2003.
———. *Sealed with an Oath: Covenant in God's Unfolding Purpose.* Nottingham, UK: Apollos, 2007.
Willimon, W. H. *A Guide to Preaching and Leading Worship.* Louisville: Westminster John Knox, 2008.
———. *Pastor: The Theology and Practice of Ordained Ministry.* Nashville: Abingdon, 2002.
———. *Worship as Pastoral Care.* Nashville: Abingdon, 1979.
Wilson, J. R. *Why Church Matters: Worship, Ministry and Mission in Practice.* Grand Rapids: Brazos, 2006.
Winner, L. F. *Mudhouse Sabbath.* Brewster: Paraclete, 2003.
Wolff, H. W. "The Kerygma of the Yahwist." *Int* 20 (1966) 131–57.
Wolterstorff, N. *Lament for a Son.* Grand Rapids: Eerdmans, 1987.
Wood, R. C. *Contending for the Faith. The Church's Engagement with Culture.* Waco, TX: Baylor University Press, 2003.
Wright, C. J. H. *Deuteronomy.* Peabody, MA: Hendrickson, 1996.
———. *God's People in God's Land: Family, Land and Property in the Old Testament.* Carlisle: Paternoster, 1997.
———. *The Message of Ezekiel.* Leicester, UK: InterVarsity, 2001.
———. *The Mission of God: Unlocking the Bible's Grand Narrative.* Downers Grove, IL: InterVarsity, 2006.
Wright, N. G. *Free Church. Free State / The Positive Baptist Vision.* Milton Keynes, UK: Paternoster, 2005.
Wright, N. T. *Jesus and the Victory of God.* London: SPCK, 1996.
———. *The Last Word: Beyond the Bible Wars to a New Understanding of the Authority of Scripture.* New York: Harper, 2005.
———. *Paul: Fresh Perspectives.* London: SPCK, 2005.
———. *Simply Christian: Why Christianity Makes Sense.* New York: HarperCollins, 2006.

Wyckoff, C. "Have We Come Full Circle Yet? Closure, Psycholinguistics, and Problems of Recognition with the *Inclusio*." *JSOT* 30 (2006) 475–505.

Yaconelli, M. *Messy Spirituality: God's Annoying Love for Imperfect People*. Grand Rapids: Zondervan, 2002.

Young, N. "Sacrament, Sign, and Unity." In *Ecumenical Theology in Worship, Doctrine, and Life: Essays Presented to Geoffrey Wainwright on His Sixtieth Birthday*, edited by D. S. Cunningham et al., 95–106. New York: Oxford University Press, 1999.

Yule, G. *The Study of Language*. 2nd ed. Cambridge: Cambridge University Press, 1996.

Ziesler, J. *Pauline Christianity*. Oxford: Oxford University Press, 1983.

Zimmerli, W. *Ezekiel 1: A Commentary on the Book of the Prophet Ezekiel, Chapters 1–24*. Translated by R. E. Clements. Hermeneia. Philadelphia: Fortress, 1979 [orig. German, 1969].

———. *Ezekiel 2: A Commentary on the Book of the Prophet Ezekiel, Chapters 25–48*. Translated by J. D. Martin. Hermeneia. Philadelphia: Fortress, 1983 [orig. German, 1969].

———. "I Am Yahweh." In *I Am Yahweh*, edited by W. Brueggemann, 1–28. Atlanta: John Knox, 1982 [orig. German 1953].

———. "Knowledge of God According to the Book of Ezekiel." In *I Am Yahweh*, edited by W. Brueggemann, 29–98. Atlanta: John Knox, 1982 [orig. German 1954].

———. "Plans for Rebuilding after the Catastrophe of 587." In *I Am Yahweh*, edited by W. Brueggemann, 111–34. Atlanta: John Knox, 1982 [orig. German 1968].

Zizioulas, J. D. *Being as Communion: Studies in Personhood and the Church*. London: Dayton, Longman & Todd, 1985.

———. *Lectures in Christian Dogmatics*. London: T. & T. Clark, 2008.